OXFORD EC LAW LIBRARY

General Editor: F. G. Jacobs
Advocate General, The Court of Justice
of the European Communities

WORKERS, ESTABLISHMENT, AND SERVICES IN THE EUROPEAN UNION

OXFORD EC LAW LIBRARY

The aim of this series is to publish important and original studies of the various branches of EC Law. Each work provides a clear, concise, and original critical exposition of the law in its social, economic, and political context, at a level which will interest the advanced student, the practitioner, the academic, and government and Community officials.

Other Titles in the Library

The European Union and its Court of Justice
Antony Arnull

The General Principles of EC Law
Takis Tridimas

EC Company Law
Vanessa Edwards

EC Sex Equality Law
second edition
Evelyn Ellis

European Community Law of State Aid
Andrew Evans

EC Competition Law
fourth edition
Daniel G. Goyder

EC Agricultural Law
second edition
J.A. Usher

Intellectual Property Rights in the EC Volume 1
Free Movement and Competition Law
David T. Keeling

The European Internal Market and International Trade
An International Analysis
Piet Eeckhout

Trade and Environment Law in the European Community
Andreas R. Ziegler

EC Employment Law
third edition
Catherine Barnard

EC Customs Law
Timothy Lyons

The Law of Money and Financial Services in the EC
second edition
J.A. Usher

EC Securities Regulation
Niamh Moloney

External Relations of the European Union
Legal and Constitutional Foundations
Piet Eeckhout

Workers, Establishment, and Services in the European Union

ROBIN C. A. WHITE

OXFORD
UNIVERSITY PRESS

OXFORD
UNIVERSITY PRESS

Great Clarendon Street, Oxford OX2 6DP

Oxford University Press is a department of the University of Oxford.
It furthers the University's objective of excellence in research, scholarship,
and education by publishing worldwide

in Oxford New York

Auckland Bangkok Buenos Aires Cape Town Chennai
Dar es Salaam Delhi Hong Kong Istanbul Karachi Kolkata
Kuala Lumpur Madrid Melbourne Mexico City Mumbai Nairobi
São Paulo Shanghai Singapore Taipei Tokyo Toronto

Oxford is a registered trade mark of Oxford University Press
in the UK and in certain other countries

Published in the United States
by Oxford University Press Inc., New York

First published 2004

British Library Cataloguing in Publication

Data Available

Library of Congress Cataloging-in-Publication Data

White, Robin C. A.
Workers, establishment, and services in the European Union/Robin C. A. White.
p. cm.—(Oxford EC law library)
Includes bibliographical refrences and index.
ISBN 0–19–826776–2 (alk. paper)
1. Freedom of movement—European Union countries. 2. Free choice of employment—European Union countries. 3. Free trade—European Union countries. I. Title. II. Series.
KJE5174.W45 2004
344.2401—dc22

2004014385

ISBN 0–19–826776–2

1 3 5 7 9 10 8 6 4 2

Typset by Kolam Information Services Pvt. Ltd, Pondicherry, India
Printed in Great Britain
on acid-free paper by
Biddles Ltd., King's Lynn

General Editor's Foreword

Citizens of the European Union—that is, the nationals of the twenty-five Member States, currently about 450 million citizens in all—enjoy various rights, and also have certain obligations, under European Union (or European Community) law. Those rights were initially founded on a single principle: the principle of freedom of movement throughout the European Community—now the European Union.

The transformation of that principle is a remarkable story in itself.

Freedom of movement in the original EEC Treaty of 1957 was essentially an economic concept. The Foundations of the Community, set out as Part Two of that Treaty, embraced the free movement of goods on the one hand and the free movement of persons, services and capital on the other. Both the context of the Treaty provisions and their content were plainly economic and mercantile.

Moreover, as a reflection of the economic character of the Treaty, the free movement of persons was confined to three matters: first, freedom of movement for workers throughout the Community; second, the freedom of establishment—the freedom for businesses to set themselves up throughout the Community; and third, freedom of movement for providers of services. So far as workers were concerned, the main efforts in the early years were directed to the very laudable but limited aim of preserving the social security rights of migrant workers.

Over the years the law has been progressively transformed. It has been developed by the case law of the European Court of Justice, by Community legislation, and by Treaty amendments. The case law recognized that even the original Treaty could be seen, as indeed may have been the ultimate intention of its authors, as creating fundamental rights for individuals. Those rights accordingly had to be broadly interpreted, and the corresponding restrictions construed narrowly.

The legislation created new rights: it provided, for example, for a variety of social and economic rights, and for the mutual recognition of professional and vocational qualifications. It also extended the categories of those entitled, first to all economically active persons and their dependants, and then even beyond those categories.

For its part, the Maastricht Treaty—the Treaty on European Union—both consolidated the past achievements and laid the foundations for further developments, Among other things, it transformed the European Economic Community into the European Community; it provided for the establishment of the European Union, embracing the Community and extending its remit; and it introduced the concept of citizenship of the European Union.

As a result of these developments, workers, providers and recipients of services and those setting up in business now benefit from a freedom which includes, among other things, substantial social and economic rights, the mutual recognition of professional and other qualifications, and an overarching principle of equal treatment covering all matters within the scope of the EC Treaty. In addition, all citizens of the European Union benefit in various ways from the Treaty provisions. All of them are entitled to freedom of movement. They also have political rights, including the right to vote in both local elections and elections to the European Parliament in the Member State in which they reside.

And all citizens—not merely economic actors—in every Member State are entitled to receive equal treatment in all fields covered by the Treaty, with that State's own nationals.

The concern of the European Union is now widely recognized as being to put the individual and the citizen first. The appearance of this book in the Oxford EC Law Library is therefore perhaps overdue, but no less welcome for that.

Francis G. Jacobs
June 2004

For Noah and Louie

Preface

My aim in writing this book has been to present a modern exposition of the law relating to the free movement of workers, and to freedom of establishment and services, without over-elaboration or over-simplification. It seemed to me that there was room in the literature on the free movement of persons for a book which presented the law in these areas in the light of the developing status of citizenship of the Union, and addressed issues flowing from the convergence of the principles adopted by the Court of Justice in dealing with internal market issues.

I decided to divide the book into three main parts after a scene-setting introduction. The general part deals with the underlying rules of entitlement, the prohibition of discrimination, the mutual recognition of qualifications, exceptions to the Treaty rules, and the development of the principle of effective enjoyment of Community rights. The next part extracts from the Treaty, the secondary legislation, and the case law of the Court of Justice, the personal rights enjoyed by individuals in exercising their rights of free movement. It roots those rights in the constitutional right to free movement which now flows from the establishment of citizenship of the Union. The final part separates out those principles which are more concerned with market access, and the limits of home or host State regulation of an activity. This synthesis of Community law seems to me to offer a means through which the divergences and convergences in the law relating to the internal market can be better explained and accommodated. It is also suggested that overall the law is more coherent that

The law is stated as at 1 April 2004. There is, as there has to be, reference to the 1 May 2004 enlargement in chapter 1, where the transitional arrangements for the ten new Member States are addressed, but the remainder of the book seeks to present a synthesis of the legal position immediately prior to enlargement. Two significant new legislative measures adopted in late April have been treated rather differently, even though both measures will enter into force in 2006. The first is Directive 2004/38/EC, the new residence directive. This is treated in some detail at a number of points since it is a modern restatement of many of the personal rights flowing from citizenship of the Union, and supports the thesis that citizenship of the Union is having a profound influence on the personal rights of citizens of the Union when in a Member State other than that of their own nationality. The second is Regulation 883/2004/EC, the simplified regulation on the coordination of social security. This is referred to at the end of chapter 9 on social security and pensions; it makes some significant changes but its entry into force is dependent upon the preparation of a new implementing regulation. As such it seemed to warrant only a passing reference in a book setting out the law as at 1 April 2004. One or two cases where judgments have been handed down after 1 April are mentioned. I believe that the inclusion of these later developments does not distort the presentation of the law as at 1 April 2004.

The encouragement and support provided by colleagues at Oxford University Press—not to mention their patience in waiting for the manuscript of this book—has been outstanding. Input from colleagues at the University of Leicester—both academic colleagues and postgraduate students—and academic colleagues elsewhere, has largely consisted of their allowing me to test a number of approaches to the presentation of a synthesis on the law relating to workers, establishment, and services in the European Union, and responding to those arguments in a way which has allowed me to refine my own views. I acknowledge my gratitude to them all.

Robin C. A. White

The University of Leicester
28 June 2004

Contents

Table of Cases

European Court of Human Rights

European Court of Justice

Alphabetical

European Court of Justice

Chronological

United Kingdom

United States

Table of Legislation

European Union

Decisions

Directives

Recommendations

Regulations

Resolutions

Treaties

France

Germany

International

Ireland

United Kingdom

United States of America

Abbreviations

CMLR	*Common Market Law Reports*
CMLRev	*Common Market Law Review*
Court of Justice	Court of Justice of the European Communities
EC	European Communities
EC (appearing after article number)	Treaty establishing the European Community (as amended)
ECHR	European Convention on Human Rights
ECR	*European Court Reports*
EEA	European Economic Area
EEA countries	Iceland, Liechtenstein and Norway
EEC	European Economic Community
EHRLR	*European Human Rights Law Review*
EHRR	*European Human Rights Reports*
EJSS	*European Journal of Social Security*
ELRev	*European Law Review*
ETS	European Treaty Series
ICLQ	*International and Comparative Law Quarterly*
ILJ	*Industrial Law Journal*
LNTS	League of Nations Treaty Series
Member States	Austria, Belgium, Denmark, Finland, France, Germany, Greece, Ireland, Italy, Luxembourg, The Netherlands, Portugal, Spain, Sweden, United Kingdom
nyr	not yet reported
OJ	Official Journal of the European Communities
TEU	Treaty on European Union
Treaty of Amsterdam	Treaty of Amsterdam of 29 March 1996 amending the Treaty on European Union, the Treaties establishing the European Communities, [1996] OJ C340/1

Treaty of Maastricht	Treaty on European Union signed at Maastricht on 7 February 1992, [1992] OJ C325/5
Treaty of Nice	Treaty of Nice of 26 February 2001 amending the Treaty on European Union, the Treaties establishing the European Communities and certain related acts, [2001] OJ C80/1

Part I

Introduction

1

Setting the scene

The context

There is still an argument that the core of the European Union remains the four freedoms, even though there are now established and detailed policies in many other areas. Free movement of goods, persons, services and capital in the European Union can properly be regarded as the hallmark of the Union.[1] Many other policies have flowed from the creation of an internal market 'characterised by the abolition, as between Member States, of obstacles to the free movement of goods, persons, services and capital'.[2] However, the Preamble to the EC Treaty does not refer to the four freedoms. It is the 'ever closer union among the peoples of Europe' which heads the list of commitments. These include the ensuring of economic and social progress by eliminating barriers which divide Europe; the removal of obstacles in order to guarantee steady expansion, balanced trade and fair competition, and progressive abolition of restrictions on international trade by means of a common commercial policy.

Article 2 EC lists three tasks for the European Community: establishing a common market; establishing an economic and monetary union; and implementing common policies or activities listed in Articles 3 and 4. In the activities listed in Article 3, which includes the establishment of the internal market, the Community is required to 'aim to eliminate inequalities, and to promote equality, between men and women'.[3]

Two further key obligations can be found in Part One of the EC Treaty: the duty of solidarity in Article 10, and the prohibition of discrimination on grounds of nationality in Article 12. In addition to the latter prohibition, there is now in Article 13 a power to enact secondary legislation to 'combat discrimination based on sex, racial or ethnic origin, religion or belief, disability, age or sexual orientation'.

[1] In the Preface to Green, N, Hartley, T, and Usher, J, *The Legal Foundations of the Single European Market* (Oxford, 1991), Professor Hartley describes the free movement of goods and persons as 'the most obvious components of the single market'.

[2] Art 3(c) EC.

[3] Art 3(2) EC.

Two key articles on the internal market follow:

Article 14

1. The Community shall adopt measures with the aim of progressively establishing the internal market over a period expiring on 31 December 1992, in accordance with the provisions of this Article and of Articles 15, 26, 47(2), 49, 80, 93 and 95 and without prejudice to the other provisions of this Treaty.

2. The internal market shall comprise an area without internal frontiers in which the free movement of goods, persons, services and capital is ensured in accordance with the provisions of this Treaty.

3. The Council, acting by a qualified majority on a proposal from the Commission shall determine the guidelines and conditions necessary to ensure balanced progress in all the sectors concerned.

Article 15

When drawing up its proposals with a view to achieving the objectives set out in Article 14, the Commission shall take into account the extent of the effort that certain economies showing differences in development will have to sustain during the period of establishment of the internal market and it may propose appropriate provisions.

If these provisions take the form of derogations, they must be of a temporary nature and must cause the least possible disturbance of the functioning of the common market.

These provisions call for some comment. First of all, the internal market, as defined in Article 14, was not achieved by 31 December 1992, and has not yet been fully achieved, though very many of the barriers flowing from internal frontiers have been removed. Furthermore, the requirement is that the internal market is an area without internal frontiers 'in accordance with the provisions of this Treaty', which itself contains permissible derogations based upon national boundaries. The second observation is that the list of articles in Article 14(1) EC makes it clear that the internal market involves both fundamental freedoms and policies. Notably, the customs union is a necessary part of the scheme for the free movement of goods. The capacity for tax policy to have an impact, most obviously[4] on the free movement of goods, is also recognized, as is the link with the common transport policy. Most significant among the policies not specifically mentioned is competition policy, but open competition in the internal market has always been seen as requiring the Community to have its own competition law and policy.

Though there was originally a clearer distinction between fundamental freedoms and common policies, the current version of the EC Treaty lists the four freedoms in Part Three of the Treaty entitled 'Community Policies'. However, prior to the amendments made by the Treaty on European Union, Part Two of the EEC Treaty was entitled 'Foundations of the Community' and covered free movement of goods,[5] agriculture,[6] free movement of persons, services and capital,[7] and transport.[8] This was followed by a separate part of the Treaty entitled 'Policy of the Community.' Sometimes the distinction between the fundamental freedoms

[4] But not exclusively. [5] Title I. [6] Title II. [7] Title III. [8] Title IV.

and common policies has been said to be that between negative and positive integration. Negative integration refers to rules based on prohibitions, whereas positive integration refers to common rules established to secure a harmonized approach to a particular area. The obligations which flow from the rules in the EC Treaty on the free movement of goods, persons, services and capital now go well beyond simply prohibitions, but the law in this area does not require every Member State to regulate every area of activity falling within the scope of the freedoms in the same way. This finds its clearest expression in the application of the rules relating to establishment and services where the Treaty refers to according treatment 'under the conditions laid down for its own nationals by the law of the country where such establishment is effected',[9] and 'under the same conditions as are imposed by that State on its own nationals'.[10]

Free movement of persons

The term 'free movement of persons' is frequently used. It appears in the wording of Title III of the EC Treaty, which reads 'Free movement of persons, services and capital'. The provisions in Title III cover in chapter 1, workers; in chapter 2, the right of establishment; in chapter 3, services; and in chapter 4, capital and payments. However, Title IV is entitled 'Visas, Asylum, Immigration and Other Policies Related to Free Movement of Persons'. It is also the case that no exposition of the law relating to the free movement of persons can ignore the rapidly developing case law flowing from Part Two of the EC Treaty on citizenship of the Union. This leads to the need for consideration of the scope of the label 'free movement of persons'.

In their book entitled *Free Movement of Persons within the European Community*,[11] Friedl Weiss and Frank Wooldridge cover workers, establishment and services, the right to residence of other persons, European citizenship, the right of third country nationals in the European Community, and international agreements and free movement. In this latter chapter, they cover the EEA Agreement and association agreements which grant certain free movement rights.

In her book, *Freedom of Movement of Persons. A Practitioner's Handbook*,[12] Joanna Apap covers workers, establishment and services, (giving particular emphasis to recognition of qualifications and social security entitlements), the rights of third country nationals particularly under association agreements, political rights, and access to justice. The latter two flow from citizenship of the European Union.

This book is much more explicitly about the law relating to workers, establishment and services in the European Union as set out in Title III of Part 3 of the EC

[9] Art 43 EC. [10] Art 49 EC.

[11] Weiss, F and Wooldridge, F, *Free Movement of Persons within the European Community* (The Hague, 2002).

[12] Apap, J, *Freedom of Movement of Persons. A Practitioner's Handbook* (The Hague, 2002).

Treaty. Inevitably, it provides coverage of citizenship of the Union in Part 2 of the EC Treaty, since this is inextricably intertwined with the Treaty rules on the free movement of workers and self-employed persons. Because of its selection of coverage for detailed exposition in the body of the book, the remainder of this chapter provides a brief overview of a number of related topics which are only considered adjectivally there.

Title IV of the EC Treaty

Title IV represents the porting across from the so-called third pillar[13] of material that is sufficiently close to the law on the free movement of persons that it was anomalous to keep it outside the EC Treaty framework.[14] It has been described as 'a curious amalgam of matters which have previously been dealt with under a range of different and fragmented instruments and frameworks.'[15]

Article 69 EC makes the operation of Title IV subject to the provisions of two Protocols on the position of the United Kingdom and of Ireland,[16] and a Protocol on the position of Denmark.[17] Under Protocol No 3, the United Kingdom and Ireland reserve the right to exercise controls at their frontiers, and both countries reserve the right to maintain the common travel area between the United Kingdom and Ireland. Under Protocol No 4, the provisions of Title IV are optional for the United Kingdom and Ireland. The starting point is that the provisions do not apply to, and do not bind, the United Kingdom and Ireland, but under Article 3 of Protocol No 4 the United Kingdom and Ireland may opt in to any proposal or initiative under Title IV. Under Article 4, these countries may also opt in to a regime in an adopted measure. In relation to Ireland only, Article 6 contains a provision permitting Ireland to give notice that it no longer wishes to be covered by the terms of the Protocol. The provisions of Protocol No 5 concerning Denmark are drafted somewhat differently, but essentially also make Title IV optional for Denmark, except for those measures determining the third countries whose nationals must have a visa when crossing the external borders of the Member States and the measures setting up a common visa policy.

Article 61 EC commits the Community to the progressive establishment of an area of freedom, security and justice.[18] This involves the adoption within five years

[13] Formerly Justice and Home Affairs, now re-named Police and Judicial Co-operation in Criminal Matters following the move of certain areas of Justice and Home Affairs to the EC Treaty.

[14] Though visa policy was covered by former Article 100c EC.

[15] Craig, P and de Búrca, G, *EU Law. Text, Cases, and Materials* (Oxford, 2003), at 752.

[16] Protocol No 3 (1997): United Kingdom and Ireland: Border Controls, and Protocol No 4 (1997): United Kingdom and Ireland: Visas, Asylum etc., annexed by the Treaty of Amsterdam to the EC Treaty and the Treaty on European Union.

[17] Protocol No 5 (1997): Denmark: Border Controls and Defence, annexed by the Treaty of Amsterdam to the EC Treaty and the Treaty on European Union.

[18] See generally Walker, N (ed), *Europe's Area of Freedom, Security and Justice* (Oxford, 2004).

from the entry into force of the Treaty of Amsterdam,[19] of 'measures aimed at ensuring the free movement of persons in accordance with Article 14, in conjunction with directly related flanking measures with respect to external border controls, asylum and immigration'. The programme also includes other measures in the field of asylum, immigration, and the safeguarding of the rights of third country nationals.

Article 62 EC concerns the removal of controls on citizens of the Union and third country nationals alike when crossing internal borders, as well as a common visa policy for stays of up to three months by third country nationals entering the Community. Article 63 EC requires the adoption of measures concerned with asylum and refugees, as well as a common visa policy for long-term visas and residence permits for third country nationals, and rights of free movement for this group of persons. Following the Tampere European Council meeting, there is a policy of bringing the rights of third country nationals lawfully resident in the territory of a Member State much more closely into line with the rights enjoyed by citizens of the Union.[20]

Article 64 EC contains important security safeguards:

1. This Title shall not affect the exercise of the responsibilities incumbent upon Member States with regard to the maintenance of law and order and the safeguarding of internal security.

2. In the event of one or more Member States being confronted with an emergency situation characterised by a sudden inflow of nationals of third countries and without prejudice to paragraph 1, the Council may, acting by qualified majority on a proposal from the Commission, adopt provisional measures of a duration not exceeding six months for the benefit of the Member State concerned.

Article 65 EC concerns judicial co-operation in civil matters about such matters as cross-border service of judicial documents, while Article 66 EC concerns general co-operation between the administrations of the Member States in the matters within Title IV. The lengthy Article 67 EC concerns voting arrangements; in the first five years of its operation the Council is very much in the driving seat and unanimity among the participating Member States is required, whereas after that period a unanimous decision may determine that the procedure in Article 251 EC be used for further measures.

Article 68 EC contains the special rules for obtaining preliminary rulings concerning the interpretation of Title IV and the validity and interpretation of acts made under it. This limits the ability to make references to those courts or tribunals 'against whose decisions there is no judicial remedy under national law'. Measures taken under Article 62(1) EC relating to the maintenance or law and order, or the safeguarding of internal security are excluded from the preliminary ruling procedure. Finally, there is a special preliminary ruling procedure under

[19] 1 May 1999.

[20] For a brief summary and comment see Editorial, 'The Tampere summit: The ties that bind *or* The Policeman's Ball' (1999) 36 CMLRev 1119.

which the Council, the Commission or a Member State[21] may request the Court of Justice to give a ruling on a question of interpretation of Title IV or acts made under it, but any ruling given in response to such a request does not apply to judgments before national courts or tribunals which have become *res judicata*.

The Schengen Arrangements

The abolition of checks at the frontiers of certain Member States which has come to be known as the Schengen arrangements can be tracked back to agreements among five European countries outside the framework of the Community. Schengen is the small town in Luxembourg where the original Schengen Agreement was signed. In June 1985, five Member States[22] signed a treaty to end internal border checkpoints and controls. There are now 15 Schengen countries:[23] Austria, Belgium, Denmark, Finland, France, Germany, Iceland, Italy, Greece, Luxembourg, Netherlands, Norway, Portugal, Spain and Sweden.[24] Norway and Iceland are not Member States, though they are parties to the EEA Agreement.[25] The territories of these 15 countries has come to known as the 'Schengen zone'. Under these arrangements, which came into effect on 26 March 1995,[26] citizens of participating countries can cross the internal borders of the participating countries at any point without checks being carried out. Any national of a country other than a participating country with a residence permit valid in one of the participating countries does not need a passport to travel for up to 90 days in another participating country. Information is collected and shared between the participating countries through the Schengen Information System (SIS),[27] which provides personal identity and other data throughout the Schengen zone.

The body of law known as the 'Schengen acquis' consists of the following acts:

- the Agreement signed in Schengen on 14 June 1985 between the Benelux countries, Germany and France of the gradual abolition of checks at their common borders;
- the Convention signed in Schengen on 19 June 1990 between Belgium, Germany, France, Luxembourg and the Netherlands implementing the Agreement of 14 June 1985 with related Final Act and common declarations;

[21] As distinct from a final court or tribunal in the national legal order of a Member State.
[22] Belgium, the Netherlands, Luxemburg, France and Germany.
[23] Negotiations with Switzerland were opened in 2001, but suspended in February 2004.
[24] That is, all the current Member States except the United Kingdom and Ireland. Both Ireland and the United Kingdom have received approval to take part in some aspects of the Schengen arrangements in relation to the collection and sharing of information under the Schengen Information System (but not to the removal of frontier checks). See below in this chapter for a comment on enlargement and the Schengen arrangements.
[25] See below in this chapter.
[26] See http://www.eurovisa.info/SchengenCountries.htm.
[27] A second generation information system known as SIS II is being developed.

- the Accession Protocols and Agreements with Italy signed on 27 November 1990, Spain and Portugal signed on 25 June 1991, Greece signed on 6 November 1992, Austria signed on 28 April 1995, and Denmark, Finland and Sweden signed on 19 December 1996, with related Final Acts and declarations;
- decisions and declarations adopted by the Executive Committee which was established by the 1990 Implementing Convention, as well as Acts adopted for the implementation of the Convention by the organs upon which the Executive Committee has conferred decision-making powers.

The implementation of the Schengen arrangements is complex because of the need for participating countries to agree a common visa policy,[28] and to provide for sharing of information by the police and judicial authorities through the Schengen Information System.

The Treaty of Amsterdam brought the Schengen arrangements within the framework of the European Union through the incorporation into the Treaty of the Schengen Protocol. The Council has taken over the role previously undertaken by the Schengen Executive Committee. The common rules for visas, asylum, checks at external borders and co-operation between police and judicial authorities have been incorporated into Title IV of the EC Treaty and Title VI of the Treaty on European Union.

The Schengen arrangements have both a positive and negative aspect. On the positive side, they represent a visionary dismantling of national frontiers and produce an area without frontiers or border controls for citizens of the participating countries. Internal borders disappear. These benefits will also accrue to those legitimately in the territory of the participating countries. But there has to be some common agreement on who is entitled to be legitimately in those countries so that decisions taken by one participating country are acceptable to all. Hence the need for a common visa policy. The downside of the arrangements is that the removal of frontiers and border controls within the group has tended to be compensated for by stricter controls on external borders. The phrase 'fortress Europe' has been coined as a catchphrase to describe the risks inherent in the development of more open internal arrangements. There have also been concerns that there is a risk of migrants with Schengen visas disappearing into the territories of the participating countries or working illegally. This is countered by the Schengen Information System, but this is such a massive information database that it is complex to administer and some regard it as too intrusive.[29] It is interesting to note that both Ireland and the United Kingdom have obtained approval to participate in the Schengen Information System without removing frontier controls or opening up their borders.

28 The visa issued under these arrangements is often referred to as a 'Schengen visa'.

29 See Colvin, M, 'The Schengen Information System: a Human Rights Audit' [2001] EHRLR 271.

The European Economic Area Agreement

In order to understand the European Economic Area, it is necessary to know a little about the European Free Trade Association (EFTA). EFTA was founded through the Stockholm Convention[30] in 1960 by seven European countries.[31] It is supported by an institutional structure consisting of the EFTA Secretariat, the EFTA Surveillance Authority, and the EFTA Court. Following accession to the European Community, a number of participating countries left EFTA, so that it now consists of four countries: Iceland, Liechtenstein, Norway and Switzerland.[32] The objectives of EFTA are to support free trade as a means of achieving growth and prosperity, and closer co-operation between the countries of western Europe. Its immediate objectives were the creation of a free trade area among its members. EFTA countries that were not members of the European Economic Community concluded free trade agreements with the Community, but these have been overtaken by the European Economic Area Agreement which entered into force in 1994. The remaining EFTA countries have negotiated a number of free trade agreements across the globe.

The European Economic Area (EEA) Agreement[33] was signed in May 1992 between the then 12 Member States and the then six EFTA countries: Austria, Finland, Iceland, Norway, Switzerland and Sweden. A referendum in Switzerland resulted in the decision of that country not to participate in the EEA Agreement. The Agreement entered into force on 1 January 1994. Three of the original EFTA countries have subsequently become Member States of the European Union, and Liechtenstein acceded to the EEA in May 1995. The end result is that there are three EEA countries: Iceland, Liechtenstein and Norway. The EEA Agreement is essentially a co-operation agreement between the EFTA countries (except Switzerland) and the European Union. It permits the EEA countries to participate in the four freedoms and certain related flanking measures without assuming full membership of the Union. It requires the EEA countries to implement the *acquis communautaire* in so far as it relates to the four freedoms into their national legal orders.

The *acquis communautaire* for the purposes of the EEA Agreement consists of Community law on the four freedoms[34] plus those provisions relevant to the four freedoms in the areas of social policy, consumer protection, the environment and company law necessary to complete the extended internal market. In addition the

[30] Convention establishing the European Free Trade Association signed at Stockholm on 4 January 1960, and entered into force on 3 May 1960. Revisions to the Convention were agreed at Vaduz on 21 June 2001 and entered into force on 1 June 2002. Convention texts are available at http://secretariat.efta.int/Web/EFTAConvention/.

[31] Austria, Denmark, Norway, Portugal, Sweden, Switzerland and the United Kingdom. Finland joined in 1961, Iceland in 1970, and Liechtenstein in 1991.

[32] With a total population for all four countries of around 12 million.

[33] An association agreement concluded under what is now Article 310 EC: see below in this chapter.

[34] Although agriculture and fisheries are only included to a very limited extent.

competition law and policy of the EEA Agreement closely parallels that of the EC Treaty. Changes in the law of the European Union are automatically included in the EEA Agreement. This is achieved through the work of the EEA Joint Committee on which the EEA countries and the European Commission are represented. All new rules adopted by the EEA Joint Committee must be incorporated into the national law of the EEA countries. The EFTA Surveillance Authority and the EFTA Court are responsible for ensuring that the EEA countries comply with their obligations under the EEA Agreement.

The position of Switzerland

Switzerland is an EFTA country which is not a party to the EEA Agreement and so is not an EEA country. Its relationship with the Community and Union has been ambivalent, but co-operation has been long-standing and Switzerland has long had a permanent mission to the European Community in Brussels. In order to avoid the adverse consequences of rejection of participation in the EEA Agreement in the referendum referred to above, Switzerland entered into negotiations in 1994 for agreements with the European Union in seven sectoral areas: (1) free movement of persons; (2) trade in agricultural goods; (3) public procurement; (4) conformity assessments; (5) air transport; (6) transport by road and rail; and (7) scientific and technological co-operation. These agreements were finalized in 1999 and approved in May 2000 in a Swiss referendum. They entered into force on 1 June 2002. All seven agreements are linked so that they entered into force on the same date, and, if terminated, will all end on the same date. Negotiations with Switzerland are under way for further bilateral agreements with the Union. The agreements are primarily of an economic nature designed to improve access for Switzerland to the market of the European Union, and vice versa.

The agreement on the free movement of persons covers rights of entry and residence, access to employment and self-employment, access to study, free movement for persons without gainful employment who have sufficient financial resources of their own coupled with adequate health insurance cover, and co-ordination of social security rules. There are detailed transitional provisions which will not be fully exhausted until 2014. The agreement also foresees a liberalization of services,[35] but this is subject to a separate agreement currently under negotiation, though there is an agreement on public procurement which touches on the area of services.

[35] For example, from 1 June 2004, cross-border provision of services by individuals and business organizations for up to 90 days a year is possible without the need for a permit. But this liberalization does not apply to the activities of employment agencies.

Other association agreements

This section looks in outline at the EC–Turkey Association Agreement, and at a number of features of the Europe Agreements concluded with the countries of central and eastern Europe as a precursor to admission to membership of the Union in so far as both refer to the free movement of persons. There are, of course, other association agreements which touch on this area of Community law.[36]

Article 310 EC is short but is the legal base for many international agreements:

> The Community may conclude with one or more States or international organisations agreements establishing an association involving reciprocal rights and obligations, common action and special procedure.

Agreements concluded under Article 310 (and its predecessor, Article 238) become part of the Community legal order, and are subject to the preliminary ruling procedure in Article 234 EC if a question of their interpretation arises.[37]

EC–Turkey Association Agreement

One of the earliest and most developed association agreements is that between the Community and Turkey signed in 1963, and known as the Ankara Agreement, with an Additional Protocol added in 1970.[38] This was an association agreement entered into as a precursor to possible membership of the Community by Turkey.[39] Under this association agreement, the Community and Turkey agree, inter alia, to be guided by the relevant articles of the EC Treaty for the purposes of progressively securing between themselves the free movement of workers, for the purpose of abolishing restrictions on freedom of establishment, and on freedom to provide services between them.[40] The progressive establishment of the free movement of workers has generated a significant body of case law. Article 36 of the Protocol

[36] See, for example, agreements with Algeria, Morocco, and Tunisia, with the CIS countries, and the Cotonou Convention with the countries of the African, Caribbean and Pacific region. See generally Weiss, F and Woodlridge, F, *Free Movement of Persons within the European Community* (The Hague, 2002), ch 10. On the Cotonou Convention, see Arts, K, 'ACP-EU relations in a new era: The Cotonou Agreement' (2003) 40 CMLRev 95.

[37] Even if the agreement is a 'mixed agreement', that is, one which has been signed and ratified by both the Community and the Member States each within their respective spheres of competence, though in such cases the Court's jurisdiction is limited to matters within the scope of the EC Treaty. See Case 12/86 *Demirel* [1987] ECR 3719.

[38] Both documents can be found at [1977] OJ L361/29. See generally Rogers, N, *A Practitioner's Guide to the EC-Turkey Association Agreement* (The Hague, 1999).

[39] See art 28 of the Ankara Agreement. Turkey applied for membership of the Community in 1987. Current deliberations on Turkish membership take place in the context of Accession Partnerships; for the most recent document see [2003] OJ L145/40.

[40] Such an obligation, being progressive in nature, does not give rise to direct effect: Case 12/86 *Demirel* [1987] ECR 3719.

envisaged the completion of the programme for the free movement of workers by 1985, but for a variety of reasons this was not achieved.

The Ankara Agreement is supported by an Association Council with power to make Decisions in the field of its application. Decision 1/80 of the Association Council contains important rules for Turkish workers in a Member State, but the rights only arise for those duly registered as belonging to the labour force of a Member State.[41] The Court of Justice has often noted that the Association Agreement does not give any entitlement to entry; this remains a matter for the Member States who can determine whether Turkish nationals are admitted for employment and the terms under which they work for the first year of their employment.[42] However, the Court has said that the provisions of the Decision represent 'a further stage in securing freedom of movement for workers based on Articles 48, 49 and 50 of the Treaty' and that it is 'essential to extend, so far as possible, the principles enshrined in those Treaty articles to Turkish workers who enjoy the rights' conferred by the Decision.[43]

Under Article 6(1), such workers are entitled, after one year's legal employment, to renewal of a permit for the same employer; after three years' legal employment and subject to priority being given for nationals of the Member States, to take up another offer of employment in the same occupation; and after four years' of legal employment, to a right of residence for the purposes of undertaking any paid employment in that State.

The *Sevince* case[44] concerned a Turkish national in the Netherlands. Sevince had been resident in the Netherlands for over a year, but he was refused an extension to the residence permit which he had initially been granted since his family circumstances had changed. He argued that he had a right of residence under Article 6(1) of Decision 1/80. He had been working while his appeal against the refusal of the extension of his residence permit had been wending its way through the Dutch courts. The Court of Justice concluded that Article 6(1) was capable of giving rise to direct effect, but also concluded that the term 'legal employment' did not include the situation of a person who was authorized to engage in work during the suspensory period of an appeal in respect of his right to reside in the Member State in question. This view was confirmed in the *Kus* case.[45] Here a Turkish national in Germany was found to be entitled to renewal of his work permit after

[41] But it is not open to a Member State to exclude whole sectors of employment where Turkish nationals meet the requirements of Decision 1/80: see Case C-98/96 *Ertanir* [1997] ECR I-5179, paras 31–35 of the judgment.

[42] See, for example, Case C-171/95 *Tetik* [1997] ECR I-379, para 21 of the judgment.

[43] See Case C-36/96 *Günaydin* [1997] ECR I-5143, para 21 of the judgment.

[44] Case C-192/89 *Sevince* [1990] ECR I-3461, affirmed in Case C-386/95 *Eker* [1997] ECR I-2697, Case C-36/96 *Günaydin* [1997] ECR I-5143, and Case C-1/97 *Birden* [1998] ECR I-7747. See also Case C-285/95 *Kol* [1997] ECR I-3069, which makes the obvious point that the rights do not attach to work under a residence permit which had been obtained fraudulently. For a recapitulation of the case law, see Case C-188/00 *Kurz, né Yüce* [2002] ECR I-10691.

[45] Case C-237/91 *Kus* [1992] ECR I-6781.

having been employed for a year, even though his right of residence had been based on admission for the purpose of marriage and by the date of renewal the marriage had been dissolved. Furthermore, the Court held that the right to a work permit would be rendered nugatory unless it included a right of residence. However, it was held in the *Eroglu* case[46] that the right to renewal of a work permit did not apply where the prior work on which the claim was predicated was under a special authorization to permit a university graduate to obtain specialized knowledge in connection with the higher education.[47]

The Court has repeatedly stated that the legality of the employment for the purposes of Article 6(1) 'presupposes a stable and secure situation as a member of the labour force of a Member State'.[48] Furthermore:

> The legality of the employment engaged in over a certain period must be determined in the light of the legislation of the host State governing the conditions under which the Turkish worker entered the national territory and is employed there.[49]

In the *Bozkurt* case, the question arose as to whether an international lorry driver was in legal employment in the Netherlands. The Dutch government did not require him to have a work permit, but he was employed by a Dutch company, and in the periods between his journeys and when he was not working, he lived in the Netherlands. The Court concluded that it was for the national court to determine whether there were sufficiently close links to the Netherlands for the Turkish national to be regarded as belonging to the labour force of the Netherlands. In doing so, they must pay full regard to the place where he was hired, the territory on which the paid employment was based, and the applicable legislation in the fields of employment and social security law. The incomplete nature of the rights enjoyed by Turkish workers under the Association Agreement is evident in this case, in which Bozkurt was seeking to remain in the Netherlands after suffering an accident at work which meant that he could no longer work. The Court ruled that there was no such right under Decision 1/80.

The parallel interpretation of the rights arising under the Association Agreement with those arising under the provisions of the EC Treaty can be seen in the *Nazli* case.[50] Nazli had lived in Germany for over 10 years, but he was subsequently convicted of involvement in drug trafficking and sentenced to a suspended term of imprisonment. He had been detained in prison pending his trial and this naturally interrupted his employment record. He was subsequently in work, but the renewal of his residence permit was refused because of his conviction. The detention did

[46] Case C-355/93 *Eroglu* [1994] ECR I-5113.

[47] The case also ruled that Art 7, dealing with the rights of children of Turkish workers within the scope of the Decision, is capable of giving rise to direct effect. See also Case C-351/95 *Kadiman* [1997] ECR I-2133, Case C-65/98 *Eyüp* [2000] ECR I-4747, Case C-210/97 *Akman* [1998] ECR I-7519, and Case C-327/97 *Ergat* [2000] ECR I-1487.

[48] For example in Case C-434/93 *Bozkurt* [1995] ECR I-1475, para 26 of the judgment.

[49] ibid, para 27 of the judgment.

[50] Case C-340/97 *Nazli* [2000] ECR I-957.

not prevent his being treated as a member of the labour force of Germany. Furthermore, Article 14 of Decision 1/80 which applies limitations based on grounds of public policy, public health and public security was to be interpreted as requiring consideration of Nazli's personal conduct. The refusal to renew the residence permit as a deterrent to other foreign workers without considering his personal circumstances was not compatible with Community law requirements.[51]

Decision 1/80 also touches on the right of establishment. Article 13 of the Ankara Agreement provides:

> The Contracting Parties agree to be guided by Articles 52 to 56 and Article 58 of the Treaty establishing the Community for the purpose of abolishing restrictions on freedom of establishment between them.[52]

Article 41 of the Additional Protocol is a standstill clause requiring the Member States to introduce no new restrictions on freedom of establishment, and provides for the setting up of a timetable for the abolition of existing restrictions. Immigration rules tend to take a more liberal approach to establishment as distinct from employment, since the establishment of new businesses is seen as contributing to the economy. It is not, however, unusual for immigration rules to indicate that a person intending to establish a business have a high level of resources available to do so, together with a detailed business plan.

The *Savas* case[53] concerned Mr and Mrs Savas who had entered the United Kingdom on tourist visas. They overstayed and Mr Savas subsequently set up a shirt factory; he later opened a fast food business. More than 10 years had gone by since their initial admission. A deportation order was made, which was contested. The Court ruled that the standstill provision was capable of giving rise to direct effect, and so could be pleaded in national courts. Like the rights to work, the Association Agreement did not give any rights of entry for the purposes of establishment, and a Turkish national's first admission to a country is determined solely by reference to national law. Any rights flowing from work, or self-employed activity, could only be pleaded if the position in the Member State was regular.

The provisions of the Association Agreement offer significant guarantees to Turkish nationals who are admitted to a Member State for work (and, by analogy, self-employment), but give no initial right of entry. In this regard, the Ankara Agreement is significantly different from the rights given to nationals of the Member States in the EC Treaty. The Member States have the choice over the admission of Turkish nationals for economic activity. Once admitted, many, but not all, of the rights which arise under the EC Treaty are extended to Turkish nationals and their families.[54]

[51] See below, ch 5. [52] The relevant Treaty articles are now Arts 43–46 and 48 EC.

[53] Case C-37/98 *ex parte Savas* [2000] ECR I-2927.

[54] So, for example, the rules co-ordinating social security among the Member States also apply to Turkish nationals under Decision 3/80. See on Decision 3/80 Case C-262/96 *Sürül* [1999] ECR I-2685.

Europe Agreements

The Europe Agreements represent a uniform approach to the development of relations with the countries of central and eastern Europe as they prepared for membership of the European Union.[55] Title IV of these agreements deals with the free movement of workers, the right of establishment and the freedom to provide services. Like the Ankara Agreement, the Europe Agreements make entry for the purposes of employment a matter for the determination of the Member State, and so continuing residence is conditioned upon lawful entry.

The *Gloszczuk* case[56] concerned the Gloszczuk family; Mr and Mrs Gloszczuk had entered the United Kingdom on tourist visas and had overstayed the period for which they have been given leave to remain. Mr Gloszczuk then worked as a builder before setting himself up in self-employment as a builder. A child was born to the couple. When the immigration authorities caught up with the family and deportation was threatened, the family sought to rely on provisions of the Europe Agreement with Poland relating to the right of establishment in order to avoid their removal from the United Kingdom.

Article 58 of the Europe Agreement states that, in relation to the provisions on the free movement of persons, nothing in the Agreement is intended to limit the Member States from applying their own laws in relation to entry and residence 'provided that . . . they do not apply them in a manner as to nullify or impair the benefits accruing to any Party under the terms of a specific provision of this Agreement'. Article 44 of the Europe Agreement with Poland deals with establishment. Article 44(3) reads:

> Each Member State shall grant . . . a treatment no less favourable than that accorded to its own nationals for the establishment of Polish companies and nationals . . . and shall grant in the operation of Polish companies and nationals established in its territory a treatment no less favourable than that accorded to its own companies and nationals.

The Court ruled that this provision is capable of giving rise to direct effect. Furthermore rights of entry and residence are corollaries of the right of establishment which is conferred on Polish nationals, but these rights are not absolute privileges because of the provisions of Article 58, since they may be limited by the rules of the host Member State governing the entry, stay and residence of Polish nationals. The Court goes on to say that the two provisions read together do not preclude a system of checks on entry in order to determine whether a person genuinely intends to take up self-employment without at the same time entering into employment, and has sufficient financial resources to do so. It is also not

[55] See generally, Böcker, A and Guild, E, *Implementation of the Europe Agreements in France, Germany, the Netherlands and the UK: Movement of Persons* (London, 2002). There are Europe Agreements with the accession countries (except for Cyprus and Malta with whom there are long-standing association agreements) and with Bulgaria and Romania.

[56] Case C-63/99 *Gloszczuk* [2001] ECR I-6369.

inconsistent with the terms of the Agreement to reject an application made under Article 44(3) on the sole ground that the applicant was residing illegally on the territory of the Member State because of false representations made on initial entry into that territory, or a failure to comply with conditions attaching to the initial grant of entry. However, this cannot preclude a later application for admission for the purposes of establishment which permit the situation of the applicant to be reviewed. This indicates, once again, that lawful entry and presence which is determined by the application of national law, is a precondition to becoming a beneficiary of the rights contained in the Europe Agreements.[57] However, the case law also makes it clear that the barriers which national rules require to be met must not be such as to render it impossible to take advantage of the benefits granted by the Europe Agreements.

The *Jany* case[58] concerned applications for residence permits in the Netherlands by two Polish nationals and four Czech nationals to enable them to carry on activities as self-employed prostitutes. The Court recapitulated its rulings under the earlier judgments on the interpretation of the Europe Agreements, but went on to conclude that the activity of prostitution in a self-employed capacity can be regarded as a service provided for remuneration, and so constitutes an economic activity. A Member State could only refuse a residence permit for such activity, if shown to be genuine, on grounds of public policy, public security or public health, and this would require the Member State to take repressive measures in respect of the activity in relation to its own nationals. Conduct which is accepted for a Member State's own nationals cannot constitute a genuine threat to public order. Ultimately, the Court left it to the national courts to determine the question of whether the women concerned were genuinely self-employed in the sense that there was no relationship of subordination concerning the choice of activity, working conditions and conditions of remuneration, that the women worked under their own responsibility, and for remuneration paid directly to them in full.

The issue of whether the provisions of the Europe Agreements preclude a Member State from establishing a system under which applications for a residence permit with a view to establishment in the host Member State may be rejected without examination where the applicant does not have a valid temporary residence permit obtained in the applicant's country of origin is before the Court in a pending case.[59] The Advocate General's Opinion in this case is consistent with the earlier authorities in recognizing a right of residence for those establishing themselves subject to initial controls on entry operated by the host Member State.

[57] See also to the same effect Case C-235/99 *Kondova* [2001] ECR I-6427, which concerned a Bulgarian national granted temporary admission as an asylum seeker, and Case C-257/99 *Barkoci and Malik* [2001] ECR I-6557, which concerned two Czech nationals, both members of the Roma community, also claiming asylum in the United Kingdom.

[58] Case C-268/99 *Jany and others* [2001] ECR I-8615.

[59] Case C-327/02 *Panayotova and others*. The Advocate General's Opinion in this case was delivered on 19 February 2004.

However, restrictions on the right of establishment must be based on objective criteria which can be known in advance by applicants and they must be susceptible to review by the courts. They must not make the exercise of the right of establishment impossible or excessively difficult. Irregularities in the past should not colour any subsequent requests for entry by making the exercise of the right impossible or excessively difficult. Furthermore, an automatic rule which rejected applications from those lawfully resident in the Member State on the sole basis that they do not hold a temporary residence permit obtained in the country from which they come is not regarded as appropriate to pursue any legitimate objective and is capable of making the exercise of the right of establishment impossible or excessively difficult. If, as seems likely, the Court follows the Advocate General's Opinion, this indicates the power of the Europe Agreements to offer nationals of the countries with whom the Union has Europe Agreements rights approaching those which obtain under the EC Treaty itself. There do remain controls on initial entry, but the application of national immigration decision-making is heavily circumscribed by Community law.

Enlargement

Ten new States joined the European Union on 1 May 2004, but there are detailed Treaties of Accession with these 10 new Member States. In relation to the law of the internal market relating to workers, establishment and services, there will be transitional periods over which the full application of the Treaty rules will be phased in. The Europe Agreements did not give a right of access to the labour markets of the Member States for nationals of the applicant countries. The result is that virtually all nationals from the new Member States who were, prior to 1 May 2004, workers in the territories of the 15 existing Member States were there as a result of the application national immigration rules or of the provisions of bilateral agreements between the countries in question.[60]

In the past, it has been common to have transitional periods for the implementation. These have been followed by, or coupled with, a period during which safeguard measures may be taken if there are serious or persistent disruption of the labour market as a result of the exercise of the free movement rights. In the case of the accession of Spain and Portugal, a transitional period of seven to 10 years for the free movement of workers was agreed, though the full operation of the Treaty provisions was achieved after six years.[61] The 2004 enlargement has been

[60] Though, as noted above, those lawfully resident in one of the Member States acquired rights under the Europe Agreements, and from 1 May 2004 acquired rights under the EC Treaty.

[61] Transitional periods for the right of establishment, and freedom of movement to provide services have not been applied on past enlargements. This is largely accounted for by provisions in agreements prior to accession which have placed the way for free movement in these sectors. There are, however, special rules in relation to posting of workers from Germany and Austria.

accompanied by a very high level of concern about the potential of labour migration to disturb the labour markets of some Member States. Such concerns have flowed from geographic proximity,[62] considerable variations in earnings levels, differential levels of unemployment, and a concern that there will be a greater propensity for labour migration than with earlier enlargements.

It is important to realize that the transitional period covers only the right of movement for the purposes of employment. There will be an immediate right to move for the purposes of study or residence.[63] The arrangements for the 2004 enlargement are as follows. Until 1 May 2006, the current Member States may choose to apply national rules to the admission of workers from the new Member States.[64] After this two-year period, the Commission will report on migration patterns and the current Member States will be required to define their position from 1 May 2006. The expectation is that some of the alarmist talk about labour migration will not materialize and that it will be possible to move to the application of Community rules on the free movement of workers. Those countries which did so would be able to apply safeguard measures for a period of three years in the event of their experiencing serious and unexpected disturbances of the labour market.[65]

From 1 May 2009, those current Member States still applying national rules would be called upon to open up their labour markets subject to the possibility of seeking safeguard measures to address serious and unexpected disturbances of the labour market. From 1 May 2011, Community rules will apply to movement of workers to all current Member States.

Free movement of workers who are nationals of the current Member States to the new Member States will take effect under the same transitional arrangements, though it is likely that some Member States will choose to apply a very liberal regime from the date of enlargement. There is a seven-year safeguard provision written into the Treaties of Accession for Malta.

Finally, there is a standstill clause, under which no Member State may introduce measures more restrictive than those in place immediately prior to 1 May 2004. There will also be a Community preference in the labour market for nationals of the new Member States over nationals from countries which are not members of the European Union.

[62] Leading to a prediction that labour migration will be concentrated in the so-called 'front-line' Member States.

[63] Subject to the requirements of Community law in relation to movement for such purposes. See below, ch 7.

[64] Except Cyprus and Malta, whose nationals enjoy full Community law rights from 1 May 2004.

[65] On previous enlargements, similar safeguard measures have been available, but they have never been invoked.

Comment

Much of the material in this chapter shows that the web of provisions drawn from the core rules on the free movement of persons to be found in the EC Treaty is large and complex. The rules on the free movement of persons are not just for the nationals of the Member States, though the Member States have generally[66] remained very firmly in control of decisions on initial entry into their territories for those who are not nationals of one of the Member States.

The approach taken in this book is to divide what the author chooses to call the core law on workers, establishment and service in the European Union into three parts. The first, or general, part examines the underlying rules of entitlement, the prohibition of discrimination, the mutual recognition of qualifications, exceptions to the Treaty rules, and the system of remedies for breach of the Community rules. The second part extracts from the EC Treaty, secondary legislation and the case law of the Court of Justice, the personal rights enjoyed by individuals in exercising their rights of free movement. The third part separates out the case law and legislative developments that are more concerned with the regulation of market access, and of business activities. This methodology offers a greater sense of coherence in the case law on workers, establishment and services, and also highlights the significant benefits the Community rules give to citizens of the Union, while not ignoring the case law on the prohibition of obstacles to the exercise of the rights of free movement.

[66] The EEA Agreement and the agreement with Switzerland are the major exceptions.

Part II

The General Part

2

Entitlement

Introduction

The law on the free movement of persons has been dominated in the literature by a treatment of the law relating to the free movement of workers. The result has been a focus on individuals as the beneficiaries of the rules. However, once the focus shifts to establishment and services, businesses are just as likely to be beneficiaries of the rules as individuals. A recurring theme in this book is the tension between, on the one hand, ensuring the fair treatment of individuals and social integration of migrant workers, and, on the other, regulating the obstacles Member States place, or tolerate in the private sector, on the exercise of the free movement of persons. This chapter focuses on entitlement to the benefit of the rules in the EC Treaty on the free movement of persons, in terms of the territorial, personal, and material scope of the provisions.

Territorial scope

Member States

In very simple terms, the rules in the Treaty apply to the territories of the 15 Member States of the European Union,[1] plus the EEA countries: Iceland, Liechtenstein and Norway.[2] However, the detail is much more complex, though in most cases it is not likely to be difficult to establish the status of a part or parts of the territory of a Member State or EEA country for the purpose of the application of the rules on the free movement of persons.

For the Member States, Article 299 EC sets out the rules of territorial application, and both extends and limits the territorial application of the Treaty rules in a number of cases. As a general proposition, the territories of the Member States would appear to include those areas of the adjacent seas over which the Member State has jurisdiction. This includes the territorial sea,[3] and it would follow also the

[1] From 1 May 2004, this will be 25 when the following new Member States join: Cyprus, Czech Republic, Estonia, Hungary, Latvia, Lithuania, Malta, Poland, Slovakia and Slovenia. In addition Bulgaria, Romania and Turkey have applied for membership of the European Union.

[2] Subject to modifications as set out in the EEA Treaty.

[3] Case 61/77 *Commission v Ireland* [1987] ECR 417, paras 46-50 of the judgment.

exclusive economic zone and continental shelf.[4] It does not appear to be the case that vessels and aircraft are equated with territory for the purpose of Community law.[5]

Article 299 EC spells out special arrangements for particular territories. There is specific provision for the application of the Treaty to the European territories for whose external relations a Member State is responsible. The best example of such a territory is Gibraltar. The Treaty applies to the French overseas departments, but special arrangements apply to the Portuguese islands of the Azores and Madeira and Spain's Canary Islands.[6] Under Article 182 EC the Member States agree to associate with the Community the non-European countries and territories which have special relations with Denmark, France, the Netherlands, and the United Kingdom listed in Annex II to the EC Treaty.[7] Article 299(3) provides that the special arrangements in Part IV of the Treaty apply to these overseas countries and territories, but the article goes on to specify that those special arrangements do not apply to British overseas countries and territories omitted from the list in Annex II.

Article 186 EC provides:

> Subject to the provisions relating to public health, public security or public policy, freedom of movement within Member States for workers from the countries and territories, and within the countries and territories for workers from Member States, shall be governed by agreements to be concluded subsequently with the unanimous approval of Member States.

In practice, this offers little to these territories, and the practical arrangements have been overtaken by Joint Declarations made under the Cotonou Convention.[8]

The Treaty does not apply to the Faeroe Islands, British sovereign bases in Cyprus, and only applies to the Åland Islands, the Channel Islands and the Isle of Man to the extent specified in the special arrangements referred to in Article 229(5) and (6) EC.[9] The status of the Isle of Man arose in the *Barr* case.[10] Montrose Holdings employed Mr Barr as a company lawyer without first obtaining a work permit for him as required by the law of the Isle of Man. This resulted in a

[4] Bleckmann, A, 'The Personal Jurisdiction of the European Community' (1980) 17 CMLRev 467, at 473.

[5] But the ruling of the Court of Justice in Case 9/88 *Mário Lopes da Veiga v Staatssecretaris van Justitie* [1989] ECR 2989, discussed below, probably secures a similar result by different reasoning.

[6] Art 299(2) EC.

[7] Greenland, New Caledonia and Dependencies, French Polynesia, French Southern and Antarctic Territories, Wallis and Futuna Islands, Mayotte, Saint Pierre and Miquelon, Aruba, Netherlands Antilles (Bonaire, Curaçao, Saba, Sint Eustasius, Sint Maarten), Anguilla, Cayman Islands, Falkland Islands, South Georgia and the South Sandwich Islands, Montserrat, Pitcairn, St Helena and Dependencies, British Antarctic Territory, British Indian Ocean Territory, Turks and Caicos Islands, British Virgin Islands, and Bermuda.

[8] Partnership Agreement between the members of the African, Caribbean and Pacific Group of States (ACP) of the one part, and the European Community and its Member States, of the other part, signed in Cotonou on 23 June 2000, [2000] OJ L317. See below in this chapter.

[9] Note also the special status of Mount Athos in Greece by virtue of a joint declaration appended to the Final Act of the Greek Act of Accession.

[10] Case C-355/89 *Department of Health and Social Security v Barr and Montrose Holdings Ltd* [1991] ECR I-3479, noted at (1992) 17 ELRev 522.

prosecution of both Barr and the employing company. The Court was called upon to interpret provisions of Protocol 3 to the Act of Accession of 1972. Article 2 of that Protocol preserves the rights of Manxmen in the United Kingdom but excludes them from the provisions on the free movement of persons and services, while Article 4 provides that the authorities of the Isle of Man shall apply the same treatment to all natural and legal persons of the Community. Barr and the company argued that the Isle of Man legislation requiring Barr to have a work permit contained provisions which, in certain cases, put nationals of the United Kingdom and the Republic of Ireland in a more favourable position than nationals of other Member States. This, it was argued, constituted a breach of the equal treatment provision in Article 4 of the Protocol and so tainted the whole legislation. The Court of Justice ruled that this was not so; just because other provisions of the legislation applied to Barr, and the company might operate in a discriminatory manner which breached Article 4 of the Protocol, did not necessarily render the whole work permit scheme in the Manx legislation invalid. The second argument sought to extend the favourable treatment accorded by the United Kingdom to Manxmen (who are not required to have work permits) to all nationals of the Member States, but the Court ruled that there was no obligation on the Isle of Man authorities to treat such nationals as favourably as the United Kingdom accorded to Manxmen in this regard. A United Kingdom argument that the equal treatment provision applied only to the free movement of goods was rejected by the Court which stated:

> [Article 4] must be interpreted as precluding any discrimination between natural and legal persons from the Member States in relation to situations which, in territories where the Treaty is fully applicable, are governed by Community law.[11]

EEA countries

Article 28(1) EEA provides that freedom of movement for workers is to be secured among the Member States and the EEA countries. There are specific provisions relating to the free movement of workers in this context, which extend the principal secondary legislation to the EEA countries.[12] Similar provisions are made for the right of establishment,[13] and the free movement of services.[14]

The application of the rules on the free movement of persons to the EEA countries must be read in the light of Articles 112 and 113 EEA which permit the EEA countries to take safeguard measures if 'serious economic, societal or environmental difficulties of a sectorial or regional nature liable to persist' arise. There are also two joint declarations relating to recognition of medical and other qualifications secured in Iceland, which note that it is common for certain parts

[11] ibid, para 17 of judgment. [12] Annex V EEA.
[13] Article 31 and Annexes VIII–XI EEA. [14] Article 36 and Annexes IX–XI EEA.

of specialist training to take place in third countries and that this should not preclude mutual recognition of those qualifications. Furthermore a unilateral declaration by Liechtenstein states that a situation justifying measures under Articles 112 and 113 EEA should be considered to exist 'in the case of an extraordinary increase in the number of nationals from the EC Member States or the other EFTA States, or in the total number of jobs in the economic, both in comparison with the number of the resident population'. A unilateral declaration by Iceland seeks to confirm that it may take safeguard measures if 'serious disturbances on the labour market through large-scale movements of labour into certain geographical areas, particular types of jobs, or branches of industry'. Such considerations do not, of course, give rise to any possibility of safeguard measures by the Member States.

Location of the economic activity

It is a condition of the exercise of the freedom of movement of persons that the activity in question takes place in a territory to which the Treaty rules apply. This does not appear to give rise to frequent problems. In the case of *Walrave and Koch*,[15] two Dutch nationals who took part in international cycle racing as pacemakers challenged rules of the Union Cycliste Internationale and the Dutch and Spanish cycling federations requiring the pacemaker to be the same nationality as the stayer.[16] As is well known, the Court ruled that the practice of sport is subject to Community law so far as it constitutes an economic activity, though the composition of national teams is not caught by the prohibition of discrimination on grounds of nationality. Absent such considerations, the prohibition did apply. The Court of Justice was invited to say whether the legal position may depend on whether the sporting competition is held within or outside the Community. The Court replied:

> By reason of the fact that it is imperative, the rule on non-discrimination applies in judging all legal relationships in so far as these relationships, by reason either of the place where they are entered into or of the place where they take effect, can be located within the territory of the Community.

It is for the national judge to decide whether they can be so located, having regard to the facts of each particular case, and, as regards the legal effect of these relationships, to draw the consequences of any infringement of the rule on non-discrimination.[17]

[15] Case 36/74 *Walrave and Koch v Association Union Cycliste Internationale, Koninklijke Nederlandsche Wielren Unie and Federacion Española Ciclismo* [1974] ECR 1405.

[16] Pacemakers offer their services for remuneration and set a pace on a motorcycle in medium distance cycle racers with the stayer (who is the competitor) cycling in the lee of the motorcycle.

[17] Case 36/74 *Walrave and Koch v Association Union Cycliste Internationale, Koninklijke Nederlandsche Wielren Unie and Federacion Española Ciclismo* [1974] ECR 1405, paras 28-9 of the judgment.

The *Prodest* case[18] concerned a simple point. Should the social insurance of an employee, a Belgian national resident in France, employed by a French company and posted temporarily to Nigeria, be maintained during that temporary absence? The Court, referring to its decision in the *Walrave and Koch* case, ruled that activities temporarily carried on outside the territory of the Community are not sufficient to exclude the application of Community law as long as the employment relationship retained a sufficiently close link with a Member State. The Court goes on to make clear that such a link was established in this case.[19]

In the *Lopes da Veiga* case,[20] the question arose as to whether the employment of a Portuguese national on a Dutch registered ship was sufficient to give the employee the status of a person employed in the Netherlands. The Court says explicitly that permanent employment provides a sufficiently close link with the territory of the State of nationality of the ship to engage Community law.

In the *Boukhalfa* case, Advocate General Léger provided a non-exhaustive list of criteria for extraterritorial application of Community law, as follows:

- an employment relationship entered into by a Community worker and an undertaking in another Member State;
- recruitment of the Community worker in a Member State;
- a Community national established in a Member State at the time of recruitment;
- employment by an employer established in the Member State of which the worker is a national;
- the employer is subject to the legal system of a Member State;
- the employment relationship is governed by the law of the Member State of which the employer is a national;
- a Community worker working for the undertaking which employs him even if it is in a non-Member country;
- the Community worker belongs to the social security system of a Member State of which his employer is a national;
- the Community worker is liable for income tax in the member State of which his employer is a national.[21]

The Advocate General warns against a process of weighing the scales by putting factors in favour on one side of the scales and factors against on the other. The proper question in every case is whether, having regard to all the circumstances of each particular case, there is a sufficiently close link with the Community.

[18] Case 237/83 *Sàrl Prodest v Caisse Primaire d'Assurance Maladie de Paris* [1984] ECR 3153.

[19] ibid, para 7 of the judgment.

[20] Case 9/88 *Lopes da Veiga v Staatssecretaris van Justitie* [1989] ECR 2989, affirmed in Case C-60/93 *Alderwereld v Staatssecretaris van Financiën* [1994] ECR 2991, and Case C-214/94 *Boukhalfa v Germany* [1996] ECR I-2263.

[21] Case C-214/94 *Boukhalfa v Germany* [1996] ECR I-2253, para 46 of the Opinion, see generally paras 35-47 of the Opinion.

Personal scope

A second requirement applicable to employment, establishment and services in order to benefit from the rules on the free movement of persons is that the beneficiary, whether individual or business entity, has the nationality of a Member State or of an EEA country.[22] The allocation of nationality to individuals is a matter for each Member State to determine, subject to very limited intervention by Community law. The allocation of nationality to 'companies or firms' is also a matter for each Member State but this is subject to Article 48 EC discussed below.

Nationality of individuals

The reservation of the attribution of nationality to the Member States and the EEA countries reflects the general position at international law encapsulated in Article 1 of the Hague Convention of 1930[23] which provides:

> It is for each State to determine under its own law who are its nationals. This law shall be recognised by other States in so far as it is consistent with international conventions, international custom and the principles of law generally recognised with regard to nationality.

Article 3 of the Council of Europe's European Convention on Nationality is remarkably similar:

> 1. Each State shall determine under its own law who are its nationals.
>
> 2. This law shall be accepted by other States in so far as it is consistent with applicable international conventions, customary international law and the principles of law generally recognised with regard to nationality.[24]

A few Member States have attached declarations to the relevant Treaty of Accession on who are to be regarded as its nationals for the purposes of Community law. The Treaty on European Union also contains a Declaration which re-affirms that any question of the possession of nationality of a Member State is to be determined solely by reference to the national law of the Member State concerned, and recognizes that Member States may declare who are to be considered their nationals for Community purposes.[25] So Germany included a declaration on accession that its nationals were to be regarded as those deemed to be its nationals

[22] Art 39(1) and (2) (ex 48) EC on workers (though it is only clear from para (2) that workers must be nationals of a Member State), art 43 (ex 52) EC on establishment, and art 49 (ex 59) EC on services.

[23] 179 LNTS 89.

[24] European Convention on Nationality, signed at Strasbourg on 6 November 1997, ETS 166. As at 23 June 1999 it has been signed by eight Member States, and ratified by only Austria from among the Member States. It requires three ratifications to enter into force. See generally, Hall, S, 'The European Convention on Nationality and the Right to have Rights' (1999) 24 ELRev 586.

[25] See Case C-192/99 *R v Secretary of State for the Home Department, ex parte Kaur* [2001] ECR I-1237.

under the Basic Law.[26] The current British declaration[27] lists three categories of person to be regarded as United Kingdom nationals for the purposes of Community law:

- British citizens;
- persons who are British subjects by virtue of Part IV of the British Nationality Act 1981 and who have the right of abode in the United Kingdom and are therefore exempt from United Kingdom immigration control;
- British Dependent Territories citizens who acquired their citizenship from a connection with Gibraltar.

Questions of nationality have been brought before the Court of Justice. The case law has established that there are limits on the capacity of other Member States to deny an individual the benefits of the nationality of one of the Member States or an EEA country. The issue arose squarely in the *Micheletti* case[28] in the context of the rules on establishment. Micheletti held dual nationality: that of Italy and of Argentina. He wished to establish himself in Spain, which refused him a residence permit, relying on a provision in the Spanish Civil Code to the effect that, in cases of dual nationality, precedence would be given to the country of the person's habitual residence immediately prior to the entry into Spain. In Michelletti's case this was Argentina. Michelletti challenged the refusal to recognize his Italian nationality, and questions were referred to the Court of Justice. The Court ruled that a Member State could not apply its internal law on nationality to deny recognition to a dual national of the nationality of another Member State.

It is also clear that Member States cannot require more than a minimum documentation to determine nationality; and this had been referred to as a factor in the *Micheletti* case. The *Giagounidis* case[29] concerned Panagiotis Giagounidis, who held a Greek national identity card of indefinite duration issued in 1967, which under Greek law does not permit a person to leave the national territory. The Greek authorities had refused to extend the validity of his Greek passport, and so in 1984 when he applied for a residence permit[30] in Germany, he presented his identity card as evidence of his nationality but this was rejected by the German authorities. The Court ruled that it should not have been. Since his identity and nationality were not contested, Giagounidis was entitled to rely on the identity card as evidence of his identity and nationality and, if he met the other conditions, to be issued with a residence permit on the basis of it.

[26] Bleckmann, A, 'German Nationality within the Meaning of the EEC Treaty' (1978) 15 CMLRev 435.

[27] [1983] OJ C23/1, and see Simmonds, K, 'The British Nationality Act 1981 and the Definition of the Term "National" for Community Purposes' (1984) 21 CMLRev 675.

[28] Case C-369/90 *M V Micheletti and others v Delegación del Gobierno en Cantabria* [1992] ECR I-4239, noted at (1993) 30 CMLRev 623.

[29] Case C-376/89 *Panagiotis Giagounidis v City of Reutlingen* [1991] ECR I-1069.

[30] A document providing evidence of his right to reside in a Member State under the provisions of the EC Treaty.

The laws of the Member States govern changes of nationality just as they govern the attribution of a nationality.

Union citizenship

Nationals of the Member States (but not of EEA countries) are by reason of that nationality declared to be citizens of the European Union.[31] This complements and does not replace national citizenship.[32] Union citizens enjoy the rights conferred by the Treaty, which are spelled out in Articles 18 to 21 EC. Principal among these is the right to move and reside freely within the territory of the Member States, 'subject to the limitations and conditions laid down in this Treaty and by the measures adopted to give it effect'. The introduction of citizenship gave rise to no new rights of free movement and it has been challenged as a citizenship without meaning.[33] The citizenship is also said to be subject to the duties imposed by the Treaty, but there are none.

An intriguing statement in the *Micheletti* case that it is 'for each Member State, *having due regard to Community law*, to lay down the conditions for the acquisition and loss of nationality'[34] takes on added significance now that possession of the nationality of a Member State passports such a person to Union citizenship, which may well develop into something meaningful in due course. Hall has argued that this means that there is now an important qualification to the power of a Member State to withdraw its nationality from individuals, since to do so will (unless they are also nationals of another Member State) deprive them of Union citizenship.[35]

A line of cases beginning with the *Martínez Sala* case[36] has indicated quite how powerful Union citizenship might be, since the existence of citizenship alone provides a basis for bringing a person within the material scope of the EC Treaty and so entitles them to equality of treatment, at least where they are already lawfully resident in a Member State other than that of which they are a national.[37]

Nationality of companies and firms

Article 48 EC refers to 'companies or firms', which are defined as 'companies or firms constituted under civil or commercial law, including cooperative societies,

[31] See generally on Union citizenship, O'Leary, S, *The Evolving Concept of Community Citizenship. From the Free Movement of Persons to Union Citizenship* (The Hague, 1996).

[32] Article 17 (ex 8) EC.

[33] See, for example, Weiler, J, 'European Citizenship and Human Rights' in Winter, J and others (eds), *Reforming the Treaty on European Union. The Legal Debate* (The Hague, 1996) at 57. But see also ch 6 below.

[34] Case C-369/90 *M V Micheletti and others v Delegación del Gobierno en Cantabria* [1992] ECR I-4239, para 10 of the judgment (emphasis added).

[35] Hall, S, 'Loss of Union Citizenship in Breach of Fundamental Rights' (1996) 21 ELRev 129.

[36] Case C-85/96 *Martínez Sala v Freistaat Bayern* [1998] ECR I-2691, noted at (1999) 24 ELRev 68.

[37] Some of these issues are considered further in chs 7 and 8 below.

and other legal persons governed by public or private law, save for those which are non-profit-making'. The definition is broad enough to encompass nearly all business entities. The exception of non-profit-making legal persons is potentially problematic. The purpose of the clause has been said to be the exclusion of organizations of a political, cultural, religious, social or charitable character, and so are not commercial in nature.[38] It is, however, clear that such entities can and do engage in economic activity.[39]

The basis on which states attribute nationality to companies and firms varies considerably, and is, of course, of much more recent vintage than the basis for attributing nationality to individuals. There appear to be two bases on which nationality is attributed to companies; the first is based on the place of incorporation, and the second is based on the 'real seat'[40] of the company.[41] It is unclear whether companies and firms can hold dual nationality, but the possibility cannot be excluded. For example, the United Kingdom would regard a company registered under English law as a United Kingdom company, whereas if that company's principal place of business and the centre of its administration was in a different Member State, that country may also accord the company its nationality. Some commentators refer to the doctrine of *siège réel* involving 'the "re-creation" of the foreign company in accordance with the requirements of the legal system of the host State' and implies a 'certain legal schizophrenia'.[42]

The Court tends not to refer to nationality when dealing with companies or firms. In *Commission v France*[43] the Court ruled that the right of establishment includes the right of companies or firms formed in accordance with the law of a Member State through having their registered office, central administration or principal place of business within the Community to pursue their activities in another Member State through an agency, branch or subsidiary. In the *Segers* case[44] the Court confirmed that 'a company formed in accordance with the law of another Member State and which conducts its business through an agency, branch or subsidiary in the Member State in which it seeks to establish itself cannot be deprived of the benefit'[45] of the rule set out in *Commission v France*. In the *Centros* case,[46] the Court of Justice affirmed that the provisions of the EC Treaty gave nationals of the Member States the freedom to establish companies under what

[38] Everling, U, *The Right of Establishment in the Common Market* (Chicago, 1964), at 69; Wyatt, D and Dashwood, A, *Wyatt & Dashwood's European Community Law*, 3rd edn, (London, 1993), at 299.

[39] As, for example, the Bhagwan community in Case 196/87 *Steymann v Staatssecretaris van Justitie* [1988] ECR 6159.

[40] *Siège réel* or *siège social* in French.

[41] See generally Drury, R, 'Migrating Companies' (1999) 24 ELRev 354.

[42] Cath, I, 'Free Movement of Legal Persons' in Schermers, H *et al* (eds), *Free Movement of Persons in Europe. Legal Problems and Experiences* (Dordrecht, 1993) 450, at 459.

[43] Case 270/83 *Commission v France* [1986] ECR 273.

[44] Case 79/85 *Segers v Bestuur van de Bedrijfsvereniging voor Bank-en Verzekeringswezen, Groothandel en Vrije Beropen* [1986] ECR 2375.

[45] ibid, para 14 of the judgment.

[46] Case C-212/97 *Centros Ltd v Erhvervs-og Selskabsstyrelsen* [1999] ECR I-1459, noted at (2000) 25 ELRev 157, and (2000) 49 ICLQ 621.

they saw as the most advantageous corporate form, and restricted the ability of Member States to refuse to recognize a company formation.[47]

The issue tends to have its greatest impact in the context of taxation questions. Such an issue arose in the *Daily Mail* case[48] in the context of the residence of a company. The Court of Justice was called upon to consider whether a company could transfer its central management and control away from the United Kingdom without HM Treasury consent while maintaining its legal personality and its status as a United Kingdom company. The Court ruled that companies, as 'legal persons', are creatures of law. The differing requirements of connecting factors to the State in which a company was registered and restrictions on the transfer from one Member State to another are not currently controlled by Community law. This means that their freedom of movement is more limited than that of individuals, though they retain a right to undertake activities in other Member States. In other words, the residence of companies, in the sense of the link to the State of incorporation or 'real seat', can result in differences of treatment from that accorded to individuals, since the current state of Community law does not regulate the control of corporations to the extent that it does individuals. The result was that a company could not use the right of establishment as the basis for moving its place of central control and management to another Member State for tax reasons without obtaining the required national consent.

There is considerable debate as to whether the Court's decisions in *Centros* and *Überseering* have over-ruled its decision in the *Daily Mail* case. But it has certainly not done so expressly.[49]

Material scope

Introduction

In the case of workers, establishment and services, a key requirement will be some form of economic activity falling within the definition of employment, establishment, or services. There are, however, limited rights available to certain groups who cannot bring themselves within the ambit of economic activity constituting employment, establishment or services. These are students, retired persons, and persons of independent means whose position is governed by three specific directives, all of which condition the exercise of free movement on the requirement that

[47] See paras 26 and 27 of the judgment. See also Case C-208/00 *Überseering v Nordic Construction Company Baumanagement* [2002] ECR I-9919, noted at (2003) 28 ELRev 528.
[48] Case 81/87 *R v HM Treasury and Commissioners of Inland Revenue, ex parte Daily Mail and General Trust plc* [1988] ECR 5483.
[49] See discussion in Dyrberg, P, 'Full free movement of companies in the European Community at last?' (2003) 28 ELRev 528, at 536–7.

the person is not dependent on public assistance from the State of residence.[50] Save for these groups, the requirement of economic activity reflects the commercially-based origins of the rights of free movement. The Court has taken a broad approach to the concept of economic activity.[51] Attempts to argue that professional sport does not constitute economic activity have found little favour with the Court, which has nevertheless accommodated competitions between national teams by permitting a requirement of a link between players and the national team they are representing and the exclusion of foreign players from such teams.[52]

In some cases, it may not be necessary to locate the economic activity precisely within one of the three heads of employment, establishment or services. The Court has said that the rights arising under the rules on these three different types of activity are based on the same principles in so far as they concern rights of entry and residence in another Member State and the prohibition of discrimination on grounds of nationality.[53] The *Roux* case[54] concerned a French national seeking to obtain a right to enter and reside in Belgium. It was unclear from the terms of her contract whether she was an employed or self-employed waitress. As the former, she would fall within the rules on workers, while as the latter she would fall within the rules on establishment. The Court ruled that the precise determination of her status was irrelevant, since it was clear that in either case she would have a right to enter and reside in Belgium. The position might well be different if rights other than entry and residence or the prohibition of discrimination on grounds of nationality were in issue.

Employment

Workers under Article 39 EC are those in employment. In order to secure the uniform application of Community law, the Court of Justice has stated that determining whether a person holds the status of worker is to be decided by applying a Community definition and not solely national criteria.[55] The case law on this issue has established a formal test and a sufficiency test. The formal test determines whether a person is an employee, while the sufficiency test determines whether the nature and quality of the work undertaken is such that a person can be regarded as engaged in effective and genuine work as an employee. The formal test

[50] Discussed further below in ch 8.

[51] See, for example, Case 196/87 *Steymann v Staatssecretaris van Justitie* [1988] ECR 6159.

[52] Case 36/74 *Walrave and Koch v Association Union Cycliste Internationale, Koninklijke Nederlandsche Wielren Unie and Federacion Española Ciclismo* [1974] ECR 1405; Case 13/76 *Dona v Mantero* [1976] ECR 1333; affirmed in Case 415/93 *Union Royale Belge des Sociétés de Football Association, ASBL and others v Jean-Marc Bosman and others* [1995] ECR I-4921.

[53] Case 48/75 *Royer* [1976] ECR 497.

[54] Case C-363/89 *Roux v Belgium* [1991] ECR I-273.

[55] Case 75/63 *Hoekstra (née Unger) v Bestuur der Bedrijfsvereniging voor Detailhandel en Ambachten* [1964] ECR 177.

was established in the *Lawrie-Blum* case,[56] which required an affirmative answer to be given to three questions:

- is the person obliged to work for another?
- is the work done for monetary reward?
- is the person subject to the direction and control of another?

If so, the person is an employee. It will not matter that the post is a training post; Deborah Lawrie-Blum was a trainee teacher. Work done for remuneration constitutes an economic activity, even though the purpose of the work is not to make a profit, as in the case of a teacher. A later case[57] established that 'monetary reward' included payment in kind, and that the condition of monetary reward should be so construed. It may, therefore, be better to think of the second condition as work done in exchange for remuneration which may take a number of forms.

The sufficiency test predates the formal test, but it is logical to determine first whether a person is an employee before considering the nature and quality of the work. The *Levin* case[58] concerned a British woman who sought a residence permit as a worker in the Netherlands on the basis of part-time work as a chambermaid in a hotel for which she earned less than the national minimum wage. The Dutch authorities did not regard her as being engaged in gainful employment. The Court of Justice confirmed that being engaged in part-time work and being low paid did not prevent a person from being a worker. The Court continued,

> It should however be stated that whilst part-time employment is not excluded from the field of application of the rule of freedom of movement for workers, those rules cover only the pursuit of effective and genuine activities, to the exclusion of activities on such a small scale as to be regarded as purely marginal and ancillary. It follows both from the statement of the principle of freedom of movement for workers and from the place occupied by the rules relating to that principle in the system of the Treaty as a whole that those rules guarantee only the free movement of persons who pursue or are desirous of pursuing an economic activity.[59]

It is for the national court to apply this test, and it will not be easy to do so in marginal cases. The case law, however, provides some illustrations which can assist. In the *Kempf* case[60] the Court took the reasoning in the *Levin* case one step further by adding that a person pursuing a part-time activity (which constitutes both employment and effective and genuine activities) may qualify as a worker even though income from the work is supplemented by recourse to public assistance. In the *Raulin* case[61] the Court gave guidance on drawing the dividing line between, on the one hand, effective and genuine activities, and, on the other, work which is

[56] Case 66/85 *Lawrie-Blum v Land Baden-Württemberg* [1986] ECR 2121.
[57] Case 196/87 *Steymann v Staatssecretaris van Justitie* [1988] ECR 6159.
[58] Case 53/81 *Levin v Staatssecretaris van Justitie* [1982] ECR 1035.
[59] ibid, para 17 of the judgment.
[60] Case 139/85 *Kempf v Staatssecretaris van Justitie* [1986] ECR 1741.
[61] Case C-357/89 *Raulin v Netherlands Ministry of Education and Science* [1992] ECR I-1027, noted at (1992) 17 ELRev 522.

so marginal and ancillary that it is not sufficient to constitute work. Two important points were made. First, the duration of the activities was a relevant factor, and, secondly, the national court should consider all the occupational activities undertaken by the person in the host Member State *but not* occupational activities pursued elsewhere in the Community. Such an approach may, however, be criticized, since it segments the territory of the Community. For example, it could operate to the disadvantage of a person who undertook work in a ski resort in Austria during the skiing season and short-term work in a number of Mediterranean resorts in different Member States over the summer months. Taken as a whole, such a person would appear easily to meet both the formal and sufficiency tests. But when the activity is disaggregated, the person might appear to be little more than a beach bum!

The facts of the *Ninni-Orasche* case[62] were somewhat different. Franca Ninni-Orasche, an Italian national married to an Austrian national, had been living in Austria. About two years after she had moved to Austria, she worked for less than three months as a waitress and cashier on a fixed-term contract; she also acquired an Italian diploma in book-keeping and commerce. A number of job applications for which she was qualified by reason of her diploma were unsuccessful. She then started a degree course in romance languages at university in Austria, and applied for financial support for her studies. In responding to questions raised by the national court, the Luxembourg Court recapitulated the key statements in its earlier case law. The Court emphasized that 'the national court must base its examination on objective criteria and assess as a whole all the circumstances of the case relating to the nature of both the activities concerned and the employment relationship in issue.'[63] The short duration of the employment against the period of residence in the host State was not relevant to the determination of whether the work was purely marginal and ancillary. The expiry of a fixed term contract does not necessarily result in the conclusion that the employee is voluntarily unemployed. Again the national court must examine all the circumstances of the case.[64] The reasoning in this case might suggest that the restrictive view expressed in the *Raulin* case is no longer the correct approach.

Finally, in the *Bettray* case[65] the Court took a surprisingly narrow view of work schemes for reformed drug addicts. A German national was seeking a right to remain in the Netherlands. He was in work on a scheme provided under the Dutch law on social employment exclusively for those under a process of rehabilitation from drug dependence. The Court held that such work was not genuine and

[62] Case C-413/01 *Ninni-Orasche v Bundesminister für Wissenschafter, Verkehr und Kunst,* Judgment of 6 November 2003, [2003] ECR nyr.

[63] Para 27 of the judgment.

[64] Note that the Advocate General, but not the Court, considered the question of whether Ninni-Orasche as a person lawfully resident had, in any event, an entitlement to equal treatment with Austrian nationals under Arts 12 and 17 EC. He concluded that she had following the decision in *Grzelczyk:* see ch 7 below.

[65] Case 344/87 *Bettray v Staatssecretaris van Justitie* [1989] ECR 1621, noted at (1989) 14 ELRev 415.

effective, since the social aspects of the work were of greater importance than the economic aspects of the activity. The case appears to turn on its rather special facts, and at least one commentator has been keen to stress that the effect of the decision is not to take all sheltered employment schemes (for example, for people with disabilities) out of the scope of the rules on the free movement of workers.[66]

Establishment

Perhaps somewhat surprisingly, the definition of establishment has given rise to less case law. This is probably because the concept is a very broad one, and includes activities by individual as well as business organizations. Article 43 EC states that 'Freedom of establishment shall include the right to take up and pursue activities as self-employed persons and to set up and manage undertakings, in particular companies or firms . . . ' In the *Gebhard* case, the Court said:

> The concept of establishment within the meaning of the treaty is therefore a very broad one, allowing a Community national to participate, on a stable and continuous basis, in the economic life of a Member State other than his State of origin, so contributing to economic and social interpenetration within the Community in the sphere of activities as self-employed persons.[67]

Establishment would appear to indicate a permanent activity of a stable and continuous nature.[68] In the *Factortame* case, the Court said that 'the concept of establishment . . . involves the actual pursuit of an economic activity through a fixed establishment in another Member State for an indefinite period.'[69] The requisite presence may be through a branch or agency, or merely an office representing the enterprise.[70] There must, however, be some element of cross-border activity.[71]

In a case concerning the interpretation of the Europe Agreements,[72] the Court took the opportunity to offer a definition of self-employment. It is clear from the Court's reasoning that the provisions of the Europe Agreements in relation to self-employment are to be interpreted on the basis that they are the same concepts as are found in the EC Treaty.[73] The person engaged in the activity must meet the following conditions for the activity to constitute self-employment:

[66] Watson, P, 'Free movement of workers: recent cases' (1989) 14 ELRev 415, at 423–4.

[67] Case C-55/94 *Gebhard v Consiglio dell'Ordine degle Avvocati e Procuratori di Milano* [1995] ECR I-4165, para 25 of the judgment.

[68] Case C-70/95 *Sodemare SA, Anni Azzuri Holdings SpA & Anni Azzuri Rezzato Srl v Regione Lombardia* [1997] ECR I-3395, para 24 of the judgment.

[69] Case C-221/89 *R v Secretary of State for Transport, ex parte Factortame* [1991] ECR I-3905, para 20 of the judgment

[70] Case C-205/84 *Commission v Germany* [1986] ECR 3755, para 21 of the judgment.

[71] Joined Cases C-54/88, 91/88 and 14/89 *Criminal Proceedings against Nino and others* [1990] ECR I-3537, para 11 of the judgment and Case C-108/98 *RI.SAN* [1999] ECR I-5219, para 23 of the judgment.

[72] Case C-268/99 *Jany and others* [2001] ECR I-8615.

[73] Para 38 of the judgment.

- there is no relationship of subordination concerning the choice of the activity, working conditions and conditions of remuneration;
- the activity is engaged under the person's own responsibility; and
- the remuneration is paid in full to the person directly.[74]

Services

Services are often regarded as a residual category of activity where something does not constitute employment or self-employment. But that is to downplay the significance of services as economic commodities rivalling goods in their extent.[75] One has only to think of the vast range of financial services currently available through giant financial institutions operating on a global scale. Article 50 EC provides:

Services shall be considered services within the meaning of this Treaty where they are normally provided for remuneration, insofar as they are not governed by the provisions relating to freedom of movement for goods, capital and persons.

'Services' shall in particular include:
(a) activities of an industrial character;
(b) activities of a commercial character;
(c) activities of craftsmen;
(d) activities of the professions.

The key distinction between establishment and services is that establishment requires a degree of permanence whereas the provision of services connotes the temporary pursuit of the activity. Services provided on a permanent scale will be governed by the rule on establishment, while services provided on a temporary basis will constitute service provision within the EC Treaty. The effect of an activity constituting services will be that the host State can become less engaged in the regulation of that activity than if the rules on freedom of establishment were engaged. Chapter 3 of Title III governs both the liberalization of specific services and the removal of restrictions on the freedom to provide services within the Community.

The Court has defined the remuneration in exchange for a service in a case involving higher education funded essentially our of public funds as follows:

. . . the essential characteristic of remuneration lies in the fact that it constitute consideration for the service in question, and is normally agreed upon between the provider and the recipient of the service.[76]

It is also clear that medical services, such as a medical termination of a pregnancy, can constitute a service.[77]

[74] Para 71 of the judgment. [75] See ch 11 below for elaboration of this point.
[76] Case C-109/92 *Wirth v Landeshaupstadt Hannover* [1993] ECR I-6447, para 15 of the judgment.
[77] Case C-159/90 *SPUC v Grogan* [1991] ECR I-4685, para 18 of the judgment.

It will be a breach of the provisions in the EC Treaty guaranteeing freedom to provide services for national legislation to be framed in such a way that provision of services is precluded.[78]

One line of cases on services has addressed the extent to which the host State can regulate the activities of service providers when the personnel of the service provider are present on their territory.[79] In the *Rush Portuguesa* case[80] non-Member State nationals were sent by Rush Portuguesa to work on construction sites in France. The French Labour Inspectorate discovered Portuguese workers on site without work permits and reports were made to the *Office national d'immigration.* That office served notices on Rush Portuguesa requiring a special contribution to the office in lieu of prosecutions. Those notices were challenged in administrative proceedings, and questions were referred to the Luxembourg Court. The Court confirmed that contractors in one Member State who secured a contract for works in another Member State were entitled to bring their own work force into the host Member State in order to perform the contract regardless of their nationality. The host Member State could, however, conduct checks to ensure that the work force is genuinely engaged in the performance of the contract, and could extend its own labour laws to the workforce. A similar situation arose in the *Vander Elst* case.[81] Here Vander Elst, a business established in Belgium, secured a one-month contract to demolish a château in Reims. Among the work force sent to undertake the work were four Moroccan nationals who held only short-stay visas. A check by the French Labour Inspectorate discovered their circumstances and referred the matter to the *Office des Migrations Nationales* who raised a notice requiring a special contribution. Vander Elst appealed against this notice and questions were referred to the Luxembourg Court on the scope of the Treaty provisions on services. Referring to its decisions in *Rush Portuguesa*, the Court of Justice, which responded,

> The answer to the questions referred to the Court must therefore be that Articles 59 and 60 [49 and 50] of the Treaty are to be interpreted as precluding a Member State from requiring undertakings which are established in another Member State and enter the first Member State in order to provide services, and which lawfully and habitually employ nationals of non-member countries, to obtain work permits for those workers from a national immigration authority and to pay the attendant costs, with the imposition of an administrative fine as the penalty for infringement.[82]

In its reasoning, the Court makes clear that such workers do not, in fact, enter the labour market of the host Member State, and do not acquire any immigration

[78] See Case C-493/99 *Commission v Germany* [2001] ECR I-8163, which concerned German legislation which required undertakings to have their seat or a branch in Germany in order to provide trans-frontier services on the German market.

[79] See Giesen, R, 'Posting: Social Protection of Workers vs. Fundamental Freedoms?' (2003) 40 CMLRev 143.

[80] Case C-113/89 *Rush Portuguesa v Office national d'immigration* [1990] ECR I-1417.

[81] Case C-43/93 *Vander Elst v Office des Migrations Internationales* [1994] ECR I-3803. See Peers, S, 'Indirect Rights for Third Country Service Providers Confirmed' (1995) 20 ELRev 303.

[82] ibid, para 26 of the judgment.

rights as against the host Member State by reason of their presence to perform their employer's contract.

The reach of the host Member State's laws for the social protection of workers was addressed in the *Arblade* case.[83] A French company secured a contract for the construction of a large sugar silo complex in Belgium. Part of the work was subcontracted to another French company, Arblade. Belgian Labour Inspectors required the French company to produce a number of documents required by Belgian social law. Arblade took the view that it remained subject to French social legislation, and was not also subject to Belgian social legislation. The questions raised before the Court of Justice essentially raised the question of the reach of Belgian social law in these circumstances. The Court deals with this question as one concerning the permissibility of a restriction on the delivery of services. The protection of workers is an overriding reason relating to the public interest, and so may be the subject of legitimate regulation by the host State so long as it goes no further than is required to meet the requirements of that aim *and* in so far as that interest is not already adequately protected by the rules to which the undertaking is subject in its home Member State. Accordingly, rules on minimum pay for workers may be applied but prosecutions for breach may only follow if those rules are 'sufficiently precise and accessible' that the nature of obligations undertaken in relation to the workforce of service providers can be readily known.[84] But where there are comparable rules in the home Member State, such as, for example, contributions to funds for the protection of workers or the keeping of records, mere differences of form rather than purpose cannot justify the imposition of a dual burden. Furthermore, a requirement that certain documents be retained in the host Member State for a period of five years and to retain them at the address of an individual rather than a business entity cannot be justified.

The judgment in the *Mazzoleni* case[85] returned to the issue of minimum pay in the context of questions referred in the course of criminal proceedings against a French enterprise for failing to comply with Belgian law on minimum pay. The French enterprise was a company which provided security guards for shopping malls. It seemed that the work patterns of the security guards might vary considerably, and that their movement across the border between France and Belgium was sporadic.[86] The employer argued that the varying work patterns meant that the overall position of their workers was not prejudiced; the French minimum pay was lower than the Belgian minimum pay, but so was the French tax charged on that pay. Though the Court confirmed its earlier case law on the applicability of

83 Joined Cases C-369/96 and 276/96 *Arblade* [1999] ECR I-8453. See also Case C-272/94 *Criminal Proceedings against Guiot* [1996] ECR I-1905.

84 ibid, para 42 of the judgment.

85 Case C-165/98 *Criminal Proceedings against Mazzoleni and Inter Serveillance Assistance SARL* [2001] ECR I-2189.

86 It was argued that for this reason Directive 96/71/EC concerning the posting of workers in the framework of the provision of services, [1997] OJ L18/1, did not apply.

minimum pay legislation in the host Member State, it qualified that case law by indicating that:

the application of such rules might . . . prove to be disproportionate where the workers involved are employees of an undertaking established in a frontier region who are required to carry out, on a part-time basis and for brief periods, a part of their work in the territory of one, or even several, Member States other than that in which the undertaking is established. It is therefore for the competent authorities in the host Member State to establish whether, and if so to what extent, application of national rules imposing a minimum wage on such an undertaking is necessary and proportionate in order to ensure the protection of the workers concerned.[87]

The *Portugaia Construções* case[88] also concerned minimum pay requirements applied by the host Member State, on this occasion Germany. A Portuguese company had posted workers to Germany, whose pay was found to be below the level set by the German collective labour agreement. The Portuguese company argued that the underlying motivation of the German rules was not compatible with Community law, since it had referred to the protection of the domestic construction industry and the need to reduce unemployment in order to avoid social tensions.[89] These, it was argued, were economic aims which could not justify a restriction on the freedom to provide services. The Court rather ducked the issue, noting that the stated aims are not conclusive and that it is for the national court[90] to determine whether, viewed objectively, the rules in question promote the protection of posted workers.[91]

The application of national laws for the protection of posted workers is now also protected by Directive 96/71/EC.[92] The Directive only applies where workers[93] are sent by their employer in one Member State to work in another Member State; it has no application where a person simply seeks employment in a Member State other than that of his or her nationality. The Directive contemplates three types of arrangement under which the worker is sent abroad to work: (1) there is a contract for the provision of services; (2) the undertaking in the home Member State has a branch or subsidiary in another Member State; and (3) placement by an employment agency in one Member State in work in another Member State. The host Member State is regarded as having an interest in checking that the posted worker is properly protected in seven areas: (1) working hours; (2) minimum pay;

[87] Case C-165/98 *Criminal Proceedings against Mazzoleni and Inter Serveillance Assistance SARL* [2001] ECR I-2189, para 41 of the judgment.

[88] Case C-164/99 *Portugaia Construções* [2002] ECR I-787.

[89] Rather than explicitly for the protection of workers.

[90] Which will virtually always be those of the Member State whose legislation is being called into question.

[91] Case C-164/99 *Portugaia Construções* [2002] ECR I-787, para 28 of the judgment.

[92] Directive 96/71/EC of 16 December 1996 concerning the posting of workers in the framework of the provision of services, [1997] OJ L18/1. See generally Davies, P, 'Posted Workers: Single Market or Protection of National Labour Law Systems?' (1997) 34 CMLRev 571.

[93] As determined by the law of the host Member State.

(3) regulation of the conditions of workers supplied by agencies; (4) health and safety requirements; (5) protection of pregnant women, young mothers, children and young persons; (6) equal treatment of men and women; and (7) other provisions on non-discrimination. Collectively agreed standards as embodied in national labour codes or collective agreements in these areas of the host Member State must be applied to posted workers. An original proposal that the Directive should only apply where the posting was for more than three months was not included in the final text, so that the provisions of the Directive apply to all postings of whatever duration. As Davies notes, this capitulates somewhat to host State regulation; they have been 'dealt . . . most of the aces'.[94] He concludes:

> . . . whilst the Directive is likely to become an ornament of social policy of the Community, those wishing that more weight had been given to the free-movement dimension will have to rely on the perhaps vain hope that, in relation to short-term postings, the rules in the Directive will not be fully reflected in what happens 'on the ground'.[95]

It remains unclear whether Article 39 EC applies to a posted worker who is a national of one of the Member States. It is submitted that the better view is that such a worker is covered by Article 39 EC. If this is correct, then there may be provisions of Directive 96/71/EC which are incompatible with Community law since they offer a different scheme of protection than that envisaged by Article 39 EC and Regulation 1612/68.[96] Similarly, there is an argument that certain provisions of Directive 97/71/EC go beyond what is permitted under Articles 49 and 50 EC.[97] The rules in the Directive may themselves constitute the application of a dual burden which is not permitted under the EC Treaty as interpreted by the Court of Justice.

Distinguishing establishment and services

The leading case on the distinction between establishment and services is the *Gebhard* case.[98] The case concerned a Germany lawyer who practised in Italy, if he was established in Italy, he would be subject to regulation by the Italian bar, but if he was only a service provider, the Italian bar would have to adopt a much more hands-off approach to the regulation of his legal practice.[99] The test to be applied is

[94] Davies, P, 'Posted Workers: Single Market or Protection of National Labour Law Systems?' (1997) 34 CMLRev 571, at 591.
[95] ibid, at 602.
[96] See ch 8 below.
[97] Davies, P, 'Posted Workers: Single Market or Protection of National Labour Law Systems?' (1997) 34 CMLRev 571, at 583–4.
[98] Case C-55/94 *Gebhard v Consiglio dell'Ordine degle Avvocati e Procuratori di Milano* [1995] ECR I-4165. The case is discussed in more detail in ch 12 below.
[99] See generally ch 10 below.

described by the Court (agreeing with its Advocate General) in the following terms:

> . . . the temporary nature of the activities in question has to be determined in the light, not only of the duration of the provision of the service, but also of its regularity, periodicity or continuity. The fact that the provision of services is temporary does not mean that the provider of services within the meaning of the Treaty may not equip himself with some form of infrastructure in the host Member State (including an office, chambers or consulting rooms) in so far as such infrastructure is necessary for the purposes of performing the services in question.[100]

The Court refers to four qualities: duration, regularity, periodicity, and continuity. This corresponds to four questions: for how long at a time? how often? over what cycles?[101] and over what total period of time has the activity been undertaken? Whereas the *Insurance* cases[102] had suggested that the presence of an office staffed on behalf of the enterprise would be sufficient to justify a conclusion that the enterprise was established in the host State, the *Gebhard* decision requires a rather closer examination of all the circumstances of the case. The Court's ruling indicates that the presence of infrastructure does not necessarily lead to the conclusion that the enterprise is established rather than providing services. The determination will be that of the national court in the light of the guidance provided by the Court of Justice.

Using Community rules against the Member State of nationality

The problem of so-called 'reverse discrimination' has dogged Community rules on the free movement of persons. The Court has consistently maintained that a person cannot invoke Community rights to secure against the State of which he is a national the benefit of more generous rights accorded under Community law than those accorded to that State's own nationals under national law. But the situation must be wholly internal to the Member State for this rule to apply, and the Court of Justice has not needed much persuading to determine that a situation is one in which there is a factor linking a person with a situation governed by Community law.

An early example of this approach arose in the *Saunders* case.[103] Vera Saunders had come from Northern Ireland to the Bristol area, where she was convicted of theft. She was bound over by the criminal courts in return for her undertaking to return to Northern Ireland and not to return to England for three years. She broke that undertaking, and in the ensuing proceedings a question arose as to whether the requirement of the undertaking was compatible with the right of workers to move freely within the Member States. The Court stated:

[100] Para 27 of the judgment. [101] For example, one week each month.
[102] Case 220/83 *Commission v France* [1986] ECR 3663; Case 252/82 *Commission v Denmark* [1986] ECR 3713; Case 205/84 *Commission v Germany* [1986] ECR 3755; and Case 206/84 *Commission v Ireland* [1986] ECR 3817.
[103] Case 175/78 *R v Saunders* [1979] ECR 1129.

The provisions of the Treaty on freedom of movement for workers cannot therefore be applied to situations which are wholly internal to a Member State, in other words, where there is no factor connecting them to any of the situations envisaged by Community law.[104]

The case of the *Surinam mothers*[105] provides a more dramatic illustration of the principle. Two Dutch nationals of Surinam origin were living and working in the Netherlands. They were visited by their mothers from Surinam. They applied for residence permits to enable them to stay in the Netherlands, and sought to rely on Article 10 of Regulation 1612/68 which gives workers a right to bring dependent relatives in the ascending line to live with them. The Dutch authorities did not consider that Community law applied to the situation and questions were referred to the Court of Justice. The Court concluded that the situation was wholly internal to a Member State, and that the rights in Regulation 1612/68 could not be invoked in this situation. The matter was governed by national law. The position has been maintained in other cases.[106] It has also been applied to the rules on services.[107] The response to indignation that Community law tolerates such a situation is that it is always open to the Member States to upgrade the rights they accord to their own nationals to meet the level demanded when they are dealing with situations where Community law does apply.

The rule that Community law does not apply to situations wholly internal to a Member State has led to arguments that a national of a Member State cannot rely on Community law against the State of which he or she is a national. This is not so, as is illustrated by the case of *Surinder Singh.*[108] Surinder Singh was an Indian national who married a British national in October 1982. From February 1983 until the end of 1985 Surinder Singh and his wife lived and worked in Germany. They returned to the United Kingdom where they ran a business which they subsequently purchased. The Immigration Appeal Tribunal ruled that Singh had a Community right to remain in the United Kingdom as the spouse of a British citizen who had a right under Community law to establish herself in the United Kingdom after having been a worker in Germany. The Home Secretary took the view that only national law governed the situation. The Court, in a decision which hinted at a new approach to the analysis of such situations, concluded that Community law did apply, and that to permit the situation to be governed solely by national law could present an obstacle to the free movement of persons under the

[104] ibid, para 11 of the judgment.

[105] Joined Cases 35 & 36/82 *Morson and Jhanjan v Netherlands* [1982] ECR 3723.

[106] See, for example, Case 180/83 *Moser v Land Baden-Württemberg* [1984] ECR 2539; Case 298/84 *Iorio v Azienda Autonomo delle Ferrovie dello Stato* [1986] ECR 247; Case 20/87 *Ministère Public v Gauchard* [1987] ECR 4879; Joined Cases C-297/88 and 197/89 *Dzodzi v Belgium* [1990] ECR I-3763; Case C-322/90 *Steen v Deutsche Bundespost* [1992] ECR I-341, affirmed in Case C-132/93 *Steen v Deutsche Bundespost* [1994] ECR I-2715; and Case C-60/91 *Criminal Proceedings against Morais* [1992] ECR I-2085.

[107] See, for example, Case 52/79 *Procureur du Roi v Debauve* [1980] ECR 833; and Case C-41/90 *Höfner and Elser v Macrotron* [1991] ECR I-1979.

[108] Case C-370/90 *R v Immigration Appeal Tribunal and Surinder Singh, ex parte Secretary of State for the Home Department* [1992] ECR I-4625, noted at (1993) 18 ELRev 527.

EC Treaty. However, the free movement right being exercised must be an economic one. In the *Werner* case,[109] the Court did not consider that Article 52 (now 43) EC on the right of establishment was engaged in Werner's circumstances. He was a German national, who possessed the degrees and qualifications required by German law to practise as a dentist and who had worked both as an employee and in his own practice as a dentist. However, he lived in the Netherlands. He was, under German law, subject to higher tax as a non-resident than he would have been had he been resident in Germany. Thus, the only fact which took the matter outside the wholly national context was his residence in the Netherlands, which was unconnected with his dental practice. It followed that there was no situation linking Werner's circumstances to one of the situations contemplated by the EC Treaty. Having regard to the broad view taken in the *Martínez Sala* case[110] of the content of citizenship of the European Union, it can be argued that the Court might now take a different view, since there was clearly discrimination based on residence in the operation of the German tax rules and Werner would now be able to claim that he was a beneficiary of rights as a Union citizen to live as a person of independent means in a Member State other than that of his nationality.[111]

It has also been suggested that the possibility of some action by a Member State having an effect in the future on the exercise of the rights of free movement will not be enough to bring the situation within one contemplated by Community law.[112] So in the *Moser* case,[113] Moser's argument was that the refusal of the Bavarian authorities to permit him to undertake teacher training would preclude his being able to qualify as a teacher and move to another Member State to teach.[114] However, the logic of the reasoning in the *Surinder Singh* case[115] that certain national rules may be obstacles to free movement may mean that a generous view will be taken to the prospect of free movement. If a United Kingdom national could show that he or she had *not* exercised a right of free movement because he or she feared that the application of the United Kingdom would prejudice his or her position under national law, then the ability to use Community law should be no different than for a person who had exercised his or her Community rights and sought to argue that the prejudice should not arise.

The Court has been generous in finding the necessary link to a situation governed by Community law where nationals of a Member State are seeking to

[109] Case C-112/91 *Werner v Finanzamt Aachen-Innenstadt* [1993] ECR I-429.

[110] Case C-85/96 *Martínez Sala v Freistaat Bayern* [1998] ECR I-2691, noted at (1999) 24 ELRev 68.

[111] See also Case C-18/95 *Terhoeve v Inspecteur van de Belastingdienst Particulieren/Ondernemingen Buitenland* [1999] ECR I-345, discussed below.

[112] Handoll, J, *Free Movement of Persons in the EU* (Chichester, 1995), paras 3.59–3.61.

[113] Case 180/83 *Moser v Land Baden-Württemberg* [1984] ECR 2539.

[114] The Court took a similar view that a hypothetical possibility of the act complained of affecting the exercise of Community rights was irrelevant in Case C-41/90 *Höfner and Elser v Macrotron* [1991] ECR I-1979.

[115] Case C-370/90 *R v Immigration Appeal Tribunal and Surinder Singh, ex parte Secretary of State for the Home Department* [1992] ECR I-4625.

raise a Community right against the Member State of their nationality. In the *Scholz* case,[116] an Italian national was able to require an Italian university to take account of her work in the public sector in Germany in scoring her points in a job competition which favoured those who had previously worked in the public sector. In the *Knoors* case,[117] a Dutch national, who married a Belgian and moved to Belgium where he practised his trade as a plumber, was able to rely on his practice of the profession in Belgium when he returned to the Netherlands and sought to have his qualifications as a plumber recognized in the Netherlands. Similarly, in the *Kraus* case,[118] a German national with a Master of Laws degree from the University of Edinburgh was found to be in a situation contemplated by the Treaty rules for the purposes of calling into question certain rules regulating the use of non-German degree titles on business cards. It seems that establishing the necessary link will not be difficult where services are concerned, particularly if the nature of the services is such that cross frontier activity cannot be ruled out. So, in the *Alpine Investments* case,[119] a Dutch company in the Netherlands was able to complain about a Dutch law which prevented their telephoning clients both in the Netherlands and beyond. It has always been established that if the services activity crosses a frontier, there need be no movement of people.

The ruling in the *Bosman* case[120] can be read as applying to a situation in which there had been no cross-frontier movement if the regulation in issue was an obstacle to free movement. Paragraph 96 of the judgment reads:

> Provisions which preclude or deter a national of a Member State from leaving the country of origin in order to exercise his right of freedom of movement therefore constitute an obstacle to that freedom even if they apply without regard to the nationality of the worker concerned.

This suggested that there might be a re-appraisal of the Community case law on the inapplicability of Community law to situations purely internal to a Member State, at least in some cases. There have, however, been cases since the *Bosman* decision which have re-stated the earlier case law.[121] In the *Uecker* case the Court did not refer to *Bosman*, but did expressly state that the advent of citizenship of the

[116] Case C-419/92 *Scholz v Opera Universitaria di Cagliari* [1994] ECR I-505, noted at (1994) 19 ELRev 309.

[117] Case 115/78 *Knoors v Secretary of State for Economic Affairs* [1979] ECR 399.

[118] Case C-19/92 *Kraus v Land Baden-Württemberg* [1993] ECR I-1663, noted at (1994) 19 ELRev 67.

[119] Case C-384/93 *Alpine Investments BV v Minister van Financiën* [1995] ECR I-1141, noted at (1995) 20 ELRev 507, and (1995) 32 CMLRev 1427.

[120] Case 415/93 *Union Royale Belge des Sociétés de Football Association, ASBL and others v Jean-Marc Bosman and others* [1995] ECR I-4921, discussed in detail in ch 3 below.

[121] See Case C-134/95 *USSL No. 47 di Biella v INAIL* [1997] ECR I-195, para 19 of the judgment; Joined Cases C-64/96 and C-65/96 *Land Nordrhein-Westfalen v Uecker* and *Uecker v Land Nordrhein-Westfalen* [1997] ECR I-3171; Joined Cases C-225/95, C-226/95 and C-227/95 *Kapasakalis v Greece* [1998] ECR I-4239; and Case C-18/95 *Terhoeve v Inspecteur van de Belastingdienst Particulieren/Ondernemingen Buitenland* [1999] ECR I-345, para 26 of the judgment.

European Union 'is not intended to extend the scope *ratione materiae* of the Treaty also to internal situations which have no link with Community law'.[122]

The *Terhoeve* case[123] raises interesting questions about the temporal aspect of claiming Community rights. In that case Terhoeve, a Dutch national working in the Netherlands for a Dutch employer, had been posted to the United Kingdom for most of 1990 to work there. The application of the Dutch social security rules resulted in his being assessed, by virtue of being non-resident for part of 1990, to higher social security contributions than if he had been resident in the Netherlands for the whole year without enjoying any additional social benefits. The Court of Justice concluded that those rules were incompatible with Article 48 (now 39) EC. Terhoeve was able to raise the issue because he had worked in the United Kingdom, and a higher assessment to social security contributions had been raised against him. In post-*Bosman* language, the rules for levying social security contributions were an obstacle to free movement of workers. Why then should it make any difference, in challenging those rules, whether a person in the position of Terhoeve complained in advance of his posting to another Member State as against his complaining after he had moved and suffered prejudice? The current state of the case law would seem to suggest that a complaint before there had been work in another Member State would be regarded as hypothetical and so wholly internal to the Netherlands. The answer might be that in those circumstances the proper remedy is to complain to the Commission who can consider the use of Article 226 EC proceedings against the responsible Member State. Similarly, it has been suggested that there is a temporal link required between the exercise of Community rights and their arising. So Handoll suggests that, although it was right to permit Surinder Singh to rely on Community rights shortly after returning from Germany, he would not be able to rely on Community rights against his own Member State some years later because the 'economic link' between the exercise of the free movement and the claiming of the Community rights would be too remote.[124]

Third country nationals

Introduction

The position of third country nationals is complex, since not all third country nationals are in the same position.

[122] Joined Cases C-64/96 and C-65/96 *Land Nordrhein-Westfalen v Uecker* and *Uecker v Land Nordrhein-Westfalen* [1997] ECR I-3171, para 23 of the judgment. The reasoning is difficult to reconcile with what the Court said later in Case C-85/96 *Martínez Sala v Freistaat Bayern* [1998] ECR I-2691.

[123] Case C-18/95 *Terhoeve v Inspecteur van de Belastingdienst Particulieren/Ondernemingen Buitenland* [1999] ECR I-345.

[124] Handoll, J, *Free Movement of Persons in the EU* (Chichester, 1995), para 3.58.

The first group who are treated as nationals of a Member State are those who are married[125] to a national of a Member State under Article 11 of Regulation 1612/68.[126] A partner who is not a European citizen and who is living together as husband and wife with a European citizen does not enjoy the same privileged status.[127] Children under 21 or dependent on the worker who are not European citizens are also treated as if they were.

A second group are those who are beneficiaries of certain association agreements which do not equate nationals of the third country with nationals of a Member State, but do give them advantages over other third country nationals.[128]

Finally, there are nationals of those countries associated with the European Union under the Cotonou Agreement[129] as successor to the Lomé Conventions.[130]

Association agreements

The most significant association agreement from the perspective of the free movement of persons is that with Turkey,[131] though there are also agreements with Algeria,[132] Morocco,[133] and Tunisia,[134] which contain provisions touching on the free movement of persons.[135]

The association agreement with Turkey and its additional protocol contains a commitment to be guided by Articles 48–50 (now 39 to 41) EC for the purpose of progressively securing freedom of movement for workers, and there are corresponding commitments in relation to establishment and services. Decision 1/80 made under Article 36 of the Association Agreement has generated a significant body of case law before the Court of Justice,[136] which extends to certain workers from Turkey treatment similar to that provided for nationals of the Member States under the provisions of the EC Treaty and its secondary legislation.

125 Case 267/83 *Diatta v Land Berlin* [1985] ECR 567; and Case 59/85 *Netherlands v Reed* [1986] ECR 1283.

126 See ch 8 below.

127 Case 131/85 *Gül v Regierungspräsident Düsseldorf* [1986] ECR 1573; but see Case 59/85 *The Netherlands v Reed* [1986] ECR 1283; [1987] 2 CMLR 448, where the rules in Regulation 1612/68 on social and tax advantages were held to extend certain rights to cohabitees.

128 See above ch 1.

129 Partnership Agreement between the members of the African, Caribbean and Pacific Group of States (ACP) of the one part, and the European Community and its Member States, of the other part, signed in Cotonou on 23 June 2000, [2000] OJ L317; see also Arts, K, 'ACP-EU relations in a new era: The Cotonou Agreement' (2003) 40 CMLRev 95.

130 See generally on association agreements and the Lomé Convention, Handoll, J, *Free Movement of Persons in the EU* (Chichester, 1995), ch 10. See also ch 1 above.

131 [1997] OJ L361/29.

132 [1978] OJ L263/2.

133 [1978] OJ L264/2.

134 [1978] OJ L265/2.

135 See above ch 1.

136 Described in Handoll, J, *Free Movement of Persons in the EU* (Chichester, 1995), paras 10.62–10.88.

The rights accruing to nationals of Algeria, Morocco, and Tunisia under the association agreements with these countries are much more limited, and give little in the way of a right of access to the labour markets of the Member States.

The Cotonou Agreement

The Cotonou Agreement runs for a period of 20 years starting on 1 March 2000. It contains no provisions on the free movement of persons giving rights of entry and residence.

Other third country nationals

When dealing with a question involving the free movement of persons in the European Union by a person who is a national of a third country, it is important to check whether the country of which the person or business entity is a national is covered by either a Partnership Agreement or a Europe Agreement which gives nationals of that country an entitlement to more advantageous treatment than nationals of countries without such an agreement. Partnership Agreements exist with certain countries formerly being part of the Soviet Union, while Europe Agreements exist with many countries of central and eastern Europe, most of which are now countries which have submitted applications for membership of the Union. The Partnership Agreements tend to mirror the provisions of the association agreements with Algeria, Morocco, and Tunisia, while the Europe Agreements are closer to the EEC–Turkey Association Agreement in paving the way for the application of the economic freedoms in the EC Treaty to the nationals of those countries.

Concluding comment

It will be clear that there is a hierarchy of rights available within the Union from the full entitlement available to nationals of the Member States to the lack of any Community entitlements for nationals of those countries which have no agreement with the Community touching on the free movement of persons. Even nationals of the Member States have additional conditions to satisfy before they are able to claim the benefit of Community rights, since there is a requirement that the situation in which they find themselves is one contemplated by the EC Treaty. Hence, there remains an inability to plead Community rights against your own Member State if there is no linking factor to the rules on the free movement of persons. There are, however, some extraterritorial benefits where there is a sufficient linking factor to a particular Member State.

3

The prohibition of discrimination

Introduction

This chapter is about the prohibition of discrimination on grounds of nationality.[1] Discrimination can take a number of forms. Let us take three situations. First, a Member States provides that only its own nationals can become surgeons. This is an example of direct discrimination on grounds of nationality. Secondly, a Member State provides that nationals of any Member State can become surgeons provided that they undertake their medical training in that Member State. This is an example of indirect discrimination. The requirement is more likely to be met by its own nationals. It is open to question why such a requirement is applied. It could be that the Member State simply favours its own medical training, or it could be that there are features of the practice of surgery in that Member State which require training there. Thirdly, a Member State provides that nationals of any Member State can become surgeons provided that they have undertaken appropriate medical training in one of the Member States equivalent to that required in the Member State in question. This is a much more open requirement. Whether it is indirect discrimination will turn on the good faith of those required to assess the equivalence of qualifications.[2] In some areas, Community law has intervened and harmonized the applicable rules,[3] but in other cases matters remain very firmly in the hands of the Member States. Even where there are harmonizing rules, there remains the issue of compliance by Member States.

Article 12 EC contains a prohibition of discrimination on grounds of nationality in the following terms:[4]

> Within the scope of application of this Treaty . . . any discrimination on grounds of nationality shall be prohibited.

Article 13 EC, added by the Treaty of Amsterdam, gives a more general power to take measures to tackle discrimination based on sex, racial or ethnic origin,

[1] See generally Arnull, A, *The General Principles of EEC Law and the Individual* (Leicester, 1990), ch 3.

[2] Note that there are Community rules on qualifications for medical practice. See ch 4 below. These are simply examples to illustrate different types of discrimination.

[3] In which case those rules take precedence over any inconsistent national rules.

[4] See generally, Dashwood, A and O'Leary, S, *The Principle of Equal Treatment in European Community Law* (London, 1997); Bell, M, *Anti-Discrimination Law and the European Union* (Oxford, 2002); and van der Mei, A, *Free Movement of Persons within the European Community. Cross-Border Access to Public Benefits* (Oxford, 2003).

religion or belief, disability, age or sexual orientation. And, of course, Article 141 EC has long required a policy of equal pay for work of equal value as between men and women, and has provided a legal base for a number of measures on equality as between men and women.[5]

Article 39(2) outlaws 'any discrimination based on nationality between workers of the Member States as regards employment, remuneration or other conditions or work and employment'. Articles 43, and 49 and 50 EC provide for the removal of restrictions on freedom of establishment and freedom to provide services which require those from other Member States than the host State to be able to engage in these activities under the same conditions as those laid down for its own nationals. These provisions are the application of the general prohibition contained in Article 12 EC in the specific context of the free movement of persons. They outlaw discrimination based on nationality. For reasons which will already be clear,[6] the rules are expressed as a prohibition of discrimination rather than a guarantee of equality.[7] Discrimination on the grounds of nationality was the first area to be tackled, since it was generally through the favouring of nationals that Member States sought to avoid the application of Community rules in the areas of the four freedoms.

The modern formulation of the prohibition recognizes that protection from discrimination on grounds of nationality is central to the concept of citizenship of the Union, Advocate General Jacobs has said:

> Freedom from discrimination on grounds of nationality is the most fundamental right conferred by the treaty and must be seen as a basic ingredient of Union citizenship.[8]

The prohibition of discrimination on grounds of nationality

In an early judgment,[9] the Court of Justice ruled that the provisions on workers, establishment and services are all based on the same principles so far as they concern, inter alia, the prohibition of all discrimination on grounds of nationality. The Court has confirmed that this is an application of the general prohibition of discrimination on grounds of nationality in respect of all matters falling within the scope of the Treaty.[10]

[5] See, for example, Docksey, C, 'The Principle of Equality between Women and Men as a Fundamental Right under Community Law' (1991) 20 ILJ 33.

[6] See, for example, the discussion of reverse discrimination in ch 2 above.

[7] See remark of Jacobs, F, 'An Introduction to the General Principles of Equality in EC Law' in Dashwood, A and O'Leary, S, *The Principle of Equal Treatment in European Community Law* (London, 1997), at 1, where he also refers to the 'over-arching significance' of the prohibition.

[8] Case C-274/96 *Bickel and Franz* [1998] ECR I-7637, para 24 of the Opinion.

[9] Case 48/75 *Royer* [1978] ECR 497, para 12 of the decision.

[10] Case 13/76 *Donà v Mantero* [1976} ECR 1333, para 6 of the decision.

The scope of the prohibition has been spelled out in more detail in the secondary legislation applicable to workers, whereas in the areas of establishment and services, greater reliance has been placed on the general prohibition of discrimination in the Treaty articles, supported by the General Programmes in those areas.[11] The two General Programmes use the term 'restrictions' rather than elaborating the scope of the principle of national treatment in terms of the language of discrimination. That said, the substance of the text of the two General Programmes is to draw attention to the prohibition of measures which treat nationals of other Member States less favourably than a Member State's own nationals.

The case law of the Court has long used the terminology of 'restrictions' or 'obstacles'. For example, in *Watson and Belmann*[12] the Court referred to the obligations in what were then Articles 48, 52 and 59 EC as 'prohibiting Member States from setting up restrictions or obstacles to the entry into their territory of nationals of other Member States'.[13]

The nature of discrimination

It is now settled case law that the prohibition of discrimination involves not only the application of different rules to similar situations, but also the application of the same rule to different situations.[14] The differential treatment of similar situations is often described as *formal* discrimination, while the equal treatment of unequal cases is described as *material* discrimination. These terms are very seldom used in Community law. In the context of nationality discrimination, nationals of different Member States are almost always regarded as being in comparable situations. The Court does, however, frequently use the terms direct and indirect (or overt and covert) discrimination. In *Commission v Belgium*,[15] the Court, citing a number of earlier authorities, said:

> . . . according to settled case-law the requirement of equal treatment . . . prohibits not only overt discrimination by reason of nationality but also all covert forms of discrimination which, by the application of other distinguishing criteria, lead in fact to the same result.[16]

Direct discrimination

The case law abounds with examples of direct discrimination, that is, where distinctions are made based on grounds of nationality. An example would be a

[11] See on establishment [1974] OJ English Special Edition, Part IX, 7; and on services [1974] OJ English Special Edition, Part IX, 3.

[12] Case 118/75 *Criminal Proceedings against Watson and Belmann* [1976] ECR 1185.

[13] ibid, para 12 of the decision.

[14] See, for example, Case C-411/98 *Ferlini v Centre hospitalier de Luxembourg* [2000] ECR I-8081, para 51 of the judgment.

[15] Case C-278/94 *Commission v Belgium* [1996] ECR I-4307.

[16] Para 27 of the judgment.

refusal to admit persons to a particular professional activity because they were not nationals of the host State.[17] In such cases, no defences are available to the Member State unless the prohibition falls within the ambit of the derogations to be found in the Treaty articles.[18] One or two examples will suffice to illustrate the point.

Commission v France[19] concerned the compatibility of a provision of the French *Code du Travail Maritime* which provided that 'such proportion of the crew of a ship as is laid down by order of the Minister for the Merchant Fleet must be French nationals'. A ministerial order provided that for general employment on a ship there must be three French nationals for every non-French national. The Commission took the view that the provisions of the French law were incompatible with Article 48 (now 39) EC and provisions of Regulation 1612/68/EEC which set out specific prohibitions on applying national preferences in the proportion of employees in particular sectors of employment to the detriment of nationals of other Member States. The French Government sought to argue that there was no discrimination *in fact* since a verbal direction had been given that, for the purposes of the application of the offending provision, nationals of other Member States were to be treated as French nationals. The Court concluded that the uncertainty created by the continuing existence of the unamended wording of the French law amounted to an 'obstacle' as regards the equality of access to employment in the French merchant fleet and so constituted a failure to fulfil the obligations in Article 48(2) (now 39(2)) EC and of Article 4 of Regulation 1612/68/EEC. Those obligations are absolute in nature.

Workers enjoy the protection of the general principles set out in this case, but in most cases Regulation 1612/68/EEC[20] contains provisions dealing with specific forms of discrimination. There is no doubt that workers can plead the right to be protected from discrimination not only against the State and emanations of the State, but also against other private parties. Member States are under an obligation to ensure the application by all within their jurisdiction of the principle of equal treatment in employment and to curb any infringement of the principle.[21]

An example of direct discrimination from the case law on establishment can be found in the *Reyners* case.[22] Jean Reyners was a Dutch national residing in Belgium. He had a Belgian diploma of *docteur en droit*, which was the necessary academic qualification for admission to the profession of *avocat*, but was denied admission because he did not hold Belgian nationality. The Court stressed the fundamental nature of the principle of equal treatment enshrined in Article 7 (now 12) EC and in Article 52 (now 43) EC, and affirmed the direct effect of the obligations

[17] As in Case 2/74 *Reyners v Belgium* [1974] ECR 63; see below in this chapter.
[18] Workers: Article 39(3) and (4) EC; establishment: Article 45 EC; and services: Article 55 EC.
[19] Case 167/73 *Commission v France* [1974] ECR 359.
[20] See below ch 8.
[21] Case C-281/98 *Angonese v Cassa di Risparmio di Bolzano SpA* [2000] ECR I-4139, para 36 of the judgment.
[22] Case 2/74 *Reyners v Belgium* [1974] ECR 631.

contained in Article 52. It followed that Jean Reyners was entitled to be treated on equal terms with Belgian nationals in seeking admission to the profession of *avocat*. The Court also indicated that the legal profession was not excluded *per se* from the ambit of this rule by reason of the exception contained in Article 55 (now 45) EC for 'activities . . . connected with the exercise of official authority'.[23]

Similarly, in the *Steinhauser* case,[24] the Court of Justice ruled that discrimination on the grounds of nationality could not be practised where the effect was to deny nationals of another Member State the means to carry on their business, so the City of Biarritz could not limit the hire of *crampottes* (a type of beach hut used for the display and sale of merchandise) to their own nationals. Steinhauser, a German national, who was a professional artist living and working in Biarritz, had been refused the hire of a *crampotte* in which to display his artistic works for sale on the grounds that he was not a French national. Though the case arose in the context of freedom of establishment, the same result would undoubtedly arise if the context were the freedom to provide services.

The requirement of equality of treatment goes beyond the equal treatment necessary to enable persons to pursue their livelihood. In *Commission v Italy*[25] the Court of Justice considered Italian rules under which only Italian nationals were allowed to obtain reduced rate mortgages. Citing the General Programme, the Court imported into the ambit of Article 52 (now 43) EC the duty to provide housing on an equal basis. This is more specifically set out for workers in Article 9 of Regulation 1612/68/EEC, and this may have influenced the Court. Italy was found to have failed to fulfil its obligations under the Treaty by withholding publicly funded housing assistance from self-employed nationals of other Member States. The justification for so concluding was that refusal to provide such assistance would distort competition between self-employed nationals of the Member State and their counterparts in other Member States. This would arise because nationals of other Member States would be obliged to spend more of their disposable income and capital on housing and so would have less to invest in their businesses.

In the area of services, the Court in one of its earliest decisions defined the prohibition of discrimination in terms which include a very wide range of obstacles. The *Van Binsbergen* case[26] concerned rules operating in the Netherlands concerning the activity of representation of a client's interest in legal proceedings. Dutch law required that only persons established in the Netherlands may act as legal representatives and advisers. Van Binsbergen's representative had, when first consulted, been habitually resident in the Netherlands but had subsequently become habitually resident in Belgium. At this juncture, the representative was precluded from representing his client; the representative took issue with the requirement which

[23] On derogations from the Treaty rules, see ch 5 below.
[24] Case 197/84 *Steinhauser v City of Biarritz* [1985] ECR 1819.
[25] Case 63/86 *Commission v Italy* [1988] ECR 29.
[26] Case 33/74 *Van Binsbergen v Bestuur van de Bedrijfsvereniging Metaalnijverheid* [1974] ECR 1299.

had this effect. The Court ruled that obstacles to be abolished under what was then Articles 59 and 60 EC included:

> . . . all requirements imposed on the person providing the service by reason in particular of his nationality or of the fact that he does not habitually reside in the State where the service is provided, which do not apply to persons established within the national territory or which may prevent or otherwise obstruct the activities of the person providing the service.[27]

An even more dramatic example illustrates the application of the prohibition of direct discrimination in the field of services. In the *Cowan* case,[28] Ian Cowan was injured when he was assaulted outside a metro station during a visit to Paris as a tourist. He claimed compensation for his injuries under the French criminal injuries compensation scheme. Unfortunately, access to that scheme was restricted to those who were French nationals or were holders of a residence permit.[29] Cowan then argued that he was within the scope of Article 7 (now 12) EC. The Court ruled that recipients of services were within the scope of the Treaty provisions on the free movement of services. It followed that Cowan's exclusion from the scheme on the basis of nationality and holding a residence permit constituted unlawful discrimination. The case indicates that there is a social element as well as an economic element in the context of the prohibition of discrimination.

Indirect discrimination

The Court has extended the concept of discrimination to include indirect discrimination, which arises where a requirement or condition is imposed whose effect is to affect adversely nationals of other Member States compared with the position of nationals. Where indirect discrimination is in issue, it can be justified if it can be shown that the application of the condition or requirement is objectively justified. Objective justification requires the party imposing the condition or requirement to show, first, that it can be justified by reference to objective criteria unconnected with nationality, and, secondly, that it is proportionate in that there is no less discriminatory measure which will secure the legitimate objective.

Under Community law, the person alleging discrimination does not have to prove that non-nationals are adversely affected by the requirement; it is sufficient to show that the application of the requirement might well have such an effect:

> . . . a provision of national law must be regarded as indirectly discriminatory if it is intrinsically liable to affect migrant workers more than national workers and if there is a consequent risk that it will place the former at a particular disadvantage. It is not necessary to find that the provision in question does in practice affect a substantially higher proportion of migrant workers.[30]

[27] ibid, para 10 of the decision. The Court did not rule that residence requirements were always unlawful but they would have to be objectively justified.

[28] Case 186/87 *Cowan v Le Trésor Public* [1989] ECR 195.

[29] A document evidencing an entitlement to reside as a worker; see ch 8 below.

[30] Case C-278/94 *Commission v Belgium* [1996] ECR I-4307, para 20 of the judgment.

In the *O'Flynn* case,[31] the Court recapitulated its case law and characterized the following conditions as potentially discriminatory on grounds of nationality, even though they were apparently irrespective of nationality:

(a) those which affect essentially migrant workers;[32]
(b) those where the great majority of those affected are migrant workers;[33]
(c) those which can more easily be satisfied by national workers than migrant workers;[34] and
(d) those where there is a risk that they might operate to the particular detriment of migrant workers.[35]

The *Spotti* case[36] concerned provisions of the German Framework Law on Higher Education[37] which specified a maximum duration for certain contracts in higher education institutions, and the Bavarian Law on Teachers in Higher Education,[38] which stated that foreign language assistants may not be employed for a period exceeding five years. Maria Spotti was a language assistant affected by this requirement. Her contract was not renewed at the end of a five-year period. She complained to the local labour court that the termination of her contract constituted discrimination contrary to Article 48(2) (now 39(2)) EC, since no such time limit applied in respect of other workers. The national court referred questions to the Court of Justice. Spotti appeared to be on strong ground since there was already a line of cases on the position of language assistants in Italian universities,[39] though that case law had left open the possibility that a different result might arise where other workers were also employed on fixed term contracts. The HRG contained provisions on a variety of university staff, not just language assistants. The university authorities in Spotti's case argued that there was objective justification for the limitation on the duration of the contract of a language assistant, in that fixed term contracts ensured a continuity of cultural exchange and contact with the country of origin.

The German authorities argued that the earlier case law could be distinguished, in that the HRG and BayHSchLG allowed not only language assistants but also other categories of staff to be engaged under fixed term contracts of employment.[40] The Court responded by noting that there was a specific requirement that the fixed term nature of the contracts for those other categories of staff had to be justified on

[31] Case C-237/94 *O'Flynn v Adjudication Officer* [1996] ECR I-2617, para 18 of the judgment.
[32] Case 41/84 *Pinna v Caisse d'Allocations Familiales de la Savoie* [1986] ECR 1, para 24 of the judgment.
[33] Case C-279/89 *Commission v United Kingdom* [1992] ECR I-5785, para 42 of the judgment.
[34] Case C-349/87 *Paraschi v Landesversicherungsanstalt Württemberg* [1991] ECR I-4501, para 23 of the judgment.
[35] Case C-175/88 *Biehl v Administration des Contributions* [1990] ECR I-1779, para 14 of the judgment.
[36] Case C-272/92 *Spotti v Freistaat Bayern* [1993] ECR I-5185.
[37] Hochschulrahmengesetz (HRG).
[38] Bayerisches Hochschullehrergesetz (BayHSchLG).
[39] See, in particular, Case 33/88 *Allué and Coonan v Università degli studi di Venezia* [1989] ECR 1591; and Joined Cases C-259/91, C-331/91 and C-332/91 *Allué and others v Università degli studi di Venezia and Università degli studi di Parma* [1993] ECR I-4309.
[40] For example, scientific assistants, staff with medical duties, and other staff performing special duties.

objective grounds, whereas there was an express provision limiting the duration of the contracts of language assistants to a maximum of five years come what may. The Court concluded:

Since the great majority of foreign-language assistants are foreign nationals, this difference of treatment is such as to place them at a disadvantage by comparison with German nationals and consequently constitutes indirect discrimination, prohibited by Article 48(2) of the EEC Treaty, unless it is justified for objective reasons.[41]

The Court then turned to the purported objective justification for the blanket limitation of five years on the duration of contracts for language assistants, and advised the national court that, in its view, the requirement is not proportionate to the stated aim. The danger of a language assistant losing contact with the first language was described as being 'slight' and, in any event, the employing institution could check this by testing the level of the language assistant's knowledge.[42]

The introduction of citizenship of the Union appears to have introduced a new way in which a person can bring themselves within the scope of the EC Treaty, and so benefit from the general prohibition of discrimination on grounds of nationality. This is best illustrated in the *D'Hoop* case.[43] The case concerned Marie-Nathalie D'Hoop, a Belgian national who had completed her secondary school education in France. She returned to Belgium where she attended university. Following graduation she applied for a State benefit for young unemployed persons seeking their first job. Her application was refused on the grounds that she had not completed her secondary education in Belgium. The Court ruled that she was not a worker as defined by the EC Treaty or Regulation 1612/68 because a person invoking the provisions of what is now Article 39 EC 'must have already participated in the employment market by exercising an effective and genuine occupational activity which has conferred on him the status of a worker within the Community meaning of that term'.[44] However, there was inequality of treatment which placed certain persons at a disadvantage because they have exercised their freedom to move in order to pursue education in another Member State. The Court noted:

35. Such inequality of treatment is contrary to the principles which underpin the status of citizen of the Union, that is, the guarantee of the same treatment in law in the exercise of the citizen's freedom to move.

36. The condition at issue could be justified only if it were based on objective considerations independent of the nationality of the persons concerned and were proportionate to the legitimate aim of the national provisions. . . .

[41] Case C-272/92 *Spotti v Freistaat Bayern* [1993] ECR I-5185, para 18 of the decision.

[42] ibid, para 20 of the decision. See also the discussion of possible grounds of objective justification in the Opinion of Advocate General Jacobs in this case.

[43] Case C-224/98 *D'Hoop v Office national de l'Emploi* [2002] ECR I-6191, noted at (2003) 28 ELRev 389. See also Case C-148/02 *Garcia Avello*, Judgment of 2 October 2003, [2003] ECR nyr.

[44] ibid, para 18 of the judgment.

Objective justification

The *Pastoors* case[45] provides a good example of the Court's approach to the question of whether a requirement applied regardless of nationality can be justified. The case arose in the context of criminal proceedings against lorry drivers. Under Belgian law[46] there was the option of paying a fixed penalty or going to court. If the driver chose to have the matter go before a court, there was a further condition which applied where the alleged offender did not have an official or permanent residence in Belgium. A substantial sum had to be deposited per breach in order to cover the amount of any fine and the legal costs involved, in default of which the driver's vehicle was impounded. This requirement was challenged in these proceedings and questions were referred to the Court of Justice. The Court characterized the situation as one of indirect discrimination, noting that residence requirements were likely to operate mainly to the detriment of nationals of other Member States. However, this did not automatically mean that there was a breach of the prohibition of discrimination on grounds of nationality in what is now Article 12 EC, since the requirement may be capable of being justified by objective circumstances. The Belgian Government argued that the differential treatment of residents and non-residents was objectively justified 'by the fact that the legal position of non-residents is different as regards prospects for enforcement of judicial decisions'.[47] The Court accepted that difficulties of enforcement against non-residents in criminal matters justified the differential treatment. That was, however, not enough to dispose of the matter. The requirement imposed must be proportionate to the aim of the measure; here it was not since it exceeded by half the amount of the fixed penalty for the offence.

In the *Clean Car Autoservice* case,[48] the Court adopted a similar analysis in advising that a requirement that the manager of a business be resident in the Member State where the business was conducted was either inappropriate for or exceeded the measures needed to ensure the business was served with notices of fines. In the *Angonese* case,[49] a private banking undertaking in Bolzano advertised jobs which required applicants to be bilingual in German and Italian. This could only be established by obtaining a qualification from the province of Bolzano. The Court ruled that this was a requirement which applied equally to Italian nationals and nationals of other Member States, but it would be much easier for Italian nationals to meet the requirement. The prohibition on establishing the required language competence by any means other than the Bolzano certificate was

45 Case C-29/95 *Pastoors and Trans-Cap GmbH v Belgium* [1997] ECR I-285.
46 Adding implementation measures to certain Community regulations.
47 Para 20 of the judgment.
48 Case C-350/96 *Clean Car Autoservice GmbH v Landeshauptmann von Wien* [1998] ECR I-2521.
49 Case C-281/98 *Angonese v Cassa di Risparmio di Bolzano SpA* [2000] ECR I-4139.

disproportionate to the aim of the requirement. It was accordingly prohibited discrimination on grounds of nationality.

So it is now clear beyond all doubt that objective justification for a measure which applies equally to nationals and non-nationals alike must meet the twin requirements of necessity and proportionality in order to avoid breaching the prohibition on discrimination. Necessity refers to the aims of the measure; it must serve a legitimate aim. Proportionality refers to the means used to achieve the end; the means must constitute the least interference with the freedom to achieve the legitimate aim it pursues.

Reverse discrimination

The limitations of the prohibition of discrimination on grounds of nationality are evidenced, in part, by the ability of a Member State to treat its own nationals less favourably than Community law requires it to treat nationals of other Member States.[50] This means that the principle of equal treatment only applies where the situation is one falling within the scope of application of the Treaty. As was seen in chapter 2, where the circumstances fall wholly within a single Member State and where there is no connecting factor to the situations contemplated by the EC Treaty, that Member State is not obliged to extend the more favourable Community rule to its own nationals.[51]

The limitations of national treatment

Unless Community law has laid down harmonizing rules, the general rule is that a national of another Member State is only entitled to undertake activities on the same terms as nationals of the host Member State. This is explicitly stated in the second paragraph of Article 43 EC in relation to the freedom of establishment, and in the final paragraph of Article 50 EC in relation to the freedom to provide services. The Court's interpretation of the prohibition of discrimination on grounds of nationality has been an expansive one designed to catch both overt and covert forms of discrimination. As the next chapter will show, the prohibition needs to be coupled with legislative harmonization or co-ordination of certain

[50] See discussion of reverse discrimination in ch 2 above.

[51] Bell uses this example as one of the omissions and weaknesses in the basic principles governing nationality discrimination which betrays its essentially market-driven nature: see Bell, M, *Anti-Discrimination Law and the European Union* (Oxford, 2002), at 36. His other example is the absence of any prohibition on discrimination against third country nationals. See also de Búrca, G, 'The Role of Equality in European Community Law' in Dashwood, A and O'Leary, S, *The Principle of Equal Treatment in European Community Law* (London, 1997), at 13.

measures, such as recognition of qualifications, since Member States have shown that they have a distinct preference for the continuation of their own way of doing things, and for their own qualifications for undertaking a wide range of activities in the field of employment and self-employment.

De Búrca has identified three possible understandings of the role of the prohibition of discrimination in Community law.[52] Her first understanding probably best represents the application of the principle in the context of the free movement of persons: it is an instrument for attaining specific Community aims. Secondly, the prohibition of discrimination can also be seen as a value 'which mediates and possibly constrains or redirects other specific Community measures or goals'.[53] Thirdly, the principle of equality could be seen as a Community goal in its own right. Her conclusion is that there are signs that there is scope for the development of this third approach as an underlying goal of Community law.[54]

Non-discriminatory obstacles

The distinction between covert or indirect discrimination and the prohibition of restrictions or obstacles to the free movement of persons is not an easy one to grasp. Nor is it always easy to categorize a particular case emanating from the Court of Justice as one involving indirect discrimination or the prohibition of non-discriminatory obstacles. As de Búrca has noted:

> In a curious reversal of the previous position, genuinely non-discriminatory restrictions on inter-state trade have now largely been excluded from the definition of a measure having equivalent effect under Article 30 EC, while Articles 48, 52 and 59 EC have been read in such a way as to include any obstacles to the free movement of persons and services, whether or not they are discriminatory.[55]

The prohibition of non-discriminatory obstacles is the subject of discussion in chapter 10 below, since this book argues that the prohibition of non-discriminatory obstacles is primarily about regulating market access in the interests of ensuring the free movement of persons. Insofar as it is possible to justify the separate treatment of such measures, they are goal-oriented in seeking to ensure that there is a genuine single market in employment, establishment, and services. To that extent they belong to the realm of positive integration. The rules more traditionally found in the specific words of the EC Treaty in the field of the four freedoms belong to the realm of negative integration. Negative integration is a process whereby there is a

52 De Búrca, G, 'The Role of Equality in European Community Law' in Dashwood, A and O'Leary, S, *The Principle of Equal Treatment in European Community Law* (London, 1997), at 13.

53 ibid at 24.

54 There is no right to equality under the Charter of Fundamental Rights of the European Union, though there is a reference in the Preamble to the 'universal value . . . of equality' as a value underpinning the European Union. See also Article I-2 of the Draft Constitution for Europe in similar terms.

55 De Búrca, G, 'The Role of Equality in European Community Law' in Dashwood, A and O'Leary, S, *The Principle of Equal Treatment in European Community Law* (London, 1997), at 21.

prohibition on rules which mitigate against the exercise of a freedom, while positive integration is a process whereby there is a requirement to harmonize rules to achieve a common objective. The distinction is a fine one, but it does provide the means for analysing the Court's case law in a way which better demonstrates its coherence.

4

Recognition of qualifications

Introduction

There is no common system of education and training among the Member States, and the routes to qualification to undertake very many trade and professional activities differ significantly both in terms of the length and content of training required. This was potentially a serious barrier to the free movement of persons, and touched upon sensitivities concerning the protection of national standards and values. The EEC Treaty recognized this problem in relation to self-employment in former Article 57 by providing for the issue of directives on the mutual recognition of qualifications. There was no similar provision in relation to workers, but Article 49 contained a power to issue directives and make regulations setting out the measures required to bring about freedom of movement for workers. So work began slowly and often painfully on harmonization and co-ordination of vocational training in the Member States.

Progress was, however, exceedingly slow. In 1993 the Green Paper on European Social Policy Options for the Union noted that work on mutual recognition of qualifications was an urgent priority.[1] Despite the success of the ERASMUS and SOCRATES programmes in securing mobility of many students and academics, there remain very significant differences in educational systems at all levels. There have, however, been advances and developments elsewhere in Community law[2] which made a new approach to the mutual recognition of qualifications possible. The starting point is now Community legislation, but, where that does not apply, there is a significant bundle of rights flowing from the case law of the Court which might be of assistance to a citizen of the Union seeking to export his or her qualifications, and should operate as an inhibition to competent bodies in the Member States in refusing recognition to qualifications from another Member State without a good faith consideration of their equivalence to national qualifications.

[1] COM (93) 551 final.

[2] Most notably in relation to free movement of goods where the concept of mutual recognition and the avoidance of dual burdens arising from the application of the standards of more than one Member State were developed in the case law of the Court of Justice.

Regulation 1612/68

Regulation 1612/68 contains little explicit content on recognition of qualifications. Article 45 provides:

The Commission shall submit to the Council proposals aimed at abolishing, in accordance with the provisions of the Treaty, restrictions on eligibility for employment of workers who are nationals of Member States, where the absence of mutual recognition of diplomas, certificates or other evidence of formal qualifications may prevent freedom of movement for workers.

Article 3 embodies the principle of equal treatment and touches on the tricky issue of linguistic competence:

1. Under this Regulation, provisions laid down by law, regulation or administrative action or administrative practices of a Member State shall not apply:

—where they limit application for and offers of employment, or the right of foreign nationals to take up and pursue employment or subject these to conditions not applicable in respect of their own nationals; or

—where, though applicable irrespective of nationality, their exclusive or principal aim or effect is to keep nationals of other Member States away from the employment offered.

This provision shall not apply to conditions relating to linguistic knowledge required by reason of the nature of the post to be filled.

Finally, Article 6 provides:

1. The engagement and recruitment of a national of one Member State for a post in another Member State shall not depend on medical, vocational or other criteria which are discriminatory on grounds of nationality by comparison with those applied to nationals of the other Member State who wish to pursue the same activity.

2. Nevertheless, a national who holds an offer in his name from an employer in a Member State other than that of which he is a national may have to undergo a vocational test, if the employer requests this when making his offer of employment.

The linguistic competence proviso in Article 3 was considered by the Court of Justice in the *Groener* case.[3] Anita Groener was a Dutch national who was working part-time as an art teacher in Dublin. She applied for a permanent, full-time position. She was offered the position but did not meet the requirement for such posts that she hold a certificate of proficiency in the Irish language.[4] She asked for but was refused an exemption from this requirement, though consent was given to her appointment if she passed the language examination. She took a course and then the examination, but failed it. Groener challenged the application in Ireland of the language requirement in judicial review proceedings. In the course of those

[3] Case C-379/87 *Groener v Minister for Education* [1989] ECR 3967.

[4] Under the Irish Constitution, Irish is the national language and the first official language, and English is recognized as the second official language (Article 8 of the Constitution).

proceedings questions were referred to the Court of Justice. In particular the question was posed whether a language requirement could be applied in cases such as this where the requirement was not necessary for the discharge of the duties attached to the post (the working language was English) but where it was imposed as part of national policy to maintain and promote the use of Irish as a means of expressing national identity and culture. The Court responded:

20. The importance of education for the implementation of such a policy must be recognized. Teachers have an essential role to play, not only through the teaching which they provide but also by their participation in the daily life of the school and the privileged relationship which they have with their pupils. In those circumstances, it is not unreasonable to require them to have some knowledge of the first national language.

21. It follows that the requirement imposed on teachers to have an adequate knowledge of such a language must, provided the level of knowledge is not disproportionate in relation to the objective pursued, be regarded as a condition corresponding to the knowledge required by reason of the nature of the post to be filled within the meaning of the last subparagraph of Article 3(1) of Regulation No 1612/68.

In assessing qualifications, there must be no discrimination and any particular requirements must be justifiable by reference to the requirements of the post in question. In many cases the general case law of the Court described later in this chapter will, if respected, ensure the fair treatment of those with qualifications for employment acquired in another Member State.

The question of linguistic competence has also been raised in the context of the freedom of establishment. In the second *Haim* case[5] the Court of Justice was called upon to consider whether a host Member State could make any decision to authorize practice as a dentist subject to a requirement for linguistic competence necessary for the exercise of the professional activity. The Court ruled:

59. As the Advocate General notes in . . . his Opinion, the reliability of a dental practitioner's communication with his patient and with administrative authorities and professional bodies constitutes an overriding reason of general interest such as to justify making the appointment as a dental practitioner under a social security scheme subject to language requirements. Dialogue with patients, compliance with rules of professional conduct and law specific to dentistry in the Member State of establishment and performance of administrative tasks require an appropriate knowledge of the language of that State.

60. However, it is important that language requirements designed to ensure that the dental practitioner will be able to communicate effectively with his patients, whose mother tongue is that of the Member State concerned, and with the administrative authorities and the professional bodies of that State do not go beyond what is necessary to attain that objective. In this respect, it is in the interest of patients whose mother tongue is not the national language that there exist a certain number of dental practitioners who are also capable of communicating with such persons in their own language.

[5] Case C-424/97 *Haim v Kassenzahnärtzliche Vereinigung Nordrhein* [2000] ECR I-5123.

Sectoral directives

The initial approach to the mutual recognition of qualifications was an attempt to harmonize the laws of the Member States in relation to particular trades and professions. These initiatives covered the medical professions and architects. They proved to be lengthy to agree, required a number of amendments following experience in practice, and could leave some relevant qualifications outside the regime set up in the directive.[6] Sectoral directives were produced covering the following professional activities and occupations: doctors,[7] general care nurses,[8] midwives,[9] veterinary surgeons,[10] dentists,[11] pharmacists,[12] architects,[13] and road haulage and passenger transport operators.[14]

The sectoral directives in relation to the medical professions and architects have been modernized by the amendments made by Directive 2001/19/EC.[15] The amendments represent a simplification of the procedures operating under the current sectoral directives, and revisions to make for ease of reference. So, for example, various provisions which were previously scattered throughout their texts are gathered into annexes as lists, and there is a more effective procedure for incorporating new diplomas into the list of recognized qualifications.

The defining characteristic of most of these directives[16] is to set out common minimum standards of training for the practice of the work to which they relate. It follows that automatic recognition of the corresponding qualification acquired in another Member State will arise. Though complex to conclude, sectoral directives do offer a regime of legal certainty for those within their terms and for the competent national authorities who are charged with determining the equivalence of qualifications as a condition of the right to practice the occupation.

In addition to these professional activities directives, there were many directives 'concerning the attainment of freedom of establishment and freedom to provide services relating to trades and other non-professional occupations'.[17] These

[6] As in the case of the architects directive: Directive 85/384/EEC [1985] OJ L223/15, as amended.

[7] Council Directive 93/16/EEC, [1993] OJ L165/1, as amended by [1997] OJ L291/35, [1998] OJ L119/15, and [1999] OJ L139/25. For infringement proceedings concerning the incorrect transposition of this Directive, see Case C-232/99 *Commission v Spain* [2002] ECR I-4235. See also Case C-110/01 *Tennah-Durez* [2003] ECR I-6239.

[8] Council Directive 77/452/EEC, [1977] OJ L176/1.

[9] Council Directive 80/154/EEC, [1980] OJ L433/1, as amended by [1980] OJ L375/74.

[10] Council Directive 78/1026/EEC, [1978] OJ L362/1.

[11] Council Directive 78/686/EEC, [1978] OJ L233/1.

[12] Council Directive 85/433/EEC, [1985] OJ L253/37, as amended by [1985] OJ L372/42.

[13] Council Directive 85/384/EEC, [1985] OJ L223/15, as amended by [1986] OJ L27/71 and [1985] OJ L376/1. See Case C-298/99 *Commission v Italy* [2002] ECR I-3129.

[14] Council Directive 96/26/EC, [1996] OJ L124/1, as amended by [1998] OJ L277/17.

[15] Directive 2001/19/EC of the European Parliament and of the Council of 14 May 2001, [2001] OJ L206/1. The date for implementation of this directive was 1 January 2003.

[16] The architects directive does not cover all diplomas governing practice as an architect.

[17] See Annex B to Directive 1999/42/EC, [1999] OJ L201/77, for a list of such directives repealed by Directive 1999/42, on which see below in this chapter.

directives, which are generally known as the liberalization and transitional directives, are now largely consolidated into a horizontal directive which is described later in this chapter.

Moving to a horizontal approach

The laborious process of finalizing sectoral directives led the Commission to move from a vertical approach to a horizontal approach. This new approach was signalled in the conclusions of the Heads of State or Government when they met at Fontainebleau in June 1984, yet it was only at the end of 1988 that the first general system directive was passed. The horizontal approach focuses not on qualifications to undertake a particular occupation, but on the nature of the qualifications which would lead to a wide range of professional activity.[18] The move was away from harmonization towards mutual recognition: the presumption is that if persons are qualified to pursue an occupation in one Member State, then they are qualified to pursue that occupation in all Member States. Competence to undertake the work becomes more important than experience, though actually carrying out the occupation for a certain period can give rise to an entitlement to recognition in other Member States. Ultimately recognition is afforded to those fully qualified to undertake the activity; in other words, it is the end product which is entitled to recognition throughout the Union. But there is less legal certainty, since each person will be seeking recognition of his or her portfolio of competence rather than relying upon being the holder of a designated vocational qualification.

There are now three general system directives:

- Directive 89/48/EEC of 21 December 1988 on a general system for the recognition of higher education diplomas awarded on completion of professional education and training of at least three years' duration ('the first general system directive');[19]
- Directive 92/51/EEC of 18 June 1992 on a second general system for the recognition of professional education and training to supplement Directive 89/48/EEC ('the second general system directive');[20] and

[18] For some background to the first general system directive, see Ross, M, 'Mutual recognition of professional qualifications' (1989) 14 ELRev 162. For infringement proceedings in relation to failure properly to transpose the Directive, see Case C-365/93 *Commission v Greece* [1995] ECR I-499; Case C-216/94 *Commission v Belgium* [1995] ECR I-2155; Case C-285/00 *Commission v France* [2001] ECR I-3801. Further infringement proceedings were instituted before the Court in 2002 against Greece in respect of incorrect implementation of the directive.

[19] [1989] OJ L 19/16, as amended by Directive 2001/19/EC, [2001] OJ L206/1.

[20] [1992] OJ L209/25, as amended by Directive 2001/19/EC, [2001] OJ L206/1. In 2002 the Commission instituted infringement proceedings before the Court of Justice against France and Italy in respect of failures to implement the requirements of this directive. See also Case C-294/00 *Gräbner* [2002] ECR I-6515.

- Directive 1999/42/EC of 7 June 1999 establishing a mechanism for the recognition of qualifications in respect of the professional activities covered by the directives on liberalization and transitional measures and supplementing the general system for the recognition of qualifications ('the third general system directive').[21]

There is a proposal for a directive on the recognition of professional qualifications which would consolidate 12 sectoral directives covering the professions of doctor, general care nurse, dental practitioner, veterinary surgeon, midwife, pharmacist, and architect, together with the three general system directives.[22]

The first general system directive

Directive 89/48/EEC entered into force on 4 January 1991.[23] It is concerned with access to regulated professions for which qualification includes study at higher education level for at least three years. Because it applies to so many different occupations, and because its terms need to cover the educational systems and qualification routes operative in all the Member States, its language is highly abstract and the directive is peppered with terms to which a Community meaning must be given.[24] The directive does not apply if there is a sectoral directive governing qualifications for admission to the occupation; in this sense, it is subsidiary to the sectoral directives.

The beneficiaries of the rules in the directive are the nationals of the Member States.[25] The qualifications covered are those awarded in the Member States, though Recommendation 89/49/EEC[26] exhorts Member States to recognize qualifications obtained by nationals of the Member States in third States.

The key qualification which is recognized is a 'diploma', which is given a special meaning by the directive.[27] It is important to note that the definition includes not only a single qualification but a portfolio of qualifications; Article 1(a) refers to 'any

[21] [1999] OJ L201/77.

[22] COM (2002) 119 final. The directive on the provision of services and the establishment of lawyers (see ch 12 below) would not be consolidated since they concern authorization to practise rather than recognition of qualifications.

[23] See generally Pertek, J, *General Recognition of Diplomas and Free Movement of Professionals* (Maastricht, 1992).

[24] Sometimes called 'an autonomous meaning'.

[25] This is one justification for including the mutual recognition of qualifications in the general part of the law in this exposition. There are, of course, strong elements both of rights for individuals and of a system of regulating market access to be found in this and the other general system directives. The directive has no application where the facts are entirely confined to a single Member State: Joined Cases C-225-7/95 *Kapasakalis, Skiathitis and Kougiagkas v Greece* [1998] ECR I-4239, which concerned claims by Greek nationals based on Greek qualifications relating to access to certain occupations in Greece.

[26] Council Recommendation of 21 December 1988 concerning nationals of Member States who hold a diploma conferred in a third State, [1989] OJ L19/24.

[27] Art 1(a) of Dir. 89/48/EEC.

diploma, certificate or other evidence of formal qualifications or any set of such diplomas, certificates or other evidence'. The diploma must have been obtained 'mainly in the Community'[28] and display the following hallmarks:

- it is awarded by a competent authority[29] in a Member State, designated in accordance with its own laws, regulations or administrative provisions;
- it shows that the holder 'has successfully completed a post-secondary course of at least three years' duration, or of an equivalent duration part-time, at a university or establishment of higher education or another establishment of equivalent level and, where appropriate, that he has successfully completed the professional training required in addition to the post-secondary course';[30]
- it qualifies the holder to take up and pursue a regulated profession in that Member State.

The *Burbaud* case[31] concerned the definition of a diploma for the purposes of the directive. Isabel Burbaud was a Portuguese national who had completed higher education qualifications in Portugal qualifying her as a hospital administrator. She subsequently completed a French doctorate in law, and became a French national. Her application for recognition as a qualified hospital manager in France was rejected by the French authorities because she had not passed the entrance examination of the French *Ecole nationale de la santé publique.* She challenged that refusal before the national courts which referred questions to Luxembourg. The first question raised by the national court asked whether passing the French examinations which led to a public appointment in hospital administration constituted a diploma and if so how the equivalence of that diploma to a qualification obtained in another Member State is to be assessed. The Luxembourg Court determined that the French requirements for admission to the profession of hospital administrator constituted a diploma within the scope of the directive. It was accordingly then for the national court to determine whether someone in Isabel Burbaud's position has a qualification which constitutes a diploma awarded in another Member State, and, if so, whether that training is equivalent to the training required in France. If there is equivalence, then it is not open to the French authorities to require that the French examination is taken and passed as a condition of admission to the profession in question. In such circumstances, there would be no justification for requiring the person holding the qualification awarded in another Member State to participate in a national competition such as the entrance examination of the *Ecole nationale de la santé publique.*

[28] Note that art 1(a) also includes the situation where 'the holder . . . has three years' professional experience certified by the Member State which recognised a third-country diploma, certificate or other evidence of formal qualifications'. Note the different position under the sectoral directives exemplified by the facts of Case C-154/93 *Tawil-Albertini v Ministre des Affaires Sociales* [1994] ECR I-451.

[29] Under art 9 each Member State is under an obligation to designate competent authorities for this purpose and to notify this information both to the Commission and the other Member States.

[30] Art. 1 (a).

[31] Case C-285/01 *Burbaud,* Judgment of 9 September 2003, [2003] ECR nyr.

The directive is only concerned with qualifications which entitle the holder to pursue a 'regulated professional activity'. This is drafted very widely to include very many professional occupations, but at its outer edges the definition is vague, and has given rise to problems. In brief, it is any activity the practice of which in a Member State is conditional on the possession of a diploma. This means that an activity does not need to be regulated in every Member State in order to constitute a regulated professional activity. Two specific examples of modes of pursuit of a regulated professional activity are set out in Article 1(d):

- pursuit of an occupation under a professional title which is reserved for those holding particular qualifications,[32] and occupations controlled by an association or organization whose purpose is to promote and maintain a high standard in that occupation and is so recognized in the Member State;
- 'pursuit of a professional activity relating to health, in so far as remuneration and/or reimbursement for such an activity is subject by virtue of national social security arrangements to the possession of a diploma'.[33]

The definition of what constitutes a regulated professional activity has been considered by the Court of Justice. The *Aranitis* case[34] concerned the attempts of Georgios Aranitis to secure recognition of his Greek qualifications in geology as equivalent to a German qualification which entitled the holder to use a particular title. It seems that Aranitis was particularly insulted by his classification in Germany as an 'unskilled assistant'[35] on the basis of his Greek qualifications. However, Aranitis would only be able to invoke the provisions of the directive if he could show that the pursuit of the occupation of geologist constitutes the pursuit of a regulated profession activity. The Court confirmed that it is the position in the host Member State[36] which determines whether the provisions of the directive apply. It appeared that in Germany, employers almost always recruited only those holding the German title *Diplom Geologe* but that the profession of geologist was not regulated because there are no provisions governing the taking up and pursuit of the profession. The Court said:

> That profession cannot be considered to be regulated merely because it is only holders of a specific higher-education diploma who seek employment in the host State. Whether or not a profession is regulated depends on the legal situation in the host Member State and not on the conditions prevailing on the employment market in that Member State.[37]

[32] Good examples are solicitors in England and Wales.

[33] See in relation to this group the non-exhaustive list in the Annex to the directive.

[34] Case C-164/94 *Aranitis v Land Berlin* [1996] ECR I-135.

[35] At the hearing before the Court of Justice, the German Government conceded that this classification was 'unfortunate': see para 10 of the judgement.

[36] That is, the Member State in which the person 'applies to pursue a profession subject to regulation in that Member State, other than the State in which he obtained his diploma or first pursued the profession in question': art 1(b).

[37] Case C-164/94 *Aranitis v Land Berlin* [1996] ECR I-135, para 23 of the judgment.

So the directive provided no assistance to Aranitis in securing recognition of his qualifications in Germany.[38]

A similar question arose in relation to a candidate for the post of restorer at the *Museo Nacional del Prado* in Madrid.[39] Teresa Fernández de Bobadilla held degrees in fine art from the University of Boston in the United States and from Newcastle upon Tyne Polytechnic.[40] She had worked for three years on a temporary contract as a restorer at the Prado, and wished to apply for a permanent post. The Prado is an autonomous administrative body attached to the Ministry of Culture in Spain. The terms for appointment to posts at the Prado are set out in a collective agreement concluded between the Prado and staff representatives. That agreement reserved employment as a restorer to those holding certain Spanish qualifications or those foreign qualifications recognized as equivalent. Fernández de Bobadilla applied to have her qualifications so recognized, but this was refused. She raised an objection to this in the national courts, who referred questions to the Luxembourg court. The question arose as to whether the profession of art restorer was a regulated professional activity in Spain. The answer to this question depended upon the status and effect of the collective agreement which governed access to the post. The Court of Justice did not feel that it had sufficient information to determine whether the collective agreement operated to constitute the activity as a regulated professional activity in Spain, but advised that a collective agreement could constitute the basis for such regulation. The matter was left for determination by the national court in the light of its further investigations.[41]

There are four possible combinations of circumstances which may arise where a person is concerned to secure recognition of qualifications acquired in one Member State in a different Member State:

- the activity is regulated in neither State;
- the activity is regulated in the home Member State but not in the host Member State;
- the activity is regulated in the host Member State but not in the home Member State; and
- the activity is regulated in both the host Member State and the home Member State.

The directive cannot apply in the first two situations, but will apply in the last two situations. However, even where the directive does not apply, the person seeking recognition may derive some benefit from general Community law principles laid down in the case law of the Court of Justice.[42]

[38] But see below in this chapter for the application of case law principles to his situation.

[39] Case C-234/97 *Fernández de Bobadilla v Museo Nacional del Prado* [1999] ECR I-4773.

[40] Her postgraduate course had been financially supported by the Prado.

[41] Note that the Court indicated that the activity may be regulated either by the first general system directive or the second general system directive. On the latter, see below in this chapter. See also below in this chapter for Fernández de Bobadilla's rights under case law principles.

[42] See below in this chapter.

The general rule,[43] which is subject to exceptions, where the activity is regulated in both the home Member State and the host Member State is that the host Member State must recognize the applicant's qualifications as entitling them to pursue that regulated professional activity in the host Member State. Such recognition generally entails the right to use the professional title for that occupation common in the host Member State.[44]

The position is slightly different if the activity is not regulated in the home Member State. Here applicants must show that they:

- have pursued the activity full-time for two years during the previous 10 years in the home Member State (or another Member State which does not regulate the activity); and
- possess evidence of formal qualifications which fall within the scope of the directive.

However, the two years of professional experience may not be required where the formal qualifications were awarded on completion of 'regulated education and training'. Such training is defined in Article 1(dd) as education and training directly geared to the practice of a defined profession and constitutes at least three years of full-time higher education.

The main exceptions arise where there is a significant difference in either the duration or the content of training in the home Member State when compared with the requirements in the host Member State.

The host Member State can only impose additional requirements on an applicant for recognition on the grounds of differences in the length of training where the difference exceeds one year or more. In such cases, the host Member State can require the applicant to undergo a period of professional experience[45] whose length will depend on whether the difference arises in the duration of the education and training,[46] or in any period of professional practice 'acquired with the assistance of a qualified member of the profession'.[47] Where the shortfall arises in the length of education and training, the host Member State cannot require professional experience exceeding twice the length of the shortfall. Where the shortfall arises in the length of any period of professional practice, the host Member State cannot require professional experience exceeding the length of the shortfall.

Where the content of the training differs substantially between the home Member State and the host Member State, the host Member State can require the applicant either to complete an adaptation period not exceeding three years in

[43] Art 3 of Directive 89/48/EEC

[44] Art 7(1) of the directive.

[45] Art 1(e) of the directive defines professional experience as 'the actual and lawful pursuit of the profession concerned in a Member State'. There is an upper limit of four years on the requirement in the host Member State for professional experience: art 4.

[46] Which includes any period of probationary practice carried out under supervision and which ends with an examination.

[47] Art 4(a) of the directive.

duration, or to undertake an aptitude test.[48] The applicant has the right to choose between an adaptation period and an aptitude test, and the host Member State must make a good faith assessment of the shortfall in content and all requirements in relation to meeting that shortfall must be proportionate to the need to develop competence in the missing material.

Definitions of the terms 'adaptation period' and 'aptitude test' are to be found in Article 1. An adaptation period is:

> the pursuit of a regulated profession in the host Member State under the responsibility of a qualified member of that profession, such period of supervised practice possibly being accompanied by further training. This period of supervised practice shall be the subject of an assessment. The detailed rules governing the adaptation period and its assessment as well as the status of the migrant person under supervision shall be laid down by the competent authority in the host Member State.[49]

An aptitude test is:

> a test limited to the professional knowledge of the applicant made by the competent authorities of the host Member State with the aim of assessing the ability of the applicant to pursue a regulated profession in that Member State.[50]

The requirements for a period of professional experience under Article 4(a) and either an adaptation period or aptitude test under Article 4(b) may not be applied cumulatively.

There are even further exceptions to the exceptions contained in Article 4(b), which arise in the case of 'professions whose practice requires precise knowledge of national law and in respect of which the provision of advice and/or assistance concerning national law is an essential and constant aspect of the professional activity'. In these cases, the host Member State need not give the applicant a choice between an adaptation period and an aptitude test, but can require one or the other. In relation to the legal profession, all Member States have elected to require an aptitude test for cross-qualification.

Article 6 makes provision for the host Member State to apply to the person seeking recognition of their qualifications certain provisions relating to their fitness to practise, financial standing, and public liability insurance. In essence any fitness to practise conditions require the host Member State to accept a certificate of good standing issued by the home Member State, or an oath or statutory declaration to this effect if such certification is not issued in the home Member State.

The second general system directive

The second general system directive parallels the provisions of the first general system directive. Hence it does not demand as detailed an exposition as is provided

[48] Art 4(b) of the directive. [49] Art 1(f) of the directive. [50] Art 1(g) of the directive.

above in relation to the first general system directive. In essence, the second general system directive extends the system of recognition contained in the first general system directive either to diplomas which involve at least one year of full-time, post-secondary education or to certain education and training courses specified in Annex C to the directive. This opens up the system of mutual recognition to a huge range of additional occupations, which must, however, still fall within the concept of regulated professional activity.

The second general system directive introduces entitlement to recognition on possession of a 'certificate' which is distinct from the notion of a 'diploma'. Article 1(b) of the directive defines a certificate as having the following characteristics:

- it is awarded by a competent authority in one of the Member States; and
- it shows that the holder has pursued an approved course other than one which would constitute a diploma leading to entitlement to professional practice.[51]

Certificate holders become entitled to recognition of their right to practise the occupation covered by the certificate in the host Member State. There are some detailed differences which apply to those falling within the second general system directive, but the underlying principles are the same.

There is no possibility of Member States making reciprocity a condition of recognition of the qualifications proffered by a national of a Member State from another Member State.[52]

The third general system directive

The third general system directive entered into force on 31 July 2001.[53] It relates to a very large group of occupations ranging from mining to hairdressing, whether pursued in an employed or self-employed capacity.[54] The directive sets up three schemes for recognition: recognition of 'formal qualifications'; recognition of professional qualifications on the basis of professional experience; and recognition of 'other professional qualifications' acquired in another Member State.

Title II deals with recognition of formal qualifications, and prohibits Member States from refusing to permit a national of another Member State from taking up and pursuing an occupation within the scope of the directive on the grounds of inadequate qualifications without first comparing the knowledge and skills reflected

[51] A good example of training which would constitute a certificate is post-admission training leading to certification earned after initial qualification.

[52] Case C-142/01 *Commission v Italy* [2002] ECR I-4541.

[53] For the United Kingdom implementing legislation, see The European Communities (Recognition of Qualifications and Experience) (Third General System) Regulations 2002 (SI 2002/1597). The Commission is bringing infringement proceedings against the following States in relation to their failure to implement, or fully to implement this directive: Austria, Finland, Germany, Greece, Ireland, Italy, the Netherlands, Portugal, Spain, and the United Kingdom.

[54] See art 1 and Annex A to the directive.

in the formal qualifications which the applicant presents with those required under its own national rules. This approach reflects that adopted in the case law of the Court of Justice, and requires a good faith assessment of the comparability of the qualifications. Where there is a substantial difference in the knowledge and skills so reflected, the host Member State must offer the applicant the opportunity to undertake an adaptation period or to take an aptitude test 'by analogy with' the first and second general system directives. But where the occupation requires the knowledge and application of the specific national rules in force, the host Member State may require an adaptation period or aptitude test taking into consideration the applicant's preference between these two forms of skills top-up.

Applications for recognition must be determined in the 'shortest possible time' and in any event within four months from the date on which full documentation is provided.[55] Reasons must be given for any refusal of recognition, and there must be a right of appeal under national law against an adverse decision or against the failure to make a decision.

Title III deals with recognition of professional qualifications acquired on the basis of professional experience acquired in another Member State, and applies where the practice of a listed occupation is subject, in the host Member State, to possession of general, commercial or professional knowledge and ability. In the cases covered by Article 4,[56] the host Member State must recognize as equivalent to the meeting of those requirements within that Member State the pursuit of the occupation in another Member State for a specified period as a self-employed person or in a managerial capacity. Shorter periods will meet the requirement where they are preceded by the specified period of formal training leading to qualification to undertake the occupation, or where there has been a period of employment followed by self-employment in the occupation.

Title IV deals with recognition of other professional qualifications obtained in another Member State. This relates mainly to requirements that the person undertaking the occupation be of good character and a fit person to carry out the activity. These provisions parallel those of Article 6 of the first general system directive.

The reluctance of some competent bodies in Member States to apply the wording and spirit of the predecessor directives to this third general system directive can be illustrated by reference to the case law. The host Member State is under a good faith obligation to accept certification from the home Member State and must not apply conditions for taking up a particular activity which render the certification from the home Member State useless, as, for example, by requiring that, where a number of related trades is in issue, each has been pursued independently for six years.[57]

[55] The competent authority in the home Member State is under a duty to certify whether the applicant's pursuit of the activity in question was genuine and real and took place over a given number of consecutive years: see Case 130/88 *Van de Bijl v Staatssecretaris van Economische Zaken* [1989] ECR 3039.

[56] There are detailed differences depending upon which list the occupation appears in.

[57] Joined Cases C-193-4/97 *de Castro Freitas and Escallier v Ministre des Classes moyennes et du Tourisme* [1998] ECR I-6747. See also Case C-58/98 *Proceedings against Josef Corsten* [2000] ECR I-7919.

Case law entitlements

In the absence of harmonizing provisions, the Court of Justice has accepted that the Member States may adopt their own national standards for admission to certain occupations, but this does not mean that they may ignore qualifications acquired in another Member State. To do so would be to apply a dual burden to a person wishing to undertake that activity in another Member State, and that would constitute an obstacle to the free movement of persons.

The Court of Justice adopted this approach in the *Thieffry* case.[58] Thieffry was a Belgian national who had obtained a doctorate in law in Belgium and had practised law in Brussels for a number of years. He then obtained recognition from a French university that his Belgian doctorate was equivalent to the corresponding French doctorate. On the basis of that recognition, he obtained a certificate of aptitude for the profession of *avocat*. His ambitions to join the Paris Bar were then frustrated by the decision of the Paris Bar to refuse to admit him to professional training because he did not have a French degree. The Court ruled that the absence of Community harmonizing measures did not preclude Community law requiring, where there was already an element of recognition,[59] Member States to act in a manner which did not present an obstacle to freedom of establishment.

The Court of Justice applied this ruling in the *Patrick* case.[60] Patrick, a United Kingdom national with a United Kingdom qualification as an architect, had secured recognition in principle of the equivalence of his qualification. He was, nevertheless, refused authorization to practise as an architect in France on the grounds that authorization was exceptional where there was no reciprocal arrangement with the country whose qualifications the applicant was seeking to import. The Court ruled that a host Member State was obliged to grant authorization to practise where a national of another Member State held certification recognized as equivalent to the host Member State certification.

The next case in this line of authority is the *Heylens* case,[61] which imposed positive obligations on the Member States to assess in good faith the equivalence of qualifications. Heylens was a Belgian national with a Belgian diploma entitling him to work as a football trainer. Football trainers in France could only undertake this activity if they held a French diploma. Heylens sought recognition of his Belgian diploma, but this was refused by the French authorities. Heylens took issue with this and the national court referred questions to the Court of Justice. The Court reaffirmed that, in the absence of harmonizing measures, the Member States were entitled to regulate the knowledge, skills, and experience required to undertake particular activities. However, it was a general requirement of Community law that

58 Case 71/76 *Thieffry v Conseil de l'Ordre des Avocats à la Cour de Paris* [1977] ECR 765.

59 The recognition of Thieffry's Belgian degree as being equivalent to the corresponding French qualification.

60 Case 11/77 *Patrick v Ministre des Affaires Culturelles* [1977] ECR 1199.

61 Case 222/86 *UNECTEF v Heylens* [1987] ECR 4097.

there must be a good faith assessment of the equivalence of qualifications obtained in other Member States. Reasons must be given for any adverse decision,[62] and such decisions had to be subject to challenge in the national legal order.

This approach is illustrated in the *Vlassopoulou* case.[63] Vlassopoulou, a Greek national with a law degree from Greece and qualified as a Greek lawyer (δικηζορος), had worked in Germany for some years. Since 1983, she had been qualified under the German regulations to advise on Greek law and European Community law. She applied for membership of the German bar, but her application was rejected because she had not taken and passed the German professional examinations. She argued that the restrictions imposed by the German regulations were excessive in the light of her obvious knowledge of German law. The Court's ruling highlights the current transitional nature of Community law in this area.

The Court began by again confirming that, in the absence of Community law on mutual recognition of qualifications, Member States could insist on a set of qualifications before individuals entered a profession. However, the national regulations must not be so restrictive as to operate as a bar to freedom of establishment. There was a duty on the authorities in Member States to take account of an applicant's pre-existing qualifications and to compare those with the national rules to see whether they were evidence of the appropriate skills required to join the equivalent profession. If this examination revealed partial qualification, then the only requirement that could legitimately be imposed must be in the nature of topping up the missing knowledge and skills.

The decision in the *Vlassopoulou* case was handed down shortly before the first general system directive entered into force, and clearly reflects the approach adopted in that directive. But the force of the reasoning in this line of cases has not disappeared following the entry into force of that legislative measure. The general rules will apply whenever the provisions of the general system directives do not assist the applicant. In both the *Aranitis* case[64] and the *Fernández de Bobadilla* case[65] discussed above, the Court was at pains to make clear that, where the first general system directive[66] did not apply, there must be a prompt, good faith assessment of the equivalence of qualifications followed by a reasoned decision which could be challenged in the national legal order. This exactly parallels such requirements in the legislative provisions where they apply.

[62] Without the articulation of reasons, the applicant would not be in a position to know whether the refusal was compatible with Community law. It is also, of course, the case that the requirement to articulate reasons acts as a check on decisions being made on improper grounds.

[63] Case 340/89 *Vlassopoulou v Ministerium für Justiz* [1991] ECR 2357. See also Case C-104/91 *Colegio Official de Agentes de la Propriedad Inmobiliaria v Aguirre Borrelli and others* [1992] ECR I-3003 (a case concerning recognition of qualifications to undertake work as an estate agent).

[64] Case C-164/94 *Aranitis v Land Berlin* [1996] ECR I-135.

[65] Case C-234/97 *Fernández de Bobadilla v Museo Nacional del Prado* [1999] ECR I-4773.

[66] And it would follow any of the subsequent general system directives; indeed specific reference was made to the second general system directive in the *Fernández de Bobadilla* case.

More recent examples of this approach can be found in the *Hocsman* case[67] and the *Dreessen* case.[68] Hocsman was of Argentine origin, acquired Spanish nationality and subsequently became a French citizen. He had qualified as a doctor in Argentina, and had then secured recognition of that qualification in Spain, where he had gone on to acquire specialist knowledge in urology. His application for authorization to practise in France was refused. Directive 93/16/EEC did not assist him since his basic diploma had been not been acquired in a Member State.[69] After reviewing the authorities outlined above, the Court said:

> . . . where, in a situation not regulated by a directive on mutual recognition of diplomas, a Community national applies for authorisation to practise a profession access to which depends, under national law, on the possession of a diploma or professional qualification, or on periods of practical experience, the competent authorities of the Member States concerned must take into consideration all the diplomas, certificates and other evidence of formal qualifications of the person concerned and his relevant experience, by comparing the specialised knowledge and abilities certified by those diplomas and that experience with the knowledge and qualifications required by the national rules.[70]

The extension in this case relates to the requirement to take account of *all* prior diplomas, including those obtained outside the European Union. There is no obligation to accord them mutual recognition but their equivalence must now be considered in good faith alongside qualifications obtained within the Union. A similar approach is taken to the recognition of franchised provision.[71]

The *Dreessen* case[72] concerned the sectoral directive on the mutual recognition of qualifications for the practice of architecture. Nicolas Dreessen, a Belgian national, held a diploma in engineering obtained in Germany after having followed an engineering course in building construction. He had worked as an employee for various architects' practices in Belgium for 25 years. When his employers went into liquidation, he applied to the Belgian authorities for authorization to practise as a self-employed architect. His application was refused, since his German qualification was not included in the relevant sectoral directive.[73] Dreessen's appeal against this refusal was eventually unsuccessful before the *Cour de Cassation*. Undeterred,

[67] Case C-238/98 *Hocsman v Ministre de l'Emploi et de la Solidarité* [2000] ECR I-6623, noted at (2001) 38 CMLRev 1587.

[68] Case C-31/00 *Conseil national de l'ordre des architectes v Dreessen* [2002] ECR I-663.

[69] See also Case C-154/93 *Tawil-Albertini v Ministre des Affaires Sociales* [1994] ECR I-451 concerning the directive in relation to recognition of qualifications in dentistry which established that the directive did not assist where the original qualification had not been awarded by a Member State even though a Member State had recognized it. See also Case C-319/92 *Haim v Kassenzahnärtzliche Vereinigung Nordrhein* [1994] ECR I-425 to similar effect.

[70] Case C-238/98 *Hocsman v Ministre de l'Emploi et de la Solidarité* [2000] ECR I-6623, para 40 of the judgment.

[71] See Case C-153/02 *Neri*, Judgment of 13 November 2003, [2003] ECR nyr.

[72] Case C-31/00 *Conseil national de l'ordre des architectes v Dreessen* [2002] ECR I-663.

[73] Litigation at the time of this refusal resulted in questions being referred to the Court of Justice, which in Case C-447/93 *Dreessen* [1994] ECR I-4087 ruled that the applicant's diploma did not fall within the terms of the sectoral directive. That reference was solely concerned with the interpretation of the provisions of the sectoral directive.

Dreessen made a further application for authorization to practise on his own account; one of his grounds at this time was that the competent body should have carried out a good faith assessment of his qualifications and experience in accordance with the principles set out in the *Vlassopoulou* case, despite his qualifications not falling within the sectoral directive. The Provincial Council[74] rejected the fresh application on the ground that it was not required to consider his qualifications or to evaluate them. On appeal, this decision was reversed and it was ordered that his name be included in the register of those authorized to practise. The National Council brought an appeal against this decision, and in the course of these proceedings the *Cour de Cassation* referred questions to the Court of Justice in Luxembourg. The Court re-stated what it had said in the *Hocsman* case. What is remarkable about this case is its demonstration of the continuing reluctance of the authorities in certain cases[75] to apply clearly established principles of Community law. This was clearly a case of professional gate-keeping by a national competent body in relation to a national of the host Member State who had obtained qualifications in another Member State and who had worked as an employee of architects for 25 years in the host Member State.

Concluding comment

A key distinction between the sectoral directives and the general system directives is that recognition under the sectoral directives is automatic, whereas recognition under the general system directives requires consideration of the individual circumstances of each applicant for recognition. This places a considerable premium on the co-operative spirit of a variety of professional bodies in the Member States. The high level of abstraction necessary in the general system directives also facilitates poor implementation. Mutual recognition requires mutual trust and the adoption of measures for according recognition which avoid protectionism.[76] The number of preliminary rulings and infringement proceedings in this area is testimony to the continuing reluctance of Member States, and professional bodies within them, to recognize qualifications obtained in other Member States.

[74] The relevant competent body.

[75] Note that the arguments of the National Council were supported by the Italian Government before the Court of Justice.

[76] See generally Pertek, J, 'Free movement of professionals and recognition of higher education diplomas' (1992) 12 YEL 293.

5

Exceptions

Introduction

Exceptions to the Treaty provisions on workers, establishment and services can be divided into two groups: those permitting Member States to exclude certain activities from the scope of the provisions and to reserve such activities for their own nationals; and those which permit a State to derogate from the Treaty freedoms in individual cases on specific grounds.

Article 39(4) EC excludes from the application of Article 39 'employment in the public service', while Article 45 EC excludes from the application of Chapter 2 on the right of establishment 'activities which in [any given Member] State are connected, even occasionally, with the exercise of official authority'. Article 55 EC applies the exception relating to the exercise of official authority to Chapter 3 on services.

Article 39(3) EC subjects the right to freedom of movement for workers to 'limitations on grounds of public policy, public security or public health'. Article 46(1) EC provides:

> The provisions of this Chapter and measures taken in pursuance thereof shall not prejudice the applicability of provisions laid down by law, regulation or administrative action providing for special treatment for foreign nationals on grounds of public policy, public security or public health.

Article 55 EC extends the application of this provision to Chapter 3 on services. The content of the limitations on grounds of public policy, public security or public health is elaborated in Council Directive 64/221.[1] These provisions have not been updated since 1964, though a significant body of case law has developed on the interpretation of Directive 64/221. The new directive,[2] bringing together the rules on residence and limitations on it, does not go beyond amendments which reflect the decisions of the Court of Justice on the interpretation of Directive 64/221. There does not appear to have been any fundamental rethink of the place of either

[1] Council Directive 64/221/EEC of 25 February 1964 on the coordination of special measures concerning the movement and residence of foreign nationals which are justified on grounds of public policy, public security or public health. [1963–4] OJ Sp Ed 117.

[2] Directive 2004/38/EC of 29 April 2004 on the right of citizens of the Union and their family members to move and reside freely within the territory of the Member States, [2004] OJ L158/77, referred to in this chapter as 'the new directive'. The new directive will repeal Directive 64/221/EEC when it enters into force in 2006.

the exclusions or the permissible derogations in the context of the formal establishment of a citizenship of the European Union.

There also remains some uncertainty as to who can rely on the derogations. In most cases, questions of the application of the limitations will arise when the State takes action to refuse entry or to remove a person as a threat to public policy, public security, or public health. But in the *Bosman* case,[3] suggestions were made that a private body may seek to rely on the limitations in derogating from the Treaty freedoms. This raises questions as to whether the purpose of the provision is solely to limit State discretion in restricting the right of free movement.

Employment in the public service

Article 39(4) (ex 48(4)) EC excludes from the application of Article 39 'employment in the public service'.[4] The extent to which the Member States have traditionally reserved particular types of employment for their own nationals has varied dramatically.[5] In some Member States it was usual for employment by State authorities to be limited to nationals of the State, whereas in other Member States a much more cosmopolitan view was taken. Despite an increasingly narrow interpretation of the employment excluded by Article 39(4) (ex 48(4)) EC, there remains a need for the Commission from time to time to bring enforcement actions against recalcitrant States in order to remind them of the need to keep within the narrow confines of this exclusion.

Some Member States had argued that the notion that employment in the public service applies to all posts within a given body, such as the State's civil service. This has been labelled the institutional approach: whether employment is in the public service is largely determined by the character of the employer. The Court of Justice has rejected this approach, which, taken to its logical extreme, would essentially permit the concept to be defined by the Member States. The Court has rejected the institutional approach in favour of a functional approach which focuses upon the nature of the tasks undertaken rather than the character of the employer.

The classic definition of what constitutes employment in the public service remains that set out in *Commission v Belgium*:

[3] Case C-415/93 *Union Royal Belge des Sociétés de Football Association ASBL and others v Bosman and others* [1995] ECR I-4921, and see below in this chapter.

[4] See, generally, Handoll, J, 'Article 48(4) EEC and Non-National Access to Public Employment' (1988) 13 ELRev 223; O'Keeffe, D, 'Judicial Interpretation of the Public Services Exception to the Free Movement of Workers' in Curtin, D and O'Keeffe, D, (eds), *Constitutional Adjudication in European Community and National Law* (Dublin, 1992), at 89; and Arnull, A and Jacobs, F, 'Applying the Common Rules on Free Movement of Persons' in Schermers, H *et al*, *Free Movement of Persons in Europe* (Dordrecht, 1993), at 272.

[5] See Beenen, N, *Citizenship, Nationality and Access to Public Service Employment. The Impact of European Community Law* (Groningen, 2001).

> . . . a series of posts which involve direct or indirect participation in the exercise of powers conferred by public law and duties designed to safeguard the general interests of the State or of other public authorities. Such posts in fact presume on the part of those occupying them the existence of a special relationship of allegiance to the State and reciprocity of rights and duties which form the foundation of the bond of nationality.[6]

The exclusion relates only to access to the employment, so that if a Member State has admitted a national of another Member State to particular employment, it cannot then seek to exclude that employee from the benefits of Article 39 EC on the basis that the employment is employment in the public service. So in the *Sotgiu* case,[7] it was not open to the German authorities, who had employed an Italian national to work for the Deutsche Bundespost, to argue that he was not entitled to the same benefits as German nationals by virtue of the work being employment in the public service.

Following this decision and that in the *Scholz* case,[8] it is clear that it is a breach of Community law for a Member State to refuse to consider a migrant worker's previous periods of comparable employment in the public service of another Member State for the purposes of access to its own public service and to matters of seniority within that service.[9] Member States have put forward a number of justifications for their restrictive approaches: rewarding loyalty; differences in career structures; reverse discrimination difficulties of comparison; and the principle of homogeneity. However, none of these justifications has been accepted by the Court.[10]

Having regard to the definition of employment in the public service and the need for 'a special relationship of allegiance', it is also questionable whether Member States could ever claim that employment was employment in the public service if they have admitted a non-national to that employment. But this point has not been tested before the Court, and there are dramatic examples of non-nationals occupying posts which would clearly be regarded by the Court as being in the public service. For example, entry requirements for the Royal Air Force are based on a range of nationality and residence requirements: so, nationals of other countries who were born in the United Kingdom who have been resident in the United Kingdom for five years are eligible, as are nationals of the Republic of Ireland not born in the United Kingdom who have been so resident. Such conditions

[6] Case 149/79 *Commission v Belgium* [1980] ECR 3881, para 10 of the judgment. See also [1982] ECR 1845 for the second phase of this case.

[7] Case 152/73 *Sotgiu* [1974] ECR 153. The point was specifically confirmed in Joined Cases 389 and 390/87 *Echternach and Moritz* [1989] ECR 723, para 14 of the judgment.

[8] Case C-419/92 *Scholz v Opera Universitaria di Cagliari and Cinzi Porcedda* [1994] ECR I-505, noted at (1994) 19 ELRev 309.

[9] Case C-15/96 *Schöning Kougebetopoulou v Frei und Hansestadt Hamburg* [1998] ECR I-47, Case C-187/96 *Commission v Greece* [1998] ECR I-1095, and Case C-195/98 *Österreichischer Gewerkschaftsbund v Austria* [2000] ECR I-10497.

[10] See generally on this issue for the Commission's view of good practice, Communication from the Commission, Free movement of workers—achieving the full benefits and potential, COM(2002) 694 final of 11 December 2002.

recognize that the required state of allegiance may arise other then through the mere possession of nationality. The Police Reform Act 2002 removed the nationality requirement in relation to service as a police officer.[11]

The Court's decision in *Commission v Belgium* reflected the need to balance recognition of the autonomy of the Member States to organize and structure their civil services in the manner they considered appropriate against the need for uniform interpretation and application of the exclusion in order to secure the free movement of workers. The first phase of this case had involved a wide range of occupations including railway workers, nurses, night-watchmen, plumbers, carpenters, electricians, gardeners, and architects. Once the Court had determined that the test for employment in the public service involved a functional test, it became apparent that there was insufficient information to make an accurate appraisal of the functions of some of the posts. So the Court adjourned making an order that the Commission and the Belgian Government re-examine certain of the posts in the light of the Court's approach. In the event, the parties were unable to agree on all the posts in issue, and the Court had to make further determinations in the second phase of the case. Since the case law has moved on, it is inappropriate to list the posts which were included and excluded from the scope of the exclusion in this case. There is no certainty that if the matter were to be litigated today, the outcome in terms of the nature of the posts would be the same, though it is certain that the Court would apply the same functional test to them.

In 1986 the Commission brought infringement proceedings against France in relation to the nationality requirement it imposed for employment as a nurse in a public hospital. Nationals of other Member States were only eligible for a temporary status.[12] France pressed the institutional approach in its arguments before the Court, and sought to re-assert the primacy of national definitions of what constituted the public service. The Court confirmed the approach it had laid down in *Commission v Belgium,* and found an infringement of the Treaty by France.

The *Lawrie-Blum* case[13] concerned a challenge by a British national to the refusal of the Bavarian authorities to admit her to teacher training on the grounds that such posts had civil service status and were only open to German nationals. The Court's decision on the application of the exclusion of employment in the public service is remarkable only for its recapitulation of the principles set out in *Commission v Luxembourg* (discussed above).

A rather more interesting issue arose the following year when the Court handed down its decision in *Commission v Italy.*[14] These proceedings concerned research workers employed by the *Consiglio Nationale delle Recherche* (CNR), an autonomous government agency which employed staff on terms governed in large part by the staff regulations for civil servants. There was, however, provision to recruit foreign

[11] Police Reform Act 2002, s 82.

[12] Case 307/84 *Commission v France* [1986] ECR 1725.

[13] Case 66/85 *Lawrie-Blum v Land Baden-Württemberg* [1986] ECR 2121.

[14] Case 225/85 *Commission v Italy* [1987] ECR 2625, noted at (1988) 13 ELRev 345.

nationals for a maximum period of five years where this was required by the particular needs of the scientific research in question. The Italian Government did not seek to contest the Commission's complaint that these posts were not excluded on grounds of their constituting employment in the public service, but the Advocate General hinted that, had the researchers not been employed by the CNR for some time, the posts might well have been covered by the Article 48(4) (now 39(4)) EC exception.[15]

The *Allué and Coonan* case[16] is part of the long-running saga of the poor treatment afforded to foreign language assistants in universities in Italy.[17] Italian legislation precluded such teachers from access to permanent posts, and their terms and conditions were much less favourable than other similar university posts. In a reference to the Court of Justice, the Italian court asked whether such posts were within the exclusion for employment in the public service. The court had little difficulty in advising that the application of the principles laid down in *Commission v Belgium* did not indicate the presence of any of the factors which would suggest that such employment constituted employment in the public service. This decision was reinforced in the *Bleis* case,[18] in which the French authorities had refused access to an examination which would lead to access to the post of secondary school teacher on the grounds that the applicant was not a French national. The Court re-affirmed its decisions in the cases of *Lawrie-Blum* and *Allué and Coonan*.

In 1988 the Commission issued a communication designed to give guidance on the application of the exception, having rejected the idea that secondary legislation amplifying the exception was needed. There were two risks inherent in secondary legislation of this issue: first that States would use the detail of any such legislation to increase the ambit of the exception, and, secondly, that such legislation would not assist the development of the idea of a citizen's Europe. The Commission action[19] focused on access to employment in four sectors: bodies responsible for administering commercial services, public health care services, teaching posts, and research for non-military purposes. These posts were generally not within the ambit of the exception. It followed that the armed forces, the police, the judiciary, the revenue and certain posts connected with the preparation of legislation would be within the exception.[20]

[15] See para 27 of the Advocate General's Opinion.

[16] Case 33/88 *Allué and Coonan v Università degli studi di Venezia* [1989] ECR 1591, noted at (1989) 14 ELRev 415.

[17] See Friedl, A, 'Fixed Term Contracts for Foreign language Lecturers—A Proportionate Restriction on Free Movement of Workers' (1996) 25 ILJ 66.

[18] Case C-4/91 *Bleis v Ministère de l'Education Nationale* [1991] ECR I-5627.

[19] Freedom of movement of workers and access to employment in the public service of Member States—Commission action in respect of the application of Article 48(4) of the EEC Treaty, [1988] OJ C72/2.

[20] See also Communication from the Commission: Free movement of workers—achieving the full benefits and potential, COM(2002) 694 final of 11 December 2002.

On 2 July 1996 the Court handed down its decisions in three sets of infringement proceedings brought by the Commission against Luxembourg, Belgium and Greece.[21] The infringement proceedings against Luxembourg concerned the reservation for Luxembourg nationals of a variety of posts in research, teaching, health, transport, and in the postal, telecommunications and utilities sectors. The Luxembourg Government argued that the Court should depart from its established case law, and regard as employment in the public service all posts which constituted public service posts under national law. Luxembourg also challenged the generic approach to the posts which had been taken by the Commission in their designation of the posts in issue. Unsurprisingly, the Court did not depart from its established case law, and also considered that the generic approach taken by the Commission was acceptable since the posts in issue were so palpably remote from the specific requirements laid down in the Court's case law on employment in the public service. The Court did recognize that education involves the protection of national identity, but concluded that this did not justify the exclusion of non-nationals from all posts in the field.

Belgium did not contest the generic approach taken by the Commission in the infringement proceedings against it which concerned workers in the bodies responsible for the distribution of water, electricity and gas. It argued that two of the employers in question were private companies over which the public authorities could exercise no authority, and that there were no national, regional or local rules requiring them to apply a nationality condition when recruiting staff. The Court upheld this limited objection to the Commission's case.

The Commission's complaint against Greece contained an exceptionally long list of employments which were reserved for Greek nationals, many of which had already been the subject of decisions by the Court of Justice.[22] The Court speedily concluded that Greece was in breach of its obligations under the EC Treaty. Apart from the attempt by Luxembourg to resurrect the institutional approach to the exclusion, these three cases are significant only for their approval of the Commission's generic approach to ranges of posts. Where the employment in issue is remote from the interests of the State, it was not necessary for the Commission to embark on a post-by-post analysis of the requirements of the post and the interests of the State.

Two decisions handed down by the Court in September 2003[23] concerned the reservation of certain posts in relation to merchant vessels registered in a Member State for its own nationals. The Spanish cases concerned a reference from a court in Spain brought by the officers' association challenging the legality of changes to

[21] Case C-473/93 *Commission v Luxembourg* [1996] ECR I-3207; Case C-173/94 *Commission v Belgium* [1996] ECR I-3265; and Case C-290/94 *Commission v Greece* [1996] ECR I-3285.

[22] For example, nurses, teachers and transport workers.

[23] Case C-405/01 *Colegio de Officiales de la Marina Mercante Española v Administración del Estado,* judgment of 30 September 2003, [2003] ECR nyr; and Case C-47/02 *Anker, Ras and Snoek v Bundesrepublik Deutschland,* judgment of 30 September 2003, [2003] ECR nyr.

Spanish law permitting other than Spanish nationals to have command of vessels registered in Spain. The German case was a challenge to provisions of German law requiring the master of a German registered vessel to be a German national. The essential argument in both cases was that the function of being the master or first officer on a merchant vessel required from time to time the exercise of powers on behalf of the State. This justified the reservation of these posts for the State's own nationals. The Court's reasoning in both cases is identical. The Court qualified the statement in the earlier cases that the exception did not apply where the employer was not the State in the following terms:

> The fact that masters are employed by a private natural or legal person is not, as such, sufficient to exclude the application of Article 39(4) EC since it is established that, in order to perform the public functions which are delegated to them, masters act as representatives of public authority, at the service of the general interests of the flag State.[24]

The exercise of public powers arose only occasionally and this was not sufficient to justify reservation of the employment to nationals of the flag State. The Court noted that the United Nations Convention on the Law of the Sea does not require the master of a ship to be a national of the State whose flag it carries.[25]

It is not possible to use qualifications for access to certain employment as a means of achieving a similar result. The *Burbaud* case[26] concerned the qualifications required for access to public employment, and arose in the context of a Portuguese national who sought admission to the profession of hospital manager in France. Her application was rejected by the Minister on the grounds that she had first to pass the entrance examination of the *École nationale de la santé publique*. The French Government argued that employment in the public service, particularly in the higher echelons, did not allow that status to be equated with a regulated profession such that the rules on mutual recognition of qualifications would apply.[27] This argument was advanced even though the French Government accepted that the employment was not employment in the public service within Article 39(4) EC. The Court concluded that the rules in the mutual recognition directive applied to this employment. If the diploma obtained by Burbaud was equivalent to the diploma required by the French authorities,[28] then the French authorities could not make access to the employment in question subject to the requirement to obtain a diploma from the *École nationale de la santé publique*.

According to one commentary, the issue of employment in the public service remains one 'which is fraught with ideological tensions about the concept of nationality and when it is legitimate for the Member States to require nationality as a condition of employment'.[29] Despite its repeated rejection by the Court of

[24] Case C-405/01, para 43 of the judgment. [25] See, in particular, art 94 of the convention.

[26] Case C-285/01 *Burbaud v Ministère de l'Emploi et de la Solidarité*, judgment of 9 September 2003, [2003] ECR nyr.

[27] Para 25 of the judgment. See also chapter 4 above.

[28] A matter for determination by the national court.

[29] Craig, P and de Búrca, G, *EU Law. Text, Cases, and Materials*, 3rd edn. (Oxford, 2003), 726.

Justice, there remain Member States with a deeply rooted affinity for the institutional approach and for a broadly-defined public sector of employment which may be reserved for its own nationals. This largely explains the continuing flow of case law in this area.

The exercise of official authority

The provision which corresponds to the exception for employment in the public service in the context of establishment and services is the exception in Article 45 (ex 55) EC. This excludes the exercise of the freedoms in respect of 'activities which in that State are connected, even occasionally, with the exercise of official authority'. There are clear parallels in the case law on employment in the public service and the exercise of official authority.

Surprisingly, the Court does not appear to have defined 'the exercise of official authority' in its judgments. So one is left to fall back on the definition used by Advocate General Mayras in the first case in which the Court was called upon to interpret the exception, the *Reyners* case:

> Official authority is that which arises from the sovereignty and majesty of the State; for him who exercises it, it implies the power of enjoying the prerogatives outside the general law, privileges of official power and powers of coercion over citizens.[30]

This definition is not particularly helpful, but the redolence with the notion of employment in the public service is clear.

The profession in issue in the *Reyners* case was that of *avocat* in Belgium; the referring court asked the Luxembourg court whether only the activities inherent in the professional activity which constituted the exercise of official authority could be excluded or whether access to the whole profession could be excluded. The Court responded by noting that as an exception to a fundamental freedom, the exception should be construed strictly.[31] The activities which involved the exercise of official authority were severable and so it would be contrary to Community law to close access to that professional activity as a whole. The fact that the professional activity involved contact with the courts on a regular basis did not mean that the *avocat* was engaged in the exercise of official authority.

In the *Thijssen* case[32] the Court rejected arguments raised by Belgium that auditors of the accounts of insurance companies were exercising official authority. There was a monitoring function and an obligation to report irregularities, but the powers were neither definitive nor final.

A number of attempts have been made to argue that certain activities constitute the exercise of official authority in the context of infringement provisions brought

[30] Case 2/74 *Reyners v Belgium* [1974] ECR 631; Advocate General's Opinion at 664.
[31] See also Case C-114/97 *Commission v Spain* [1998] ECR I-6717, para 34 of the judgment.
[32] Case C-42/92 *Thijssen v Controledienst voor de Verzekeringen* [1993] ECR I-4047.

by the Commission. These have invariably failed, and often seem to be a token effort at defence of an indefensible position. So Greece failed in its argument that the activities of a traffic-accident expert fell within the exception,[33] and Italy argued unsuccessfully that operating a computer system for the national lottery[34] and the activities of transport consultants[35] were protected by the exception. In *Commission v Spain*[36] and *Commission v Belgium*[37] the application of the exception was touched on in the context of the activity of security staff, notably the use of surveillance techniques. The Court's response was short and sharp in both cases. No real evidence had been adduced to establish that the activities in issue constituted the exercise of official authority; activities which made a contribution to public security and occasionally involved assisting the police did not constitute the exercise of official authority.

Compatibility of the exceptions with citizenship of the European Union

The future of these two exceptions—or their ambit—might be considered to be in doubt following the introduction of citizenship of the European Union, since this provides some bond between nationals of all the Member States and the European Union. The contrary argument is that the European Union is not concerned to replace nationality and national identities, and the link between the State and certain activities is such that those activities can continue to be reserved for that State's own nationals. The case law demonstrates the lingering tension between the requirements of an open market in employment and self-employment and a closed market in certain jobs and activities. Writing in 1992 David O'Keeffe said:

> . . . this view of the public service exception is founded on a conception of nationality which may face increasing strain. It is based on a very traditional notion of loyalty to the State and finds its parallel in the denial of foreigners of political rights. . . . [38]

An example of an activity which would currently clearly fall within the ambit of both exceptions will illustrate the point. Eligibility for many first-tier judicial appointments in England and Wales is a five-year practising qualification as a lawyer. Why should such appointments only be open to United Kingdom nationals holding such qualifications? Is United Kingdom nationality a prerequisite for the determination of first instance disputes on unfair dismissal, or entitlement to social

[33] Case C-306/89 *Commission v Greece* [1991] ECR I-5863.
[34] Case C-272/91 *Commission v Italy* [1994] ECR I-1409.
[35] Case C-263/99 *Commission v Italy* [2001] ECR I-4195.
[36] Case C-114/97 *Commission v Spain* [1998] ECR I-6717.
[37] Case C-355/98 *Commission v Belgium* [2000] ECR I-1221.
[38] O'Keeffe, D, 'Judicial Interpretation of the Public Service Exception to the Free Movement of Workers' in Curtin, D and O'Keeffe, D, *Constitutional Adjudication in European Community and National Law* (Dublin, 1992) at 105.

security benefits? Surely what is relevant is whether an applicant for such an appointment has the skills and qualifications necessary to be a good judge?

It is clear that access to employment in the public service or to activities involving the exercise of official authority varies from Member State to Member State. Some focus more on qualifications to undertake the task, whereas others argue that the bond of nationality and the activity are much more closely related. This is an area where there is considerable variation of practice. It is, therefore, not unreasonable to expect that the introduction of citizenship of the Union will lead, over time, to calls for a further narrowing of the use of these two exceptions. Perhaps it would be timely for the Commission (or an academic team) to conduct a comparative investigation into the activities which are closed to non-nationals in some Member States but open to them in others.

Exceptions justified on grounds of public policy, public security, and public health

The exceptions for employment in the public service and for the exercise of official authority take qualifying activities outside the scope of the provisions of the EC Treaty. The exceptions to be found in Articles 39(3), 46(1) and 55 EC allow Member States to deny to particular individuals the benefits which flow from the rules on the free movement of persons. The necessity for a careful consideration of the individual circumstances of each and every case is a prerequisite for the use of these exceptions. None of the terms used in the Treaty is defined there, though there is secondary legislation to assist together with a rich case law from the Court of Justice.

The elaboration of the exceptions in Directive 64/221/EEC[39] is of special importance in determining the scope of these exceptions. The objective of the directive is to offer safeguards and procedural guarantees when a Member State proposes to rely upon one of these exceptions to deny the application of Community rights. Article 1 of Directive 64/221 provides that it applies to any national of a Member State who resides in or travels to another Member State as a worker, a self-employed person, or as a provider or recipient of services. The provisions equally apply to spouses and members of the family who acquire rights under the rules on free movement of persons. The scope of the directive covers all those situations in which an adverse decision may be made: decisions on entry to the territory of a Member State, issue and renewal of residence permits, and expulsions from the territory of a Member State. The exceptions can never be invoked 'to service

[39] Council Directive of 25 February 1964 on the coordination of special measures concerning the movement and residence of foreign nationals which are justified on grounds of public policy, public security or public health (64/221/EEC), [1963–64] OJ Eng. Sp. Ed. 117, which will be replaced in due course by provisions in the new directive.

economic ends'.[40] So, for example, it will never be open to a Member State to seek to close its borders to those from other Member States seeking work there on the grounds that unemployment in that State is at a high level.

In July 1999 the Commission issued a Communication[41] offering guidelines on the application of the exceptions in the light of the introduction of citizenship of the Union, and of a number of specific problems which had been identified from the complaints received by the Commission over the years. There are also a number of improvements of wording and clarification reflecting judgments of the Court of Justice to be found in the new directive on the right of citizens of the Union and their family members to move and reside freely within the territory of the Member States.[42]

Who can rely on the exceptions?

In the overwhelming majority of cases, it will be the State which is seeking to rely on the exceptions, because their application will arise in the context of an immigration decision or on application for the issue or renewal of the Community residence permit. But in the *Bosman* case,[43] which concerned rules applied by national and international football associations, the Court said:

> There is nothing to preclude individuals from relying on justifications on grounds of public policy, public security or public health. Neither the scope not the content of those grounds of justification is in any way affected by the public or private nature of the rules in question.[44]

As Fernández Martín has noted,[45] that extension is troublesome if it means that private parties can seek to justify discriminatory practices by references to public interest criteria. Such an approach has no basis in the Treaty, in Directive 64/221/EEC (which refers to measures adopted by States) or in the prior case law of the Court of Justice. He posits the attractive proposition that the scope of private party reliance on the public interest exceptions is limited to organizations charged with 'regulating the conditions of employment in a collective manner' and so are exercising a semi-public regulatory function.

[40] Art. 2(2) of Directive 64/221/EEC. See also Case 352/85 *Bond van Adverteerders and others v The Netherlands* [1988] ECR 2085, para 34 of the judgment.

[41] Commission Communication to the Council and the European Parliament on the Special Measures concerning the Movement and Residence of Citizens of the Union which are Justified on Grounds of Public Policy, Public Security or Public Health, COM(1999) 372 of 30 July 1999. This document is referred to in this chapter as 'the Commission Communication'.

[42] See n 2 above.

[43] Case C-415/93 *Union Royal Belge des Sociétés de Football Association ASBL and others v Bosman and others* [1995] ECR I-4921, noted at (1996) 21 ELRev 313.

[44] Para 86 of the judgment.

[45] (1996) 21 ELRev 313, at 323–4.

Public policy

Most difficulties arise with the application of the exception based on considerations of public policy. What is a ground of public policy is determined by national courts, subject to the secondary legislation in Directive 64/221 and to guidance from the Court of Justice. As an exception to a broad freedom, it is interpreted restrictively. It is also accepted that what amounts to a ground of public policy will vary from Member State to Member State. In the *Van Duyn* case[46] the Court ruled that 'the concept of public policy may vary from one country to another and from one period to another'[47] and added 'it is . . . necessary to allow the competent national authorities an area of discretion within the limits imposed by the Treaty.'[48] Some assistance on what is and is not included in the concept of public policy and public security is provided by Article 3 of the directive. This stresses that personal conduct of the migrant is the sole issue for consideration, that previous convictions do not alone amount to a ground of public policy, and that expiry of documentation cannot justify expulsion from the territory.

The classic definition of 'public policy' is contained in the *Bouchereau* case:

> Recourse by a national authority to the concept of public policy presupposes . . . the existence . . . of a genuine and sufficiently serious threat to the requirements of public policy affecting one of the fundamental interests of society.[49]

There is a significant body of case law on the topic. The Court of Justice has held that the exclusion by the United Kingdom of a scientologist was justified on grounds of public policy in the *Van Duyn* case.[50] This was because the cult was considered socially harmful, even though there was no restriction on the practice of scientology by nationals. The Court said:

> A Member State in imposing restrictions justified on grounds of public policy, is entitled to take into account, as a matter of personal conduct of the individual concerned, the fact that the individual is associated with some body or organisation the activities of which the Member State considers socially harmful but which are not unlawful in that State, despite the fact that no restriction is placed upon nationals of the said Member State who wish to take similar employment with these same bodies or organisations.[51]

The decision has lost some of its force (though it has not been departed from) as a result of the *Adoui and Cornuaille* case,[52] where the expulsion of waitresses alleged to be involved in prostitution was in issue. The Court ruled that a Member State was not entitled to exclude or expel a national of another Member State for conduct which, if it had been conduct of one of its own nationals, would not have been subject to any repressive measures or effective and genuine measures to combat it.

[46] Case 41/74, *Van Duyn* [1974] ECR 1337. [47] Para 18 of the judgment
[48] ibid. [49] Case 30/77, *Bouchereau* [1977] ECR 1999, para 18 of the judgment.
[50] Case 41/74, *Van Duyn* [1974] ECR 1337. [51] Para 24 of the judgment.
[52] Joined Cases 115–6/81, *Adoui and Cornuaille v Belgian State* [1982] ECR 1665.

> Although Community law does not impose upon the Member States a uniform scale of values as regards the assessment of conduct which may be considered as contrary to public policy, it should nevertheless be stated that conduct may not be considered as being of a sufficiently serious nature to justify restrictions on the admission to or residence within the territory of a Member State of a national of another Member State in a case where the former Member State does not adopt, with respect to the same conduct on the part of its own nationals, repressive measures intended to combat such conduct.[53]

The Commission Communication stresses that the concept of public policy (as well as those of public security and public health) should 'not be artificially limited by trying to give exact and exhausting [sic] definition'. It also stresses that as European integration advances, national differences in definition and approach 'may gradually approach each other'.[54]

The *Rutili* case[55] concerned an Italian national living in France. In 1967 and 1968 he took part in political and trade union activities that made him unpopular with the authorities, who took the view that his presence in certain *départements* was 'likely to disturb public policy'. In 1968 he was subject first to a deportation order, but later to an order requiring him to live in a particular *département* and in 1970 was prohibited from living in any of four *départements*, one of which was his place of normal residence where he lived with his family. He challenged this restriction before the French courts and a reference was made to the Court of Justice on the compatibility of the restrictions with Community law. The Court of Justice ruled that the exceptions in the Treaty must be construed strictly since they were derogations from freedom of movement. The Court also noted the limitations on movement which might be justified under provisions of the European Convention on Human Rights. On the substantive question, the Court ruled that the restriction in the Treaty could only be imposed in relation to the whole of the national territory. Furthermore under Article 7 EEC (now Article 12 EC) it was not open to a Member State to impose a restriction in relation to freedom of movement on a national of another Member State exercising rights under the Treaty which was not available in respect of its own nationals.

This ruling has been considered in the *Olazabal* case.[56] The case concerned a proposal by the French authorities to require Olazabal, who was considered to have involvement with ETA terrorists activity, not to live in 31 *départements* with the object of keeping him away from the Spanish border. The Court ruled that such measures were permissible within the public policy provisions provided that three conditions were met: (1) such measures were justified on grounds of public policy or public security having regard to the personal conduct of the person concerned; (2) those reasons could otherwise justify excluding the person from the territory of the Member State altogether; and (3) the conduct which the State wishes to prevent is the subject of punitive or other genuine and effective measures in respect of its own nationals designed to combat such conduct.

[53] Para 8 of the judgment. [54] Commission Communication, p 10.
[55] Case 36/75, *Rutili* [1975] ECR 1219.
[56] Case C-100/01 *Ministre de l'Intérieure v Olazabal* [2002] ECR I-10981.

Article 3(2) of Directive 64/221/EEC provides that deportation cannot be an automatic consequence of a criminal conviction; this was confirmed in the *Bouchereau* case, which concerned a French national convicted twice in the space of six months for possession of cannabis, where the Court advised:

> The existence of a previous conviction can therefore only be taken into account in so far as the circumstances which gave rise to that conviction are evidence of personal conduct constituting a present threat to the requirements of public policy.
>
> Although, in general, a finding that such a threat exists implies the existence in the individual of a propensity to act in the same way in the future. It is possible that past conduct alone may constitute such a threat to the requirements of public policy.[57]

The question of expulsion following conviction for a criminal offence has proved to be problematic.[58] It is not uncommon for criminal justice systems to include as part of the sentence of imprisonment a recommendation or order that a person is removed from the territory on completion of the sentence of imprisonment.[59] Such conditions must always be proportional to the offence.[60] The *Calfa* case[61] underlines the requirement of proportionality in balancing the interests of the State and the fundamental nature of free movement. Donatella Calfa was charged and convicted of possession of drugs while staying in Crete as a tourist. She was sentenced to three months' imprisonment followed by expulsion from Greece for life. This was an automatic consequence of the offence of which she had been convicted. The Court said that the order could only be made if it was established that Calfa presented a sufficiently serious threat to one of the fundamental interests of society to justify so extensive an exclusion. The conditions for the application of such a lengthy sanction required by Directive 64/221 were not present.[62]

The Commission Communication reminds Member States that the question of whether there is a sufficiently serious threat to one of the fundamental interests of society must be determined at the time expulsion is contemplated. In the cases where there is a lapse of time between a recommendation or decision and its implementation, this requires an individual assessment of the character, behaviour and rehabilitation of the offender.[63] Consideration must also be given to the person's present personal circumstances, including his or her ties with the Member

[57] Case 30/77 *Bouchereau* [1977] ECR 1999, para 28 of the judgment.

[58] See Joined Cases C-482/01 and C-493/01 *Orfanopoulos and Oliveri*, Judgment of 29 April 2004.

[59] See for example, Case 131/79 *ex parte Santillo* [1980] ECR 1685. Santillo had been convicted of violent sexual attacks for which he was sentenced to a period of imprisonment on completion of which he was to be returned to Italy.

[60] See also the new directive, art 27(2) which includes reference to the principle of proportionality alongside the requirement that the conduct relied on to justify exclusion or expulsion must be personal conduct.

[61] Case C-348/96 *Criminal Proceedings against Donatella Calfa* [1999] ECR I-11.

[62] Under the new directive, provision is made for applying for any exclusion orders to be lifted no later than three years after they take effect.

[63] See also later in this chapter on the procedural safeguards in Directive 64/221/EEC.

State contemplating expulsion. This will require consideration of the circumstances of any spouse and children.[64]

The conduct must always be personal to the individual concerned and not an assumption based on activities of groups as a genre, nor can the penalty of expulsion be used in order to provide an example to others. The *Bonsignore* case[65] illustrated this. Carmelo Bonsignore, an Italian national working in Germany, accidentally shot and killed his brother as a result of careless handling of a firearm, possession of which was unlawful. The German Court showed mercy in imposing no penalty having regard to the tragedy which had occurred, but ordered Bonsignore's deportation as a deterrent against other aliens possessing firearms. Its purpose was of a general preventive nature. The Court of Justice held that deportation on such grounds was inconsistent with the requirements of Article 3(2) of Directive 64/221/EEC, which prohibited consideration of grounds extraneous to the individual case. Only the personal conduct of the individual can be taken into consideration.

The Commission Communication recognizes that some circumstances may not easily permit a full individual consideration. Examples given are large sports events, rock concerts, political demonstrations and other organized protests.[66] Nevertheless measures seeking to exclude those likely to cause violence and hooliganism should still be measures targeted at individuals, or exceptionally, groups of individuals and should not merely be general preventive measures.

Public security

Public security relates to the protection of a Member State from terrorism, serious crime, espionage and activities leading to the destabilization of the State. Surprisingly, there is no case law expressly on the issue of public security, possibly because it is even more limited in scope than public policy and is, in essence, a particular aspect of it. But it may also be that the Member States are considered to have a greater discretion when dealing with matters involving the security of the State, particularly in a context where a number of Member States have been victims of terrorist attacks. The Commission Communication stresses the particular need for transparency in relation to decisions made on this ground.

Public health

There are detailed provisions on the public health exception in Directive 64/221; these have something of an old-fashioned look to them. The Commission Communication comments:

[64] The new directive makes it clear that a check prior to expulsion must always be made in order to test that the grounds on which the original order was made remain valid.

[65] Case 67/74, *Bonsignore* [1975] ECR 297.

[66] Commission Communication, p 16.

The public health grounds are somewhat outdated given the current level of integration of the European Union and the development of new means to handle public health problems. Therefore, restrictions on free movement can no longer be considered as necessary and effective means of solving public health problems. The situation has changed radically from what it was in 1964, even though the concept of public health still forms part of Community law.[67]

Article 4 of Directive 64/221 provides that it is only those diseases specified in the Annex to the directive which can justify refusal of entry into a Member State or refusal of a first residence permit. Development of the diseases after entry cannot be used as a grounds for refusal to renew a residence permit or expulsion from the Member State. There is a prohibition on the introduction of new provisions or practices which are more restrictive than those contained in the directive.

The Annex contains two lists. The first lists diseases which are regarded as endangering public health, such as tuberculosis, diseases which are subject to quarantine under World Health Organization rules, syphilis, and other contagious diseases 'if they are the subject of provisions for the protection of nationals of the host country'. The second lists conditions which might threaten public policy or public security; these are drug addiction and serious mental illnesses. An issue which has arisen is whether measures can be taken by Member States in relation to those with HIV/AIDS. The Community has stated its policy in relation to this group of securing full respect for their free movement and for equality of treatment.[68]

The new directive considerably simplifies the public health exceptions. It retains reference to diseases 'with epidemic potential' under World Health Organization rules, and to infectious diseases or contagious parasitic diseases provided that they are subject to control measures applicable to nationals. The other conditions listed in the Annex to Directive 64/221 disappear.

Procedural safeguards

Articles 5 to 9 of Directive 64/221/EEC establish a detailed system of procedural guarantees and remedies in the context of free movement of persons. These apply whenever refusal of entry, refusal of a residence permit, or expulsion is in issue. Since derogation from the provisions of Directive 68/360/EEC[69] is only permitted on grounds of public policy, public security or public health, the procedural

[67] P 12.

[68] See Conclusions of the Council and of the Representatives of the Governments of the Member States meeting within the Council on 15 May 1987 concerning AIDS, [1987] OJ C178/1. See also Van Overbeek, P, 'AIDS/HIV infection and the free movement of persons in the European Economic Community' (1990) 27 CMLRev 791. The SARS epidemic in 2003 does not seem to have caused any restrictions on free movement within the European Union, but any measures could probably have been justified under Annex A.3.

[69] Council Directive of 15 October 1968 on the abolition of restrictions on movement and residence within the Community for workers of Member States and their families (68/360/EEC), [1968] III OJ Eng Sp Ed 485, as amended.

safeguards in Directive 64/221/EEC will also apply where a residence permit is refused.

Migrants may experience difficulties when they apply for a residence permit. Article 5 concerns the issue of residence permits, and requires decisions to be taken 'as soon as possible and in any event not later than six months from the date of application for the permit'. An applicant is allowed to remain in the territory pending a decision on the application. Enquiries may be made (though not as a matter of routine) of the Member State of origin and, if relevant, of other Member States, concerning an applicant's police record. Replies must be provided within two months.

The Commission Communication expressed concern about undue delays in examining applications for residence permits. The residence permit gives no rights which the applicant does not already have under the provisions of the EC Treaty, but merely provides evidence of the existence of those rights. Nevertheless the Commission stresses the importance of compliance with the timescale envisaged by Article 5.

Any person subject to the application of the exceptions is entitled under Article 6 to be informed of the grounds of public policy, public security or public health upon which a decision to refuse a residence permit or to deport is based. The only exception is where the interests of the security of the State would be adversely affected. This right to information is a right to receive details of the exact nature and consequences of any proposed measure. In the *Rutili* case, the Court said that this was an entitlement to be given a 'precise and comprehensive statement of the grounds for the decision, to enable him to take effect measures to prepare his defence.'[70]

Anyone faced with refusal of a residence permit or deportation must be given at least 15 days' notice under Article 7 except in cases of urgency. A good example of such a situation might be exclusion of a known football hooligan seeking to travel to the venue of a football match where the giving of notice would defeat the interests of public order the Member State is seeking to protect because the match would have taken place before the end of the period of notice.

Articles 8 and 9 detail the procedures which must be available to enable a person to challenge any adverse decision. The application and interaction of these guarantees are complex.

Under Article 8 a person must be afforded the same legal remedies as are available to nationals of the Member State concerned in respect of acts of the administration. This is simply an extension of existing remedies to such decisions, but it does not mean that a national of another Member State has access to exactly

[70] Case 36/75, *Rutili* [1975] ECR 1219, para 39 of the judgment. Similar wording was used in Joined Cases 115–6/81, *Adoui and Cornuaille* [1982] ECR 1665, para 19 of the judgment. The new directive requires these reasons to be given in writing. This may already be needed in order to enable a person to take effective measures to defend themselves, but the requirement is not laid down anywhere. The court or tribunal before which any appeal is to be taken must also be specified.

the same remedies as those who might be regarded as in a cognate situation in the national legal order. In the *Pecastaing* case[71] the Court said that the provision 'imposes upon the Member States the obligation to make available to any person affected by such acts the same legal remedies as are available to nationals in respect of acts of the administration'.[72] But the article does not indicate which courts are to have jurisdiction in respect of such appeals; this is a matter for the organization of the courts of the Member States.

The notion of the 'same remedies' was raised in the *Shingara and Radiom* cases.[73] Shingara was a French national of Sikh origin. His admission to the United Kingdom was refused in 1991 by personal direction of the Home Secretary on the grounds that his presence in the United Kingdom was not conducive to the public good because of his alleged links with the activities of Sikh extremists. Such persons do not have rights of appeal through the normal appeal system concerning contested immigration decisions,[74] but do have access to judicial review. In July 1993 he entered the United Kingdom at Dover, but was arrested in Birmingham a few days later. He was granted leave to apply for a judicial review of the Home Secretary's decision.

Radiom held both Iranian and Irish nationality. In May 1983 he was granted indefinite leave to remain as an employee in the Iranian consular service in the United Kingdom. In 1989, following the severance of diplomatic relations between the United Kingdom and Iran, he was required to leave the country. He did so. In 1992 he sought entry into the United Kingdom on the basis of his Irish nationality. When this was refused, he too sought a judicial review of the decision of the Home Secretary.

Both applicants argued that there was a lack of similar treatment of those in comparable situations and this violated the requirements of Article 8. Their argument was based upon a comparison of their own situation with that of a United Kingdom national whose immigration status was in issue. The latter would have access to the appeal to an immigration adjudicator, whereas they did not. The real distinction, however, related to personal decisions made by the Home Secretary on the grounds that a person's presence was not conducive to the public good, and 'ordinary' decisions whether in respect of United Kingdom or other nationals, where appeals went through the immigration appeal system. The Court referred to its decisions in the *Van Duyn* case[75] and the *Adoui and Cornuaille* case[76] in which it had noted that there were necessarily distinctions to be drawn in the treatment of a Member State's own nationals and those of other Member States, since a Member

[71] Case 98/79 *Pecastaing v Belgian State* [1980] ECR 691.

[72] Para 10 of the judgment.

[73] Joined Cases C-65/95 and C-111/95 *R v Secretary of State for the Home Department, ex parte Shingara and Radiom* [1997] ECR I-3343, noted at (1998) 35 CMLRev 519 and (1998) 23 ELRev 157.

[74] That is, appeal to an immigration adjudicator, followed by an appeal to the Immigration Appeal Tribunal.

[75] Case 41/71 *Van Duyn v Home Office* [1974] ECR 1337.

[76] Joined Cases 115/81 and 116/81 *Adoui and Cornuaille v Belgian State* [1982] ECR 1665.

State had no authority to expel or refuse admission of its own nationals. It followed that there need not be access to exactly the same remedy, as long as there was access to the same remedies as those generally available. This decision might be regarded as an unnecessary accommodation to Member State procedures, since the real issue was whether cases like that raised by Shingara and Radiom should not be treated in the same way as more routine immigration decisions. The comparison in Article 8 is not with remedies available to nationals of the host State but to the 'same remedies as those available against acts of the administration generally in that Member State'.

Article 8 is silent on the question of whether the remedy must have a suspensory effect, although Article 9 contains additional protection where the Article 8 remedy 'cannot have suspensory effect'. In the *Pecastaing* case,[77] the Court had this to say on the suspensory effect of Article 8 remedies:

> . . . Article 8 contains no specific obligation concerning any suspensory effect of applications available to persons covered by the directive. If that provision requires that the person concerned should be able to appeal against the measure affecting him if must be inferred, as the Court stated in its judgment in the *Royer* case (paragraph 60 of the decision), that the decision ordering expulsion may not be executed—save in cases of urgency—before the party concerned is able to complete the formalities necessary to avail himself of the remedy. However, it cannot be inferred from that provision that the person concerned is entitled to remain on the territory of the State concerned throughout the proceedings initiated by him. Such an interpretation, which would enable the person concerned unilaterally, by lodging an application, to suspend the measure affecting him, is incompatible with the objective of the directive which is to reconcile the requirements of public policy, public security and public health with the guarantees which must be provided for the persons affected by such measures.[78]

Article 9 applies in three situations: (a) where there is no right of appeal to a court of law; or (b) where the appeal may only be taken in respect of the legal validity of the decision; or (c) where the appeal cannot have suspensory effect. The article contains minimum standard guarantees, which differ according to the status of the person concerned. Article 9(1) applies where a person already has a residence permit[79] and is either refused a renewal of that permit or is subject to expulsion. The relationship of Articles 8 and 9 was considered in the *Royer* case.[80] The judgment in this case supports a number of important propositions. Where an Article 8 remedy is available but does not have suspensory effect, then the guarantees in Article 9 must also be applied. The person affected by an Article 8 decision which does not have suspensory effect cannot be removed before he or she is able to 'avail himself of the remedy'. The Article 9 guarantee must also be applied.

[77] Case 98/79 *Pecastaing v Belgian State* [1980] ECR 691.

[78] Para 12 of the judgment.

[79] Since it was held in Case 48/75 *Royer* [1976] ECR 497, that the residence permit was merely evidence of entitlement to enter and reside in the territory of a Member State other than that of the claimant's nationality, this term must be read as including a person who is entitled under the secondary legislation to the issue of a residence permit. See also Case C-174/94 *R v Secretary of State for the Home Department, ex parte Gallagher* [1995] ECR I-4253.

[80] Case 48/75 *Royer* [1976] ECR 497.

Where the person has a residence permit which is not being renewed, or where the holder of a residence permit is being expelled, the expulsion cannot take place until the opinion of a 'competent authority' has been obtained. The judgment in the *Royer* case refers to the 'opportunity of appealing to the authority designated in Article 9'.[81] However, Article 9 is in mandatory terms rather than permissive terms; it provides:

> . . . a decision refusing renewal of a residence permit or ordering the expulsion of the holder of a residence permit from the territory *shall not be taken* by the administrative authority, save in cases of urgency, until an opinion has been obtained from a competent authority.[82]

The mandatory nature of the reference for an opinion of a competent authority would appear to be confirmed in the *Pecastaing* case, where the Court said:

> . . . if a Member State has applied Article 9 in order to compensate for the fact that the appeals to the courts which are available do not carry suspensory effect that provision would be rendered nugatory if, always save in cases of urgency, execution of the expulsion order contemplated were not suspended until that authority has given its opinion (*Royer* case, paragraph 61 of the decision).[83]

If there were any doubt about the interaction of the Article 8 and Article 9 remedies, this is removed by the next paragraph of the Court's judgment:

> It follows from Article 9 therefore that as soon as the opinion in question has been obtained and notified to the person concerned an expulsion order may be executed immediately, subject always to the right of that person to stay on the territory for the time necessary to avail himself of the remedies accorded by Article 8 of the directive.[84]

Article 9(2) applies where no initial decision authorizing admission to a Member State has been made or where no first residence permit has been issued. However, this second provision must be read in the light of the Court's case law noted above making it clear that the residence permit is merely evidence of rights flowing from the Treaty. It is also clear that, where a person has been admitted temporarily pending determination of their immigration status, such a decision is not a decision concerning entry which attracts the procedural guarantees. But if there is a significant lapse of time before a final decision is made, then the person affected will be entitled to the procedural guarantees in Article 9.[85]

Where a decision is taken to refuse the *renewal* of a residence permit or ordering the expulsion of the *holder* of a residence permit, that decision cannot be taken, 'save in cases of urgency' until 'an opinion has been obtained from a 'competent authority' of the host State (different from that which made the contested decision) at which the person is to be afforded 'such rights of defence and of assistance or representation as the domestic law of that country provides for'.

[81] Para 61 of the judgment. [82] Author's emphasis added.
[83] Case 98/79 *Pecastaing v Belgian State* [1980] ECR 691, para 17 of the decision.
[84] Para 18 of the judgment.
[85] Case C-357/98 *R v Secretary of State for the Home Department, ex parte Yiadom* [2000] ECR I-9265.

Where a decision refusing the issue of a *first* residence permit, or expelling a person *before* the issue of a first residence permit, is made, Article 9(2) requires that the decision must, at the request of the affected person be referred to a 'competent authority' of the host State (different from that which made the contested decision) at which the person is to be afforded 'such rights of defence and of assistance or representation as the domestic law of that country provides for' and must be permitted to submit his defence in person 'except where this would be contrary to the interests of national security'.

The difference between these two situations is that there must always be consideration by a 'competent authority' where the person already has rights of residence or already holds a residence permit, whereas in a case where initial entry or a first residence is sought, the minimum procedural guarantee only applies if the person 'so requests'.

In both cases, the immigration authorities must take the views of the review body into account, but are not bound by them. In the *Royer* case, it was ruled that the procedure under both Article 8 and Article 9 meant that the decision to exclude someone from the territory of a Member State could not be put into effect until the procedures under these articles had run their course.[86] The key difference between the requirements of paragraphs (1) and (2) is not qualitative, but temporal. The same procedural safeguard applies, but in the circumstances envisaged by paragraph (1), the opinion must be obtained before the decision to expel the person is taken, whereas under paragraph (2) the requirement for the opinion is triggered by the claimant's request and may be obtained after the decision to expel has been made.[87]

So what constitutes a 'competent authority'? The Court was first called upon to consider this question in the *Santillo* case.[88] Santillo, an Italian national, had been convicted in the United Kingdom of serious sexual offences and, in January 1974, sentenced to imprisonment for eight years with a recommendation for deportation when he was released from prison. Santillo sought to challenge the decision made in September 1978 shortly before his release that he should be deported on his release from prison. The Court of Justice concluded that a recommendation for deportation made by a criminal court at the time of conviction may constitute an opinion by a competent authority for the purposes of Article 9 of the Directive. Indeed the Court said:

> Any public authority independent of the administrative authority called upon to adopt one of the measures referred to by the directive, which is so constituted that the person concerned enjoys the right of representation and defence before it, may be considered as such an authority.[89]

However, the opinion of the competent authority must be proximate in time to the decision to expel, and the passage of time amounting to several years between

[86] Case 48/75 *Royer* [1976] ECR 497, paras 57–61 of the judgment.

[87] Joined Cases C-65/95 and C-111/95 *R v Secretary of State for the Home Department, ex parte Shingara and Radiom* [1997] ECR I-3343, paras 107–9 of the Advocate General's Opinion.

[88] Case 131/79 *R v Secretary of State for the Home Department, ex parte Santillo* [1980] ECR 1585.

[89] Para 19 of the judgment.

the recommendation and the implementation of that recommendation might deprive the original recommendation of its status as an opinion within Article 9. The Court said:

It is indeed essential that social danger resulting from a foreigner's presence should be assessed at the very time when the decision ordering expulsion is made against him as the factors to be taken into account, particularly those concerning his conduct, are likely to change in the course of time.[90]

On receiving the Court of Justice's decision on the questions referred, the national court decided, and the Court of Appeal subsequently confirmed, that a delay of four and a half years did not produce a situation in which the recommendation of the Crown Court was not proximate in time to the decision taken by the Home Secretary to implement recommendation for deportation.[91] It is at least arguable that this was not a correct application of the Court of Justice's judgment, since it is difficult to see how anyone could be certain that Santillo continued to represent a significant danger to public order without an individual assessment in 1978.

The Court of Justice also gave advice on the qualities of the competent authority in the *Adoui and Cornuaille* case[92] and in the *Dzodzi* case.[93] In both cases, the Court emphasized that the competent authority need neither be a court nor be composed of judges; nor need it be a permanent body. Key qualities were 'absolute independence' from the administrative authority taking the decision which required that the competent authority is not in any way subject to any control by the administrative authority whose decision is in issue. If these qualities are present, absolute independence is not compromised even if the costs of the 'competent authority' fall on the Government department which is the administrative authority making the decision on which the competent authority's opinion is sought. Article 9 does not lay down any procedural requirements save in relation to the receipt of representations from the person affected; it is for each Member State to lay down the procedure for reference of relevant decisions to the competent authority. Although the outcome must be communicated to the person affected, neither the identity of the members of the authority nor their professional status need be disclosed.

The nature of the competent authority arose in other circumstances in the *Gallagher* case.[94] This case concerned an expulsion decision made on the personal

[90] Para 18 of the judgment.

[91] *R v Secretary of State for the Home Department, ex parte Santillo* [1981] 2 WLR 362. In his usual trenchant language Lord Denning MR captured the mood of the Court of Appeal when he said, 'The lapse of time here—four and a half years—was not such as to invalidate the recommendation for deportation. The applicant had spent all those years in prison. That was because he was such a bad man, and there was a risk of his offending again. It does not deprive the recommendation of its force in the slightest' (at 373).

[92] Joined Cases 115–6/81, *Adoui and Cornuaille* [1982] ECR 1665, paras 16–19 of the judgment.

[93] Joined Cases C-297/88 and C-197/88 *Dzodzi v Belgian State* [1990] ECR I-3763, paras 64–6 of the judgment.

[94] Case C-174/94 *R v Secretary of State for the Home Department, ex parte Gallagher* [1995] ECR I-4253, noted at (1996) 33 CMLRev 777 and (1996) 21 ELRev 241.

authority of the Home Secretary under anti-terrorism legislation because he was satisfied that Gallagher was a person who 'is or has been concerned in the commission, preparation or instigation of acts of terrorism connected with the affairs of Northern Ireland'. For family reasons, Gallagher consented to his immediate removal to Ireland, since he wanted to be with his pregnant girlfriend. Following his removal, he elected within the requisite 14-day period to make representations objecting to the grounds of his removal and requesting a personal interview with a person or persons nominated by the Home Secretary.[95] Under this procedure the Home Secretary is required to receive the representations of the person concerned and the advice of the person conducting the personal interview together with the report of that interview in reconsidering the decision to exclude the person concerned.

Gallagher was interviewed at the British Embassy in Dublin by an adviser nominated by the Home Secretary. The identity of the adviser was not disclosed to Gallagher and no further particulars of the ground on which the Home Secretary had expelled Gallagher were provided. The Home Secretary subsequently refused to vary the initial decision. Gallagher then sought a judicial review of the Home Secretary's decision. In the course of these proceedings two questions were referred to the Luxembourg Court. The first question essentially asked whether the Home Secretary was required by Article 9 of the directive to await the opinion of the adviser before making the exclusion order. The second question essentially asked whether the nomination of the adviser by the Home Secretary offered sufficient guarantee of independence as required by Article 9.

The Court of Justice concluded that Article 9(1) of the directive applied to Gallagher, and accordingly the opinion should have been obtained before the decision to expel Gallagher was taken.[96]

Responding to the second question, the Court re-stated the qualities of the competent authority to which it had referred in its earlier case law noted above. In any judicial review proceedings, the reviewing court should be advised of the identity and functions of the member or members constituting the competent authority in order to be able to satisfy themselves as to their independence and impartiality, but there is no requirement that these matters be communicated to the person concerned in connection with the representations themselves.[97] It did not matter that the competent authority was appointed by the administrative authority provided that the guarantees of independence and impartiality were present.[98]

[95] In accordance with provisions in Sch. 2, para 3 to the Prevention of Terrorism (Temporary Provisions) Act 1989.

[96] Case C-174/94 *R v Secretary of State for the Home Department, ex parte Gallagher* [1995] ECR I-4253, para 22 of the judgment.

[97] Para 25 of the judgment.

[98] Note that Advocate General Colomer in his Opinion in Joined Cases C-65/95 and C-111/95 *R v Secretary of State for the Home Department, ex parte Shingara and Radiom* [1997] ECR I-3343, suggests that the development of the concept of effective judicial protection requires decision-makers to be more concerned with substance and not simply with formal requirements: see paras 68–103 of his Opinion.

Concluding comment

The existence both of exclusions from the provisions of free movement and of exceptions based on grounds of public policy, public security, and public health offer some accommodation to the interests of Member States in both the reservation of activities for their own nationals and the control of the conduct of nationals of other Member States. Those accommodations tend to disguise the tensions between different national approaches to the nature of employment and which activities can only effectively be carried out by its own nationals. The exclusions and exceptions are not mandatory and there are significant differences of approach in relation to reliance on both areas. The basic rules have not changed since the early days of the Community, and there is no political will to change the provisions of the EC Treaty. There have been developments in the case law, but these are really fine-tuning of the interpretation of the Treaty provisions.

Citizenship of the Union appears to have had very little impact on the operation of the exclusions and exceptions, though there might be developments in this area as substance is given to citizenship rights.

It is, however, possible to detect an increasing emphasis on fundamental rights in the procedural safeguards which surround the application of the exceptions based on public policy, public security, and public health. These have an impact not only on procedure which must offer a fair trial within the meaning of Article 6 of the European Convention on Human Rights, but also on the substance of the decision in terms of family unity under Article 8 of the Convention.

6

Remedies

Introduction

This chapter provides a brief overview of the remedies available in Community law for those who believe that they have not been accorded the rights to which they are entitled under Community law. Over time, the Court has developed a Community right to the effective enjoyment of those rights granted by the Treaty which must be secured through both national institutions and the institutions of the European Union.

This chapter does not restate the settled case law on the supremacy of Community law; that is taken for granted.[1] The proposition which is now universally recognized is that whenever there is an inconsistency between Community law and national law, Community law prevails.

The requirement for reasoned decisions

The Court has, in a number of decisions,[2] affirmed as a general principle a right to a reasoned decision where Community rights are in issue. This requires the decision-maker to explain the basis upon which a decision is taken which curtails or denies a Community right. The purpose is to enable persons affected to be in a position to assert their Community law rights effectively in the national courts through some process of judicial review. The establishment of the right also has the effect of requiring decision-makers to address their minds to the possible Community law entitlement in making the decision. If this is done, there is a greater chance that the correct decision is made in the first instance. This case law has arisen primarily in the context of the recognition of qualifications. The articulation of reasons for the refusal of recognition better enables the person seeking recognition either to know where their qualifications fall short of those required by the national authority or the basis upon which they can challenge the decision as being in breach of their Community rights. So, for example, reasons which indicated that the ground for

[1] See, generally, Craig, P and de Búrca, G, *EU Law. Text, Cases, and Materials*, 3rd edn (Oxford, 2003), ch 7; or Douglas-Scott, S, *Constitutional Law of the European Union* (Harlow, 2002), ch 7.

[2] For example, Case 222/86 *UNECTEF v Heylens* [1987] ECR 4097; Case 340/89 *Vlassopoulou v Ministerium für Justiz* [1991] ECR 2357; and Case C-234/97 *Fernández de Bobadilla v Museo Nacional del Prado* [1999] ECR I-4773, discussed in ch 4 above and ch 8 below.

refusal amounted to discrimination on grounds of nationality would be relatively easy to challenge, whereas detailed reasons on the equivalence of qualifications might well be much more difficult.

Enforcing Community law before national courts

Direct effect

It has long been held that individuals can plead a rule of Community law in national courts where the provisions of the rule of Community law give them rights. Such a rule is said to give rise to direct effect. Whether a rule of Community law gives rise to direct effect is a matter of interpretation initially for national courts, but in cases of doubt for determination by the Court of Justice.

The conditions for direct effect are said to be:[3]

- that the provision is clear and unconditional;
- that the rights given are expressed with sufficient precision;
- if rights are in a directive, the date for implementation must have passed.

This application of direct effect is often described as a matter of interpretation, or sometimes as a matter of justiciability.

There is comparatively little difficulty in the application of this doctrine to Treaty provisions and regulations, since they have direct applicability in the national legal orders of the Member States. The position is, however, rather more complicated where the provisions of directives are concerned.

If a directive is fully and properly implemented in the national legal order, then an individual can rely upon national law to secure the rights given by Community law in the directive. However, the directive might not be fully and properly implemented, or a Member State may believe that it has implemented the directive fully but has been mistaken about its scope. In these cases, an individual can (once the date for implementation of the directive has passed) rely on the directive itself in asserting the Community law rights, even though, under Article 249 EC, it is addressed to Member States.[4]

The first possibility is to argue for an interpretation of the national legislation which is consistent with the requirements of the directive. National courts are obliged to interpret national law, so far as possible, in a manner which is compatible with Community law. This obligation flows from Article 10 EC.[5]

[3] Case 26/62 *van Gend en Loos* [1963] ECR 1; Case 41/74 *Van Duyn* [1974] ECR 1337; and Case 43/75 *Defrenne v SABENA* [1976] ECR 455.

[4] Case 148/78 *Ratti* [1979] ECR 1629.

[5] See below in this chapter. See generally Temple Lang, J, 'The Duties of National Courts under Community Constitutional Law' (1997) 22 ELRev 3; and Temple Lang, J, 'The Duties of National Authorities under Community Constitutional Law' (1998) 23 ELRev 109.

The second possibility is to rely on a rule in the directive itself, provided that the right granted by the directive is clear and precise, that the date for implementation has passed, and that it is unconditional. However, in this situation reliance can only be placed on the directive if the other party is the State, or an 'emanation of the State'.

The requirement that the other party be the State or an emanation of the State flows from a rejection of the proposition that rules in directives bind all. It has been held that rules in directives may only be pleaded where there is a vertical relationship between the individual and the other party; such a relationship arises where the other party is the State or an emanation of the State.[6] Emanations of the State are, broadly speaking, organs closely linked with the State and exercising some form of public function; the precise ambit of emanations of the State remains a matter of considerable controversy. In *Foster v British Gas*, the Court said:

> It follows from the foregoing that a body, whatever its legal form, which has been made responsible, pursuant to a measure adopted by the State, for providing a public service under the control of the State and has for that purpose special powers beyond those which result from the normal rules applicable in relations between individuals is included in any event among the bodies against which the provisions of a directive capable of having direct effect may be relied upon.[7]

This is not always an easy test to apply. Some organs in some Member States appear clearly to fit the requirements for being treated as emanations of the State, whereas in other Member States the matter is much more controversial. A good example is whether universities are emanations of the State. You will get different answers from nationals of different Member States because of the way in which higher education is organized in each Member State.

The Court of Justice has rejected the idea that the direct effect of a rule in a directive can be pleaded where the other party is a private individual. Such a relationship is said to be horizontal, and it is frequently stated that there is no 'horizontal direct effect' of directives. The reasons for this are both practical and principled. First, it would be excessively burdensome to require private parties to monitor directives to determine whether they gave rise to any obligations for them and to check whether any implementing national measures fully met the requirements of the directive. Secondly, it is said that to allow horizontal direct effect would amount to the assimilation of directives to regulations.[8]

The situation can be illustrated by reference to Helen Marshall's 13-year struggle to secure the benefits of Community equality law.[9] Helen Marshall had worked as a dietitian for the health authority for 14 years; she was dismissed in 1980 on the grounds that she had passed the normal retirement age applicable for women. The written policy of the health authority fixed a retirement age of 60 for women and

[6] Case C-188/89 *Foster v British Gas* [1990] ECR I-3133. [7] Para 20 of the judgment.

[8] Case C-91/92 *Faccini Dori* [1994] ECR I-3325.

[9] Case 152/84 *Marshall v South-West Hampshire AHA (Marshall I)* [1986] ECR 723; and Case C-271/91 *Marshall v South-West Hampshire AHA (Marshall II)* [1993] ECR I-4367.

65 for men; this corresponded to the ages at which entitlement to a State retirement pension arose. The relevant national legislation, the Sex Discrimination Act 1975, appeared to exempt matters relating to retirement from its scope. But Helen Marshall argued that the principle of equal treatment in Article 2 of Directive 76/207[10] when applied under Article 5(1) of the directive to conditions relating to dismissal meant that she had an enforceable Community right to be treated equally with men in the matter of a compulsory retirement age. The Court of Appeal referred questions to the Court of Justice.

The Court of Justice ruled that the rights in the directive were clear and unconditional, and so Helen Marshall could rely on them if she was taking action against the State or an emanation of the State. The health authority was considered to meet the criteria for being an emanation of the State and could be obliged to give to its employees the rights guaranteed by the directive even though national law had failed to implement the directive correctly in the circumstances of this case.

A further question arose as to the remedy for compulsory retirement in breach of the rights contained in the directive. Article 6 appeared to be broadly drafted:

> Member States shall introduce into their national legal systems such measures as are necessary to enable all persons who consider themselves wronged by failure to apply the principle of equal treatment to pursue their claims by judicial process, possibly after recourse to other competent authorities.

Earlier cases tended to support the view that the rights in this article did not meet the text of unconditionality and clarity required for direct effect.[11]

Following the ruling of the Court of Justice, an industrial tribunal[12] assessed compensation at £18,405 including £7,710 by way of interest. The problem was that national legislation at the time limited the award of compensation to a maximum of £6,250 and it was far from clear whether the tribunal had any power to award interest. The case made its way to the House of Lords who referred further questions to the Court of Justice on the extent of reparation to which Helen Marshall was entitled. The United Kingdom cap on compensation and the apparent inability to award interest were considered to be incompatible with the concept of remedies in Article 6 where the national measure adopted to secure respect for the principle of equal treatment was financial compensation for the loss and damage suffered.

In summary, the provisions of directives which contain rights for individuals which are sufficiently clearly expressed to make interpretation of the right granted clear and unambiguous may, after the date for their implementation has passed, be

[10] Council Directive 76/207/EEC of 9 February 1976 on the implementation of the principle of equal treatment for men and women as regards access to employment, vocational training and promotion, and working conditions. [1976] OJ L39/40.

[11] See Case 14/83 *Von Colson* [1984] ECR 1891; and Case 79/83 *Harz* [1984] ECR 1921, although the later Case 224/84 *Johnston* [1986] ECR 1651 suggested that in some circumstances it would have direct effect.

[12] As they were then known, now employment tribunals.

pleaded against the State or an emanation of the State, but not against another private party. They are said to have vertical direct effect, but no horizontal direct effect.

This leaves a stark difference in the enjoyment of rights. If you are compulsorily retired by a private sector employer in breach of the principle of equal treatment of men and women in Directive 76/207, you cannot rely upon the directive. If you are, however, employed by the State or an emanation of the State, you can challenge your compulsory retirement. This distinction is far from satisfactory.

Furthermore, if the provisions of a directive do not meet the tests of clarity and precision in the expression of rights, they cannot be pleaded against either the State, an emanation of the State, or a private party. It will be for the Commission to exercise its discretion to bring the defaulting State before the Court of Justice under the enforcement jurisdiction in Article 226 EC,[13] unless the principle of interpretation described by commentators as 'indirect effect' enables effect to be given to the provision of the directive.

Indirect effect

One way in which the potential problems illustrated above can be addressed is through the principle of interpretation of national law.

The *Von Colson* case[14] also concerned the implementation—this time in Germany—of Directive 76/207. Two women had applied for posts as social workers in a German prison. They had been refused the jobs on grounds of sex in breach of the German law which purported to implement the requirements of the directive. The remedies open to the German labour courts appeared to be limited in this case to the reimbursement of travelling expenses to the interview at which they were subjected to discrimination on grounds of sex. A question was referred to the Luxembourg Court about the adequacy of the remedies in the light of the requirements of the directive. The Court of Justice said that national courts must interpret the provisions of national law 'in the light of the wording and purpose of the directive'[15] and, if it had discretion to do so, to exercise its powers in such a way that the remedies for sex discrimination operated as a clear sanction likely to deter such conduct.

The *Von Colson* case concerned the interpretation of national legislation intended to implement the directive. The underlying rationale could therefore be said to be the duty of solidarity in Article 10 (ex 5) EC. But what of earlier legislation? Did the duty to interpret national legislation to meet the requirements of Community law equally apply here? Furthermore did the rule of interpretation

[13] See below in this chapter. There is also the possibility that State liability will be incurred; see later in this chapter.
[14] Case 14/83 *Von Colson* [1984] ECR 1891.
[15] ibid, para 26 of the judgment.

apply where there was a horizontal relationship? After all the situation in the *Von Colson* case was a vertical relationship involving a provision of a directive which was arguably not sufficiently clear and precise to give rise to direct effect. Both issues came up in the *Marleasing* case,[16] which was litigation in Spain between two private companies. The Court of Justice ruled that it mattered little whether the national legislation pre-dated or post-dated the Community obligation; nor did it make any difference that the litigation was between two private parties. All national law had to be interpreted in order to secure compatibility with Community law.

The position is therefore that there is now a general rule flowing from Article 10 EC that national authorities, including courts, must apply an interpretation of national law which secures compatibility with Community law.[17] This is so regardless of the source of the Community law; it is not just a rule to ameliorate the unfairness of limiting the direct effect of directives to those with a grievance against the State or an emanation of the State.

There are, however, limits to the power of interpretation to overcome the limitations of the doctrine of direct effect, and the frailties of national implementation of Community law.

First, no criminal liability will flow, by reason of interpretation, from the provisions of a directive which has not been implemented in the Member State.[18] Nor could an unimplemented directive give rise to obligations for an individual.

Secondly, the Court has accepted that there are limits to interpretation as a correctional measure, and that there is no obligation to go beyond a possible interpretation of national law in order to secure consistency with the requirements of Community law.[19] However, the power of forced interpretation is well illustrated in the British case of *Webb v EMO Cargo*,[20] which concerned dismissal on grounds of pregnancy.

Indirect effect is, however, of no assistance if there is no national legislation to which interpretation can attach. Here a person or company which has suffered loss and damage at the hands of another private party by reason of the failure of the State properly to implement the requirements of a directive or otherwise to honour the requirements of Community law remains in a dramatically worse position than where the relationship is a vertical one. How has the Court of Justice responded to this gap in the uniform application of Community law? The development of a

[16] Case C-106/89 *Marleasing* [1990] ECR I-4135.

[17] This obligation applies to all national authorities including courts: see Temple Lang, J, 'The Duties of National Courts under Community Constitutional Law' (1997) 22 ELRev 3; and Temple Lang, J, 'The Duties of National Authorities under Community Constitutional Law' (1998) 23 ELRev 109.

[18] Case 80/86 *Criminal Proceedings against Kolpinghuis Nijmegen BV* [1987] ECR 3969.

[19] Case C-168/95 *Criminal Proceedings against Arcaro* [1996] ECR I-4705, especially para 42 of the judgment.

[20] Case C-32/93 *Webb v EMO Air Cargo* [1994] ECR I-3567; see also [1992] 2 All ER 43 (Court of Appeal) and [1993] 1 WLR 49 (House of Lords).

uniform remedy in the form of State liability for breach of Community law provides a partial answer to the question.

State liability

In 1991 the Court of Justice decided in the *Francovich* case[21] that the legal system of every Member State must provide a new form of remedy: the claim for compensation for loss or damage caused by the State in acting in breach of Community law. This was a dramatic development of major constitutional significance.

Earlier case law had begun with the proposition of respect for national procedural autonomy. This refers to the requirement that national remedies must be extended to cover claims for breach of Community law, but that Community law did not require the introduction of new national procedures.[22] These propositions were modified by requirements that national procedural law must be changed if it has the effect of rendering reliance on Community rights practically impossible.[23]

The Italian Government had failed to implement Directive 80/987 which required the establishment of a system for guaranteeing to employees the payment of their unpaid wages in the event of the insolvency of their employer. Indeed the Italian Government had been condemned in an enforcement action for its failure to implement the directive.[24] The two claimants had both lost wages when their employer went into insolvency. They sued the Italian State claiming that the Italian Government was liable to pay them their lost wages either by way of having the guarantees in the unimplemented directive enforced against the State, or by way of damages from the State for failing to implement the directive.

Questions were referred by the national court to the Court of Justice. The Court of Justice found that the provisions of the directive lacked sufficient clarity and precision to render them capable of direct effect. However, the directive clearly intended employees in the circumstances of the two claimants to be beneficiaries of a system of protection set out in the directive.

The Court went back to the *van Gend en Loos* case and *Costa v ENEL,* recalling the new legal order created by the EEC Treaty which was intended to create rights and obligations for individuals as well as the Member States. Since then a principle of ensuring that those rules have full effect and protect the rights which they confer on individuals has been established. It would be inconsistent with this principle of the full effectiveness of Community rules if individuals were denied compensation

[21] Joined Cases C-6/90 and C-9/90 *Francovich and Boniface v Italy* [1991] ECR I-5357.

[22] See Case 33/76 *Rewe-Zentralfinanz* [1976] ECR 1989 (respect for national procedural autonomy), and Case 158/80 *Rewe-Handesgesellschaft Nord* [1981] ECR 1805 (no obligation to create new remedies).

[23] Case 213/89 *Factortame I* [1990] ECR I-2433 (abolition of restriction on interim relief against the Crown), and Case C-271/91 *Marshall v South-West Hampshire AHA (Marshall II)* [1993] ECR I-4367 (removal of ceiling on compensation payments or limits on award of interest).

[24] Case 22/87 *Commission v Italy* [1989] ECR 143.

when they suffered loss as a result of a infringement of their rights for which a Member State can be held responsible. The Court then stated:

It follows that the principle of State liability for harm caused to individuals by breaches of Community law for which the State can be held responsible is inherent in the system of the Treaty.[25]

The Treaty foundation for this new principle of State liability was said to be Article 5 (now 10) EC, which includes 'the obligation to nullify the unlawful consequences of a breach of Community law'.[26]

Of course, the distinction between the creation of a new remedy and the development of an existing one is a fine one. But the significance of the *Francovich* judgment is the requirement that each Member State must recognize a *Community* remedy for breaches of Community law available within the national legal orders of all Member States, and not simply the application of a national remedy. The requirement makes it much riskier for a Member State not to implement a directive, since it will not only be liable to action under Article 226 EC at the instance of the Commission,[27] but also to liability to all who suffer loss as a result of their failure to implement the directive. The remedy is available even where the directive lacks the quality of direct effect.

The conditions of liability laid down in the *Francovich* case will depend on the nature of the breach of Community law giving rise to the loss.[28] However, where the breach is failure to implement a directive, there are three conditions:[29]

- the result prescribed by the directive entails the grant of rights to individuals;
- it is possible to identify the content of those rights on the basis of the provisions of the directive; and
- there is a causal link between breach of Community law by the Member State and the loss and damage suffered by the injured party.

There was a nod in the direction of national procedural autonomy when the Court said:[30]

. . . it is in accordance with the rules of national law on liability that the State must make reparation for the consequences of the harm caused. In the absence of any Community legislation, it is a matter for the internal legal order of each Member State to determine the competent courts and lay down the detailed procedural rules for legal proceedings intended fully to safeguard the rights which individuals derive from Community law. . . .

[25] Joined Cases C-6/90 and C-9/90 *Francovich and Boniface v Italy* [1991] ECR I-5357, para 35 of the judgment.
[26] ibid, para 36 of the judgment.
[27] See below in this chapter.
[28] Joined Cases C-6/90 and C-9/90 *Francovich and Boniface v Italy* [1991] ECR I-5357, para 38 of the judgment.
[29] ibid, para 40 of the judgment.
[30] ibid, para 42 of the judgment.

This decision left open a number of questions about the scope of State liability: in particular, was this a remedy of last resort in the case of unimplemented directives? Was it available for breaches of Community law arising other than from directives? Was the basis of liability fault, or no-fault? Did the principle apply to courts? Some commentators suggested that the Court would derive assistance from the standard of non-contractual liability laid down in Article 288 (ex 215) EC.[31]

Clarification of the basis of liability was provided by the Court in its decisions in *Brasserie du Pêcheur and Factortame III*.[32]

The *Brasserie du Pêcheur* litigation involved claims by a French brewery against Germany for loss of profits it had incurred when its beer was kept off the German market because it did not comply with the German beer purity law. That law had been found to be incompatible with Community law on the free movement of goods.[33]

The *Factortame III* litigation was the claim by Spanish fisherman for the losses they had incurred in not being able to secure access to British fishing quotas in breach of Community law on the freedom of establishment, which had been determined in the second reference in this long-running saga.[34]

A number of questions were raised in these two references. Among them was whether the principle of State liability applied to breaches flowing from legislative measures: in Germany it was the beer purity law, and in the United Kingdom it was Part II of the Merchant Shipping Act 1988. Questions also related to whether the remedy was available where directly effective Community law was in issue since in such cases national remedies would be available, and to the conditions of liability.

The Court responded quite briefly that the principle of State liability is available *whenever* there is a breach of Community law by the State which causes harm. This included breaches of the Treaty itself as in the two cases referred to the Court of Justice. The Court further explained the basis for the principle which had been set out in the *Francovich* decision. There the principle was said to flow from Article 5 EC. In these cases, the Court referred also to Article 164 (now 220) EC requiring the Court to ensure that the law is observed, and to Article 215 (now 288) EC on the non-contractual liability of the Community.

It was also Article 215 which provides the inspiration for the elaboration of the conditions for liability in *Brasserie du Pêcheur and Factortame III*. As a result the

[31] See, for example, Steiner, J, 'From Direct Effect to *Francovich*' (1993) 18 ELRev 3; and Craig, P, '*Francovich*, Remedies and the Scope of Damages Liability' (1993) 109 LQR 595.

[32] Joined Cases C-46/93 and C-48/93 *Brasserie du Pêcheur and Factortame III* [1996] ECR I-1029. See Tridimas, T, 'Liability for breach of Community law: growing up and mellowing down' (2001) 38 CMLRev 301; and Anagnostaras, G, 'Not as unproblematic as you might think: the establishment of causation in governmental liability actions' (2002) 27 ELRev 663.

[33] Case 178/84 *Commission v Germany* [1987] ECR 1227.

[34] Case 221/89 *Factortame II* [1991] ECR I-3905.

threefold test expressed in *Francovich* as relevant where failure to implement a directive gives rise to liability was restated as a new threefold test:[35]

- the rule of Community law infringed must be intended to confer rights on individuals;
- the breach must be 'sufficiently serious';
- there is a direct causal link between the breach of the Community obligation and the damage sustained by the injured party.

The Court added that a breach of Community law will be 'sufficiently serious' where the Member State concerned 'manifestly and gravely disregarded the limits of its discretion'.[36] Paragraph 57 of the judgment provided:

> . . . a breach of Community law will clearly be sufficiently serious if it has persisted despite a judgment finding the infringement in question to be established, or a preliminary ruling or settled case law of the Court on the matter from which it is clear that the conduct in question constituted an infringement.

The Court also considered the basis of liability. It seems clear that the notion of a 'sufficiently serious breach' imports some connotation of fault, but the Court stressed that that alone is the test of liability. There seems to be no room for further consideration of fault. Whether there is a direct causal link between the relevant Community right and the loss claimed is to be determined by national courts.[37]

How has this seminal decision been applied in subsequent cases? In two cases, a failure fully to implement a directive where the directive could have been clearer in its requirements was not regarded as a sufficiently serious breach to engage State liability.[38] But a complete failure to implement a directive is likely to constitute a sufficiently serious breach.[39] Similarly, a restriction on the free movement of goods where the Member State in question cannot substantiate the basis of its concerns is likely to render the imposition of such restrictions a sufficiently serious breach of Community law to attract State liability.[40]

The position of courts has been clarified in the *Köbler* case.[41] The Court of Justice confirmed that the principle of State liability applies to courts including final appeal courts, and that it is for the national law of Member States to determine the form of action for claiming damages for a breach of Community law by such a court. The *Brasserie du Pêcheur* conditions apply, but the breach must be particularly manifest in the case of a court.

[35] Joined Cases C-46/93 and C-48/93 *Brasserie du Pêcheur and Factortame III* [1996] ECR I-1029, para 51 of the judgment.

[36] Para 55 of the judgment.

[37] Para 63 of the judgment.

[38] Case C-392/93 *ex parte British Telecom* [1996] ECR I-1631; and Joined Cases C-283, 291 and 292/94 *Denkavit* [1996] ECR I-5063.

[39] Joined Cases 178–9/94, 188–190/94 *Dillenkofer* [1996] ECR I-4845; [1996] 3 CMLR 469.

[40] Case C-5/94 *ex parte Hedley Lomas* [1996] ECR I-2553.

[41] Case C-224/01 *Köbler v Republik Österreich*, judgment of 30 September 2003, [2003] ECR nyr.

Preliminary rulings

The jurisdiction of the Court of Justice is usually divided into direct actions[42] and indirect actions.[43] Direct actions refer to those jurisdictions where a party brings a dispute direct to the Court. A good example is an action under Article 226 EC by the Commission against a Member State arguing that the Member State has violated its obligations under the Treaty, for example, by failing to transpose a directive into national law within the time limit allowed by the directive.[44] Another example is the judicial review jurisdiction of the Court under which the legality of Community legislation can be challenged.[45] Direct actions brought by private individuals or companies are now dealt with by the Court of First Instance, but the Court of Justice has jurisdiction where such actions are brought by a Community institution or by a Member State.

Indirect actions are references for preliminary rulings under Article 234 (ex 177) EC made by national courts seeking an authoritative statement from the Court of Justice on the interpretation of Community law (including provisions of the Treaties), on the direct effect of Community law, and on the validity of legislative acts of the Community institutions.[46] Under this jurisdiction, any court or tribunal in a Member State, which finds itself faced with a point of Community law which is relevant to the determination it is called upon to make, is able to refer questions to the Court of Justice for its authoritative ruling. The decision to refer is for the court or tribunal in the Member State, and not for the parties to the litigation in the Member State. Of course, the parties can argue that a reference is needed (or not needed), but it is for the national court alone to decide whether to make the reference. Courts, other than final appeal courts, have a discretion as to whether or not a reference is made, but where a question of Community law is raised before a final appeal court which it is necessary to answer in order to determine the question before that court, there is an obligation to make a reference.[47]

Where a reference is made, it has the effect of adjourning the case before the national court or tribunal until the decision of the Court of Justice is given. When the Court of Justice delivers its opinion, the national court or tribunal reconvenes and is obliged to follow the ruling of the Court of Justice on the content or validity of the Community law in issue in the case. The Court of Justice advises on the meaning of Community law, and the national court or tribunal applies that advice to the case before it.

[42] Or contentious business. [43] Or non-contentious business.

[44] See below in this chapter.

[45] Under Art 230 EC. All Community legislation must be based on a provision of the EC Treaty and may be challenged, inter alia, if it is outside the scope of the provision claimed to be its legal base.

[46] See Arnull, A, 'References to the European Court' (1990) 15 ELRev 375; and O'Keeffe, D, 'Is the Spirit of Article 177 under Attack? Preliminary References and Admissibility' (1998) 23 ELRev 509.

[47] Hartley, T, *The Foundations of European Community Law*, 5th edn (Oxford, 2003), ch 9.

The Court of Justice has emphasized that the objective of the preliminary ruling procedure is a partnership between national courts and tribunals and the Court of Justice.[48] The Court of Justice has indicated that any attempt by national authorities to restrict the discretion of national courts or tribunals in making references is contrary to Article 234 EC.[49] Five propositions emerge from consideration of the case law of the Court of Justice:[50]

1. It is for the national court or tribunal to decide at what stage of the proceedings it is appropriate for a preliminary ruling to be requested.
2. In order to assist the Court of Justice, it is essential for the national court or tribunal to define the legal context in which the reference is made.
3. This suggests that in some cases it might well be appropriate for the facts in the case to be settled at the time of the reference.
4. Attempts to fetter or limit the discretion of the national court or tribunal are inconsistent with Community law.
5. The decision to refer is that of the court or tribunal and not that of the parties.

Practice in English courts and tribunals has been influence by guidelines expressed by Lord Denning in *Bulmer v Bollinger*,[51] but these are not binding on any court or tribunal and aspects of them are inconsistent with statements made by the Court of Justice, which in 1996 itself issued notes for guidance on references by national courts for preliminary rulings.[52] It is important that the question posed relates to Community law, and that the question is posed as a general question of interpretation or validity rather than as a request to the Court to tell the national court or tribunal the decision it should make. The Court of Justice is fastidious in only advising on the Community law issue raised, leaving it for the national court to apply this in the case before it. However, in some cases its advice is so specific that there is little room for choice in the determination of the question before the national court. The question or questions posed should be self-contained and self-explanatory, since they will be notified to the Commission, Council, and all the Member States, who may choose within two months to submit written observations on the questions raised. Though the only formal requirement is the formulation of a question or questions for the Court of Justice, the Court finds it helpful to have the following information included in the reference:

- the facts of the case;
- the relevant provisions of national law;
- the provisions of Community law thought to be relevant;

[48] Case 166/73 *Rheinmuhlen* [1974] ECR 33, 38. [49] ibid.

[50] See Case 166/73 *Rheinmuhlen* [1974] ECR 33; Joined Cases 36 and 71/80 *Irish Creamery Milk Suppliers Association v Ireland* [1981] ECR 735; Case 72/83 *Campus Oil v Minister for Industry and Energy* [1984] ECR 2727; and Case 14/86 *Pretore di Salo v Persons Unknown* [1987] ECR 2545.

[51] [1974] Ch 401.

[52] Available on the Court's website: curia.eu.int.

- a summary of the contentions of the parties on the question or questions referred; and
- if necessary, the reasons why the answers to the questions posed are considered necessary to decide the case.

The case law of the Court of Justice is replete with examples of important principles of Community law on the free movement of persons, which have been established as a result of references made by national courts. For example, the concept of a worker within Article 39 EC was established in the *Levin* case;[53] and the distinction between establishment and services was clarified in the *Gebhard* case.[54]

Enforcing Community law at Community level

Commission enforcement

Article 226 EC provides that the Commission may bring proceedings against a Member State which it regards as having failed to fulfil an obligation arising under the EC Treaty.[55] The procedure set down in Article 226 EC contains an administrative phase and a judicial phase. The Commission must first raise the alleged breach with the Member State and seek its observations.[56] If in the light of the Member State's response (or failure to respond), the Commission remains concerned, it may issue a reasoned opinion setting out in some detail its conclusions about the Member State's failure to fulfil its obligations under the EC Treaty. If the Member State does not comply with the requirements of this reasoned opinion within the period set by the Commission, the Commission may bring the alleged breach before the Court of Justice. The use of the enforcement procedure is discretionary; the Commission enjoys a broad discretion in deciding which infringements to pursue.

In its annual reports, the Commission has repeatedly stated that a significant number of breaches are identified as a result of complaints made to it by individuals who feel that they have been denied a right to which they are entitled under the EC Treaty. That said, the primary purpose of the Article 226 procedure is to provide a means by which Member State compliance with Community law can be required

[53] Case 53/81 *Levin v Staatssecretaris van Justitie* [1982] ECR 1035; see ch 2 above.

[54] Case C-54/94 *Gebhard v Consiglio dell'Ordine degle Avvocati e Procuratori di Milano* [1995] ECR I-4165; see ch 2 above.

[55] See, generally, Audretsch, H, *Supervision in European Community Law*, 2nd edn (Amsterdam, 1986); Gil Ibáñez, A, *The Administrative Supervision and Enforcement of EC Law* (Oxford, 1999); Hartley, T, *The Foundations of European Community Law*, 5th edn (Oxford, 2003), ch 10; Dashwood, A and White, R, 'Enforcement Actions under Article 169 and 170 EC' (1989) 14 ELRev 388; and Rawlings, R, 'Engaged Elites, Citizen Action and Institutional Attitudes in Commission Enforcement' (2000) 6 ELJ 4.

[56] Sometimes described as the pre-contentious stage.

rather than with providing a remedy for aggrieved citizens.[57] Any Member State found to have failed to fulfil its obligations under the EC Treaty is required to take the necessary measures to comply with the judgment of the Court which so concludes.[58] Any failure to comply can result in the matter being brought before the Court again with the possibility that a pecuniary penalty may be imposed.[59]

The reasoned opinion defines the nature of the breach, and it is not open to the Commission to vary the case against the Member State at a later stage of the proceedings.[60] But the proceedings do not fall simply because the Member State complies after the matter has been referred to the Court by the Commission.[61]

Breaches of Community law which might attract the attention of the Commission include:

- failure to implement a directive;[62]
- breach of the duty of solidarity in Article 10 EC; and
- failure to give proper effect to the requirements of Community law.

Complaining to the Commission is one avenue which might be taken by a person who feels they have not been accorded a Community right by a Member State, but it must be remembered that the Commission enjoys a considerable discretion in whether or not to take up the complaint, and that the main purpose of the procedure is to ensure the application of Community law by Member States rather than to provide a remedy for individuals.

Some examples of infringement proceedings in which issues relating to the free movement of persons have arisen will give an impression of the range of issues which have been dealt with under this procedure. In 1974, France was found to be in breach of Community law in not formally changing its *Code du travail maritime* in order to remove discrimination on the grounds of nationality, and failed in its argument that it had taken informal measures to ensure that the nationality provisions were not applied to nationals of the Member States.[63] In 1988, Italy was condemned for its failure to treat nationals of other Member States who were self-employed in the same manner as Italian nationals in granting access to housing

[57] See Rawlings, R, 'Engaged Elites, Citizen Action and Institutional Attitudes in Commission Enforcement' (2000) 6 ELJ 4.

[58] Art 228(1) EC.

[59] Art 228(2) EC. See also Case C-387/97 *Commission v Greece* [2000] ECR I-5047, which imposed a daily penalty on Greece of €20,000 in respect of its failure to comply with the requirements of Community law directives on the management of toxic and dangerous waste in the Chania region of Crete. See also Theodossiou, M, 'An analysis of the recent response of the Community to non-compliance with Court of Justice judgments' (2002) 27 ELRev 25.

[60] See, for example, Case 124/81 *Commission v United Kingdom* [1983] ECR 203, para 6 of the judgment.

[61] See, for example, Case 240/86 *Commission v Greece* [1988] ECR 1835, para 14 of the judgment.

[62] One of the commonest sources of art 226 actions.

[63] Case 167/73 *Commission v France* [1974] ECR 359, discussed in ch 3 above.

subsidies.[64] In 2000, the Court clarified the extent of the exception for employment in the public service in relation to security guards in the infringement proceedings against Belgium.[65]

Petitioning the European Parliament

Article 194 EC provides:

Any citizen of the Union, and any natural or legal person residing or having a registered office in a Member State, shall have the right to address, individually or in association with other citizens or persons, a petition to the European Parliament on a matter which comes within the Community's fields of activity and which affects him, her or it directly.

This provision provides a formal legal base for arrangements which were in place prior to the introduction of this adjunct of citizenship of the Union.[66] The way in which petitions are dealt with is set out in the Rules of Procedure of the European Parliament. Petitions are forwarded to the Committee on Petitions and filed in a public register. The Committee will investigate admissible petitions, and may request opinions from other institutions, such as the Commission. The outcome of a petition might be as follows:

- submission of a report on the petition to the European Parliament;
- a request that the President of the European Parliament approach the national authorities in a Member State in order to resolve the matter;
- referral to other Parliamentary committees for further consideration;
- referral to the European Ombudsman;
- referral to the Commission or the Council of Ministers with its opinion on the petition.

Complaining to the European Ombudsman

Article 195 EC sets out the process for the appointment of a European Ombudsman and spells out the ombudsman's role.[67] This role is markedly different from that encompassed by complaints to the Commission or petitions to the European Parliament. The ombudsman is concerned with complaints of maladministration in the activities of the Community institutions or bodies, other than the Court of Justice and the Court of First Instance. Whereas the overwhelming majority of complaints to the Commission and petitions to the European Parliament concern violations of Community law by Member States, petitions to the ombudsman can only concern violations by Community institutions which amount to maladminis-

[64] Case 63/86 *Commission v Italy* [1988] ECR 29, discussed in ch 3 above.
[65] Case C-355/98 *Commission v Belgium* [2000] ECR I-1221, discussed in ch 5 above.
[66] See art 21 EC.
[67] Also an adjunct of citizenship of the Union: art 21 EC.

tration.[68] Examples of maladministration are unfairness, discrimination, abuse of power, and inexcusable delay. The outcome of an admissible petition is a report on the investigation of the complaint which may include recommendations to the institution concerned. It will not include redress for the person complaining.

A strategy for enforcing Community rights

Securing rights granted by Community law will almost always be a favoured solution as against obtaining damages for loss after a denial of Community rights. So the opening gambit should always be to look to ways in which Community rights can be enforced.

If the rights flow from directly applicable Community law (Treaty articles or regulations), the task will simply be to interpret—and to persuade a court to agree with a particular interpretation of—the provision to determine whether it grants rights with sufficient clarity and precision that a national court will recognize them and enforce them.

If the Community instrument is a directive, matters are more complex. If there has been an attempt at implementation or if there is some existing national law which may be capable of interpretation in order to secure the rights, then that is probably the best starting point. The national authority or court will be reminded of its duty to interpret national law to secure the effective enjoyment of Community rights.

If there is nothing which can be interpreted, it will be necessary to establish whether there is a vertical or horizontal relationship with the party against whom Community rights are being asserted. Rights set out clearly and precisely in a directive may be enforced after the date of implementation against the State or an emanation of the State, but not against another private party.

Although it is clearly not formally a remedy of last resort, it would seem that State liability will in practice be a remedy of last resort, since it concerns compensation for losses after a denial of Community rights where there has been a sufficiently serious breach of Community law causing the loss suffered.

However, if the sole consideration is the volume of principles of Community law which have been developed, it is clear that the most significant procedure is the preliminary ruling procedure. This has proved to be an exceptionally important vehicle for ensuring Community law rights. Its success flows from the assertion by individuals of their Community law rights in national courts, and the willingness of those courts to work co-operatively with the Court of Justice in Luxembourg in order to deliver the rights flowing from the EC Treaty to the beneficiaries of those rights.

[68] Nearly three-quarters of petitions to the European Ombudsman concern matters outside his competence.

Part III

Personal Rights

7

Citizenship of the European Union

Background

Although much of the development of the law on free movement of persons is predicated on the economic activity of the mover,[1] Community law has always regarded workers as more than simply a source of labour. The result is that the entitlements enjoyed by those taking advantage of the rights of free movement have always gone beyond the minimum necessary to facilitate free movement. They have contained a bundle of social rights designed to contribute to the integration of the mover into the social fabric of the country of residence. These have been most developed in the context of workers, but many of the rules apply either directly or by analogy to those moving as self-employed persons. This can be seen in the comments of the Advocate General Trabucchi in an early case on the entitlement of the children of workers to social security benefits, where he said:

> If we want Community law to be more than a mere mechanical system of economics and to constitute instead a system commensurate with the society which it has to govern, if we wish it to be a legal system corresponding to the concept of social justice and to the requirements of European integration, not only of the economy but of the people, we cannot disappoint the Belgian court's expectations, which are more than those of legal form.[2]

The concept of European citizenship as part of the political development of the Community appears to have been mentioned first at the Paris Summit in October 1972.[3] It was elaborated in the Tindemans Report on European Union.[4] The Tindemans Report saw two key developments contributing to the development of the European Union: the development of a passport union, and of political rights taking effect across national frontiers. The former notion has come to nothing, though development may in future take place under Title IV of the EC Treaty on visas, asylum, immigration and other policies related to the free movement of

[1] See Everson, M, 'The Legacy of the Market Citizen' in Shaw, J and More, G (eds), *New Legal Dynamics of the European Union* (Oxford, 1995), 73.

[2] Case 7/75 *Mr and Mrs F* [1975] ECR 679, at 697.

[3] For detail on the background, see Handoll, J, *Free Movement of Persons in the EU* (Chichester, 1995), ch 9; O'Leary, S, *The Evolving Concept of Community Citizenship. From the Free Movement of Persons to Union Citizenship* (The Hague, 1996); Weiss, F and Wooldridge, F, *Free Movement of Persons within the European Community* (The Hague, 2002), ch 8.

[4] *Report of the Commission on the European Communities on European Union (Tindemans Report)*, EC Bulletin 7/75.

persons. The latter is now reflected in the Treaty provisions on citizenship of the Union.

The Fontainebleau European Council of June 1984 set up an ad hoc committee chaired by Pietro Adonnino which issued two reports on a people's Europe.[5] The first report presented to the Brussels European Council in March 1985 concerned extended rights of free movement, while the second, presented to the Milan European Council in June 1985, dealt with special rights for citizens and the creation of a more clearly understood European identity. The first real step in the establishment of citizenship of the Union is credited to the Spanish Government in September 1990,[6] and the idea is also reflected in position papers from the Commission and the Danish Government shortly afterwards. The Spanish proposal was to bring existing rights together with new rights so that the privileged position of the economic migrant would become entitlements of a citizen of the European Union. The Commission's position paper referred to fundamental rights arising under the European Convention on Human Rights. But it was also clear that Union citizenship would be additional to nationality and citizenship of a Member State. This dual system of national and Union citizenships has plagued the debate about the value of citizenship of the Union.[7]

Part Two of the Treaty on European Union now contains the provisions on citizenship of the Union. There have also been some significant case law developments on the rights which flow from the introduction of this citizenship, which suggest that it may have a greater potential than at first sight appears.

Treaty-based rights

Articles 17 to 22 EC now contain the provisions on citizenship of the Union. These are much the same as the provisions which were formerly in Articles 8 to 8c inserted by the Treaty of Maastricht. Article 17 provides:

1. Citizenship of the Union is hereby established. Every person holding the nationality of a Member State shall be a citizen of the Union. Citizenship of the Union shall complement and not replace national citizenship.

2. Citizens of the Union shall enjoy the rights conferred by this Treaty and shall be subject to the duties imposed thereby.

[5] See EC Bulletin 7/75.

[6] *Towards a European Citizenship,* Council Document SN 3940/90 of 24 September 1990.

[7] This is not the place to recount the debate on whether Union citizenship is a genuine citizenship, or simply an ill-judged attempt to create a European identity where none exists. For a flavour of the debate see Weiler, J, 'To be a European Citizen: Eros and civilization' in Weiler, J, *The Constitution of Europe* (Cambridge, 1999); Shaw, J, 'The Many Pasts and Futures of Citizenship in the European Union' (1997) 22 ELRev 554; Davis, R, 'Citizenship of the European Union . . . rights for all?' (2002) 28 ELRev 121; and Barber, N, 'Citizenship, nationalism and the European Union' (2002) 28 ELRev 241.

Citizenship in its classical sense involves duties as well as rights: typically to serve in the armed forces of the State of citizenship if called upon to do so, and to pay taxes. There are no duties currently attached to citizenship of the European Union.

Citizenship is additional to citizenship of the State of nationality and is not intended to replace it. It is the holding of the nationality of one of the Member States which automatically gives rise to citizenship of the Union. Each Member State is free to have its own rules for the grant of nationality. But it is not open to a State to use its internal rules to deny recognition of the nationality of another Member State.[8] An example is rules in some Member States which do not recognize one of a number of nationalities where the centre of the individual's activities has not been in that State, because they have never lived there, and have little connection with that State.[9]

The case of *ex parte Kaur*[10] raised the question of citizenship of the Union in a more central way. Manjit Kaur was a British Overseas Citizen under the immigration and nationality legislation of the United Kingdom. She was born in Kenya. British Overseas Citizens hold British passports, but do not thereby have any right to enter the United Kingdom free from immigration control. She first entered the United Kingdom in 1990 and stayed for several temporary periods of residence. In September 1996 she applied for leave to remain in the United Kingdom; this was refused and she sought judicial review of the decision. She said she wished to remain and obtain work in the United Kingdom, and from time to time to go to other Member States to make purchases of goods and services, and possibly to seek work.

The High Court referred the question of whether a British Overseas Citizen was a person holding the nationality of a Member State and so acquired the status of a citizen of the European Union. At the time of British accession, the United Kingdom government had filed a declaration defining the concept of British nationality; this was amended in 1982 following the passing of the British Nationality Act 1981, which did not include British Overseas Citizens among those defined as holding British nationality for the purposes of the application of the EC Treaty.

The Court said that Community law did not preclude a Member State from defining nationality under its own laws and that, in determining whether Manjit Kaur was a citizen of the European Union, it was appropriate to refer to the definitions of nationality in the two declarations filed by the United Kingdom government.

The Advocate General had side-stepped the issue by ruling that what is now Article 18(1) EC does not apply either to a national of one of the Member States who is not present in the territory of another Member State since the matter is

[8] See discussion of the allocation of nationality in ch 2 above.

[9] Case C-369/90 *M V Micheletti and others v Delegación del Gobierno en Cantabria* [1992] ECR I-4239, noted at (1993) 30 CMLRev 623.

[10] Case C-192/99 *R v Secretary of State for the Home Department, ex parte Kaur* [2001] ECR I-1237.

wholly internal to that Member State, or to a person holding the nationality of a non-member country.

Article 22 EC provides:

> The Commission shall report to the European Parliament, to the Council and to the Economic and Social Committee every three years on the application of the provisions of this Part. This report shall take account of the development of the Union.
>
> On this basis, and without prejudice to the other provisions of this Treaty, the Council acting unanimously on a proposal from the Commission and after consulting the European Parliament, may adopt provisions to strengthen or add to the rights laid down in this Part, which it shall recommend to the Member States for adoption in accordance with their respective constitutional requirements.

It should be noted that the rights attaching to citizenship of the Union can only be expanded under this provision; they cannot be reduced. However, Member State caution in this area is reflected in the use of the consultation procedure for the adoption of provisions enhancing citizenship of the Union.[11]

Movement and residence

Article 18(1) EC provides:

> Every citizen of the Union shall have the right to move and reside freely within the territory of the Member States, subject to the limitations and conditions laid down in this Treaty and by the measures adopted to give it effect.

The right to be free from immigration control is a classic incident of nationality. Subject to limited exceptions, international law precludes the removal from their territory of one of its own nationals. International law also requires a State to admit its own nationals to its territory. Article 18(1) EC is a step in the direction of recognition of such a right, but it is expressed to be subject to the limitations and conditions in the Treaty and in Community secondary legislation. This would appear to have added nothing to existing rights of free movement.[12] That said, by the time this provision found its way into the Treaty, there was a portfolio of provisions which gave a substantial proportion of the nationals of the Member States the right to move and reside in the country of their choice. Those who are, or have been for the requisite qualifying period, economically active are covered by the rights given to workers, the self-employed, and service providers and recipients by the EC Treaty.[13] Those who are not economically active are covered by the free movement directives governing retired persons, students, and persons of independent means.[14]

[11] Note that measures under art 18 are to be adopted using the co-operation procedure except in relation to passports, identity cards, residence permits and similar documents, and social security and social protection.

[12] But see the case law developments described later in this chapter.

[13] See generally ch 2 above on entitlement, and ch 8 below on rights attaching to free movement.

[14] Council Directive 90/365/EEC of 28 June 1990 on the right of residence for employees and self-employed persons who have ceased their occupational activity, [1990] OJ L180/28; Council Directive

The purpose of the retired persons directive is to permit those who do not have the right under other provisions of Community law[15] to retire with their families after working in the Member State of their choice. The directive governing persons of independent means grants a choice of Member State of residence to those not falling within the scope of the retired persons directive who are of independent means. In the case of both directives, the applicant must have sufficient resources 'to avoid becoming a burden on the social assistance system of the host Member State during their period of residence'.[16] Such means are defined in Article 1 of Directive 90/364/EEC and in Article 1 of Directive 90/365/EEC as follows:

> The resources referred to . . . shall be deemed sufficient where they are higher than the level of resources below which the host Member State may grant social assistance to its nationals, taking into account the personal circumstances of the applicant and, where appropriate, the personal circumstances of persons admitted pursuant to paragraph 2 [family members admitted with the applicant].
>
> Where [the above paragraph] cannot be applied in a Member State, the resources of the applicant shall be deemed sufficient if they are higher than the level of the minimum social security pension paid by the host Member State.

The Commission has established guidelines on the application of the sufficient resources test in these directives.[17] Member States should only require evidence up to the level of minimum resources applicable under the directives and should not investigate the general financial situation of the applicant. In particular, pensions are seen as a stable source of income; if the amount of a pension exceeds the sufficient resources threshold, no further evidence should be sought. The nature and provenance of the resources is irrelevant as long as the applicant has free and effective access to them. The resources of partners should be treated in the same way as the Member State treats such resources in internal situations. Finally, family members dependent on the applicant must be able to invoke the resources coming from the applicant.

The applicant must also be covered by sickness insurance in respect of all risks in the host Member State. The requirement is expressed in very general terms, and will be satisfied through private insurance, or social insurance arising either in the host Member State or elsewhere.

Those within the scope of these directives are entitled to a Community residence permit[18] lasting for five years, though it may be subject to revalidation after the first two years.

93/96/EEC of 29 October 1993 on the right of residence for students, [1993]OJ L317/59 (replacing Dir 90/366/EEC which had been annulled by the Court of Justice in Case C-295/90 *European Parliament v Council* [1992] ECR I-4193 since it had not been made under the correct legal base); and Council Directive 90/364/EEC of 28 June 1990 on the right of residence (sometimes referred to as the 'Playboy Directive'), [1990] OJ L180/26. These directives are now consolidated into Directive 2004/38/EC, [2004] OJ L158/77, which will come into force in 2006.

[15] Such as Regulation 1251/70/EEC on the right of workers to retire in the Member State in which they have worked. See ch 8 below.

[16] Art 1 of Directive 90/365/EEC and art 1 of Directive 90/364/EEC.

[17] COM (1999) 127 final.

[18] Under Directive 68/360/EEC. For more detail, see below ch 8.

The Court of Justice confirmed in *Commission v Italy*[19] that Member States must adopt a flexible approach to the documents required to establish an entitlement under these directives. Limiting the types of proof of entitlement and requiring certification of documentation by another Member State went beyond what was permitted under these directives.

The students directive is somewhat different, since it provides for a temporary right of residence for the purposes of education. It is designed to ensure free movement of students and their families in order to guarantee them access to vocational education in any Member State. The rights in the directive are subsidiary to the rights which flow from other provisions of Community law.[20] There are three conditions which must be satisfied:

- The student must have been accepted to attend a vocational training course in another Member State at a recognized educational establishment, and be enrolled on that course.
- The student must have sufficient resources to avoid becoming a burden on the social assistance system of the host Member State during their period of residence.
- The student must be covered by sickness insurance in respect of all risks in the host Member State.

So long as the principal purpose of the residence is to follow the vocational training course, it does not appear to matter that the course is part-time rather than full-time, as long as the other conditions are met.[21] The host Member State's enquiry into the student's possession of sufficient resources is different from the other directives. Article 1 of the students directive merely provides that 'the student assures the relevant national authority, by means of a declaration or by such alternative means as the student may choose that are at least equivalent' that he or she possesses sufficient resources to avoid becoming a burden on the host Member State. However, Article 3 makes clear that the student is not entitled, under the directive, to receive any maintenance grant from the host Member State. Those who meet the requirements of the directive are entitled to a Community residence permit 'which may be limited to the duration of the studies or to one year where the course lasts longer; in the latter event it shall be renewable annually'.[22]

In *Commission v Italy*,[23] the Court of Justice ruled that Italy had gone beyond the limits of its discretion under the students directive in specifying the level of resources a student must show and the manner in which his or her possession of those resources must be proved. The Court appeared to approve comments made

[19] Case C-424/98 *Commission v Italy* [2000] ECR I-4001.

[20] For example, those relating to the education of the children of migrant workers. See ch 8 below.

[21] Note that a person working part-time and studying part-time would almost certainly be a worker within art 39 EC and be governed by rights flowing from his or her worker status.

[22] Art 2 of Directive 93/96/EEC.

[23] Case C-424/98 *Commission v Italy* [2000] ECR I-4001.

in argument by the Commission that a more relaxed approach to resources is justified in relation to students because it is far easier for students to supplement resources by income from work, but that it would be difficult to produce proof in advance that a student will supplement income in this way.[24]

The term 'vocational training course' is not defined in the directive, but it is clear from case law of the Court of Justice that this is to be interpreted widely. It would appear to cover any form of education which prepares a person for a profession, trade or employment including university courses save only for those courses undertaken by individuals for their general knowledge rather than to prepare them for an occupation.[25]

Standing and voting in elections

Article 19(1) EC gives 'every citizen of the Union residing in a Member State of which he is not a national' the right to vote, and to stand as a candidate, at municipal elections in the Member State of residence under the same conditions as apply to nationals of that member State.[26]

Article 19(2) gives corresponding rights to vote, and to stand as a candidate, in elections to the European Parliament.[27] There is a limitation in the implementing legislation which permits the host Member State to derogate from the granting of voting and standing rights where the proportion of nationals of other Member States reaches one-fifth of the relevant electorate. In such circumstances, a residence requirement may be attached to the eligibility to vote[28] and to the eligibility to stand as a candidate.[29]

These provisions do give new rights by decoupling eligibility to stand and vote in these elections from the holding of the nationality of the Member State in which the elections are held. Note that the extension of voting rights and eligibility to stand does not extend of voting and standing in national elections.

[24] See para 45 of the judgment.

[25] See Case 293/83 *Gravier v City of Liège* [1985] ECR 59 and Case 24/86 *Blaizot v City of Liège* [1988] ECR 379.

[26] The article goes on to indicate that this entitlement is to be subject to detailed arrangements adopted by the Council. These can be found in Council Directive 94/80/EEC of 6 December 1994 on the right to vote and stand in municipal elections, [1994] OJ L368/38 as amended by Council Directive 96/30/EEC, [1996] OJ L122/12. Certain posts, such as those of mayor and deputy mayor, may be reserved for nationals of the Member State.

[27] Again the right is subject to implementing measures adopted by the Council. These can be found in Council Directive 93/109/EEC of 6 December 1993 on exercising the right to vote in European Parliament elections, [1993] OJ L329/34, and see the resolution of the European Parliament on the implementation of the directive, [1994] OJ C44/159. Weiss and Wooldridge suggest that a refusal to grant the right to vote in such elections in the Member State of residence may constitute a violation of Article 3 of Protocol 1 to the European Convention on Human Rights following the decision of the Strasbourg Court in *Matthews v United Kingdom* (App. 24833/94), judgment of 18 February 1999; (1999) 30 EHRR 361.

[28] Up to a maximum of five years.

[29] Up to a maximum of 10 years.

Diplomatic and consular protection

Article 20 EC provides for diplomatic and consular representation to be afforded by the representatives of any other Member State in a country where the Member State of his or her nationality has no such representation. Member States are required to 'establish the necessary rules among themselves and start the international negotiations required to secure this protection'.[30]

The wording of this provision may not accord with the generally understood position in relation to the obligation of States to exercise diplomatic and consular protection. International law recognizes the entitlement of the State to exercise such protection but does not require them to do so; it is a matter for the discretion of the State. The wording of Article 20 EC suggests that diplomatic and consular protection is an entitlement of Union citizens as a matter of Community law. This was almost certainly not intended, and an interpretation which conforms to well-understood propositions of international law in this regard is likely to be preferred. The reference in the article to enjoyment of the rights on the same condition as nationals would justify such an interpretation.

Complaints mechanisms

Article 21 EC recognizes the right of citizens of the Union to petition the European Parliament under Article 194 EC and to apply to the ombudsman established under Article 195 EC.[31] Finally the article provides that every citizen may write to the European Parliament, the Council, the Commission, the Court of Justice, the Court of Auditors, the Commission of the Regions, the Economic and Social Committee, and the ombudsman in one of the official languages[32] of the Union and have an answer in the same language.

The Charter of Fundamental Rights of the European Union

On 7 December 2000 at the European Council in Nice, the European Parliament, the Council and the Commission solemnly proclaimed the Charter of Fundamental

[30] For Community implementing measures, see Council Decision 95/553/EEC of 28 December 1995 regarding protection for citizens of the European Union by diplomatic and consular representations, [1995] OJ L315/73. See also Decision of the Representatives of the Governments of the Member States, meeting within the Council of 6 July 1996 on the establishment of an emergency travel document. For guidance on the assistance which can be expected, see http://europa.eu.int/scadplus/citizens/en/uk/010993.htm.

[31] The ombudsman has jurisdiction to consider complaints of maladministration by the institutions of the Union other than the Court of Justice and the Court of First Instance acting in their judicial capacity.

[32] Currently Danish, Dutch, English, Finnish, French, German, Greek, Irish, Italian, Portuguese, Spanish and Swedish.

Rights of the European Union.[33] This has been described as a 'creative distillation of the rights contained in the various European and international agreements and national constitutions on which the ECJ had for some years already been drawing'.[34] The Charter had been drafted by a Convention which did not know whether it was drafting a declaratory or a legally binding document;[35] its current status is declaratory, although its final status is to be determined as part of the Intergovernmental Conference in 2004.[36] Chapter V, entitled 'Citizens' Rights', reflects the rights to be found in Articles 17 to 22 EC as follows:

- Article 39. Right to vote and to stand as a candidate at elections to the European Parliament.
- Article 40. Right to vote and stand as a candidate at municipal elections.
- Article 41. Right to good administration.
- Article 42. Right of access to documents.
- Article 43. Ombudsman.
- Article 44. Right to petition.
- Article 45. Freedom of movement and residence.
- Article 46. Diplomatic and consular protection.

All but Articles 41 and 42 begin with the words 'Every citizen of the Union . . . ' or 'Any citizen of the Union . . . ' emphasizing that such rights accrue only to nationals of the Member States who thereby qualify as citizens of the European Union. Article 41 on the right to good administration begins 'Every person . . . ' so making this a right which applies regardless of nationality. Article 42 rightly provides that access to documents is a right both for citizens of the Union and for 'any natural or legal person residing or having its registered office in a Member State'. Indeed it is not difficult to conceive of there being a legitimate interest in seeing such documents by an individual or business affected by them who does not reside or have its registered office in a Member State. There are rights to be found elsewhere which might properly be regarded as citizens' rights. A good example is Article 34 on social security and social assistance where the beneficiaries are 'everyone residing and moving legally within the European Union'.[37]

The Court of Justice has not yet referred to the Charter as the basis for any of its decisions, though the Advocates General have alluded to its significance in a number of cases, and the Court has made passing reference to it.[38] There would

[33] [2000] OJ C364/1.

[34] Craig, P and de Búrca, G, *EU Law. Text, Cases, and Materials* (Oxford, 2002), 359.

[35] See de Búrca, G, 'The Drafting of the European Union Charter of Fundamental Rights' (2001) 26 ELRev 126.

[36] See deliberations of the Convention especially the Working Group on Fundamental Rights.

[37] This formulation no doubt takes account of proposals to extend the rights in Regulation 1408/71/EEC to third country nationals. See ch 9 below.

[38] See Case C-254/01 *RTL*, judgment of 23 October 2003, para 38 of the judgment; Case C-101/01 *Lindqvist*, judgment of 6 November 2003, para 35 of the judgment; and Joined Cases C-204/00 P and others, *Aalborg Portland A/S*, judgment of 7 January 2004, para 94 of the judgment.

appear to be three possible approaches that might be taken by the Court. First, it could simply regard the Charter as devoid of any significance. That seems highly unlikely given its provenance. Over the years the Court has sought inspiration for its case law on the protection of fundamental rights in the Community legal order from a variety of sources. Secondly, the Court might have little difficulty in regarding an instrument signed by the Presidents of the Commission, the Council and the European Parliament as binding on them. Thirdly, the Court might seek inspiration in the Charter in defining and clarifying the general principles of Community law, and assistance in interpreting Community legislation.

In any event, the Charter provides support for the approach taken in this book of seeking to divide Community law on workers, establishment, and services into two streams, one of which is primarily concerned with personal rights for individuals, and the other of which is primarily concerned with regulating the market to secure access to the business environment of other Member States.

The provisions of the Charter of Fundamental Rights are incorporated as Part II of the Draft Constitution for Europe. If adopted, this would, of course, give the Charter provisions explicit legal effect.

The case law

There has been significant case law on the content of citizenship of the Union. Some of it is rather tentative and cautious in approach, but other cases are destined to become classic examples of judicial interpretation of the Treaty.

The mere holding of citizenship of the Union does not engage the Treaty rules; there must still be some factor connecting the circumstances to a situation covered by the Treaty. So citizenship of the Union does not extend the scope of the Treaty to situations which are wholly internal to a Member State and where there is no link with Community law.[39]

In the *Bickel and Franz* case[40] the Court linked Article 18 and the prohibition of discrimination in Article 12. Bickel, an Austrian national, was prosecuted in Italy for driving his lorry while under the influence of alcohol. Franz, a German national, was a tourist who was prosecuted in Italy for possession of a prohibited knife. The prosecutions were taken in the province of Bolzano, which has a significant German-speaking community of Italians. This group was entitled to require German to be the language of any criminal proceedings. Neither Bickel nor Franz spoke Italian; they requested but were refused trials in German. The national court referred questions to the Court of Justice on their entitlement to be tried in

[39] Joined Cases C-64/96 and C-65/96 *Uecker and Jacquet* [1997] ECR I-3171, para 23 of the judgment; see also Case C-148/02 *Garcia Avello*, judgment of 2 October 2003, [2003] ECR nyr, para 26 of the judgment.

[40] Case C-274/96 *Criminal Proceedings against Bickel and Franz* [1998] ECR I-7637.

the language of their choice where such a right existed for Italian nationals.[41] The Court found that the situation of both Bickel and Franz fell within the material scope of the Treaty since both were likely to be the recipient of services in Italy. Furthermore—and this is the point where the Court links the entitlement to citizenship rights—Article 18 gives persons the right to move and reside freely in other Member States which would be 'enhanced if the citizens of the Union are able to use a given language to communicate with the administrative and judicial authorities on the same footing as nationals'.[42] The implication is that such rights flow directly from Article 18, though, of course, the service provisions in the EC Treaty had also been engaged according to the Court.

It is now clear that the necessary link with the EC Treaty to engage the Treaty provisions may be provided by the provisions on citizenship where rights under the EC Treaty have been exercised in the past. This is well illustrated in the *D'Hoop* case.[43] Marie-Nathalie D'Hoop, a Belgian national, had undergone her education in both France and Belgium. Following her graduation from university in Belgium, she applied for a Belgian State benefit which provided financial support for graduates who were seeking their first jobs. Her application was refused on the grounds that she had not completed her secondary education in Belgium. The Court concluded that she could not rely on the Treaty provisions and secondary legislation on the free movement of workers, since she was not a worker. Nor in her circumstances could she rely on derived rights conferred on family members. An alternative was rooted in the provisions on citizenship. Since D'Hoop had exercised her Community rights to study in another Member State, that was enough to engage the Treaty provisions and to protect her against discrimination on grounds of nationality. The Court first addressed the temporal question concerning reliance on the citizenship provisions, since D'Hoop had studied abroad in 1991 prior to the entry into force of the Treaty provisions on citizenship. The Court concluded that these provisions must be applied to the 'present effects of situations arising previously'.[44] She was accordingly protected against differential treatment.

> In that a citizen of the Union must be granted in all Member States the same treatment in law as that accorded to the nationals of those Member States who find themselves in the same situation, it would be incompatible with the right of freedom of movement were a citizen, in the Member State of which he is a national, to receive treatment less favourable than he would enjoy if he had not availed himself of the opportunities offered by the Treaty in relation to freedom of movement.[45]

[41] The facts are reminiscent of those in Case 137/84 *Ministère Public v Mutsch* [1985] ECR 2681, which related to the language of trial in Belgium. But in that case Mutsch was a worker and so entitled to equal treatment under Art 7(2) of Regulation 1612/68/EEC, on which see ch 8 below.

[42] Case C-274/96 *Criminal Proceedings against Bickel and Franz* [1998] ECR I-7637, para 16 of the judgment.

[43] Case C-224/98 *D'Hoop* [2002] ECR I-6191.

[44] ibid, para 25 of the judgment.

[45] ibid, para 30 of the judgment.

In the circumstances in which D'Hoop found herself, she was treated less favourably than her fellow Belgians who had completed their secondary education in Belgium; she was penalized for having moved as a student. The Belgian requirement was an obstacle to free movement which could only be justified if its objective was to serve a legitimate aim and if this was the only way to meet that legitimate aim. The Court concluded that it was not. The citizen who has moved must not be disadvantaged as a consequence of that movement unless the rules resulting in less favourable treatment can be objectively justified.

The *Garcia Avello* case[46] shows the generosity with which the Court finds the necessary link with a situation contemplated by Community law. Mere residence was enough in this case, which concerned the application of Belgian rules on surnames to the children of a Spanish father and Belgian mother resident in Belgium. Where Community law is engaged, and where the national rules apply conditions for the award of some benefit in order to meet a legitimate aim, then the normal rules on necessity and proportionality will apply. In the *Collins* case,[47] the United Kingdom rules requiring a person to establish habitual residence in the United Kingdom as a condition of entitlement to means-tested social security benefits was in issue. Collins was born in the United States and held Irish nationality in addition to his American nationality. He came to the United Kingdom in 1998 and claimed a means-tested social security benefit, but this was refused on the grounds that he was not habitually resident in the United Kingdom. The Court concluded that it was legitimate for a Member State to grant a means-tested benefit for those seeking work only 'after is has been possible to establish that a genuine link exists between the person seeking work and the employment market of that State'.[48] The Court continued:

genuine link

> However, while a residence requirement is, in principle appropriate for the purpose of ensuring such a connection, if it is to be proportionate it cannot go beyond what is necessary in order to attain that objective. More specifically, its application by the national authorities must rest on clear criteria known in advance and provision must be made for the possibility of a means of redress of a judicial nature. In any event, if compliance with the requirement demands a period of residence, the period must not exceed what is necessary in order for the national authorities to be able to satisfy themselves that the person concerned is genuinely seeking work in the employment market of the host Member State.[49]

In relation to citizenship of the Union, the *Calfa* case[50] is more significant for what the Court did not do than for what it did. The case concerned Donatella Calfa, an Italian national, who was charged with drugs offences while on holiday in Crete. She was sentenced to three months' imprisonment and thereafter to expulsion for life from Greece. She took issue solely with the expulsion order, relying on the rights to move to receive services in Article 59 (now 49) EC and the Treaty

[46] Case C-148/02 *Garcia Avello*, judgment of 2 October 2003, [2003] ECR nyr.
[47] Case C-138/02 *Collins*, judgment of 23 March 2004, [2004] ECR nyr.
[48] ibid, para 69 of the judgment. [49] ibid, para 72 of the judgment.
[50] Case C-348/96 *Criminal Proceedings against Donatella Calfa* [1999] ECR I-11.

provisions on citizenship. The Court decided the case on the limits of the derogations permitted from the rules on the free movement of persons in the Treaty, which, said the Court, rendered it unnecessary to consider the claims based on citizenship of the Union. Automatic expulsion for life was a disproportionate response to the offence.

A trio of cases has significantly moved the debate about the content of citizenship of the Union forwards. The social aspects of citizenship are overtaking the economic aspects of citizenship.

The *Martínez Sala* case[51] concerned Maria Martínez Sala, a Spanish national, who was lawfully resident in Germany and found herself in need of financial support from the State. The Court ruled that the prohibition of discrimination on grounds of nationality applied in this case, and that Maria Martínez Sala was entitled to obtain social assistance on the same basis as German nationals. The referring court had conceded that her residence in Germany was lawful, and so the Luxembourg Court did not need to consider the limitations referred to in Article 18 EC. This suggested that perhaps the decision turned on its own special facts but the *Grzelczyk* case showed that this was not so.

The *Grzelczyk* case[52] is much more significant. Rudy Grzelczyk was a French national and a student at a university in Belgium. For the first three years of his course, he managed to maintain himself. He had undertaken some periods of work in Belgium to supplement his income. At the start of his fourth year, he found things tougher and applied for social assistance. This was initially awarded, but when the social assistance agency sought reimbursement from the Belgian Government, it was refused because Grzelczyk was a Community national enrolled as a student. When Grzelczyk challenged this decision, the Labour Tribunal referred questions to the Luxembourg Court.

The Court noted that, from the file submitted by the national court, it was clear that the national court considered that Grzelczyk did not meet the requirements for being treated as a worker with the meaning of Community law. The question the Court addressed was whether the Belgian authorities could make entitlement to social assistance conditional on a national of another Member State being a worker, when no such condition applied to nationals. The Court noted that this was prima facie discrimination on grounds of nationality which is prohibited by the Treaty. The Court said that Article 12 EC must be read in conjunction with the Treaty rules on citizenship of the Union. The Court said:

> Union citizenship is destined to be the fundamental status of nationals of the Member States, enabling those who find themselves in the same situation to enjoy the same treatment in law irrespective of their nationality, subject to such exceptions as are expressly provided for.[53]

[51] Case C-85/96 *Martínez Sala v Freistaat Bayern* [1998] ECR I-2691; see also O'Leary, S, 'Putting Flesh on the Bones of European Union Citizenship' (1999) 24 ELRev 68.

[52] Case C-184/99 *Grzelczyk v Centre public d'aide sociale d'Ottignies-Louvain-la-Neuve* [2001] ECR I-6193. See also Jacqueson, C, 'Union citizenship and the Court of Justice: something new under the sun? Towards social citizenship' (2002) 27 ELRev 260.

[53] Para 31 of the judgment.

And went on:

There is nothing in the amended text of the Treaty to suggest that students who are citizens of the Union, when they move to another Member State to study there, lose the rights which the treaty confers on citizens of the Union.[54]

Directive 93/96/EEC[55] on the free movement of students indicates that they are not entitled to maintenance grants, but does not 'preclude those to whom it applies from receiving social security benefits' on equal terms with nationals of the State of residence.[56] It would follow that a student who starts a course not needing to have recourse to public funds, is not precluded from making a claim if his or her circumstances change.

This is a significant enhancement of the position of citizens of the European Union in countries other than their country of nationality. Equality of treatment in all matters is required unless there is some exception applicable to their circumstances. This moves the case law on from the earlier decisions, and would seem to give direct effect to Article 18(1) EC since Grzelczyk had no other Treaty-based entitlement to reside in a Member State other than that of his nationality. Article 18(1) seemingly gives an independent right to reside subject only to the limitations and conditions in the Treaty and in the measures to give effect to it. The Court limited the circumstances in which a Member State can deprive a person of an entitlement arising under the students directive. Grzelczyk's unexpected need to resort to public funds was not such as would automatically remove his entitlement to be present in Belgium as a student. Some commentators have speculated that the decision could apply to those seeking work.[57]

The *Baumbast* case[58] concerned two families, but for the purposes of this exposition the circumstances of the Baumbast family will suffice to indicate the importance of the case. Mr Baumbast was a German national. He married Mrs Baumbast, a Colombian national, in 1990. There were two daughters, one a Colombian national (the child of an earlier relationship) and the other a dual national of Colombia and Germany. Mr Baumbast was an employee in the United Kingdom, followed by a period as a self-employed person, between 1990 and 1993. Mr Baumbast held a residence permit valid for five years, and the other members of the family held immigration documents giving them corresponding rights of residence. Mr Baumbast's business failed, and he then worked in China and Lesotho for German companies. Throughout the material period, the family

[54] Para 35 of the judgment. [55] See above in this chapter.

[56] Including social assistance.

[57] And so reversing the Court's decision in Case 316/85 *Centre public d'aide sociale de Courcelles v Lebon* [1987] ECR 2811. See O'Leary, S, 'Putting Flesh on the Bones of European Union Citizenship' (1999) 24 ELRev 68, at 76, and Jacqueson, C, 'Union citizenship and the Court of Justice: something new under the sun? Towards social citizenship' (2002) 27 ELRev 260, at 277.

[58] Case C-413/99 *Baumbast and R v Secretary of State for the Home Department* [2002] ECR I-7091. See Dougan, M and Spaventa, E, 'Educating Rudy and the non-English patient: A double-bill on residency rights under Article 18 EC' (2003) 28 ELRev 699.

owned a home in the United Kingdom, and the daughters went to school in England. They never claimed any social benefits, and the family had comprehensive medical insurance in Germany. They travelled there from time to time for medical treatment.

In May 1995 Mrs Baumbast applied for indefinite leave to remain in the United Kingdom for herself and other members of her family. The Secretary of State subsequently refused to renew Mr Baumbast's residence permit and the residence documents of Mrs Baumbast and the daughters. In January 1998 an appeal against that refusal came before an immigration adjudicator. The Court of Justice summarized the decision of the adjudicator as follows:

> He found that Mr Baumbast was neither a worker nor a person having a general right of residence under Directive 90/364. As regards the children, the Adjudicator decided that they enjoyed an independent right of residence under Article 12 of Regulation 1612/68. Moreover, he held that Mrs Baumbast enjoyed a right of residence for a period co-terminous with that during which her children exercised rights under Article 12 of that regulation. According to the Adjudicator, Mrs Baumbast's rights flowed from the obligation on Member States under that provision to encourage all efforts to enable children to attend courses in the host Member State under the best possible conditions.[59]

Mr Baumbast then appealed this decision to the Immigration Appeal Tribunal which referred questions to the Luxembourg Court. In brief, the Court decided that the children (including a child from a previous relationship of one of the spouses) of a person who has been a worker, are entitled to remain in the Member State for the purposes of completing their education under Article 12 of Regulation 1612/68.[60] The primary carer of the children, irrespective of nationality, is also entitled to remain in the Member State in order to facilitate the exercise of the right. The most dramatic finding relates to Mr Baumbast's circumstances; the Court ruled:

> A citizen of the European Union who no longer enjoys a right of residence as a migrant worker in the host Member State can, as a citizen of the Union, enjoy there a right of residence by direct application of Article 18(1) EC. The exercise of that right is subject to the limitations and conditions referred to in that provision, but the competent authorities and, where necessary, the national courts must ensure that those limitations and conditions are applied in compliance with the general principles of Community law and, in particular, the principle of proportionality.[61]

possible gaps!

On the face of it a series of gaps in Community law appeared to exclude Mr Baumbast from enjoying the rights of free movement enshrined in the EC Treaty and in the secondary legislation. He had ceased to be a worker in the United

[59] At para 21 of the judgment.

[60] Article 12 provides, 'The children of a national of a Member State who is or has been employed in the territory of another Member State shall be admitted to that State's general educational, apprenticeship and vocational training courses under the same conditions as nationals of that State, if such children are residing in its territory.
Member States shall encourage all efforts to enable such children to attend these courses under the best possible conditions.'

[61] Answer to the third question posed by the national court.

Kingdom, but, because he was employed by a German company to work abroad, clearly retained the status of a worker within the European Union. Could he nevertheless be regarded as a person of independent means in the United Kingdom? Unfortunately, he could not bring himself within the terms of Directive 90/364 because of the condition in that directive requiring beneficiaries of its provisions to be 'covered by sickness insurance in respect of all risks *in the host Member State*'.[62] The Baumbast family was covered by such insurance in Germany, which was not the host Member State. The Advocate General noted that Community law had not kept pace with modern social realities relating to modern family relationships where divorce and remarriage are common, to changes in the work cycle and place of work, and to globalization. Regulation 1612/68 was 'adopted at the high water mark of industrial mass production when employment conditions were relatively stable'.[63] Such considerations pointed to a gap in entitlement which at face value might lead to the conclusion that an economically active migrant worker, like Mr Baumbast, was excluded from the personal scope of Community law. Both the Advocate General and the Court of Justice resolved this dilemma by breathing new substance into Article 18(1) EC, taking by analogy the rights granted to nationals of the Member States in slightly different but cognate circumstances.

So Mr Baumbast enjoyed an independent right of residence flowing from Article 18(1) EC. We can now read this case in the light of the two earlier citizenship cases of *Martínez-Sala* and *Grzelczyk*.[64] There is a significant enhancement of the position of citizens of the European Union in countries other than their country of nationality by reason of these decisions. Equality of treatment in all matters is required unless there is some exception applicable to their circumstances.

Concluding remarks

From an unpromising beginning, in which it seemed that citizenship of the Union was a hollow shell attached to national citizenship which offered nothing which had not already been granted by the EC Treaty, the Court has fashioned a citizenship of real substance.

There will undoubtedly be further challenges based on the principle of equal treatment to rules currently applied in Member States. One example can be found in a case pending before the Court of Justice,[65] which invites re-consideration of the current rules on financial support for students. Whereas there can be no discrimination in relation to tuition fees, it has been accepted that there can be

[62] Article 1, first paragraph of Directive 90/364. Emphasis added.

[63] Opinion of Advocate General Geelhoed, at para 24; see generally paras 22–27 of the Opinion.

[64] Case C-85/96 *Martínez Sala v Freistaat Bayern* [1998] ECR I-2691; and Case C-184/99 *Grzelczyk v CPAS* [2001] ECR I-6913.

[65] Case C-209/03 *Bidar* [2003] OJ C171/13. See also Pending Case C-95/03 *Piliego* [2003] OJ C101/27.

differential treatment in relation to entitlement to financial support for studies since such matters fall outside the scope of the EC Treaty.[66] The continued exclusion of financial support for students is being questioned in a reference from the United Kingdom High Court which asks whether, in the light of developments in the field of citizenship and education, subsidized loans and educational grants fall outside the scope of the application of the EC Treaty. If they are no longer excluded, the court asks whether the conditions governing eligibility are based on objectively justifiable considerations not dependent on nationality.

It is not fanciful to see the end result of an extended case law being a conclusion that citizens of the Union are free from immigration control in all Member States; their rights of movement will be unfettered. They will also have a right to equality of treatment wherever they find themselves within the territory of the Union. These twin rights of freedom from immigration control and entitlement to equal treatment would give nationals of each Member State rights equal to those of nationals of every other Member State when resident in that State. The bundle of rights would not be the same in every Member State, but the differences of living in different Member States would be cognate with the differences of living in different regions within a Member State.

[66] See Case 39/86 *Lair* [1988] ECR 3181; and Case 197/86 *Brown* [1988] ECR 3205.

8

Benefits for movers

Introduction

This chapter sets out the rights which free movers enjoy. The broad term 'free movers' is used, since this chapter looks at the rights of those engaging in economic activity as well as the rights enjoyed by those not so engaged. The case law of the Court of Justice on citizenship of the European Union is making the enjoyment of certain benefits less dependent upon the exercise of economic activity than was formerly the case. However, there remain important distinctions in the rights enjoyed by those who come within the freedom of movement provisions of Articles 39 to 55 EC as against those not engaged in economic activity.

The right to be protected against discriminatory treatment is not considered in this chapter since it is so central to the whole area covered by this book that it has been given special emphasis in chapter 3. The rules on the co-ordination of social security schemes are the subject of the next chapter in this book.

The Community has recently modernized the legal instruments governing the rights which attach to free movement. Directive 2004/38/EC[1] will replace nine directives and two articles of one regulation[2] when it enters into force in 2006. Directive 2004/58/EC is primarily about entry and residence, and the ability of Member States to restrict these matters on grounds of public policy, public security or public health. It covers free movement whatever its basis and seeks in a single instrument to deal with qualified residence (that is, for example, residence as a retired person) as well as the free movement of the employed, the self-employed, and service providers and recipients. The structure of Directive 2004/38/EC is to define its subject matter and the groups of persons within its scope, before addressing (a) the right of movement and the right of residence for up to six months, (b) the right of residence for more than six months, and (c) the right of permanent residence. Chapter V deals with provisions common to the right of

[1] Directive 2004/38/EC of 29 April 2004 on the right of citizens of the Union and their family members to move and reside freely within the territory of the Member States, [2004] OJ L158/77.

[2] Directive 64/221, Directive 68/360, Directive 72/194, Directive 73/148, Directive 75/34, Directive 75/25, Directive 90/364, Directive 90/365, Directive 93/95, and Articles 10 and 11 of Regulation 1612/68. The provision of Directive 2004/38/EC corresponding to the provisions of these instruments is given in square brackets after footnoted references to specific provisions of the above directives.

residence and the right of permanent residence, while Chapter VI deals with restrictions based on grounds of public policy, public security and public health.[3]

The substantive rights of workers outside the areas of entry and residence remain to be found in Regulation 1612/68. Although this only applies to workers and there is no corresponding instrument dealing with the rights of self-employed persons, it is now clear from the case law of the Court of Justice that the prohibition of discrimination accords to self-employed persons much the same protection as the legislation on workers to be found in Regulation 1612/68.

Departure, entry and residence

Article 39 EC contains the right to move freely within the territory of the Member States for the purpose of accepting offers of work actually made, to stay in the Member State for the purpose of employment, and to remain in the territory of the Member State after a period of employment in accordance with the conditions set out in implementing legislation. Article 43 EC states that 'freedom of establishment shall include the right to take up and pursue activities as self-employed persons'. Article 50 EC provides that a service provider may temporarily pursue his activity in the host State on the same conditions as for nationals of that State. This implies a right of free movement for the purpose of providing services. Although a right of free movement as a *recipient* of services is not mentioned in the EC Treaty, it is referred to in the General Programme on the abolition of restrictions in relation to services.[4] Any residual doubt about this was resolved by the Court of Justice in its decision in the *Luisi and Carbone* case.[5] Rights of entry and residence flow from the Treaty itself; the secondary legislation deals with matters of detail in establishing some elements of a Community migration system.[6]

Directive 68/360 is the current instrument dealing with entry and residence rights for workers only, since it was made under Article 49 (now 40) EC. It governs movement rights of those within the material scope of Regulation 1612/68/EEC. Directive 73/148/EEC[7] is the corresponding provision which governs self-employment and movement in connection with the provision of services.

[3] The provisions concerning the application of the exceptions in the interests of public policy, public order and public health are referred to in chapter 5 above.

[4] It is also mentioned in art 1(1)(b) of Directive 73/148, see below in this chapter.

[5] Joined Cases 286/82 and 26/83 *Luisi and Carbone v Ministero del Tesoro* [1984] ECR 377.

[6] Note in this regard Regulation 539/2001/EC of 15 March 2001 listing the third countries whose nationals must be in possession of visas when crossing the external borders and those whose nationals are exempt from that requirement, [2001] OJ L81/1, as amended by Regulation 453/2003/EC of 6 March 2003, [2003] OJ L69/10.

[7] Council Directive of 21 May 1973 on the abolition of restrictions on movement and residence within the Community for nationals of Member States with regard to establishment and the provision of services (73/148/EEC), [1973] OJ L172/14.

Article 2 of both directives sets out the right to leave the Member State of nationality simply on production of a valid identity card or passport. The article contains a right to renewal of the identity card or document which must be valid for all Member States and for a period of five years. The use of exit visas or similar documents is prohibited.

Article 3 of both directives requires nationals of Member States exercising their rights under the Treaty provisions to be admitted to the territory of the Member State of work solely on production of a valid identity card or passport. Again the use of entry visas or similar documents is prohibited except for members of the worker's family who are not nationals of a Member State.[8] In these cases Member States 'must accord to such persons every facility for obtaining the necessary visas'.[9] On production of a valid identity card or passport and confirmation of engagement from the employer or a certificate of employment, the immigration authorities must grant a right of residence to the worker. In the case of self-employment or service provision, persons would appear to be entitled to admission solely on production of a valid identity card or passport coupled with a claim that they are established or wish to be established in a Member State other than that of the person's nationality in order to pursue activities as a self-employed person, or are engaged in the provision of services.[10] Members of the worker's family have a similar right on production of a document 'issued by the competent authority of the State of origin or the State whence they came, proving their relationship' or in the case of those dependent on the worker 'testifying that they are dependent on the worker or that they live under his roof in such country'.[11]

Article 6 of Directive 68/360[12] introduces the residence permit, which is a document of evidential value and not one which confers rights. These flow from the Treaty itself.[13] The issue of such permits is to be free of charge 'or on payment of an amount not exceeding the dues and taxes charged for the issue of identity cards to nationals'.[14] No other conditions for their issue can be demanded save a valid national identity card or passport and, in the case of employees, evidence of employment. So a refusal to issue a permit before a person could establish their affiliation to the social security system of the host State would breach Community law.[15] In the normal case the residence permit is valid for five years throughout the territory of the host State and is automatically renewable; members of the mover's

[8] Any such visa required must be free of charge: art 9(2) of Directive 68/360 and art 7(2) of Directive 73/148 [Art 5(1) and (2) of Directive 2004/38/EC].

[9] Art 4 of Directive 68/360 and art 3(2) of Directive 73/148 [Art 5(2) of Directive 2004/38/EC].

[10] Proof of self-employment or service provider status is only required under Directive 73/148 at the point of application for a residence permit: art 6(b) [Art 8 of Directive 2004/38/EC].

[11] Article 4 of Directive 68/360 and art 6 of Directive 74/148 [Arts 2(2) and 10 of Directive 2004/38/EC].

[12] And Art 4 of Directive 73/148 in relation to the self-employed and service providers.

[13] Case 48/75 *Royer* [1976] ECR 497, para 33 of the judgment.

[14] Article 9(1) of Directive 68/360 and art 7(1) of Directive 73/148.

[15] Case C-363/89 *Roux* [1991] ECR I-273, para 16 of the judgment.

family are entitled to a residence permit having the same validity as that issued to the mover. Article 5 makes it clear that obtaining a residence permit is not a condition of starting work, while Article 6(2) provides that breaks in residence not exceeding six consecutive months and absence on military service do not affect the validity of the residence permit. Nor does sickness, invalidity or involuntary unemployment affect the validity of the residence permit, although a worker who has been involuntarily unemployed for a period of more than 12 months may have the renewal of the residence permit limited to a period of one year rather than the normal five.[16]

There is no entitlement to a residence permit for employees whose work is not expected to last more than three months, for frontier workers,[17] or for seasonal workers. Those whose work is expected to last more than three but less than 12 months are entitled to a temporary residence permit which lasts as long as the expected duration of the work. A service provider whose stay in another Member State is expected to exceed three months is entitled to be issued with a document called 'a right of abode'.[18]

Since the residence permit is merely evidence of rights flowing from the EC Treaty, it follows that any failure to comply with legal formalities concerning access cannot justify expulsion.[19] However, this does not mean that any form of administrative requirement is unlawful. The only express reference in Directive 68/360 to such measures is in Article 8(2) which provides that short-term workers may be required to report their presence in the territory of the host State.

Commission v Belgium[20] illustrates how, even as late as 1995, certain Member States were not complying with the requirements of Community law on the issue of residence permits and allied documentation. Belgium required those seeking employment who had not found work to leave their territory without exception after three months, refused to issue a residence permit to those with employment lasting more than one year during the first six months of the employment, and required payment for the document issued to seasonal workers and short-term workers. All were found to be clear breaches of Community law.

[16] Article 7(2) of Directive 68/360. The corresponding provisions of Directive 73/148 do not refer to involuntary unemployment.

[17] Defined in art 8(b) of Directive 68/360 as a 'worker who, while having his residence in the territory of a Member State to which he returns as a rule, each day or at least once a week'. Such workers are entitled to a 'special permit valid for five years and automatically renewable'.

[18] Article 4(2) of Directive 73/148.

[19] Case 48/75 *Royer* [1976] ECR 497, para 38 of the judgment. See also Case 8/77 *Sagulo* [1977] ECR 1495, and Case 157/79 *Pieck* [1980] ECR 2171. In *Sagulo*, the Advocate General suggested that the penalty imposed on an Italian in Germany whose residence permit was no longer valid could not exceed the penalty available in respect of a German national whose identity card had expired. This case also makes clear that the only permit that can be required is the Community residence permit provided for in Directive 68/360/EEC; a person exercising rights under Article 39 EC cannot be required to obtain the sort of residence permit required of nationals from other States which are not members of the Community.

[20] Case C-344/95 *Commission v Belgium* [1997] ECR I-1035.

The permissibility of administrative measures ostensibly designed to enable a State to count migrant workers arose in the *Watson and Bellmann* case.[21] Ms Watson, who appears to have been some sort of *au pair,* failed to comply with an Italian requirement to report to the police within three days of entering the country. Mr Belmann, an Italian national for whom she was working, also failed to notify her presence in his house within 24 hours of her arrival. The possible penalties on conviction included imprisonment and deportation of non-nationals. The Italian court referred questions to the Luxembourg Court on the compatibility of such measures with Community law. The Court of Justice ruled that deportation would negate the right of free movement, and so was not an available penalty for failure to comply with administrative regulations.[22] The Court continued:

> As regards other penalties, such as fines and detention, whilst the national authorities are entitled to impose penalties in respect of a failure to comply with the terms of provisions requiring foreign nationals to notify their presence which are comparable to those attaching to infringement of provisions of equal importance by nationals, they are not justified in imposing a penalty so disproportionate that it becomes an obstacle to the free movement of persons.[23]

The same provisions were in issue in the *Messner* case.[24] Though the Court of Justice had already said that formalities of this type were compatible with Community law, in this case the Court of Justice said that the three-day time limit for reporting was unreasonably short. The person exercising the rights must travel from the port of entry to final destination and then make enquiries of the competent authorities. A three-day time limit for such activities was not long enough. This shows that the Court will take a tough line on the proportionality both of any requirement and of the penalties available in the event of non-compliance; such arrangements must respect the fundamental nature of the free movement of persons.

Infringement proceedings against Belgium show the subtle distinctions which can arise.[25] The case concerned the requirement sometimes imposed on nationals of other Member States to produce their residence permit in addition to a valid national identity card or passport on entry into Belgium, and at other times while in the country. The Court ruled that a Member State could not require more than the production of the identity document at the point of entry into the country, but that a Member State could check the residence permit within its territory when there was a corresponding obligation on its own nationals to present on demand a valid national identity card. Furthermore, such controls must not be carried out in a 'systematic, arbitrary or unnecessarily restrictive manner'. Since the evidence was that such controls were exercised only 'sporadically and unsystematically', there was no infringement of Community law.[26] Infringement proceedings were taken against Germany some years later in relation to similar requirements to produce a

[21] Case 118/75 *Watson and Bellmann* [1976] ECR 1185.
[22] Para 20 of the judgment.
[23] Para 21 of the judgment.
[24] Case C-265/88 *Messner* [1989] ECR 4209.
[25] Case 321/87 *Commission v Belgium* [1989] ECR 997.
[26] Paras 15–16 of the judgment.

national identity card, or passport or residence permit.[27] The operation of the checks was not in issue, but the Commission considered that the differences in the basis of liability and the penalties imposed for failure to produce the documents constituted a disproportionate difference in the treatment of nationals as against migrant workers.[28] The Court found a violation ruling that the nature of the penalties imposed on nationals and non-nationals could not be disproportionately different.

When Directive 68/360/EEC, which establishes a common framework of immigration control for workers, was adopted by the Council, the Member States minuted an interpretative declaration that those seeking work would be allowed to enter another Member State for a period of three months in order to look for work, provided that they could support themselves without recourse to social assistance. The text of the statement is set out in the *Levin* case:[29]

> The Member States adopted an interpretative declaration at the meeting of the Council at which Regulation No 1612/68 and Directive 68/360 were adopted. Under the terms of that declaration, 'the persons referred to by Article 1 (of Directive 68/360), that is to say nationals of a Member State who move to another Member State in order to find employment, have a minimum period of three months in which to do so; if at the end of that period they have not found employment, their stay in the territory of that other Member State may be terminated. However, if during that period the above-mentioned persons become dependent on public support (social assistance) in that other Member State they may be requested to leave its territory.'

In both the *Royer*[30] and *Levin* cases the Court of Justice combined reference to those with offers of employment and those seeking employment in defining the term, worker. However, minuted statements of the kind made by the Council do not create law. The Court's view is that the right to enter for the purpose of seeking employment arises under Article 39 (ex 48) EC and not under Directive 68/360.[31]

The precise status of work seekers arose in the *Antonissen* case,[32] where the Court of Justice had to consider the rights of those who entered a Member State in order to seek work. The Court confirmed the view that those seeking work had a right of entry for that purpose for a limited period in order to appraise themselves of job opportunities corresponding to their qualifications. Clearly if the job search is successful, the individual will be able to claim the full rights given by Article 39 EC. But what of the status of a person who exhausts the period without securing employment? The United Kingdom immigration rules permit nationals of other Member States a stay of six months for job search purposes. Antonissen had used up

[27] Case C-24/97 *Commission v Germany* [1998] ECR I-2133.

[28] The maximum penalty for migrant workers was five times that applicable to a national found not to be in possession of a valid identity card.

[29] Case 53/81, *Levin* [1982] ECR 1035, at 1043.

[30] Case 48/75, *Royer* [1976] ECR 497.

[31] Case C-138/02 *Collins*, judgment of 23 March 2004, [2004] ECR nyr, paras 34–44 of the judgment. See also Case C-171/91 *Tsiotras* [1992] ECR I-2925.

[32] Case C-292/89 *Antonissen* [1991] ECR I-745.

this time. The Court of Justice, on a reference from the High Court in England, ruled that if, after the period of six months expires, applicants can nevertheless show on the balance of probabilities that they have a genuine chance of obtaining employment, immediate deportation would be inappropriate. This decision reflects the increasing emphasis placed by the Court on free movement as existing independently of economic activity.

However, the *Lebon* case[33] underlines the lesser status of work seekers by making clear that they have no claim to the full range of benefits available in the Member State where they are seeking work, even though those benefits must be granted to those who are workers on the same basis as they are granted to nationals of that Member State. It is, however, now at least arguable that the Court would look more closely at the circumstances in which the person claiming certain rights found themselves in a Member State. If there was a sufficient period of residence to constitute lawful residence in the host State, then entitlement to equal treatment in relation to social assistance might flow from his or her status as a citizen of the European Union following the decision in the *Martínez Sala* case.[34]

Three directives passed in 1990 extended rights of residence to persons of independent means[35] retired persons,[36] and students,[37] and to members of their families.[38] Directive 90/366 grants a right of residence to those who have been employees or self-employed persons who have ceased their occupational activity as a result of retirement whether in the normal course of events or by reason of illness or injury, and to members of their families. Such persons may choose to reside in any Member State. Directive 90/364 grants a similar right to a residual class of persons who do not have any right of residence under any other provision of Community law.[39] For those covered by these two directives, it is a condition of the exercise of the right of residence that the person has sufficient resources in order not to become a financial burden on the host Member State. These two directives indicate that the threshold is the level at which social assistance would become available in the State of residence.[40] The Commission[41] has indicated that Member

[33] Case 316/85 *Centre public d'aide sociale de Courcelles v Lebon* [1987] ECR 2811, confirmed in Case C-138/02 *Collins*, judgment of 23 March 2004, [2004] ECR nyr.

[34] Case C-85/96 *Martínez Sala* [1998] ECR I-2691, discussed in ch 7 above.

[35] Council Directive of 28 June 1990 on the right of residence (90/364/EEC), [1990] OJ L180/26.

[36] Council Directive of 28 June 1990 on the right of residence for employees and self-employed persons who have ceased their occupational activity (90/365/EEC), [1990] OJ L180/28.

[37] Council Directive of 28 June 1990 on the right of residence for students (90/366/EEC), [1990] OJ L180/30. This Directive was annulled in Case C-295/90 *European Parliament v Council* [1992] ECR I-4193 because it was made on the wrong legal base. It was replaced by Council Directive of 29 October 1993 on the right of residence for students (93/96/EEC), [1993] OJ L317/59, as amended by Decision 95/1/EC, [1995] OJ L1/1.

[38] The provisions of these directives are consolidated in Directive 2004/38/EC of 29 April 2004. See art 7 of the new directive.

[39] Sometimes referred to as the 'Playboy Directive'.

[40] Article 1 of Directive 90/364 and art 1 of Directive 90/365.

[41] Commission Report to European Parliament and Council on the application of Directives 90/364, 90/365 and 93/96, COM(1999) 127 final of 17 March 1999.

States should not be unnecessarily demanding in checking the financial resources of persons exercising the right of entry and residence under these directives. It was not necessary to see bank statements or tax returns. Pensions are considered a particularly stable source of income.

It is also a condition that those exercising the rights 'are covered by sickness insurance in respect of all risks in the host Member State'.[42] This requirement is both general and specific. It is general in that its terms can be met by a variety of means, including both private insurance and social insurance. It is specific in requiring the cover to be 'in respect of all risks in the host State',[43] though it does not appear to matter whether the cover is provided by an insurer within the host State or from elsewhere.

The requirements of the students directive are similar, but have the aim of encouraging non-discriminatory access to vocational training throughout the Community. There is a right of entry and residence for the duration of the course for students enrolled in a recognized educational establishment in order to pursue a vocational course.[44] Students must provide an assurance that they have financial resources which will avoid their becoming a financial burden on the host State.[45] The directive gives no entitlement to a maintenance grant in the host State.[46]

The Commission took infringement proceedings against Italy in respect of the demands it was making of those seeking to exercise the rights of entry and residence granted by these directives.[47] In its judgment, the Court stated that the use of identical wording in the three directives in relation to the sufficiency of resources required for a person not to be a burden on the public purse did not mean that the amount of those resources needed to be the same in all the situations contemplated by the directives.

The documentary requirements imposed by Member States must not constitute obstacles to the exercise of the rights set out in the directives. This meant that Member States were obliged to permit a variety of means of establishing the conditions for the exercise of the rights in the directives, and could not require that certain documents be issued or certified by an authority of a Member State, for example, by requiring certification through consular authorities.

The Court's judgment in relation to the requirement imposed by Italy concerning the amount of a student's resources makes a fine distinction. It seems that the Italian authorities required that students have a specific amount at their disposal 'not

[42] Art 1 of Directive 90/364 and art 1 of Directive 90/365.

[43] This proved to be problematic in Case C-413/99 *Baumbast and R v Secretary of State for the Home Department*, judgment of 17 September 2002, [2002] ECR I-7091, see ch 7 above.

[44] It would seem that this may be a full-time or part-time course as long as the principal purpose is to pursue the vocational education: art 1.

[45] But note the entitlement which may flow from citizenship of the Union as established in Case C-184/99 *Grzelczyk v Centre public d'aide sociale d'Ottignies-Louvain-la-Neuve* [2001] ECR I-6193. See ch 7 above.

[46] Article 3 of Directive 93/96.

[47] Case C-424/98 *Commission v Italy* [2000] ECR I-4001.

being lower than the minimum amount laid down by the Italian compulsory general insurance scheme'. This was found by the Court to exceed the limits of the State's discretion having regard to the wording of the students directive. Whereas the retired persons directive and the persons of independent means directive both require the person to *have* sufficient resources to avoid becoming a burden on the State, the students directive merely requires the student to *provide an assurance* by means of a declaration or such alternative means as the student may choose that he or she has sufficient resources to avoid becoming a burden. The Advocate General explained the difference in wording as follows:

diff. students and others

There are several reasons for the differences between Directive 93/96 and the other two. Firstly, in the great majority of cases a student's period of residence is limited to the duration of his studies and there is, therefore, less danger that he will become dependent on the social assistance system of the host State. Secondly, Member States may limit the validity of a residence permit to one year, renewable annually, so that they have greater capacity to intervene in the event that the applicant becomes dependent on the social assistance system. Thirdly, if a student is short of money, he is better placed than the beneficiaries of the other Directives to supplement his income by doing small temporary or part-time jobs, even though it may be impossible to prove, in advance, that he will find himself in that position.[48]

The right to remain

Article 39(3)(d) EC provides for a right to remain in the territory of a Member State after having been employed in that State 'subject to conditions which shall be embodied in implementing regulations to be drawn up by the Commission'. The right to remain is implemented in Regulation 1251/70.[49] The object of the right to remain is to reflect the social integration in the host State which might well have occurred as a result of a person's residence and employment there.

The *Nani Givane* case[50] concerned the application of the right to remain in the United Kingdom. Givane, a Portuguese national, had entered the United Kingdom in 1992 to work as a chef and had obtained a five-year residence permit. In 1995 he went to India for 10 months. He returned in February 1996 with his wife and their three children, all of whom held Indian nationality. Givane died in November 1997. The members of the family sought to remain in the United Kingdom in reliance on the provisions of Article 3(2) of the regulation. This provides that there is a right to remain for relatives of a worker who has died during his working life if the worker had at the date of his death resided continuously in the territory of the Member State for at least two years. The Home Secretary had refused leave to remain because as at the date of his death, Givane had not been resident for a period

48 Para 28 of the Opinion.

49 Commission Regulation of 29 June 1970 on the right of workers to remain in the territory of a Member State after having been employed in that State (1251/70/EEC), [1970] II OJ Eng Sp. Ed. 402.

50 Case C-257/00 *Nani Givane* [2003] ECR I-345.

of two years immediately preceding his death. This was a case in which the different language versions of the regulation were not consistent.[51] The Court looked at the object and purpose of the provision, and concluded that the proper interpretation of the provision required the two years' residence to have immediately preceded the worker's death.[52] Advocate General Alber had come to a different conclusion in his Opinion.

There is no corresponding Treaty right to remain after a period of self-employment, but Directive 75/34 contains such a right.[53]

Broadly speaking the right to remain arises when a person reaches retirement age, or has to cease work by reason of illness or disablement. There are also rights of permanent residence for family members after the worker or self-employed person dies. There are detailed rules on the length and continuity of residence required before these rights arise. Again in broad terms, persons remaining under these rules are entitled to equality of treatment just as if they were workers or self-employed persons.

Directive 2004/38/EC

Directive 2004/38/EC applies to citizens of the European Union who move to or reside in a Member State other than that of which they are a national. The rights extend to family members. These are defined as (a) the spouse, or (b) 'the partner with whom the Union citizen has contracted a registered partnership, on the basis of the legislation of a Member State, if the legislation of the host Member State treats registered partnerships as equivalent to marriage'[54] together with (c) the direct descendants of the citizen, spouse or partner, and (d) the direct relatives in the ascending line of the citizen, spouse or partner. The prohibition of discrimination on grounds, among others, of sexual identity means that this will include same sex partners subject to the conditions set out in Directive 2004/38/EC. The entry and residence of dependent relatives who do not fall within this list and of other family members where there are serious health or humanitarian grounds for admission shall be facilitated.[55]

[51] ibid, para 35 of the judgment.

[52] Despite referring in para 45 of the judgment to the need for respect of family life, which suggests that members of a worker family should 'as a rule' be entitled to reside in the territory of the host Member State on the worker's death.

[53] Council Directive of 17 December 1974 concerning the right of nationals of a Member State to remain in the territory of another Member State after having pursued therein an activity in a self-employed capacity (75/34/EEC), [1975] OJ L14/10. This directive was made under the reserve power in Article 235 (now 305) EC. Its provisions are consolidated in Directive 2004/38/EC.

[54] Article 2(2) of Directive 2004/38/EC.

[55] Article 3(2) of Directive 2004/38/EC.

Chapter II of Directive 2004/38/EC deals with the right of entry and residence for up to six months. This is unconditional save that a valid identity card or passport must be produced, and persons so admitted may be required to report their presence in the territory within a time limit which may not be less than 15 days.

Chapter II deals with the rights of residence for more than six months. This right is available to Union citizens who:

(a) are employed or self-employed persons; or
(b) are recipients of services; or
(c) have sufficient resources not to become a burden on welfare assistance in the host Member State and have comprehensive sickness insurance cover in the host Member State; or
(d) are enrolled as students at an accredited educational establishment for the principal purpose of following a course of study and have comprehensive sickness insurance cover in the host Member State.[56]

The status of being an employee or self-employed person is retained in the following circumstances:

(a) they are temporarily unable to work as a result of illness or injury; or
(b) they are involuntarily unemployed and have registered as a jobseeker;[57] or
(c) they embark on vocational training.[58]

Registration in the host State may be required which entitles the Union citizen to the issue of a registration certificate on the spot; failure to register may attract only administrative penalties.[59]

The right of residence of those who are family members of a Union citizen but who are not themselves Union citizens is to be evidenced by the residence card, which is to be valid for at least five years.[60]

Chapter IV concerns the right of permanent residence. Article 14(1) gives a right of permanent residence to Union citizens 'who have resided legally for a continuous period of five years in the host Member State' and this right 'shall not be subject to the conditions provided for in Chapter III'. Under Article 17 the right of permanent residence may arise sooner in the detailed circumstances set out there. Article 19 introduces a permanent residence document.

[56] Directive 2004/38/EC is silent on the resources a student is required to have.

[57] The requirement to register as an unemployed person is new. If the unemployment results from the ending by the passage of time of a fixed-term contract of less than a year, then the duration of the retention of worker status is to be not less than six months, but where unemployment benefits are in payment the duration of the extended right of residence is for such period as the entitlement to unemployment benefit runs.

[58] Unless the person concerned is involuntarily unemployed, retaining worker status requires that the training be related to their previous occupation.

[59] Article 8 of Directive 2004/38/EC.

[60] Articles 10 and 11 of Directive 2004/38/EC. Art 12 deals with the right of residence by family members following the death or departure of the Union citizen, while art 13 deals with the consequences of divorce or annulment of marriage or the termination of partnership.

There are, of course, corresponding rights for family members of Union citizens in the circumstances set out above.

Even this cursory overview of Directive 2004/38/EC indicates that it reflects the rights which attach to citizenship of the European Union much more than the exercise of economic activity.

Equality of treatment with nationals

Chapter 3 of this book examined the prohibition of discrimination which is at the heart of the law on the fundamental freedoms. The Treaty prohibition on discrimination on grounds of nationality finds expression in a number of articles of Regulation 1612/68.[61] In particular Titles I and II of the regulation provide for equality of access to employment, eligibility for consideration for employment, and in the conditions of employment. A number of the rights contained in this regulation are considered in more detail below.

Social and tax advantages

Article 7(2) of Regulation 1612/68[62] has become central to the equal treatment of workers. Its drafting is simplicity itself:

> [The worker] shall enjoy the same social and tax advantages as national workers.

The benefit of these provisions applies both to the worker and to members of a worker's family.[63]

Social advantages

The Court has, over time, taken a more expansive view of what constitutes a social advantage; it is important to note that the term used is social advantages rather than social rights.[64] Its early case law required a much closer link to the contract of employment than its later case law.[65] The modern, if somewhat inelegant, definition of what constitutes a social advantage was first stated in the *Even* case:[66]

[61] For example, Arts 1(2), 7, 8, 9, and 10.

[62] See O'Keeffe, D, 'Equal Rights for Migrants: The Concept of Social Advantage in Article 7(2), Regulation 1612/68' (1985) 5 YEL 93; and Ellis, E, 'Social advantages: A new lease of life?' (2003) 40 CMLRev 639.

[63] See, for example, Case 32/75 *Cristini (Fiorini)* [1975] ECR 1085.

[64] And so covers benefits which are discretionary in nature based on need as well as those entitlement to which is mandatory. See comment by Advocate General Slynn in Case 65/81 *Reina v Landeskreditbank Baden-Württemberg* [1982] ECR 33, at 51.

[65] For an example of the early case law, see Case 76/72 *Michel S* [1973] ECR 437.

[66] Case 207/78 *Criminal Proceedings against Even* [1979] ECR 2019.

. . . the advantages which this regulation extends to workers who are nationals of other Member States are all those which, whether or not linked to a contract of employment, are generally granted to national workers or by virtue of the mere fact of their residence on the national territory and the extension of which to workers who are nationals of other Member States therefore seems suitable to facilitate their mobility within the Community.

This definition has been rather more elegantly restated by the Court:

. . . the advantages which [Article 7(2)] extends to workers of other Member States are all those which, whether or not linked to a contract of employment, are generally granted to national workers primarily because of their objective status as workers or by virtue of the mere fact of their residence on the national territory and whose extension to workers who are nationals of other Member States therefore seems likely to facilitate the mobility of such workers within the Community.[67]

Advantages within the provision include the predictable and the somewhat surprising. So, it includes childbirth loans,[68] and minimum means of subsistence for the worker.[69] But it also includes having your unmarried partner live with you if such rights are available to nationals,[70] and the right to have proceedings against you heard in your own language (again if there are language choices available to nationals).[71] However, it does appear to be a requirement that the advantage being claimed can be identified with sufficient precision. Although the Advocate General in the *Ferlini* case[72] concluded that the fixing of scales of fees for medical and hospital maternity care was capable of constituting a social advantage within Article 7(2),[73] the Court concluded that it did not.[74]

Several cases have concerned the availability of some advantage for a family member, since an advantage accorded to a family member may constitute an advantage for the worker. In the *Deak* case[75] the Court explained that the article was also intended to prevent discrimination against the descendants of a worker who are dependent on him. The extension of advantages to the children or workers was an advantage to them, and any refusal to extend such advantages would be an obstacle to the free movement of workers. So the Hungarian son of an Italian national working in Belgium was entitled to unemployment benefits on being unable to find employment on completion of his education. The same view has been taken in relation to benefits for those in the ascending line of relationship.[76]

[67] Case 249/83 *Hoeckx v Openbaar Centrum voor Maatschappelijk Welzijn* [1985] ECR 973, para 20 of the judgment.
[68] Case 65/81 *Reina v Landeskreditkbank Baden-Württemberg* [1982] ECR 33.
[69] Case 249/83 *Hoeckx v Openbaar Centrum voor Maatschappelijk Welzijn* [1985] ECR 973.
[70] Case 59/85 *The Netherlands v Reed* [1986] ECR 1283.
[71] Case 137/84 *Ministère Public v Mutsch* [1985] ECR 2681.
[72] Case C-411/98 *Ferlini v Centre hospitalier de Luxembourg* [2000] ECR I-8081.
[73] Para 59 of the Opinion.
[74] Paras 45–6 of the judgment.
[75] Case 94/84 *Office national de l'emploi v Deak* [1985] ECR 1873.
[76] Case 157/84 *Frascogna v Caisse des depots et consignations* [1985] ECR 1739.

Since there is no corresponding secondary legislation for the self-employed and service providers or recipients, the corresponding rights of this group flow from the general law prohibiting discriminatory treatment, which finds particular expression in Articles 43 and 50 EC on an entitlement to undertake such activities on the same conditions as nationals of the host State. This is also made clear in the two General Programmes for the abolition of restrictions on freedom of establishment and on freedom to provide services, each of which contains detailed lists of areas where equality of opportunity in access to activities as self-employed persons or service providers can be found.[77]

Two illustrations from the case law of the Court of Justice show the sort of difficulties that can be met in practice. In the *Steinhauser* case,[78] the Court of Justice ruled that discrimination on the grounds of nationality could not be practised where the effect was to deny the person from another Member State the means of carrying on their business. So the City of Biarritz could not limit the hire of *crampottes*[79] to their own nationals. Steinhauser, a German national, who was a professional artist living and working in Biarritz had been refused the hire of a *crampotte* because he was not a French national. But it is also clear that equality of treatment goes beyond the equality needed to enable a person to pursue their livelihood. In *Commission v Italy*[80] the Court of Justice considered Italian rules whereby only Italian nationals were allowed to purchase or lease housing built or renovated with the aid of public funds, or to obtain reduced rate mortgages. Citing the General Programme, the Court imported into the ambit of Article 52 (now 43) EC the duty to provide housing on an equal basis, which is more specifically set out for workers in Article 9 of Regulation 1612/68. The Court found that Italy had failed to fulfil its obligations under the EC Treaty by withholding publicly funded housing assistance from self-employed nationals of other Member States. The justification was that refusal to provide such assistance would distort competition between self-employed nationals of the Member State and those of other Member States carrying on the same economic activity. Nationals of other Member States would have to spend more on their housing and so would have less money to devote to the development of their businesses.

In the area of services, the Court, in one of its earliest decisions in the area, defined the prohibition of discrimination in terms which include a very wide range of obstacles. In the *Van Binsbergen* case,[81] the Court ruled that the obstacles to be abolished under Articles 59 and 60 (now 49 and 50) EC included:

[77] General Programme for the Abolition of Restrictions on Freedom to Provide Services, [1962] IX OJ Eng Sp. Ed. 3; and General Programme for the Abolition of Restrictions on Freedom of Establishment, [1962] IX OJ Eng Sp. Ed. 7

[78] Case 197/84 *Steinhauser v City of Biarritz* [1985] ECR 1819.

[79] A type of beach hut used for the display and sale of works of art.

[80] Case 63/86 *Commission v Italy* [1988] ECR 29.

[81] Case 33/74 *Van Binsbergen v Bestuur van de Bedrijfsvereniging voor de Metaalnijverheid* [1974] ECR 1299.

> . . . all requirements imposed on the person providing the service by reason in particular of his nationality or of the fact that he does not habitually reside in the State where the service is provided, which do not apply to persons established within the national territory or which may prevent or otherwise obstruct the activities of the person providing the service.[82]

The application of the principle in wide terms to a recipient of services is illustrated by the *Cowan* case.[83] Ian Cowan, a British tourist, was attacked outside a Paris metro station, and claimed compensation for his injuries under the French criminal injuries compensation scheme. He was refused access to the scheme, since he was neither a French national nor the holder of a residence permit. The Court noted that he was a recipient of services and was therefore entitled to equal treatment with French nationals in access to the scheme. There was no residence requirement attaching to access by French nationals to the scheme, and so no such requirement could be applied to Cowan whose activities fell within the scope of the EC Treaty. This case is authority for the proposition that a provider or recipient of services must enjoy not only rights directly related to the provision of the services but also equal treatment in all areas regarded as running with that freedom. There need be no direct link between those areas and free movement if the denial of the equal treatment is capable of being an obstacle to the exercise of the freedom.

The *Meeusen* case[84] shows just how close the regimes governing workers and self-employed persons are in substance. Chantal Meeusen was the daughter of Belgian parents who lived in Belgium but worked in the Netherlands. Her father was the proprietor of a company he set up and her mother an employee of that company. Chantal was refused a grant to support her studies of chemistry in Antwerp in the Netherlands. The Court ruled that the close family relationship between employer and employee did not preclude Chantal's mother from being a worker within the meaning of the Treaty. Furthermore, a grant for educational purposes was a social advantage to the worker under Article 7(2) of Regulation 1612/68, and, finally:

> . . . the dependent child of a national of one Member State who pursues an activity as a self-employed person in another Member State while maintaining his residence in the State of which he is a national can obtain student finance under the same conditions as are applicable to children of nationals of the State of establishment, and in particular without any further requirement as to the child's place of residence.[85]

As the range of persons entitled to social advantages has been widened, and as the range of benefits constituting social advantages has also been widened, it is probably inevitable that the Court would be faced with more complex questions relating to the conditions of entitlement to the benefits.[86] In addressing these questions, the Court has drawn on its general approach to questions of indirect

[82] Para 10 of the judgment. [83] Case 186/87 *Cowan v Le Trésor Public* [1989] ECR 195.

[84] Case C-337/97 *Meeusen v Hoofddirectie van de Informatie Beheer Groep* [1999] ECR I-3289.

[85] Para 30 of the judgment.

[86] See Peers, S, ' "Social Advantages" and Discrimination in Employment: Case Law Confirmed and Clarified' (1997) 22 ELRev 157.

discrimination. The *O'Flynn* case[87] concerned an Irish national who had worked for many years in the United Kingdom and had retired there. In 1988 his son died and he arranged for him to be buried in the family grave in Ireland. He claimed a funeral payment, a social security benefit aimed at providing financial assistance in meeting the cost of a burial. This was refused on the grounds that such payments were only available for burials in the United Kingdom. The question was whether this condition was indirectly discriminatory in that there would be a greater likelihood of nationals meeting the condition. The Court concluded that the provisions would run the risk of being discriminatory if they (a) affected essentially migrant workers, or (b) where the great majority of persons affected by the condition were migrant workers, or (c) where they can more easily be satisfied by national workers than migrant workers, or (d) where there is a risk that they may operate to the particular detriment of migrant workers.[88] The discriminatory effect could only be avoided if the requirements 'are justified by objective considerations independent of the nationality of the workers concerned, and if they are proportionate to the legitimate aim pursued by the national law'.[89] The arguments put forward by the United Kingdom Government to justify the requirement were not considered to meet the test of objective justification.

Tax advantages

Article 7(2) also applies to tax advantages, and the notion of objective justification for various national tax rules has featured large in the Court's decision in this area.[90]

The *Bachmann* case[91] concerned a German national who worked in Belgium. He made contributions to a voluntary German pension scheme to which he had belonged prior to moving to work in Belgium. He claimed tax relief in Belgium on the pension contributions, but the Belgian tax authorities disallowed this. The Advocate General concluded that the disallowance was discrimination against migrant workers which was not justified, but the Court disagreed. Though they found that there was discrimination against workers, the Court nevertheless concluded that it was justified 'by the need to preserve the cohesion of the applicable tax system'.[92] Reliance on this justification represents something of an accommodation between the general interests of national taxation systems and the rights of free movers.

[87] Case C-237/94 *O'Flynn v Adjudication Officer* [1996] ECR I-2617.
[88] Para 18 of the judgment. [89] Para 19 of the judgment.
[90] See Wattel, P, 'The EC Court's Attempts to Reconcile the Treaty Freedoms with International Tax Law' (1996) 33 CMLRev 223, and Vanistendael, F, 'The Consequences of *Schumacker* and *Wielockx*: Two Steps forward in the Tax Procession of Echternach' (1996) 33 CMLRev 255.
[91] Case C-204/90 *Bachmann v Belgium* [1992] ECR I-249.
[92] Court's ruling, at 296. It is clear that the word 'cohesion' is a translation error and should read 'coherence'. See also Case C-300/90 *Commission v Belgium* [1992] ECR I-305, decided on the same day as *Bachmann*.

The situation which faced the Court in the *Schumacker* case[93] concerned a claim to personal allowances in Germany by a German tax payer who lived in Belgium. The basis of the national rules was that habitual residents in Germany were granted full allowances, but those who were not so resident did not receive such allowances because it was assumed that they would be subject to a charge to tax elsewhere and would have personal allowances that could be set off against the charge to tax. In fact, almost all of Schumacker's income arose in Germany and he was not subject to tax in Belgium at all. The Court found that there was discriminatory treatment here, which could not be justified on the grounds of the coherence of the tax system. There was no possibility of any reconsideration of Schumacker's tax situation in Belgium since he had no tax liability there. One commentator has described this as 'a narrow exception to the *Bachmann* approach'.[94]

The Court echoed its judgment in the *Schumacker* case in its judgment in the *Wielockx* case.[95] A Belgian national resident in Belgium derived his income from self-employed activities in the Netherlands. He was not allowed to set off his liability for tax in the Netherlands against contributions to a voluntary pension reserve. Dutch residents were able to do so. This was a straightforward case of discrimination since the deduction was available to residents of the Netherlands. Many cases of this type turn on the terms of double taxation agreements, and it has been suggested that the Court misunderstood the agreement in this case.[96]

The *Asscher* case[97] concerned differential rates of tax depending upon the source of the income and liability to pay social insurance contributions in a context where the Court concluded that the tax payer was a self-employed person. The tax rules constituted a form of indirect discrimination which could not be justified. One commentator describes the outcome as 'entirely predictable'[98] while others regard it as providing 'unsatisfactory answers to most of the issue'.[99]

Finally, the *Zurstrassen* case[100] concerned the income tax regime applicable to the Zurstrassen family where both husband and wife were Belgian nationals. Mr Zurstrassen lived and worked in Luxembourg, but his wife and children lived in Belgium. Mrs Zurstrassen did not work. All but two per cent of Mr Zurstrassen's income derive from his employment in Luxembourg. The remaining two per cent derived from his teaching for the Catholic University of Louvain in Belgium. The Luxembourg authorities treated Mr Zurstrassen as a single person, and refused to tax him as a family. He drew comparisons with situations which he argued were comparable in which the approach to taxation of income was more favourable. The

[93] Case C-279/93 *Finanzamt Koln-Alstadt v Schumacker* [1995] ECR I-225.

[94] Williams, D, *EC Tax Law* (London, 1998), at 111.

[95] Case C-80/94 *Wielockx v Inspecteur der Directe Belastingen* [1995] ECR I-2493.

[96] See Williams, D, *EC Tax Law* (London, 1998), at 129, especially n.47.

[97] Case C-107/94 *Asscher v Staatssecretaris van Fiancien* [1996] ECR I-3089, noted at (1997) 344 CMLRev 713.

[98] Stanley, P, 'Note on *Asscher*' (1997) 34 CMLRev 713, at 723.

[99] Williams, D, *EC Tax Law* (London, 1998), at 116.

[100] Case C-87/99 *Zurstrassen* [2000] ECR I-3337.

Court considered that it was dealing with taxation under Article 7(2) of Regulation 1612/68, and that it was a breach of the provisions of that article not to extend to someone in Mr Zurstrassen's circumstances the joint assessment to tax on the grounds that both spouses were not resident in Luxembourg.

Family unity

It would be an obstacle to the free movement of persons if the person entitled to move could not move with his or her family. This has been recognized from the earliest days of the Community and there has always been a right for family members to accompany the employed or self-employed person, even when that person is not a national of one of the Member States.[101]

Title III of Regulation 1612/68 contains important provisions relating to the families of workers. Article 10 permits the following family members to accompany the worker:

(a) any spouse;
(b) descendants under the age of 21;
(c) descendants above that age who are dependent on the worker;
(d) dependent relatives in the ascending line.

Member States must under Article 10(2) facilitate the entry and residence of other relatives of the worker who are dependent upon him or who live in the same household in the country form which the worker comes. In all cases the worker must have housing available for his family members 'considered as normal for national workers in the region'. Article 11 gives the spouse and family members a right to work in the host State even if they are not nationals of a Member State, and Article 12 guarantees access to education for relevant family members living with the worker.

These provisions have spawned case law. The first issue is who constitutes a spouse. In the *Reed* case,[102] both the Advocate General and the Court rejected arguments that unmarried companions should as far as possible be treated as spouses. Though recognizing the changing nature of relationships, the Court felt that legal certainty and the uniform application of Community law required that the term spouse refers only to a marital relationship.[103]

The *Diatta* case[104] had earlier considered the impact of separation on the rights of spouses to reside in a Member State. Aissatou Diatta was the Senegalese wife of a

[101] The provisions of Directive 2004/38/EC which modify the current law on family unity have already been alluded to earlier in this chapter. This section focuses on the current provisions unless otherwise stated.
[102] Case 59/85 *The Netherlands v Reed* [1986] ECR 1283.
[103] Paras 8–16 of the judgment.
[104] Case 267/83 *Diatta v Land Berlin* [1985] ECR 567.

French national. The couple had lived and worked in Germany for a number of years. The couple separated and Diatta moved into different accommodation. The issue arose on her application for renewal of her residence permit whether she retained an entitlement to reside in Germany. The Court concluded that, since the couple was only separated, they remained married and so Diatta remained the spouse of a worker. There was no requirement for a married couple to live together, and until such time as the marriage was ended, there was a possibility that there might be a reconciliation. Consequently, Diatta retained her rights as the non-national spouse of a worker.[105] It would seem to follow that, once divorced, she would not retain those rights. Though it is nowhere explicitly stated, this is confirmed by the *Baumbast and R* case.[106] R was a United States citizen who was divorced from her French husband and was residing in the United Kingdom. The whole discussion of her rights of residence proceeds on the basis that she retained no rights of residence following her divorce.[107]

There are, however, two possible routes through which an unmarried partner and a divorced person may nevertheless have rights of residence. The unmarried partner may be able to argue that his or her residence constitutes a social advantage for the worker.[108] The divorced person may retain rights of residence as the primary carer of children of the family where otherwise, as a consequence of the non-nationals requirement to leave the country, access of the children to both parents would be severely compromised.[109]

A further issue which has arisen is what constitutes dependency. The Court indicated in the *Lebon* case that this was a factual question for the national court.[110] The Court said:

> . . . the status of dependent member of a worker's family . . . is the result of a factual situation, namely the provision of support by the worker, without there being any need to determine the reasons for recourse to the worker's support.[111]

The application of the housing condition in Article 10(3) has generated infringement proceedings.[112] The requirement applies only once, namely at the point at which the worker seeks to bring his family to live with him. It is not open to a

[105] The same would appear to be true where a decree nisi of a divorce exists: Case 370/90 *R v Secretary of State for the Home Department, ex parte Surinder Singh* [1992] ECR I-4265, para 12 of the judgment. Note that this case arose in the context of freedom of establishment rather than the free movement of workers.

[106] Case C-413/99 *Baumbast and R v Secretary of State for the Home Department*, judgment of 17 September 2002, [2002] ECR I-7091.

[107] Paras 64–75 of the judgment. The Advocate General noted that 'Mrs R is no longer a member of the family of a migrant worker and cannot assert a right o residence on that ground' (para 78 of the Opinion).

[108] See below in this chapter.

[109] The outcome for Mrs R in Case C-413/99 *Baumbast and R v Secretary of State for the Home Department* [2002] ECR I-7091.

[110] Case 316/85 *Centre public d'aide sociale de Courcelles v Lebon* [1987] ECR 2811.

[111] Para 24 of the judgment.

[112] Case 249/86 *Commission v Germany* [1989] ECR 1263.

State to refuse the renewal of a residence permit on the grounds that the worker's housing is no longer suitable for his family unless sanctions of a comparable severity were applicable to nationals of the Member State. It is difficult to envisage the circumstances in which this proviso might apply.

The broad scope of Article 11 was raised in the *Gül* case.[113] This case concerned the German rules on registration for medical practice, which only granted permanent rights to non-national spouses of German nationals. The Court of Justice ruled that it was unlawful for the German authorities to refuse permanent registration to Dr Gül, a Cypriot national married to a British citizen working in Germany.

Article 12 is designed to secure the integration of the family into the host State. It has been supplemented by a directive dealing with language tuition in the language, or one of the languages, of the host State.[114] The scope of the rights in Article 12 was clarified in the *Echternach and Moritz* cases.[115] The scope of education is to be construed broadly, and includes all forms of further and higher education.[116] A child of a worker is entitled to remain even after the worker parent has left the country to complete a course on which the child has embarked if the child could not pursue that course in the State of origin. In the *Baumbast and R* case,[117] it was held that the children of the two families had rights of residence in order to complete the education they had begun in the host State. The right remains even after the worker parent has died.[118]

There is also a whole bundle of social rights connected with education which have been read into Article 12.[119] So in the *Echternach and Moritz* cases[120] it was held that the article included a right of access to assistance to cover the costs of a student's education and maintenance on the same conditions as applied to children of nationals of the host State. This extends to financial support to study abroad, even in the State of which the student is a national.[121]

The *Humbel* case[122] illustrates the boundaries both of the requirement of equal treatment and of the benefits in Article 12. Humbel's parents were French, but lived and worked in Luxembourg. They sent their son to school in Belgium. They

113 Case 131/85 *Gül v Regierungspräsident Düsseldorf* [1986] ECR 1573.

114 Council Directive of 25 July 1977 on the education of the children of migrant workers (77/486/EEC), [1977] OJ L199/32.

115 Joined Cases 389 and 390/87 *Echternach and Moritz v Netherlands Minister for Education and Science* [1989[ECR 723.

116 It also includes education to meet special educational needs: Case 76/72 *Michel S* [1973] ECR 437.

117 Case C-413/99 *Baumbast and R v Secretary of State for the Home Department* [2002] ECR I-7091.

118 Case 42/87 *Commission v Belgium* [1988] ECR 5445.

119 Mainly inspired by the requirement of equality in respect of social and tax advantages in Article 7(2) of Regulation 1612/68 which is discussed below. See Case 9/74 *Casagrande v Landeshaupstadt München* [1974] ECR 773.

120 Joined Cases 389 and 390/87 *Echternach and Moritz v Netherlands Minister for Education and Science* [1989] ECR 723.

121 Case C-308/89 *Di Leo v Land Berlin* [1990] ECR I-4185. See also Case 235/87 *Matteucci v Communauté Français de Belgique* [1988] ECR 5589.

122 Case 263/86 *Belgium v Humbel and Edel* [1988] ECR 5365.

were charged an enrolment fee, but the children of nationals of Luxembourg were not required to pay this fee when they enrolled their children in Belgian secondary schools. The Court noted that the education in issue in this case was not vocational training.[123] This left only Article 12 of Regulation 1612/68 to be considered. This did not apply since the obligations it contains only lie on the Member State in which the migrant worker resides.[124]

However, where there is no link to the free movement of persons, entitlement to financial support for education is not a matter within the scope of the EC Treaty.[125]

Using Community law to avoid national immigration controls

As we have seen, Article 10 of Regulation 1612/68 grants the spouse[126] of a worker who is not a national of one of the Member States a right to reside with the worker.[127] The same is undoubtedly true of the spouse of a self-employed person who is not a national of one of the Member States.[128] Such persons are exempt from national immigration controls and have automatic rights of entry and residence on establishing the marriage to the Community national. The *Carpenter* case[129] extends this approach to new limits. Mary Carpenter was a Phillipine national who entered the United Kingdom as a visitor, and overstayed the terms of her leave to enter. She subsequently married a United Kingdom national, and there were no suggestions that the marriage was a sham. Mr Carpenter ran a business selling advertising space in medical and scientific journals, and a significant amount of his business was with advertisers established in other Member States. He travelled to other Member States on an occasional basis for the purpose of his business. He had two children from his first marriage. Mrs Carpenter was required to leave the United Kingdom by the immigration authorities. In the course of proceedings challenging the deportation order, Mary Carpenter claimed to have a right to reside in the United Kingdom under Community law:

She maintained that since her husband's business required him to travel around in other Member States, providing and receiving services, he could do so more easily as she was looking after his children from his

[123] Had it been, then any discrimination on grounds of nationality would be prohibited on the application of what was then Arts 7 and 128 EC: see Case 293/83 *Gravier v City of Liège* [1985] ECR 593.

[124] Case 263/86 *Belgium v Humbel and Edel* [1988] ECR 5365, para 24 of the judgment.

[125] See Case 39/86 *Lair* [1988] ECR 3181; and Case 197/86 *Brown* [1988] ECR 3205.

[126] And other family members.

[127] See generally, Barrett, G, 'Family Matters: European Community Law and Third-Country Family Members' (2003) 40 CMLRev 369.

[128] Article 4(3) of Directive 73/148/EEC. See also Case C-370/90 *ex parte Singh* [1992] ECR I-4265.

[129] Case C-60/00 *Carpenter* [2002] ECR I-6729, noted at (2003) 28 ELRev 398.

first marriage, so that her deportation would restrict her husband's right to provide and receive services.[130]

The Court agreed:

. . . Article 49 EC, read in the light of the fundamental right to respect for family life, is to be interpreted as precluding, . . . , a refusal, by a Member State of origin of a provider of services established in that Member State who provides services to recipients established in other Member States, of the right to reside in its territory to that provider's spouse, who is a national of a third country.[131]

The effects of this decision get very close to a constitutional right to residence of a spouse, of whatever nationality, wherever the national of the Member State can show that he or she is a provider or recipient of services. There is no indication in the case of when or how frequent that contact with a situation contemplated by the EC Treaty must be, or whether it should arise in the course of business as distinct from recreation. However sympathetic one might be for the family circumstances in this case, it is easy to see how this decision is likely to be problematic for national immigration authorities.

The case law shows that it is difficult to use Community law abusively. The Court said in the *Singh* case that:

. . . the facilities created by the Treaty cannot have the effect of allowing persons who benefit from them to evade the application of national legislation and of prohibiting Member States from taking measures to prevent such abuse.[132]

However, in the *Akrich* case[133] it was ruled that national rules designed to combat abuses must not give rise to a limitation of the fundamental freedoms guaranteed by the Treaty and must not prejudice the uniform application of Community law. Where the supposed advantage arises from the exercise of a fundamental right, 'the intentions of the person making use of the EC right may not be enquired into',[134] as long as there is 'a genuine intention of pursuing employment at the time of residence in [another Member State]'.[135] Later in his Opinion, the Advocate General said that 'the dividing line between abuse and use for a purpose not contemplated by the legislature is hard to define.'[136] He concluded that 'in the situation arising in the main proceedings there can be no question of a misuse of Community law.'[137] The Court concluded, after the briefest of reasoning, that use of Community law rights in order to obtain the benefit of the application of those rights could not be tainted by issues of motive.

[130] ibid, para 17 of the judgment. [131] ibid, para 46 of the judgment.

[132] Case C-370/90 *R v Immigration Appeal Tribunal and Surinder Singh, ex parte Secretary of State of the Home Department* [1992] ECR I-4265, para 24 of the judgment.

[133] Case C-109/01 *Secretary of State for the Home Department v Akrich*, judgment of September 23, 2003, [2003] ECR nyr, noted at (2004) 29 ELRev 385.

[134] Para 102 of the Opinion.

[135] ibid.

[136] Para 173 of the Opinion.

[137] Para 184 of the Opinion.

Motive was not relevant to any assessment of their legal rights where the marriage is genuine.[138] However, Article 10 of Regulation 1612/68 did not apply where the parties had entered into a marriage of convenience in order to circumvent the provision relating to entry and residence of nationals of non-Member States.[139]

The facts of the *Akrich* case are dramatic. Hacene Akrich badly wanted to get to the United Kingdom. He was a Moroccan citizen born in 1967. He first came to the United Kingdom in February 1989 on a tourist visa. He overstayed that visa and his application to remain as a student was refused in July 1989. In June 1990 he was convicted for attempted theft and the use of a stolen identity card. His appeal against the immigration decision was dismissed in August 1990. He was deported to Algeria in January 1991. He returned in January 1992 using a false French identity card. He was arrested and again deported in June 1992. Less than a month later he 'clandestinely returned to the United Kingdom'.[140] He continued to reside in the United Kingdom as an illegal immigrant. In June 1996 he married a British national, and applied for leave to remain as the spouse of a British citizen. Akrich was detained under the Immigration Act 1971 in January 1997. His wife moved to Ireland in June 1997 where she obtained full-time work in a bank. Akrich was deported in August 1997 to Dublin at his own request. He found a variety of jobs in Ireland. In January 1998 Akrich applied for revocation of the deportation order and sought entry clearance as the spouse of a person settled in the United Kingdom. There was evidence that work was available in the United Kingdom for Mrs Akrich from August 1998 and that her brother had offered the couple accommodation. In interviews with the immigration authorities, Mr and Mrs Akrich indicated that they were applying for entry clearance in reliance on Community rights.

The Court managed to find a solution to the dilemma which raises as many questions as it answers. The Court's starting point was that a non-national spouse of a national of a Member State must be lawfully resident in a Member State when he or she moves to another Member State to which the Member State national is migrating in order to be able to plead Community law on return to that State.[141] This means that lawful residence of a national of a third country in a Member State is a precondition to the exercise of the generous rights which Community law grants to such persons when they are members of the family of a citizen of the European Union. It would seem that no rights can flow from Regulation 1612/68 unless and until the residence of the third country national in a Member State is lawful. The Court then used the language of fundamental rights to give some crumb of comfort to the national of the non-Member State since the 'competent authorities . . . , in assessing the application by the spouse to enter and remain in that Member State, must none the less have regard to the right to respect for family life under Article 8 of the Convention, provided that the marriage is genuine.'[142]

[138] Presumably determined by the application of national rules.
[139] Para 57 of the judgment.
[140] Advocate General's Opinion, para 31.
[141] Para 50 of the judgment.
[142] Para 61 of the judgment.

This reference to the right to family life in the European Convention on Human Rights is significant. It represents a further endorsement of respect for the values and principles set out in the European Convention in the application and implementation of Community law. The Court was at pains to draw attention to the limits imposed by the requirement that any interference with family life must be 'necessary in a democratic society' even in the context of those who have committed criminal offences.[143] This necessarily circumscribes the freedom of a Member State to use its immigration law without having regard to questions of fundamental rights both of the third country national and of the citizen of the European Union. An individual assessment made under national law must not only have regard to fundamental rights but also to Community law as a whole.

A right to reasoned decisions

We have already seen in chapter 5 that Directive 64/221 includes important procedural guarantees where decisions are taken on the grounds of public policy, public security and public health which are adverse to a free mover. However, a more general right to reasoned decision which flows from the case law of the Court of Justice is sometimes overlooked. The *Heylens* case[144] introduced as a general principle a requirement of due process in decisions taken concerning entry and residence and other matters affecting the enjoyment of rights under the Treaty provisions on the free movement of persons. Heylens was a Belgian national who was employed as a professional football trainer. He was prosecuted in France for engaging in the activity without being the holder of the diploma recognized by French law or any qualification regarded as its equivalent. Heylens had applied for recognition of his Belgian diploma, but this was refused without any reasons being given. A reference was made to the Luxembourg Court which ruled that the free movement of workers required that a decision refusing to recognize qualifications issued in another Member State must be accompanied by reasons and must be subject to judicial review in order that the legality of the decision under Community law can be measured.[145]

Concluding remarks

This chapter has outlined the significant bundle of rights which Community law affords to free movers, most of which are designed to facilitate the integration of the

[143] The Court cites two judgments of the Court of Human Rights: *Boultif v Switzerland*, (App 54273/00), (2001) 33 EHRR 1179, and *Amrollahi v Denmark* (App 56811/00), judgment of 11 July 2002.

[144] Case 222/86 *UNECTEF v Heylens* [1987] ECR 4097.

[145] See also Case 340/89 *Vlassopoulou v Ministerium für Justiz* [1991] ECR 2357 and Case C-234/97 *Fernández de Bobadilla v Museo Nacional del Prado* [1999] ECR I-4773, both discussed in ch 4 above.

migrant into the population of the host Member State. By far the most important are rights of entry and residence, since once these are established, it is now clear that a Member State will bear a heavy burden of proof if it proposes to treat the migrant in any manner differently from the way it treats its own nationals. Indeed, it could be argued that the recent case law on equal treatment of those Union citizens lawfully resident in a Member State other than that of their own nationality makes much of the secondary legislation discussed in this chapter otiose. After all, the Court has managed to reach much the same conclusions in favour of self-employed persons (in respect of whom there is no regulation) as arise for workers under Regulation 1612/68. It has even made some inroads into national decision-making in the sacred area of direct taxation.

9

Social security and pensions

Introduction

Two principal features of social security systems would constitute obstacles to the free movement of person if Community law did not require the co-ordination of social security systems. These are nationality and residence requirements, and the territorial nature of many aspects of social security entitlement.

Nationality and residence requirements are common features of conditions of entitlement to State social security benefits. In order to meet the conditions of entitlement, the claimant must be a national of the State in question and be resident there. Examples of obstacles arising from the territoriality of social security can be even more striking. The benefit may only be payable within the territory of the State in question, and the rules surrounding entitlement to it may also be tied to a particular territory. So, entitlement to a long-term benefit may require the claimant to have been resident and insured under the law of the awarding State for a lengthy period. Someone who has been insured under the social security systems of two or more States may either receive no entitlement in either country or the total entitlements may be less than if that person had remained in a single State.

The territoriality principle, under which a State is responsible for social protection within its own territory and for its own nationals, has produced rules which present serious obstacles to obtaining entitlement if a person has lived and worked in more than one country. Examples of the application of the territorial principle are as follows. The State may require that the risk against which the person is insured or otherwise protected must arise in the territory of the State awarding the benefit. A State may require a continuous and lengthy period of insurance and residence as conditions of entitlement. Finally, once entitlement has been established to a long-term benefit, it might be lost if the person leaves the territory of the awarding State. These unilateral rules can produce startling results. Suppose that one country requires all those resident in its territory to pay social security contributions, while a neighbouring State makes the requirement to contribute conditional upon working there. In these circumstances, a person living in the first State but working in the second would be required to pay two sets of social security contributions. By contrast, a person living in the second State but working in the first would not be required to pay social security contributions at all. This might seem a considerable benefit to such a person, but it would not seem so if that person needed to fall back on the protection of social security benefits.

Another dramatic illustration relates to contributions towards a retirement pension. United Kingdom rules are based on paying contributions throughout a working life, roughly 40 years, and there is no entitlement unless a person has contributed for 10 years. Suppose that a person worked for eight years in each of five different countries, all of which had the same rules as the United Kingdom. That person would have no entitlement to a retirement pension despite having contributed throughout a working life, unless there was some system under which the contributions paid in the five different countries could be aggregated.[1]

Recognition of the problems which arise where workers pay contributions in more than one country is not something first identified by the European Community. Co-ordination provisions were a feature of many bilateral trade treaties in order to protect those moving under the treaties. These often operated on the basis of reciprocity. The International Labour Organisation has also concerned itself with the issue, but multilateral treaties seeking to co-ordinate social security arrangements often suffer two problems: if they are sufficiently general to attract a significant number of ratifications, they do not address real issues faced by claimants. On the other hand, if they are too detailed, they do not attract sufficient ratifications to become of widespread application.[2] The Council of Europe has also adopted treaties on social security, particularly in its early days, though these have had a disappointing impact.[3]

This chapter shows how the Community has responded to the obstacles to free movement of persons that would exist if it did not concern itself with social security entitlements. It also looks at the harmonizing work of the Community in the field of equal treatment in social security entitlements, and briefly touches on the broader issue of how Community law has involved itself in the question of pension entitlements.

Co-ordination and harmonization

In order to understand the Community approach to social security, it is necessary to appreciate the difference between co-ordination and harmonization. Social security, like taxation, is a matter dear to the hearts of the Member States, and there remain very significant differences both in the approach to social security and in the

[1] As we shall see, rules of aggregation are central to systems of co-ordination precisely to avoid this type of situation arising.

[2] For an overview of ILO work on social security, see *Facts on Social Security* available on the ILO website www.ilo.org.

[3] For a brief account, see Pennings, F, *Introduction to European Social Security*, 4th edn (Antwerp, 2003), at 14–16.

level of benefits paid across the Member States. Any legislative measures in the field of social security currently require unanimity among the Member States.[4]

The concept of co-ordination which lies at the heart of the Community rules is not defined in Community legislation and has never been defined in abstract terms by the Court of Justice. Co-ordination is the process by which differences in the various national social security systems are accommodated. Adjustments are made so that the systems can work together, rather than with the objective of making them more similar. It is a process which regulates transnational questions which arise when a person become subject to more than one social security system. It is sometimes said that co-ordination requires bridges to be built between differing sets of rules so that they can work together. On the other hand, harmonization is a process by which different systems are brought more into line by requiring each to adapt their rules so that they adopt the same approach. Harmonization requires change, while co-ordination merely requires accommodation of differences. This distinction has frequently been emphasized by the Court of Justice. For example, in the *Pinna* case the Court said:

> . . . Article 51 of the Treaty provides for the co-ordination, not the harmonization, of the legislation of the Member States. As a result, Article 51 leaves in being differences between the Member States' social security systems and, consequently, in the rights of persons working in the Member States. It follows that substantive and procedural differences between the social security systems of individual Member States, and hence in the rights of persons working in the Member States, are unaffected by Article 51 of the Treaty.[5]

Although the Court of Justice has consistently recognized that the requirements of Community law in this field do not amount to a requirement for harmonization, it has indicated that there are limits to the freedom of action of the participating countries as a result of the link with the free movement of workers. So, in the *Kalsbeek* case, the Court of Justice said:

> Article 51 . . . cannot allow [national] regulations to fall short of the objectives which it sets, which are intended to favour freedom of movement for workers and which would be incompatible with any reduction in their rights.[6]

The requirement that workers should not lose advantages in the field of social security has come to be known as 'the Petroni principle' following its elaboration in the *Petroni* case, where the Court said:

> The aim of Articles 48 to 51 would not be attained if, as a consequence of the exercise of their right to freedom of movement, workers were to lose advantages in the field of social security guaranteed to them in any event by the laws of a single Member State.[7]

[4] See Arts 42 and 137 EC.

[5] Case 41/84 *Pinna v Caisse d'allocation familiales de la Savoie* [1986] ECR 1, at 24–5.

[6] Case 100/62 *Kalsbeek (née van der Veen) v Bestuur der Sociale Verzekeringsbank and nine other cases* [1964] ECR 565, at 574.

[7] Case 24/75 *Petroni v Office National des Pension pur Travailleurs Salariés (ONPTS)* [1975] ECR 1149, para 13 of the judgment.

Co-ordination of social security systems must address four issues:

1. the allocation of the rules of a national social security system to particular individuals and circumstances;
2. a prohibition on unequal treatment on grounds of nationality;
3. the consequences of loss of continuity of membership of a single State's social security system; and
4. the consequences of the application of the territorial principle on the acquisition of benefits and entitlement to payment of those benefits.

The Community's co-ordinating regulations address these issues by adopting a system under which one country only is regarded as the competent State for dealing with any claim to a social security benefit within the scope of the regulations; by prohibiting discrimination on grounds of nationality; by treating periods of insurance or residence in another country as constituting periods of insurance or residence for entitlement to the benefit in the competent State; and by permitting certain benefits which have been acquired in one participating country to be exported to another participating country.

First steps and many developments

Article 51 EEC recognized the need to co-ordinate social security systems and provided:

The Council shall, acting unanimously on a proposal from the Commission, adopt such measures in the field of social security as are necessary to provide freedom of movement for workers; to this end, it shall make arrangements to secure for migrant workers and their dependants:

(a) aggregation, for the purpose of acquiring and retaining the right to benefit, of all periods taken into account under the laws of the several countries;
(b) payment of benefits to persons resident in the territories of Member States.

The current version of the provision is to be found in Article 42 EC and provides:

The Council shall, acting in accordance with the procedure referred to in Article 251, adopt such measures in the field of social security as are necessary to provide freedom of movement for workers; to this end, it shall make arrangements to secure for migrant workers and their dependants:

(a) aggregation, for the purpose of acquiring and retaining the right to benefit and of calculating the amount of benefit, of all periods taken into account under the laws of the several countries;
(b) payment of benefits to persons resident in the territories of Member States.

The Council shall act unanimously throughout the procedure referred to in Article 251.

So very little has changed in the basic requirements of the article since its introduction in the Treaty of Rome, though the expansion of the coverage of the regulations made under Article 51 has required the Community to use the reserve power in Article 235 (now 308) EC as the legal base of, for example, the extension of the regulations to cover self-employed people.[8]

The third and fourth regulations made by the European Economic Community sought to co-ordinate the social security systems of the original six Member States.[9] This reflects not only the importance of the subject for the free movement of workers, but also that the text of the Convention on social security for migrant workers had, at the time, recently been prepared in connection with Article 69(4) ECSC.[10] Regulation 3 was superseded by Regulation 1408/71, while Regulation 4 was replaced by Regulation 574/72;[11] both have subsequently been amended a number of times.[12] The origins of these two regulations lay in the removal of obstacles to the free movement of workers as required by Article 51 of the Treaty of Rome. But the personal scope of the regulations has been widened by successive developments and amendments such that the two superseding regulations are now much more of a code for the co-ordination of social security rules in their field of application for a much broader group of people. Nationals of Iceland, Liechtenstein and Norway are covered under arrangements made by the EEA Treaty, and nationals of Switzerland are covered as the result of an agreement which entered into force on 1 June 2002.[13] In addition to this broadening of the nationality base of the regulations,[14] they have also been widened to include more than workers. They now cover employed persons, self-employed persons, family members of these persons, their survivors, students, and civil servants. In essence, all persons who are, or have been, insured under the social security systems of one of the participating countries[15] are almost certainly within the personal scope of the regulations. Furthermore, from 1 June 2003, Regulation 859/2003/EC[16] extends the application of the co-ordinating rules to:

> nationals of third countries who are not already covered by those provisions solely on the ground of their nationality, as well as to members of their families and their survivors, provided they are legally resident in the territory of a Member State and are in a situation which is not confined in all respect within a single Member State.[17]

[8] See Regulation 1390/81/EEC, [1981] OJ L143/1.

[9] Regulation 3/58/EEC, [1958] JO 561, and its accompanying implementation Regulation 4/58/EEC, [1958] JO 597.

[10] See Pennings, F, *Introduction to European Social Security*, 4th edn (Antwerp, 2003), at 21, n17.

[11] A consolidated text of both regulations was issued in Regulation 118/97/EC, [1997] OJ L28.

[12] By Reg 1290/97/EC, [1997] OJ L176/1; Reg 1223/98/EC, [1998] OJ L168/1; Reg 1606/98/EC, [1998] OJ L209/1; Reg 307/99/EC, [1999] OJ L307/99; Reg 1399/99/EC, [1999] OJ L164/1; Reg 89/2001/EC, [2001] OJ L14/16; Reg 1386/2001/EC, [2001] OJ L187/1; and Reg 410/2002/EC, [2002] OJ L62/17.

[13] Agreement between the European Community and its Member States, of the one part, and the Swiss Confederation of the other, on the free movement of persons, [2002] OJ L114/6.

[14] The regulations also cover stateless persons and refugees.

[15] Throughout this chapter, the term 'participating country' is used to refer to the Member States, Iceland, Liechtenstein, Norway and Switzerland.

[16] [2003] OJ L124/1.

[17] Article 1. The requirement that the situation is not confined within a single Member State means that the third country national must have been insured in at least two participating countries for the regulation to assist them.

However, despite these developments, the regulations are not a comprehensive code of co-ordination of social security benefits among the participating countries.[18] The regulations only cover those benefits within the material scope of the regulations, though they do cover benefits in kind, as well as cash benefits.[19] A key distinction drawn in the regulations is between social security and social assistance. The former is included, but the latter is not. Determining what constitutes social security and what constitutes social assistance has not been easy. The term 'social security' as a conceptual label appears to have been used first in the United States when Congress passed the Federal Social Security Act 1935.[20] It signalled a broadening of nineteenth-century social insurance schemes, which provided only for insured persons, to include the provision of social protection for all who were in need of assistance howsoever arising. Insurance based schemes were generally concerned with the social risks of those in work: that they might become sick and unable to work, that they might lose their employment for some other reason which was not their fault, or that they might be injured at work. Other aspects of social insurance were related to incidents of life which were much more likely to occur: the birth of children, retirement, and the needs of dependants on the death of the bread-winner.

The distinction between social insurance and social assistance used to be more clear cut than it is today. Those exposed to the sorts of social risks set out above would insure against them—in the United Kingdom notionally through the payment of national insurance contributions—and on the occurrence of the risk would have an entitlement to a benefit without the application of any means test. By contrast, social assistance looked to need, and would be more likely to be discretionary requiring a decision of some authority on the suitability of the applicant for support. The distinction became blurred as entitlement to social assistance has tended to become a matter of right rather than discretion, and as the burden of funding social insurance has resulted in moves to require a test of means even for some insurance-based benefits. A third type of benefit has also achieved some prominence. This is the benefit which displays aspects of both social insurance and social assistance. The face of social insurance is presented by the recognition of a social risk (for example, suffering an injury or illness which results in permanent disability), and the benefit might be paid as of right to those meeting tightly defined conditions of entitlement without any means test. On the other hand the benefit is not dependent on the payment of contributions, and for many recipients, the benefit represents their means of subsistence.

[18] For a more detailed treatment of Regulation 1408/71, see Pennings, F, *Introduction to European Social Security Law*, 4th edn (Antwerp, 2003); White, R, *EC Social Security Law* (Harlow, 1999); and van der Mei, A, *Free Movement of Persons within the European Community. Cross-Border Access to Public Benefits* (Oxford, 2003).

[19] This has raised problems in the context of health care benefits.

[20] See generally Watson, P, *Social Security Law of the European Communities* (London, 1980), ch 1.

Two other types of benefit should be identified. The first are universal benefits, which are paid to all regardless of the payment of contributions and in circumstances where the social risk is common. Child benefits, paid to all families regardless of means, fall into this category. The second are what have been termed social compensation schemes. In the United Kingdom vaccination damage payments would fall within this category. The common feature of such schemes is government funding of compensation for victims of certain misfortunes for which the State collectively feels the need to take responsibility. There is often a link between a sense of responsibility on the part of the government for not avoiding the risk and the creation of the benefit.

The predominant model of benefits which can be found in European social security regulation is that of social insurance, and in many cases it will be vital to determine whether the benefit in issue constitutes social insurance, social assistance or a mixed benefit. In its purest form social assistance is not covered by Community social security legislation, but the Court of Justice has taken a generous view of the classification of benefits which Member States have sought to categorize as social assistance where the benefit serves a dual purpose. It is therefore fair to say that European social security law regulates all three types of benefit.

We will now consider which benefits are covered in more detail before examining the obligations which arise for participating countries under the co-ordination regulations.

Which benefits are covered

Article 4 of Regulation 1408/71 provides that the regulation applies to all legislation concerning the specified branches of social security. The term 'legislation' is defined in very broad terms in Article 1(j)[21] to mean 'statutes, regulations and other provisions and all other implementing measures, present or future' relating to the specified branches of social security. The eight specified branches of social security are:

- sickness and maternity benefits;
- invalidity benefits, including those intended for the maintenance or improvement of earning capacity;
- old-age benefits;
- survivors' benefits;
- benefits in respect of accidents at work and occupational diseases;
- death grants;
- unemployment benefits; and
- family benefits.

[21] Described by the Court as 'remarkable for its breadth' in Case 87/76 *Bozzone v Office de Sécurité Sociale d'Outre-Mer* [1977] ECR 687, para 10 of the judgment.

This list is exhaustive, and a benefit which is not connected with one of the risks set out above will not be within the material scope of the regulation.[22] Some guidance is provided as to whether a particular benefit in a particular State is covered by the declarations which participating countries are required to make under Article 5 specifying the legislation and schemes referred to in a number of articles of the regulation. Such declarations are, however, only indicative of coverage and are not legislative in character;[23] they are not always kept completely up to date.

The Court has said that the distinction between benefits which are excluded from the material scope of the regulation and those which come within it 'rests entirely on the factors relating to each benefit, in particular its purpose and the conditions for its grant'.[24]

Article 4(4) excludes social and medical assistance, and benefit schemes for victims of war or its consequences.[25] All general and special social security schemes are included, whether contributory or non-contributory. Special non-contributory benefits (other than in the excluded areas) are included where they are intended to provide supplementary, substitute or ancillary cover against the risks covered by the specified branches of social security, or where they are provided solely as provision for disabled people. It follows that the range of benefits covered is wide. The important distinction between social security schemes and social and medical assistance is not elaborated in the regulation and identifying the dividing line between the two has been left to the Court of Justice. The Court has said that social security legislation covering one of the specified risks:

> which confers on the beneficiaries a legally defined position which involves no individual or discretionary assessment of need or personal circumstances comes in principle within the field of social security within the meaning of Article 51 of the Treaty and of Regulations Nos 3 and 1408/71.[26]

This approach was followed in the *Hoeckx* case[27] which concerned a claim to the *minimex* in Belgium. This was a benefit which provided assistance to those without means irrespective of periods of work, or contributions or affiliation to any social security body. Need was the essential criterion for entitlement. The Court

[22] Case C-249/83 *Hoeckx v Openbaar Centrum voor Maatschappelijk Welzijn, Kalmthout* [1985] ECR 973, para 12 of judgment.

[23] Case 100/63 *Kalsbeek (née van der Veen) v Bestuur der Sociale Verzekeringsbank and nine other cases* [1964] ECR 565, 573. See also Case 70/80 *Vigier v Bundesversicherungsanstalt für Angestellte* [1981] ECR 229, para 15 of the judgment; Case 251/89 *Athanasopoulos and others v Bundesanstalt für Arbeit* [1991] ECR I-2797, para 28 of the judgment; and Joined Cases 102/95 and 103/95 *Martínez Losada and others v Instituto Nacional de Empleo and Instituto Nacional de le Seguiridad Social* [1997] ECR I-869, para 21 of the judgment.

[24] Case 9/78 *Directeur Régional de la Sécurité Sociale de Nancy v Gillard and Caisse Régionale d'Assurance Maladie du Nord-Est, Nancy* [1978] ECR 1661, para 12 of the judgment.

[25] See Case 9/78 *Directeur Régional de la Sécurité Sociale de Nancy v Gillard and Caisse Régionale d'Assurance Maladie du Nord-Est, Nancy* [1978] ECR 1661.

[26] Case 79/76 *Fossi v Bundesknappschaft* [1977] ECR 667, para 6 of the judgment.

[27] Case C-249/83 *Hoeckx v Openbaar Centrum voor Maatschappelijk Welzijn, Kalmthout* [1985] ECR 973.

concluded that the *minimex* was a 'general social benefit' and could not be considered one of the branches of social security listed in Regulation 4.[28]

The narrow dividing line between social security and social assistance can be discerned from the *Piscitello* case.[29] Paola Piscitello was in receipt of a *pensione sociale* in Italy which was terminated when she moved to Belgium. The benefit was paid by reference to lack of means and did not prescribe any requirements as to periods of employment, affiliation or insurance. But the Court noted that no provision was made for individual assessment (a feature of social assistance) and that the legislation conferred a legally defined status on recipients entitling them to a benefit analogous to an old-age benefit. The *pensione sociale* was accordingly a benefit within the scope of Article 4(1), and was not excluded by Article 4(4). The Court did concede that the legislation fulfilled a dual purpose of providing assistance to those entirely outside the social security system and of providing a social security top-up benefit.[30] However, it seems that the presence of an objectively constructed means test will not equate with the concept of individual assessment.[31]

The starting point for any enquiry concerning the applicability of the rules in Regulation 1408/71 to a particular benefit is to consider the benefit's link to one of the risks specified in Article 4(1) having regard to its purpose and the conditions for its grant. In its early case law, the Court appeared to require that the benefit was granted on the occurrence of one of the risks set out in Article 4(1),[32] but the Court has developed that position such that the benefit need now only have a link with one of the risks set out in Article 4(1).[33] The conditions of grant of the benefit must result in the conferring of a legally defined position on the beneficiary.

Two examples from the case law of the Court will illustrate the application of this approach.

The *Heinze* case[34] concerned a benefit paid 'to encourage and ensure the recovery of invalids'; in particular, it concerned payment of a benefit in connection with the prevention of the spread of tuberculosis. The Court took the view that there was a sufficient link to sickness benefits for the regulation to apply. The prophylactic and preventive nature of the measures did not preclude this.[35]

The *Campana* case[36] concerned an Italian national who had worked in Germany and who had applied to the German authorities for vocational training assistance

[28] See generally, Watson, P, 'Minimum income benefits: social security and social assistance' (1985) 10 EL Rev 335.

[29] Case 139/82 *Piscitello v Istituto Nationale della Previdenza Sociale (INPS)* [1983] ECR 1427.

[30] ibid, paras 11–13.

[31] See Case C-78/91 *Hughes v Chief Adjudication Officer, Belfast* [1992] ECR I-4839.

[32] Case 33/65, *Dekker v Bundesversicherungsanstalt für Angestellte* [1965] ECR 901, 905.

[33] Case C-249/83 *Hoeckx v Openbaar Centrum voor Maatschappelijk Welzijn, Kalmthout* [1985] ECR 973.

[34] Case 14/72 *Heinze v Landesversicherungsanstalt Rheinprovinz* [1972] ECR 1105.

[35] See also Case 15/72 *Land Niedersachsen v Landesversicherungsanstalt* [1972] ECR 1127, and Case 16/72 *Allgemeine Ostkrankenkasse Hamburg v Landesversicherunsanstalt Schleswig-Holstein* [1972] ECR 1141. See also Case 818/79 *Allgemeine Ostkrankenkasse Mittelfranken v Landeseversicherungsanstalt Ober- und Mittelfranken* [1980] ECR 2729.

[36] Case 375/85 *Campana v Bundesanstalt für Arbeit* [1987] ECR 2387.

after a period working in Italy. The question arose as to whether vocational training assistance constituted an unemployment benefit within Article 4(1)(g). The Court had regard to the fundamental aim of Article 51 EC in concluding:

> . . . in the light of the present economic situation the Member States have established assistance for vocational training intended both to enable persons in employment to improve their qualifications to avoid the threat of unemployment and to enable unemployed persons to retrain and find new employment. Both types of benefit are intended to combat unemployment.[37]

However, the Court went on to note that the assistance could have other purposes, such as improving the personal circumstances of recipients or satisfying certain special need of the economy. Therefore, Article 4(1)(g) should be restricted to assistance for vocational training which concerned persons already unemployed or persons still in employment but threatened by unemployment.[38] It is for the national authorities to assess in each case whether this is so.

Though the Court has been creative in its interpretation of those benefits which fall within the material scope of Article 4, some of the benefits which flow from that classification have been removed by legislative developments. There are also limits to the extent to which an approach which seeks to link a benefit to one of the risks referred to in Article 4(1) can accommodate all new benefits introduced in the Member States. There may therefore be a need for amendment to the regulation to include new types of benefit.

One type of benefit which has already proved to be problematic is the early retirement benefit. Where the State accommodates early retirement arrangements by lowering the age of retirement for certain categories of persons, that would present no difficulties in terms of consideration of the benefit as one linked to old-age benefits. However, many States accommodate early retirement by adjustments to the conditions of entitlement to unemployment benefits. Typically, the requirement (which might be seen as the essential link for the risk of unemployment) to be available for work is waived. If this is so, is the benefit still one linked to unemployment? And should the territorial limits characteristic of unemployment insurance still apply?

In *Valentini v ASSEDIC*[39] the Court had to consider the effect of an early retirement scheme on the rules concerning the overlapping of benefits. The Court said that the essential characteristic of old-age benefits was that they are intended to safeguard the means of subsistence of person who, when they reach a certain age, leave their employment and are no longer required to be available for work. By contrast guaranteed income schemes for those who retire early, though similar to old-age benefits, differ both in the methods for funding them and in their policy objectives, which are frequently to release posts held by workers near retirement age for the benefit of younger unemployed persons as a response to the level of

[37] ibid, para 9 of the judgment. [38] ibid, para 12 of the judgment.
[39] Case 171/82 *Valentini v ASSEDIC, Lyon* [1983] ECR 2157.

unemployment in Member States. The early retirement scheme in question was not an old-age benefit.

Similar issues arose in an enforcement action against the Netherlands.[40] The Commission took enforcement action against the Netherlands because it considered that there was a breach of the EEC Treaty and Regulation 1408/71 occasioned by the refusal of the Netherlands to pay family allowances to employed persons who had retired early and were resident outside the Netherlands. Such residents, if they were recipients of an old-age pension or were employed or unemployed persons, would receive family allowances. The Dutch authorities took the view that those who had taken early retirement did not come within any of these groups. The Court concluded that, even though those who had taken early retirement remained insured under the Dutch social security scheme, they were not 'employed persons' for the purpose of Article 73 of Regulation 1408/71 which gave employed persons the right to receive family allowances in the Member State in which they resided just as if they were residing in the Netherlands. An alternative argument that the Dutch rules constituted indirect discrimination could not be pursued since the Commission had not included this ground of objection in its reasoned opinion under Article 169.

Adaptation allowances granted to certain employees in declining industries have also caused difficulties. In Germany certain employees in the coal-mining industry who had been laid off between particular dates following closure or rationalization of the mines for reasons not attributable to them who were within five years of entitlement to a retirement pension were entitled to an adaptation allowance. A question arose as to whether an invalidity benefit awarded in the Netherlands should be taken into account in determining entitlement to the adaptation allowance. But the Court of Justice ruled that there were insufficient links to the risks listed in Article 4 of Regulation 1408/71 for the adaptation allowance to be regarded as a social security benefit within the scope of the regulation.[41]

Benefits for disabled people have also caused difficulties. Provision of social security specifically for people with disabilities is often by means of special non-contributory benefits. Where these exhibit characteristics of protection against one of the risks set out in Article 4(1), they are included. The *Costa* case[42] concerned 'an allowance for the handicapped' under Belgian law claimed by an Italian national married to a Belgian national. The Court noted the mixed nature of the benefit, but went on to conclude that for those within the personal scope of the regulation, the benefit was a social security benefit within Regulation 3 because of its link to invalidity.[43] A similar approach was adopted in the *Inzirillo* case,[44] where an Italian national living and working in France claimed an 'allowance for handicapped

[40] Case 198/90 *Commission v the Netherlands* [1991] ECR I-5799.

[41] Case C-25/95 *Otte v Bundesrepublik Deutschland* [1996] ECR I-3745.

[42] Case 39/74 *Costa, spouse Mazzier v Belgium* [1974] ECR 1251.

[43] ibid, para 11 of the judgment.

[44] Case 63/76 *Inzirillo v Caisse d'Allocations Familiales de l'Arrondissement de Lyon* [1976] ECR 2057.

adults' on behalf of his son who had been born in September 1948. The first issue was whether the benefit fell within Regulation 1408/71, and the second whether this could be of assistance to an adult family member who had never worked. The Court's decision combined two provisions in concluding that the benefit was within the scope of the regulation and that there was no bar to entitlement to the benefit because the son had never worked. The Court first restated what it had said in the *Costa* case on the nature of the benefit, then went on to state that the equality of treatment provisions of the regulation mean that the benefit could not terminate when the son ceased to be a minor 'if the child by reason of his handicap is prevented from himself acquiring the status of employed person within the meaning of the regulation'.[45] Finally, the Court referred to the obligation to extend all social and tax advantages to workers under Article 7(2) of Regulation 1612/68/EEC as relevant to the son's entitlement to the benefit.[46]

The dual nature of certain benefits, however, came to be recognized by the Court of Justice such that it was able to refer back to its decision in the *Giletti* case[47] and say in the *Newton* case:

> The Court has held on several occasions that, whilst it may seem desirable from the point of view of applying Community regulations on social security to establish a clear distinction between legislation schemes that fall respectively within social security and assistance, the possibility cannot be excluded that by reason of the persons covered, its objectives and its methods of application, national legislation may, at one and the same time, have links to both those categories.[48]

Newton, a United Kingdom national, was working as a self-employed person in France when he was involved in a serious road traffic accident, which left him paralysed. He returned to the United Kingdom where he claimed and was awarded mobility allowance, a flat-rate, weekly, non-means-tested cash benefit.[49] He subsequently returned to France, but after 26 weeks' absence the mobility allowance was terminated in accordance with the United Kingdom legislation. One issue was whether a mobility allowance was a benefit linked to invalidity within Article 4(1). The Court concluded that, in the circumstances of this case, it was.

Such a broad interpretation of the material scope of Regulation 1408/71 led to a 1992 legislative amendment to the regulation which deals specifically with special non-contributory benefits by the addition to Article 4 of paragraphs 2a and 2b.[50] Article 4(2a) confirms that such benefits are subject to the co-ordinating rules in Regulation 1408/71, but are nevertheless payable only on the territory of the

45 ibid, para 16 of the judgment. 46 On Art 7(2), see below.

47 Joined Cases 379-381/85 and 93/86 *Caisse Régionale d'Assurance Maladie de Rhône-Alpes v Giletti and others* [1987] ECR 955, para 9 of the judgment; see also Case 1/72 *Frilli v Belgium* [1972] ECR 457, para 13 of the judgment; Case 187/73 *Callemeyn v Belgium* [1974] ECR 553, para 6 of the judgment; and Case 24/74 *Caisse Régionale d'Assurance Maladie de Paris v Biason* [1974] ECR 999, para 9 of the judgment.

48 Case C-356/89 *Newton v Chief Adjudication Officer* [1991] ECR I-3017, para 12 of the judgment.

49 Replaced in 1992 with the mobility components of a disability living allowance.

50 Regulation 1247/92/EC, [1992] OJ L136/1.

Member State granting them.[51] In other words territoriality in the payment of the benefit is resurrected. This does not entirely exclude the international effect of these benefits since the rules relating to the acquisition of entitlement to the benefits are subject to the co-ordinating rules in the regulation.

Problems do, however, remain, as is indicated by the *Snares* case,[52] which concerned disability living allowance, a United Kingdom non-contributory cash-based weekly benefit payable at various rates to those with disabilities which result in their having defined care and mobility needs. The new benefit was introduced in April 1992 to replace mobility allowance, and, for those over 65, attendance allowance. Kelvin Snares had worked for many years in the United Kingdom as an employee, when he suffered an accident which resulted in a serious impairment of his mobility. He was awarded the middle rate of the care component and the higher rate of the mobility component of a disability living allowance for life. He also received the contributory benefit known as invalidity benefit, which from April 1995 became incapacity benefit. Mr Snares decided to move to Tenerife on a permanent basis, and he so advised the social security authorities. The result was that his entitlement to a disability living allowance was terminated with effect from the date of his departure from Great Britain. The claimant sought to argue that because the United Kingdom had not updated its Article 5 declaration in order to specify a disability living allowance as a special non-contributory benefit falling within Article 4(2a), it could not rely on the rules restricting its exportability, notwithstanding its inclusion in the United Kingdom declaration in Annex IIa. The Court did not accept that argument, referring to its earlier case law on the effect of Article 5 declarations.

However, the mere fact that a benefit is listed in Annex IIa is not sufficient to render the benefit payable only on the territory of the paying State under Article 10a; in each case the constituent elements of the benefit[53] must be examined. This is because the provisions limiting the exportability of benefits in Article 10a of the regulation are derogations from the general rule of exportability and so must be construed strictly.[54] In the *Jauch* case, the Court ruled that an Austrian care insurance benefit was not of a special nature despite its being included in the benefits listed in Annex IIa, while in the case of *Leclere and Deaconescu* the Court ruled that a Luxembourg maternity allowance was similarly not a special non-contributory benefit. Analysis of these two judgments together with deliberations of the Administrative Commission[55] suggests that the following factors will be relevant to the determination of whether a benefit is recognized by the Court as being a special non-contributory benefit. First, the prime objective of the benefit

[51] See art 10a of Reg 1408/71.

[52] Case C-20/96 *Snares v The Adjudication Officer* [1997] ECR I-895. See similarly in relation to attendance allowance Case C-297/96 *Partridge v The Adjudication Officer* [1998] ECR I-3477.

[53] Its special nature and its non-contributory nature.

[54] See decisions of the Court in Case C-215/99 *Jauch* [2001] ECR I-1901, and Case C-43/99 *Leclere and Deaconescu* [2001] ECR I-4265.

[55] See [2001] OJ C44/13, which predates the decisions of the Court in the cases of *Jauch* and *Leclere and Deaconescu*.

must be to respond to the financial need of a person in order to ensure that they have a minimum level of income. Where the benefit is for disabled people, it must be concerned primarily with meeting their need for support to enable their social integration. The benefit must also be genuinely non-contributory benefit, that is, funded out of general taxation. Finally, the benefit must not be one which can be regarded as a modern form of conventional social security benefits.

The obligations to co-ordinate

Allocating jurisdiction to a single State

The benefits of having a system of co-ordination would be seriously diminished if there were no rules for determining which social security system applied to any given claim. Thus, the potential conflict between residence-based systems and activity-based systems could lead to both States claiming insurance contributions. This would be a very real possibility since the Netherlands has a residence-based system whereas its neighbour, Belgium, has an activity-based system; many workers live in one of these countries and work in the other. This and other potential problems are resolved through the rules in Regulation 1408/71 on the determination of the applicable legislation. In the traditional language of the conflict of laws, the rules in Title II of Regulation 1408/71 determine both which country has jurisdiction in any given claim and which law is applied. In virtually every case, the country with jurisdiction will be applying its own social security rules subject to the requirements of the regulation. Article 13 of the regulation could hardly be clearer in providing that 'persons to whom this regulation applies shall be subject to the legislation of a single Member State only.' That State has exclusive jurisdiction, and the applicable law is determined by reference to the rules set out in Title II. The Court of Justice has repeatedly stressed the mandatory nature of the rules for determining which State is the competent State.[56] It has also indicated that the purpose of the rules is to avoid any unnecessary duplication of contributions and liabilities, as well as inadvertent exclusion from systems of social protection.[57] As with all situations involving the application of rules of the conflict of laws, there must be some international element present before the rules will apply.

Perhaps one deficiency of the rules, especially now that the range of persons governed by the regulation is so wide, is that there is no entitlement under the regulation to be affiliated to the social security system of at least one State. The easiest example of such a person would be a student in the United Kingdom whose earnings fell below the lower earnings limit for being required to make national

[56] See, for example, Case 60/85 *Luitjen v Raad van Arbeit* [1986] ECR 2365, at 2372–3.

[57] Case 50/75 *Caisse de Pension des Employées Privés v Massonet* [1975] ECR 1473, para 15 of the judgment. See also Case 196/90 *Fonds voor Arbeidsongevallen v De Paep* [1991] ECR I-4815.

insurance contributions. Even though this work would be sufficient to make the competent State the United Kingdom, the student would not be insured in the United Kingdom because they would not be required to make contributions. The problem is compounded by the absence of any rules for determining the applicable legislation in relation to students generally.

The basic rule gives priority to the place of work.[58] Both employed[59] and self-employed persons[60] who live in one participating country but work in another participating country are subject to the legislation of the country in which they work. This rule applies even if the registered office or place of business of the employer is in a different participating country.

Special rules deal with certain special cases. Those working on vessels are subject to the legislation of the flag State.[61] Civil servants and persons treated as such are, unsurprisingly, subject to the legislation of the country to which the administration employing them is subject.[62] A similar rule applies to those called up to service in the armed forces, or for civilian service.[63] This rule is needed because several participating countries still retain a system of national service in the armed forces, and in some cases may allow substitute civilian service. There are special rules in Article 13(2)(e) which avoid breaks in the continuity of contributions for those called up for such service.

Normally the competent State for a person who has worked in one Member State and moves to another Member State will remain the State in which that person has worked until they undertake an occupational activity in a different State. An amendment to Article 13(2)(f) of Regulation 1408/71 now makes it clear that this is not a permanent situation; a person who ceases all occupational activity and moves to another State will become subject to the legislation of the State in which they 'reside'.[64] Though this solved one problem, it raised another. In what circumstances does a person cease all occupational activity, so that the Member State in which they last worked can exclude them from their social security systems? In the case of those who have reached retirement age, it is certainly feasible to assume that they have ceased all occupational activity, But in other cases, the position will be far from clear. This is illustrated in the *Kuusijärvi* case.[65] Anna Kuusijärvi ceased occupational activity in Sweden and returned to Finland, where she was initially unemployed until the birth of her child when she claimed child allowance and parental benefit. Was Finland or Sweden the competent State? The Swedish rule which excluded her from the social security system of that State provided that a person who is covered by the Swedish system and who leaves Sweden only

[58] Often referred to by the Latin tag *lex loci laboris*. [59] Article 13(2)(a).
[60] Article 13(2)(b). [61] Article 13(2)(c). [62] Article 13(2)(d). [63] Article 13(2)(e).
[64] 'Reside', in the context of Regulation 1408/71, means 'habitual residence' whereas 'stay' means 'temporary residence'. The concept of 'habitual residence' requires that the person's centre of interest in the place of residence has an appropriate degree of permanency about it. See also Case C-138/02 *Collins*, judgment of 23 March 2004, [2004] ECR nyr.
[65] Case C-275/96 *Kuusijärvi v Riksförsäkringsverket* [1998] ECR I-3419.

continues to be covered by the Swedish system if the stay abroad is not intended to exceed one year. The Court concluded that the amendment contained in Article 13(2)(f) was sufficiently broad to permit a State to make the continued applicability of its social security system dependent upon the person's continued residence in that country. So the exception is sweeping rather than narrow, and the participating countries will have little exposure to continuing liability for those who work in their countries and move to another country. Either the person will become subject to the social security system of another country because they work there, or they will become subject to it by reason of rules in the first country which limit subjection to that social security system where occupational activities have ceased. There is, accordingly, a very real risk that participating countries will take advantage of this provision to exclude from their social security systems those who move by reason of short interruptions of their work arising, for example, by reason of unemployment or child bearing.

There are many special rules in Title II, which covers most situations likely to be met, including the obscure provision relating to undertakings which 'straddle' the common frontier of two countries.[66]

The requirement that a person is insured in the country in which they work could cause problems where people go to work for a short period in another participating country. The administrative costs of affiliation to the social security systems of several countries could outweigh any advantages, and the Commission would argue that it could hamper the free movement of persons. To accommodate such situations, there is an important exception to the rule that persons are insured in their place of work in the case of posted workers. Workers are posted when their employer sends them temporarily to work abroad. As long as the rules in Regulation 1408/71 are observed, they will remain insured for the period of their posting under the system in the State from which they are sent. The normal maximum period of posting is 12 months, but this can be extended to 24 months. Any cases falling outside this period where it is in the interests of the worker to remain affiliated to the social security system of the sending State can only be accommodated through the completion of agreements between the sending State and the receiving State under Article 17 of Regulation 1408/71. The status of a posted worker is attested in Form E101, which should protect workers from being subject to a requirement to pay social security contributions in the State to which they are sent.

The capacity of the system to be used as a vehicle to bypass the payment of high social security contributions in a participating country was raised before the Court of Justice in the *Fitzwilliam* case.[67] The company which was established in Ireland

[66] Article 14(3) and 14a(3). The provision is thought to relate to one or two situations in which farms straddle the border between two countries.

[67] Case C-202/97 *Fitzwilliam Executive Search Limited, trading under the name of Fitzwilliam Executive Services v Bestuur van het Landelijk Instituut Social Verzekeringen* [2000] ECR I-883. See also Case 35/80 *Sàrl Manpower v Caisse Primaire d'Assurance Maladie Strasbourg* [1970] ECR 1251, and Decision 162 of the Administrative Commission, [1976] OJ L241/28.

was in business providing migrant labour in the agricultural and horticultural sectors mainly in Ireland and in the Netherlands. When they placed workers in the Netherlands, they sought Forms E101 for them. The Court ruled that an undertaking must normally carry on its activities in the sending State habitually and to a significant extent in order to gain the benefit of the posted workers provisions. Furthermore the receiving State was obliged to accept the matters certified in the Form E101. In the case of suspected fraud or other irregularity, the receiving State should raise the matter with the sending State which should investigate the matter in good faith. The Court ruled that, as long as the certificate had not been withdrawn or declared invalid, the receiving State was obliged to recognize the situation to which it attested.

In the *Banks* case,[68] the Court of Justice was asked whether the receiving State can question the validity of the Form E101 or the entitlement of the holder to the status which it certifies. The Court re-affirmed its ruling in the *Fitzwilliam* case that the receiving State must accept the validity of the Form E101, and must also accept the determination of status, so that, if musicians are employees in the sending State and are posted to work in a State where musicians are treated as self-employed, the receiving State cannot, in these circumstances, use their own classification as the basis for claiming social security contributions. This is logical, because under the posting rules the law of the receiving State is not applied to the persons protected by the Form E101.

Prohibiting discrimination

The co-ordinating regulations take the general prohibition of discrimination to be found in Article 12 EC and apply it specifically to the context of social security. Article 3(1) of Regulation 1408/71 provides:

> Subject to the special provisions of this Regulation, persons resident in the territories of one of the Member States to whom this Regulation applies shall be subject to the same obligations and enjoy the same benefits under the legislation of any Member State as the nationals of the State.

The requirement of equal treatment has been given a broad interpretation by the Court of Justice, which has consistently stated that it covers not only overt forms of discrimination but also covert forms of discrimination under which certain requirements and conditions which are not on their face based on nationality in effect operate to discriminate between nationals of the participating countries. An example of direct discrimination arose in the *Allué and Coonan* case[69] where foreign language assistants (who were invariably nationals of other Member States) were wrongly treated as self-employed with the result that they were responsible for

[68] Case C-178/97 *Banks and others v Théâtre de la Monnaie* [2000] ECR I-2005.
[69] Case 33/88 *Allué and Coonan v Università degli studi di Venezia* [1989] ECR 1591.

social security payments that would be met by the employer if they were treated as employed persons.

Indirect discrimination will arise not only where the requirements of national law, in effect, treat non-nationals less favourably than nationals, but also where those requirements are liable to treat non-nationals less favourably. In deciding whether there is indirect discrimination on grounds of nationality, it is appropriate to consider the Community authorities on indirect discrimination on grounds of sex.

In the *Toia* case the Court said:

> . . . the rules on equality of treatment . . . prohibit not only patent discrimination, based on the nationality of the beneficiaries of social security schemes, but also all disguised forms of discrimination which, by the application of other distinguishing criteria, lead in fact to the same result.[70]

So a condition of entitlement to French family benefits payable to a mother which required that the children be of French nationality indirectly discriminated against nationals of other Member States than France, since the nationality provisions of many Member States linked the nationality of children to that of their parents. The requirement could not be justified on objective grounds, and the rules in Regulation 1408/71 precluded the French Government from relying on the demographic policy of increasing the birth rate which was the social purpose of the benefit.

The Court has ruled that Article 52 EC on freedom of establishment precludes a participating country from charging those within the personal scope of Regulation 1408/71, who are by virtue of rules in the regulation not required to pay contributions to its national social insurance scheme even though resident in that country, a higher rate of income tax in order to offset the advantage to this group of its not being required to pay national social insurance contributions in the country of residence.[71]

The prohibition of discrimination also applies to Community institutions. In the *Pinna* case[72] the Court of Justice ruled that Article 73(2) of Regulation 1408/71 (as it then existed) operated to make an unjustified distinction between French nationals subject to French legislation and non-French nationals subject to the same legislation.[73]

It is also arguable that Regulation 1408/71 prohibits 'reverse discrimination': this phrase is used to describe a situation in which a participating country, in effect, treats its own nationals less favourably because it is required to grant nationals of

[70] Case 237/78 *Caisse Régionale d'Assurance Maladie (CRAM), Lille v Diamante Paterno, née Toia* [1979] ECR 2645, 2653. See also Case C-349/87 *Paraschi v Landesversicherungsanstalt Württemberg* [1991] ECR I-4501.

[71] Case C-107/94 *Asscher v Staatsecretaris van Financiën* [1996] ECR I-3089, see also Case C-169/98 *Commission v France* [2000] ECR I-995 and Case C-34/98 *Commission v France* [2000] ECR I-1049.

[72] Case 41/84 *Pinna v Caisse d'allocation familiales de la Savoie* [1986] ECR 1; Case 359/87 *Pinna v Caisse d'allocation familiales de la Savoie* [1989] ECR 585.

[73] See Watson, P, 'Equal treatment in the award of family allowances' (1989) 14 ELRev 346.

other participating countries certain rights which it need not accord to its own nationals.[74]

Requiring aggregation of periods of insurance or residence

If there were no co-ordination of the social security systems of the participating countries, those who have worked in more than one such country could find that they suffer serious disadvantages in social security provision. This is most obvious in respect of retirement pensions. For example, in Luxembourg there is a 10-year qualifying period during which insurance contributions must be paid, whereas in Greece you must have worked 4,500 days.[75] But in all cases, the amount of the pension is dependent upon the number of years worked. If each system operated only on its own territory, a person might lose a pension entitlement by reason, for example, of the fact that a period of employment in Luxembourg fell short of that country's qualifying period. Equally, if the period in Luxembourg could not be taken into account elsewhere, the number of insured years would be lower which could reduce the amount of any retirement pension. To avoid these difficulties, Community social security rules require periods of insurance or residence in different countries to be aggregated. The relevant provision in relation to old age and death benefits is Article 45(1) of Regulation 1408/71, which reads:

> where the legislation of a Member State makes the acquisition, retention or recovery of the right to benefits . . . subject to the completion of periods of insurance or of residence, the competent institution of that Member State shall take account, where necessary, of the periods of insurance or residence completed under the legislation of any other Member State. . . . For that purpose, it shall take account of these periods as if they had [been] completed under its own legislation.

The objective of this principle, which applies equally to other benefits within the regulation, is that the impact of living and working in several participating countries on social security entitlements is minimized.

One consequence of aggregation could be that a participating country faces the burden of meeting a benefit based on many years of contribution to the social security scheme of one or more other countries. The principle inelegantly but frequently described as 'proraterization' addresses this issue; apportionment would be a more easily understood term to use. Under this principle, participating countries pay long-term benefits in proportion to the respective periods of

[74] See Case 1/78 *Kenny v Insurance Officer* [1978] ECR 1489, and Wyatt, D, 'Social security benefits and discrimination by a Member State against its own nationals' (1978) 3 ELRev 488. But see, to the contrary, Case C-153/91 *Petit v Office National des pensions (ONP)* [1992] ECR I-4973.

[75] See European Commission, *Your social security rights when moving within the European Union. A practical guide* (Luxembourg: Office for Official Publications of the European Communities, 2002 update).

insurance in each affected country.[76] For short-term benefits, provision is made for reimbursement of benefits paid.[77]

Permitting the export of acquired benefits

If a person has acquired entitlement to a social security benefit in one country but loses that entitlement on moving to another participating country, that could constitute an obstacle to the free movement of persons. The co-ordinating regulations accommodate this by providing for such benefits to be exported when the person moves to another country. However, this restriction on the territoriality of benefits has been eroded considerably by changes made to the Community social security rules. The basic rule is to be found in Article 10 Regulation 1408/71:

invalidity, old-age or survivors' cash benefits, pension for accidents at work or occupational diseases and death grants acquired under the legislation of one or more Member States shall not be subject to any reduction modification, suspension, withdrawal or confiscation by reason of the fact that the recipient resides in the territory of a Member State other than that in which the institution responsible for payment is situated.

The Court has consistently stated that this provision means that an acquired benefit cannot be withdrawn if the recipient moves to another participating country, and that the provision includes a right not to be prevented from acquiring a right by reason of residence in the territory of another country. So a provision in national legislation requiring a person to be incapable of work for a specified period in a particular country cannot operate to defeat entitlement in the event of that person moving to another country before the completion of the qualifying period. Time would continue to run.[78]

Over time this principle of the extra-territoriality of benefits has been eroded by the increasing number of benefits which are payable only to those resident in a particular participating country. The justification for this derogation from the waiver of residence requirements contained in Article 10 is that many of these benefits are paid at a rate which reflects the cost of living in a particular country. That is not wholly convincing. Regulation 1247/92[79] amended Regulation 1408/71 inserting a new Article 10a on special non-contributory benefits which would be payable only in the territory of the country of residence. The detail preserved the ability to have various qualifying periods which had accrued in another country taken into account, and where entitlement depends on diagnosis of disability in the territory of the participating country, the condition is to be deemed fulfilled if the diagnosis was made for the first time in any participating country.

[76] An example is spelled out in ch 6 in relation to retirement benefit.

[77] See, in relation to unemployment benefits, art 70, Reg 1408/71.

[78] See Case 92/81 *Caracciolo (née Camera) v Institut national d'assurance maladie-invalidité and Union nationale des mutualités socialistes* [1982] ECR 2213 and Joined Cases 379-381/85 and 93/86 *Giletti and others* [1987] ECR 955.

[79] Regulation 1247/92/EEC, [1992] OJ L136/1.

Links with policies on social protection

Rules of co-ordination do not raise the standard of social protection in the Community; they merely provide a mechanism under which different rules can work together where a person has contact with the social security systems of more than a single State. However, another part of the EC Treaty[80] is concerned with raising the standard of social protection. Article 137 EC contains a commitment by Community institutions to work with the Member States to secure improvement in 'social security and social protection of workers'.[81] Provision is made later in the article for directives to be passed to achieve the objectives of the chapter on social provisions. The Community Social Charter spawned two recommendations,[82] but these have had little impact. The Commission does from time to time produce reports on social protection within the Community.[83] The modern agenda appears to reflect concern at the costs of social protection[84] and places an emphasis on reducing unemployment.[85]

The European Councils in Lisbon in March 2000 and in Nice in December 2000 resulted in the creation of the Social Protection Committee. The emphasis of the discussion and its being put into practice was on modernizing the European social model, investing in people, and combating social exclusion. The favoured method is the so-called 'open method of co-ordination' which has been defined as 'a mutual feedback process of planning, examination, comparison and adjustment of the . . . policies of Member States, all of this on the basis of common objectives.'[86] This approach seems to offer greatest promise in the field of pensions.[87] Concerns over the level of spending on social protection as a share of gross domestic product[88] and the constraints on public spending imposed by participation in Economic and Monetary Union have caused some to question whether future developments might be in the direction of a reduction in the level of benefit payments rather than improved social protection.[89]

[80] Material originally included in the Community Social Charter of 1989.

[81] Article 137(1)(c).

[82] Recommendation 92/441/EEC and 92/442/EEC, [1992] OJ L245/46, discussed in Barnard, C, *EC Employment Law*, 2nd edn (Oxford, 2000), at 326–8.

[83] See, for example, *Social Protection in Europe 2001* (Brussels, European Commission, 2002).

[84] See, for example, the European Commission's report *Modernising and Improving Social Protection in the European Union*, COM(97) 102.

[85] See, for example, Resolution of the Council and of the representatives of the governments of the Member States, meeting within the Council of 2 December 1996, on the role of social protection systems in the fight against unemployment, [1996] OJ C386/3.

[86] See Berghman, J and Okma, K, 'The Method of Open Co-ordination: Open Procedures or closed circuit? Social policy making between science and politics' (2002) 4 EJSS 331.

[87] See below.

[88] This was 27.5 per cent of GDP in 1999, though the range was from 33 per cent in Sweden down to 15 per cent in Ireland. Source: *Social Protection in Europe 2001* (Brussels, European Commission, 2002).

[89] See Guild, E, 'How can social protection survive EMU? A United Kingdom perspective' (1999) 24 ELRev 22.

The equal treatment directives

The Community institutions recognized that moves to secure the principle of equal treatment for men and women would be incomplete without the inclusion of provisions for dealing with statutory social security schemes and occupational pensions. These are to be found in Directive 79/7/EEC[90] on the progressive implementation of the principle of equal treatment for men and women in matters of social security and in Directive 86/378/EEC[91] on the implementation of the principle of equal treatment for men and women in occupational social security schemes. Both directives are made as part of the policy of equal treatment rather than as part of the programme for securing the free movement of persons. As such, there is no need to exercise particular rights under the EC Treaty in order to be a beneficiary of the provisions.

Unfortunately a number of concepts in the directive have been interpreted differently from what might be regarded as corresponding provisions of Regulation 1408/71. Furthermore, the coverage of Directive 79/7 is not the same as that of Regulation 1408/71 in terms of the benefits covered.

The personal scope of the Directive is very different from that of Regulation 1408/71. Article 2 provides:

> This Directive shall apply to the working population—including self-employed persons, workers and self-employed persons whose activity is interrupted by illness, accident or involuntary unemployment and persons seeking employment—and to retired or invalided workers and self-employed persons.

Directive 79/7 is very much concerned with those benefits linked to employment and self-employment: this is what is meant by the reference to the working population and those who have retired from work by reason of age or some earlier illness or injury which renders them incapable of future work. These risks are defined in Article 3:

- sickness
- invalidity
- old age
- accidents at work and occupational diseases
- unemployment

The test for whether the benefit is within the directive is whether the benefit provides direct and effective protection against the risks specified in Article 3(1) rather than incidental protection. In the absence of such an approach, it could be argued that most forms of cash benefit offer protection against unemployment.[92] In

[90] [1979] OJ L6/24.

[91] [1986] OJ L225/40, as amended by Directive 96/97, [1997] IJ L46/20.

[92] Joined Cases C-245/94 and C-312/94 *Hoever and Zachow v Land Nordrhein Westfalen* [1996] ECR I-4895, and Case C-228/94 *Atkins v Wrekin District Council and the Department of Transport* [1996] ECR I-3633.

some cases, a failure to bring a benefit within the material scope of Directive 79/7 may not exclude Community law affecting the terms on which it is awarded. Directive 76/207,[93] known as the 'equal treatment directive', contains a requirement similar to that in Directive 79/7 to secure equal treatment of men and women. A challenge under Directive 76/207 that discriminatory arrangements in relation to access to child care costs under a United Kingdom social security benefit for those in work was held to constitute a 'working condition' under the equal treatment directive.[94]

The directive has no application to anyone who has never worked, nor to a person who gives up work for reasons not related to the risks covered, for example, in order to care for children.[95]

The key obligation is to be found in Article 5 which requires Member States to take the measures necessary to ensure that 'any laws, regulations and administrative provisions contrary to the principle of equal treatment are abolished'. The principle of equal treatment is spelled out in Article 4:

> 1. The principle of equal treatment means that there shall be no discrimination whatsoever on ground of sex either directly, or indirectly by reference in particular to marital or family status, in particular as concerns:
>
> —the scope of the schemes and the conditions of access thereto,
> —the obligation to contribute and the calculation of contributions,
> —the calculation of benefits including increases due in respect of a spouse and for dependants and the conditions governing the duration and retention of entitlement to benefits.
>
> 2. The principle of equal treatment shall be without prejudice to the provisions relating to the protection of women on grounds of maternity.

The Court of Justice has ruled that Article 4 outlaws both direct and indirect forms of discrimination. In enforcement proceedings against Belgium, the Court summarized the requirements of Article 4 as follows:

> Article 4(1) of Directive 79/7 precludes less favourable treatment from being accorded to a social group when it is shown to be made up of a much greater number of persons of one or other sex, unless the provision in question is 'based on objectively justified factors unrelated to any discrimination on grounds of sex'.[96]

Article 7 of the directive contains a number of exceptions. The most commonly invoked exception, which has been a source of a number of references to the Court

[93] Council Directive 76/207/EEC of 9 February 1976 on the implementation of the principle of equal treatment for men and women as regards access to employment, vocational training and promotion, and working conditions, [1976] OJ L39/40.

[94] Case C-116/94 *Meyers v Adjudication Officer* [1995] ECR I-2131.

[95] See Joined Cases 48, 106 and 107/88 *Achterberg-te Riele and others v Sociale Verzekeringsbank, Amsterdam* [1989] ECR 1963, Joined Cases C-87/90, 88/90 and 89/90 *Verholen and others v Sociale Verzekeringsbank, Amsterdam* [1991] ECR I-3757, and Case C-31/90 *Johnson v Chief Adjudication Officer* [1991] ECR I-3723.

[96] Case C-229/89 *Commission v Belgium* [1991] ECR I-2205, para 13 of the judgment.

of Justice from United Kingdom courts and tribunals, is the exclusion from the scope of the directive of 'the determination of pensionable age for the purposes of granting old-age and retirement pensions and the possible consequences thereof for other benefits.' The Court has consistently required that, where a State claims that the possible consequences of differential retirement ages of men and women justify unequal treatment, the difference in treatment must be 'necessarily linked' to the difference in statutory pensionable age.[97]

Pension issues

Occupational pensions are provided for by employers for their employees in connection with their employment.[98] They are to be distinguished from the State retirement pension which is provided for by the State on the basis of social security contributions made throughout a working life. Occupational pensions can be a replacement for, or a supplement to, the State retirement pension. This was the justification for applying provisions similar to those in Directive 79/7 to occupational pensions through Directive 86/738. Such pensions are those which provide protection against the same risks as are covered by Directive 79/7 and those protected by the occupational pensions directive are almost identical to those within the personal scope of Directive 79/7. The prohibition of discrimination is spelled out in Article 5:

1. Under the conditions laid down in the following provisions, the principle of equal treatment implies that there shall be no discrimination on the basis of sex, either directly or indirectly, by reference in particular to marital or family status, especially as regards:

—the scope of the schemes and the conditions of access to them;
—the obligation to contribute and the calculation of contributions;
—the calculation of benefits, including supplementary benefits due in respect of a spouse or dependants, and the conditions governing the duration and retention of entitlement to benefits.

2. The principle of equal treatment shall not prejudice the provisions relating to the protection of women by reason of maternity.

The occupational pensions directive contains derogations, but these have been significantly narrowed by decisions of the Court of Justice, such that the directive was amended in 1997, and the derogations now apply principally to self-employed

[97] See Case C-9/91 *R v Secretary of State for Social Security, ex parte Equal Opportunities Commission* [1992] ECR I-4297; Case C-139/95 *Balestra v Istituto Nazionale della Previdenza Sociale (INPS)* [1997] ECR I-549; Case C-328/91 *Thomas v Secretary of State for Social Security* [1993] ECR I-1247; Case C-92/94 *Secretary of State for Social Security v Graham and others* [1995] ECR I-2521; Case C-137/94 *R v Secretary of State for Health, ex parte Richardson* [1995] ECR I-3407; and Case C-382/98 *R v Secretary of State for Social Security, ex parte Taylor* [1999] ECR I-8955.

[98] See generally Hanlon, J, 'Pensions integration in the European Union' (2004) 29 ELRev 74.

persons. These developments flowed from judgments which brought occupational pensions within the definition of pay in Article 119 (now 141) EC,[99] though only in relation to periods of employment on or after 17 May 1990.[100] In the *Barber* case, the Court ruled that payments made under occupational pension schemes constituted pay for the purposes of Article 119 EEC.

It followed from the *Barber* judgment that discrimination which appeared to be justified by the derogations in Article 9 of Directive 86/738 (as originally drafted) were unlawful, since rights granted by the Treaty could not be over-ridden by provisions of a directive. This resulted in the amendment of Directive 86/738 in order to adapt its provisions to the post-*Barber* world in which occupational pensions constituted pay.

There has also been concern that problems over the portability of occupational pensions could constitute an obstacle to the free movement of persons. Directive 98/49/EC[101] seeks to alleviate some of these problems by requiring Member States:

> . . . to ensure the preservation of vested pension rights for members of a supplementary pension scheme in respect of whom contributions are no longer being made to that scheme as a consequence of their moving from one Member State to another, to the same extent as for members in respect of whom contributions are no longer being made, but who remain within the same Member State.[102]

It is clear that the issue remains one of concern to the European Commission, which has issued a second stage consultation among the social partners on measures to improve the portability of occupation pension rights which will be followed up in 2004.[103]

Concluding remarks

In so far as there is something which might be described as European social security law, it is a mix of measures of co-ordination and limited harmonization, of hard and soft law, and of law and policy. Nevertheless, there is probably within the European social security 'club' greater co-ordination of social security entitlement than anywhere else in the world. There is, however, recognition that Regulation 1408/71 is too complex an instrument and a proposal for a simplified regulation is slowly and with shuffling gait working its way through the decision-making

[99] For a more detailed account of this case law, see Barnard, C, *EC Employment Law*, 2nd edn, (Oxford, 2000) at 354–68.

[100] The date of the Court's judgment in Case C-262/88 *Barber v Guardian Royal Exchange Assurance Group* [1990] ECR I-1889. Protocol No 2 attached to the Treaty of Maastricht re-states this position.

[101] Directive 98/49/EC of 29 June 1998 on safeguarding the supplementary pension rights of employed and self-employed persons moving within the Community, [1998] OJ L209/46.

[102] Article 4.

[103] *Mid-Term Review of the Social Policy Agenda*, COM(2003) 312 (Final), at para 5.4.

process.[104] The new open method of co-ordination is being used to try to ensure greater mobility and portability of pensions, where the Commission's favoured instrument would be a collective agreement at European level. Progress will inevitably be slow.

[104] See COM(1998) 779 Final of 21 December 1998. See now Regulation 883/2004/EC of 29 April 2004 on the coordination of social security systems, [2004] OJ L166/1. This regulation will largely replace Regulation 1408/71, and is expected to enter into force some time in 2006 when a new implementing regulation replacing Regulation 547/72 has been drafted and enters into force.

Part IV

Regulating Market Access

10

Prohibiting obstacles to free movement

Context

Reading the articles of the EC Treaty on free movement of persons at face value suggests that the framers of the Treaty were primarily concerned with the prohibition of discrimination based on nationality. Article 39(2) EC provides that free movement of workers 'shall entail the abolition of any discrimination based on nationality between workers of the Member States'. Though Article 43 EC refers to a prohibition of 'restrictions on the freedom of establishment of nationals of a Member State in the territory of another Member State', the second paragraph of that article provides that establishment is to be permitted in the host State 'under the conditions laid down for its own nationals'. The provisions of chapter 3 on services mirror those on establishment. Article 50 EC refers to the temporary pursuit of an activity 'under the same conditions as are imposed by that State on its own nationals'.

The principle of national treatment apparent on the face of the words of the relevant Treaty articles has, however, been expanded in the case law of the Court of Justice not only to include acts of indirect discrimination,[1] but also to apply similar principles to the free movement of persons that the Court has applied to obstacles to the free movement of goods. In this way, obstacles which apply equally to nationals of the host State and nationals of other Member States[2] may be challenged for compliance with the underlying purpose of the provisions on the free movement of persons. This might be labelled the 'obstacles approach' as contrasted with the principle of national treatment.

The convergence of underlying principles on the free movement of goods and of persons has taken place notwithstanding a number of structural differences between the Treaty provisions on the free movement of goods and the free movement of persons. Most notable among these is that the provisions on free movement of goods are directed at State measures, whereas the provisions on the free movement of persons apply to all restrictions whether imposed by the State or by employers or other private regulatory bodies.[3]

Developments in the case law on the free movement of persons have also displayed a convergence of the principles applicable to workers, establishment

[1] See ch 3 above. [2] So-called non-discriminatory obstacles.
[3] Such as, for example, professional bodies.

and services. This has not gone unchallenged, since there are arguments that the interests of a migrant worker may not be same as those of an enterprise delivering services or seeking to establish itself in another Member State.[4] This chapter explores the concept of non-discriminatory obstacles and the distinction between the prohibition of discrimination on grounds of nationality and the prohibition of obstacles to access to the market of other Member States. It argues that the former is primarily concerned with granting individual rights, whereas the latter is primarily concerned with controlling the regulators of activities. Of course, it is possible to argue that the prohibition of discrimination is simply the crudest form of regulating market access. However, the case law of the Court of Justice has clearly moved beyond crude distinctions, and has, it is argued, not simply replaced the prohibition of discrimination with a rule prohibiting restrictions on access to activities governed by the law on the free movement of persons.

Home State *versus* host State regulation

A number of cases which might be regarded as falling within the obstacles approach to promoting the free movement of persons concern competition between two regulatory systems: that of the home State and that of the host State. Armstrong[5] has posited three approaches for ensuring market access and market regulation.[6] The first is based on host State regulation provided that nationals of other Member States are treated in the same manner as nationals of that State. This model places the host State in control but the market remains segmented along national boundaries. There is also a potential multiple burden in that an enterprise wishing to be active in one or more other Member States must comply with the regulatory scheme of each Member State in which it operates. The second approach is that of home State control. In the language of *Cassis de Dijon*,[7] if a person is qualified to carry on an enterprise in one Member State, then in principle that person is qualified to carry on the enterprise in any other Member State. The problem here[8] is that although there is compliance with only one system of regulation, the actual scheme of regulation applicable in any given Member State is likely to differ in some respects because home State control is imported into the host State. As Armstrong

[4] Contrast Johnson, E and O'Keeffe, D, 'From Discrimination to Obstacles to Free Movement: Recent Developments concerning the Free Movement of Workers 1989-1994' (1994) 31 CMLRev 1313, and Weatherill, S, 'After *Keck:* Some Thoughts on How to Clarify the Clarification' (1996) 33 CMLRev 885, with Daniele, L, 'Non-Discriminatory Restrictions to the Free Movement of Persons' (1997) 22 ELRev 191.

[5] Borrowing from Maduro's models of market integration as espoused in Poiares Maduro, M, *We The Court: The European Court of Justice and the European Economic Constitution* (Oxford, 1998), ch 4.

[6] Armstrong, K, 'Mutual Recognition' in Barnard, C and Scott, J, *The Law of the Single European Market. Unpacking the Premises* (Oxford, 2002), at 225.

[7] Case 120/78 *Rewe-Zentrale AG v Bundesmonopolverwaltung für Branntwein* [1979] ECR 649.

[8] Apart from the improbability of such a standard being acceptable to Member States.

says, 'different goods and services will have complied with different home state controls'.[9]

A third model envisages the harmonization of standards by replacing differing national standards with a single set of harmonized regulatory requirements.

One way through the conflicting claims of these models is mutual recognition:

> The principle of mutual recognition seeks to manage market access under conditions of regulatory pluralism by negotiating between the application of home and host state regulatory controls. Mutual recognition recognises that the regulatory history of a product, service or worker acquired in the home state cannot be ignored when it comes to considering what legitimate regulatory controls may be applied in the host State.[10]

Armstrong says that *Cassis de Dijon* has traditionally been interpreted as mandating home state control, whereas he argues that it can be interpreted as providing one means of policing the application of host state controls. He concludes that 'mutual recognition has an important—albeit limited—role to play in the assessment of the necessity and proportionality of host state measures'.

This analysis is helpful in providing some insight into the tensions between home State and host State regulation of access to an activity and to its exercise.

Avoiding dual burdens

Illustrations of the application of the principle of mutual recognition can be seen in a line of cases in which the Court of Justice has indicated that dual burdens must be avoided in the area of the free movement of persons just as in the area of the free movement of goods. The *Van Wesemael* case[11] concerned a requirement of Belgian law which provided that foreign employment agencies for entertainers may not place anyone in employment in Belgium except through a fee-charging employment agency holding a licence. Prosecutions under this law were challenged as being incompatible with the provisions of the EC Treaty on freedom to provide services. The Court concluded that these provisions required the host State to permit the activity where the person concerned held a licence in the home State, 'under conditions comparable to those required by the State in which the service is provided and his activities are subject in the first State to proper supervision covering all employment agency activity whatever may be the Member State in which the service is provided'.[12]

[9] Armstrong, K, 'Mutual Recognition' in Barnard, C and Scott, J, *The Law of the Single European Market. Unpacking the Premises* (Oxford, 2002), at 229.

[10] ibid, at 230.

[11] Joined Cases 110 and 111/78 *Ministère Public v Van Wesemael* [1979] ECR 35.

[12] Para 30 of the judgment.

The situation in the *Webb* case[13] was a little different but also concerned a prosecution for failure to hold a licence in the host State where the services of placing technical staff were undertaken. The enterprise held a licence as an employment agency in the United Kingdom. The Court followed its decision in *Van Wesemael,* but added a gloss:

> . . . the freedom to provide services is one of the fundamental principles of the treaty and may be restricted only by provisions which are justified by the general good and which are imposed on all persons or undertakings operating in the said State in so far as that interest is not safeguarded by the provisions to which the provider of the service is subject in the Member State of his establishment.[14]

The language of the judgment is very much that of mutual recognition; the host State's ability to regulate the activity is subject to its taking into account the evidence and guarantees already provided through the system of registration in the home State. The effect is to prevent the service provider from being required to meet a dual burden. Where the registration schemes serve the same purpose, there cannot be a requirement to register in the host State. Where there are differences in the purposes of registration, then a licence may be required before the service can lawfully be provided in the host State. Note, however, that the requirement of mutual recognition is much stronger in the field of services[15] than in the field of establishment where greater deference to host State regulation is permitted.

The notion of non-discriminatory obstacles

The case law described in chapter 3 treats the prohibition of discrimination broadly, but a note of caution should be sounded. Under that case law, the Court has taken a relatively narrow view requiring a functional link between the discriminatory treatment and the exercise of the Treaty right. So cases like the proceedings against Italy concerning housing subsidies for self-employed persons[16] are unusual, because most of the case law seems to require a closer link between the subject matter of the alleged discriminatory treatment and the exercise of the right of free movement. In other words, the economic aspects outweigh the social aspects.

Just as the Court of Justice has interpreted the provisions of the Treaty relating to the free movement of goods as going beyond the prohibition of discrimination in pursuit of the goal of market integration,[17] so too in regulating the free movement of persons, the Court of Justice has moved in the same direction. There have also

[13] Case 279/80 *Criminal Proceedings against Webb* [1981] ECR 3305.
[14] Para 17 of the judgment.
[15] But see discussion of the position of posted workers in the framework of services in ch 2 above.
[16] Case 63/86 *Commission v Italy* [1988] ECR 29, discussed in ch 8 above.
[17] See, for example, Weatherill, S, *Law and Integration in the European Union* (Oxford, 1995), ch 7.

been legislative measures designed to level the playing field, particularly in the area of recognition of qualifications under Article 47 EC.[18]

The rationale of the developments in the principles established in the case law on the free movement of goods is that simply to prohibit direct and indirect discrimination on grounds of nationality would not have opened up the markets of the Member States to the products of other Member States. There was a need to tackle the regulation of national markets through national rules which, although equally applicable to domestic and imported products, offered the opportunity to protect the domestic market. The truly seminal decision in the *Cassis de Dijon* case[19] contained two rules which together have a powerful integrationist effect while permitting an appropriate level of national regulation of the market. Cassis de Dijon is the famous blackcurrant liqueur produced in France, and drunk traditionally as a mixer with wine or champagne. The producer wished to sell Cassis in Germany, but was refused an authorization to do so because the drink did not meet the requirements of German law on the marketing of alcoholic drinks.[20] Questions were referred by the national court to the Court of Justice on the compatibility of the German rules on the marketing of alcohol with the rules in the EC Treaty on the free movement of goods. The nub of the Court's ruling was that there is a presumption that goods lawfully produced and marketed in one Member State may be introduced into the markets of the other Member States. The significant effect of this ruling was to sweep away the threats of inappropriate harmonizing measures converting the great variety of European products into their lowest common denominators in order to ensure their acceptability in all the Member States. The second part of the Court's ruling was that certain measures fall outside the prohibition in what is now Article 28 EC. So national regulatory rules are permissible where they apply equally to domestic and imported products; where they have a legitimate aim serving a mandatory requirement;[21] and where they are proportionate in that they interfere to the least extent possible with the free movement of goods.[22]

However, some six years earlier, the Court had handed down its decision in the field of services in the *Van Binsbergen* case, which recognized the capacity for regulation to achieve the continued segmentation of the market which would have defeated the objective of the freedoms described in the treaty.

The *Van Binsbergen* case[23] concerned rules surrounding the activity of legal representation in the Netherlands. Van Binsbergen was involved in a social security

[18] See ch 4 above.

[19] Case 120/78 *Rewe-Zentrale AG v Bundesmonopolverwaltung für Branntwein* [1979] ECR 649.

[20] For the—at first sight—strange reason that its alcoholic content was too low for it to be classified as a liqueur.

[21] The words 'mandatory requirement' are an inappropriate translation of the French *exigences imperatifs*.

[22] A number of commentators describe this as the rule of reason.

[23] Case 33/74 *Van Binsbergen v Bestuur van de Bedrijfsvereniging voor de Metaalnijverheid* [1974] ECR 1299.

dispute which had been brought before the social security tribunal in Roermond. He was represented by Kortmann, a Dutch national established in the Netherlands. At some point during the proceedings, Kortmann moved his habitual residence to Belgium; he ceased to be permanently established in the Netherlands. The effect of this move was that he lost his right under the rules of procedure of the Netherlands social service courts to act as Van Binsbergen's representative; the rules of procedure provided that only persons established in the Netherlands could act as legal representatives or advisers. Paragraphs 11 to 17 of the Court's judgment are couched in terms which are remarkably similar to the underlying reasoning in *Cassis de Dijon* and recognize the need to secure the objective of market integration by drawing regulatory matters which apply equally to nationals and non-nationals within the scope of the freedom to provide services while also setting up a test for the permissibility of legitimate national regulation. The Court began by acknowledging the capacity of a rule like that in issue in the case to conflict with the abolition of restrictions required by what was then Article 59 EC. But restrictions which flow from regulatory rules which 'have as their purpose the application of professional rules justified by the general good' might escape the prohibition. To do so, the requirement must be 'objectively justified by the need to ensure observance of professional rules of conduct connected . . . with the administration of justice and with respect for professional ethics'. But this requires that the activity is surrounded by detailed professional rules within the host State. The restriction must ultimately be proportionate to the legitimate aim pursued; if some lesser restriction can be identified which equally serves that purpose, then the restriction will breach Article 59. This decision balances the promotion of market integration against the protection of the consumer by placing limits on the methods of control which the national authorities can use to protect the consumer.

The early case law

As early as 1975 in the *Watson and Belmann* case,[24] the Court of Justice recognized that certain administrative arrangements for recording the presence of other nationals in a Member State were permissible, but required that the penalties for failure to comply with them must be proportionate to the administrative nature of the matter. If they were too onerous, they would be capable of hindering free movement of persons and would breach Article 48 (now 39) EC.

In 1978, the Court of Justice hinted that national regulation could operate as an obstacle to the free movement of persons. The *Choquet* case[25] concerned the requirement that nationals of other Member States should hold a driving licence issued by the host Member State. At the time the Court was not willing to view

[24] Case 118/75 *Criminal Proceedings against Watson and Belmann* [1976] ECR 1185.
[25] Case 16/78 *Criminal Proceedings against Choquet* [1978] ECR 2293.

national requirements on the issue of driving licences as sufficiently harmonized to require mutual recognition. It followed that the requirement to hold a national driving licence would not, of itself, be an obstacle to free movement since the requirement could be justified. But the Court did add[26] that the process of conversion of licences from other Member States must be the least intrusive to secure the objective of proper certification of drivers, and so all the conditions had to meet the test of being in 'due proportion to the requirements for the safety of highway traffic'.[27] Requirements that went beyond this test of proportionality would constitute unlawful obstacles to the free movement of persons.

In 1983 the Court ruled that a national provision applicable to both nationals and non-nationals alike could not be used to deny the right of establishment.[28] There was a rule in France that a lawyer could only establish a single office. Klopp, a lawyer practising in Germany as a *Rechtsanwalt* but also qualified to practise as an *avocat* in France, wished to open an office in France. Under the French rules, he was precluded from doing so while retaining his office in Germany. The Court ruled that it was contrary to Article 52 (now 43) EC for France to maintain a rule which denied the exercise of the rights contained in that article.

An enormously important, but complex, series of cases relating to the operation of the insurance industry and known collectively as the *Insurance* cases[29] has put forward a test for the compatibility of professional regulatory rules which bears striking similarities with the doctrine contained in the *Cassis de Dijon* line of authority which applies to the free movement of goods.

The litigation arose in the context of enforcement proceedings brought by the Commission alleging that the defendant Member States were infringing Articles 59 and 60 (now 49 and 50) EC and a directive on the provision of insurance services by maintaining in effect rules regulating the provision of insurance services which operated as restrictions on the free movement of services. One of the rules called into question was a requirement that a company or person providing direct insurance must be established as authorized for the sale of such insurance in the Member State in which the service was provided. The effect of such a rule would be to segment the market on national lines, whereas the direct selling of insurance may not need to be so segmented. The Court provided important guidance on the distinction between establishment and services,[30] and went on to note that the requirements of the EC Treaty in relation to services required the removal of all discrimination based on nationality and all restrictions on freedom to provide services by reason of the fact that the undertaking providing those services is

[26] See particularly paras 6–8 of the judgment. [27] Para 8 of the judgment.

[28] Case 107/83 *Ordre des Avocats v Klopp* [1984] ECR 2971.

[29] Case 220/83 *Commission v France* [1986] ECR 3663; Case 252/83 *Commission v Denmark* [1986] ECR 3713; Case 205/84 *Commission v Germany* [1986] ECR 3755; Case 206/84 *Commission v Ireland* [1986] ECR 3817. See also Edward, D, 'Establishment and Services: an Analysis of the Insurance Cases' (1987) 12 ELRev 231.

[30] See ch 2 above.

established in a Member State other than that in which the services are provided. The Court ruled that national rules could only be applied to undertakings established in another Member State which were delivering services in the host Member States where those rules can be justified by imperative reasons relating to the public interest, where the public interest is not already protected by the rules of the Member State in which the person or undertaking is established,[31] and where the same result cannot be achieved by less restrictive rules.[32]

So it would follow that a requirement of establishment in a Member State before services could be provided there would be a complete denial of the freedom to provide services. Authorization could, however, be justified if, for example, its purpose was to ensure that appropriate reserves were held in order to protect policyholders and insured persons.

The Court has also gone beyond the basic requirements of national treatment in its case law on the mutual recognition of qualifications. In the *Vlassopoulou* case,[33] the Court of Justice demonstrated that national approaches to the equivalence of qualifications required that the powers of regulatory bodies be exercised fairly and with due regard to the promotion of the free movement of persons.

The modern line of cases

In 1991 the Court handed down the case which is often regarded as the first in the modern line of cases on obstacles to free movement of persons in its decision in *Säger*.[34] Weatherill and Beaumont call it 'one of the clearest expressions of the use of the deregulatory influence of the *Cassis de Dijon* principle in the services sector.'[35] Dennemeyer, a United Kingdom company, found its business of providing patent renewal services hindered in Germany by the German licensing requirements. These applied equally to German and non-German enterprises, but, in practice, licences were only available to those offering German professional qualifications. The Court concluded that such requirements could only be applied to Dennemeyer where it could be shown that they were justified by 'imperative reasons relating to the public interest'[36] and where the restrictive effect was no more severe than necessary to achieve the object pursued. This involved a demonstration that the concern underlying the rules was not adequately addressed by the regulatory system of the home State (in this case, the United Kingdom). The objective of the German system of regulation was the protection of the consumer from harm that could be caused by inadequately qualified advisers.

[31] Often referred to in this sort of context as 'the home State'.
[32] See, for example, Case 205/84 *Commission v Germany* [1986] ECR 3755, para 29 of the judgment.
[33] Case 340/89 *Vlassopoulou v Ministerium für Justiz* [1991] ECR 2357, discussed in ch 4 above.
[34] Case C-76/90 *Säger v Dennemeyer* [1991] ECR I-4221.
[35] Weatherill, S and Beaumont, P. *EU Law*, 3rd edn, (London, 1999), at 686.
[36] Case C-76/90 *Säger v Dennemeyer* [1991] ECR I-4221, para 15 of the judgment.

The requirements of the German licensing scheme were not considered to be the least restrictive means of achieving this permissible objective.

By 1993 the issue of fundamental rights was also featuring in considerations of the deliberations of the Court, most often through the Opinions of the Advocates General. In the *Konstantinidis* case,[37] which concerned the transliteration of the Greek letters of Christos Konstantinidis' name into the Roman alphabet, the Advocate General concluded that the requirement for Konstantinidis to use a transliteration of his name[38] which distorted it was a violation of his fundamental rights which was for that reason not compatible with the provisions of the EC Treaty. The Court did not follow him on this point, choosing to conclude that the provisions of the EC Treaty must be interpreted as not permitting the application of rules which might lead to confusion by customers in their dealings with him. It was not necessary to show that there was a restrictive effect; their potential for such an effect was sufficient.

The *Säger* principle was applied in the *Schindler* case,[39] which concerned restrictions imposed at the time in the United Kingdom on the sale of lottery tickets. Agents of a Germany lottery placed advertisements in English magazines and sold lottery tickets for the German lottery. A mailshot about the lottery was sent to certain people in the United Kingdom from the Netherlands. The mail shot was intercepted and confiscated by customs officers at Dover. The Schindler bothers contested the confiscation order arguing that the United Kingdom legislation was in breach of Article 30 (now 28) EC on the free movement of goods and Article 59 (now 49) EC on the freedom to provide services. The Court ruled that lottery activities were not activities relating to goods, but constituted services under Article 59 EC. The price of the lottery ticket was remuneration for the services provided by the operator of the lottery to enable purchasers of tickets to participate in a game of chance with the hope of winning a prize. Lotteries were not governed by any other provisions of the EC Treaty. So was the United Kingdom legislation an obstacle to the free movement of services? In the United Kingdom, activities similar to lotteries were permitted: bingo and the football pools, and lotteries with small prizes were permitted. Despite this, the Court ruled that the United Kingdom legislation was non-discriminatory. The United Kingdom's arguments for banning lotteries[40] were to prevent crime, to ensure the honest treatment of gamblers, to avoid stimulating demand in the gambling sector which has damaging social consequences when taken to excess, and to ensure that lotteries could not be operated for personal and commercial profit, but only for charitable purposes. Ultimately, the Court found that the prohibition in United Kingdom law was

[37] Case C-168/91 *Konstantinidis* [1993] ECR I-1191, noted at (1994) 31 CMLRev 395.

[38] Albeit one applying the Convention on the Representation of Names and Surnames in Registers of Civil Status of 13 September 1973 to which Germany is a party.

[39] Case C-275/92 *HM Customs & Excise v Schindler* [1994] ECR I-1039.

[40] These make interesting reading now that a national lottery has been introduced in the United Kingdom.

not inconsistent with Article 59 EC in view of the concerns about social policy and the prevention of fraud. Indeed the Court seems to be unwilling to challenge issues of social policy.[41]

The *Kraus* case[42] again shows the Court showing deference to national preferences in regulatory schemes; the Advocate General had been much bolder in his Opinion. Dieter Kraus was a German national who successfully completed a one-year, taught master's degree in law at the University of Edinburgh. German law makes the use of any foreign qualification in a title[43] subject to prior authorization by the Ministry of Education and Science of each *Land*. The penalty for failure to comply was punishable with up to one year in prison or, alternatively, a fine. The application for authorization had to be accompanied by a fee of 130 Deutsche Marks. In Germany postgraduate qualifications can enhance the reputation of practitioners as evidence of further study and an interest in comparative, Anglo-American or European Law. Academic qualifications are a common feature of notepaper and business cards used by professional people in Germany.

The Court's ruling was excessively cautious. The Court said that, in the absence of harmonized rules relating to the conditions attached to the use of university titles, each Member State is free to regulate their use on their own territory. They must not, however, through the system of regulation adopted, deprive persons of any useful benefit to be derived from the guaranteed freedoms in Articles 39 and 43 EC. The public interest in regulating the use of university titles was accepted, but the means must be proportional to the objective. The Court also stressed that reasons must be given for any refusal to permit their use so that any such decision can be challenged by the aggrieved party.

It can be argued that Advocate General van Gerven's Opinion is much more *communautaire*. He doubted whether there was any public policy reason to regulate the use of university titles; the general law on fraud was enough to protect people against their wrongful use. He also considered that the requirements in Germany were out of all proportion to the aim to be achieved. Some system under which any use of title was accompanied by an indication of the awarding institution would make the pedigree of the degree clear to the consumer. Nor was this a case where national rules on qualification took precedence, since the LLM did not qualify Kraus to practise in Germany; it merely enhanced his prospects of success in his chosen profession.

This case perhaps shows the Court at the crossroads, still wedded to notions of equal treatment and the application of national standards on the one hand, and yet

[41] See also Case C-124/97 *Läära* [1999] ECR I-6067; Case C-67/98 *Zenatti* [1999] ECR I-7289; and Case C-6/01 *Associação Nacional de Operadores de Máquinas Recreativas (Anomar) and others v Portugal*, Judgment of 11 September 2003.

[42] Case C-19/92 *Kraus v Land Baden-Württemberg* [1993] ECR I-1663, noted at (1994) 19 ELRev 67.

[43] Such as putting the letters LLM (Edinburgh) after your name.

alert to the capacity for non-discriminatory national standards to operate as barriers to free movement.

The *Alpine Investments* case[44] concerned the practice in the Netherlands of making unsolicited telephone calls to members of the public to try to sell them securities investments.[45] Dutch law prohibited this in response to complaints from investors who had made unfortunate investments in the financial sector as a result of cold calling. Alpine Investments was a company established in, and operating from the Netherlands. The Court of Justice found a sufficient connection with Community law in the need to communicate with potential clients in the Netherlands and in other Member States in order to sell its services. The Court also had little difficulty in characterizing telephone selling of financial products as an offer to provide services. So the issue in the case[46] was whether the ban was a restriction on services. The Court applied its now familiar test: did the ban serve a legitimate purpose? Did the ban meet the test of proportionality as the least restrictive means of attaining a legitimate aim? The Court allowed a considerable margin of appreciation to the home State in concluding that the ban could be sustained. It could be argued that a ban was not the least restrictive method of protecting investors, since a cooling-off period during which an investor could withdraw from the investment with impunity might have met the concerns to protect the consumer. Such provisions are common in door-to-door selling of goods and services.

The Court decided the *Gebhard* case in the same year.[47] Gebhard was a German lawyer who moved to Italy with his Italian wife in 1978. He practised law first in collaboration with other lawyers in Milan, but in 1989 set up in practice on his own account. A key feature of the case is the distinction between services and establishment, since at the time there was a directive on lawyers' services, but no directive on lawyers' establishment. If Gebhard was merely a service provider, the services directive would apply which granted him certain rights, but if he was established then host State regulation would apply to him.[48] It soon became clear that Gebhard was almost certainly established in Italy. The Court then advised the national court on the test it should apply in determining whether any non-discriminatory rule of professional practice or conduct would constitute a barrier to freedom of establishment under the EC Treaty. The Court said:

36. Where the taking up or pursuit of a specific activity is subject to such conditions [as qualification for use of a particular professional title] in the host member State, a national of another Member State

[44] Case C-384/93 *Alpine Investments v Minister van Financiën* [1995] ECR I-1141, noted at (1995) 20 ELRev 507 and (1995) 32 CMLRev 1427.

[45] A practice known as 'cold calling'.

[46] The decision not to follow the *Keck* line of case law under which certain selling arrangements were not within the prohibition in Art 28 EC is not considered here. Suffice it to say that the Court decided that there was no parallel situation in relation to the selling of services to that which had been identified in relation to the selling of goods. See ch 11 below for further discussion of this issue.

[47] Case C-55/94 *Gebhard v Consiglio dell'Ordine degli Avvocati e Procuratori di Milano* [1995] ECR I-4165, noted at (1996) 21 ELRev 247.

[48] See ch 12 below for a case study on the regulation of legal practice.

intending to pursue that activity must in principle comply with them. It is for this reason that Article 57 provides that the Council is to issue directives, such as Directive 89/48, for the mutual recognition of diplomas, certificates and other evidence of formal qualifications or, as the case may be, for the coordination of national provisions concerning the taking-up and pursuit of activities as self-employed persons.

37. It follows, however, from the Court's case-law that national measures liable to hinder or make less attractive the exercise of fundamental freedoms guaranteed by the Treaty must fulfil four conditions: they must be applied in a non-discriminatory manner; they must be justified by imperative requirements in the general interest; they must be suitable for securing the attainment of the objective which they pursue and they must no go beyond what is necessary in order to attain it . . .

In the *Bosman* case[49] the Court of Justice applied the obstacles approach to the free movement of workers. At issue was the transfer system developed by national and transnational football associations. A football club which sought to employ a footballer whose contract with another club had come to an end had to pay the club from which the player came a transfer fee before the player could be registered to play for the new club. The transfer fee arrangements were collateral to the arrangements between the player and his new club concerning his personal terms. Bosman was playing for the third division Belgian club, Olympic de Charleroi, and wanted to move to the French club, Dunquerque. Bosman's argument was that the system of transfer payments prevented him from securing employment with the French club. The Court considered that it was dealing with a non-discriminatory rule which was capable of restricting the free movement of workers. As such, the system would only avoid breaching Article 39 EC if it could be justified as serving a legitimate aim required by pressing reasons of public interest.

It was argued that the system of transfer fees was necessary to maintain a financial and competitive balance between clubs and to support the search for and development of new football talent. The Court accepted that these were legitimate aims but went on to apply the ubiquitous proportionality text. Here the means were not the least restrictive to meet the aim; there were other mechanisms which would achieve the aim without inhibiting the free movement of workers.

So following this line of cases it is possible to posit the following proposition in relation to the free movement of persons. National rules regulating economic activity will not breach Articles 39, 43 and 49 where they:

- apply equally to all engaged in the activity;
- are justified by compelling reasons relating to the public interest;[50]
- are objectively necessary to safeguard that public interest;

[49] Case C-415/93 *Union Royale Belge des Sociétés de Football Association, ASBL and others v Bosman and others* [1995] ECR I-4921, noted at (1996) 21 ELRev 313 and (1996) 33 CMLRev 991. See also Case C-176/96 *Lehtonen* [2000] ECR I-2681; and Case C-51/96 *Deliège* [2000] ECR I-2549.

[50] And which are compatible with the EC Treaty: Case C-250/95 *Futura Participations SA* [1997] ECR I-2471, para 26 of the judgment.

- are not already the subject of safeguards under rules applying in the home Member State; and
- are the least restrictive necessary to secure the legitimate objective.

National rules which do not meet this testing standard will constitute unlawful obstacles to the free movement of persons and breach the relevant provision of the EC Treaty. Whereas regulation is a feature of undertaking professional activities and providing services, it is less likely to apply in the context of employment. The employer will normally be responsible for ensuring compliance with regulatory schemes. In the employment context, it is most likely to be some sort of collateral arrangement which brings the situation within the ambit of the *Bosman* decision.

This would appear to be confirmed in the *Terhoeve* case.[51] The case concerned the tax treatment of the earnings of a posted worker. Terhoeve, a Dutch national, had been posted to the United Kingdom for less than a year; for the remainder of the year he was resident in the Netherlands. Under a double taxation treaty, his income in the United Kingdom was not subject to income tax in the Netherlands. However, for the purpose of his liability for social security contributions, it was taken into account and he was issued with two notices of assessment.[52] Such contributions were levied at the rate of 22.1 per cent.[53] The effect was that he paid a higher rate of social security contributions than would have been the case had he received a single assessment which would have been subject to a ceiling on the amount of his contributions. Terhoeve argued that there was indirect discrimination on grounds of nationality in that those subject to dual assessment paid higher contributions and were mainly nationals of other Member States. The Court concluded that the provisions in issue were capable of being a restriction on free movement in that they could deter a national of a Member State from leaving the State of nationality in order to pursue an activity in another Member State. The Court went on to recognize the legitimacy of a State determining its own rules for the collection of income tax and social security contributions, and for simplifying and co-ordinating those rules. But such rules must not undermine rights which the Treaty grants to individuals.[54] There could be no justification for the differential treatment of those resident in the Netherlands for the whole year as against those whose income arose in another Member State as well as the Netherlands. Since this was a case where there was a ceiling on social security contributions where all the income in the calendar year arose in the Netherlands, it would be a simple matter to

[51] Case C-18/95 *Terhoeve v Inspecteur van de Belastingdienst Particulieren* [1999] ECR I-345. See also Case C-320/98 *Sehrer v Bundesknappschaft* [2000] ECR I-4584; and Case C-385/00 *de Groot v Staatssecretaris van Financiën* [2002] ECR I-11819.

[52] One for his period of stay in the United Kingdom and one for the balance of the calendar year when he was back in the Netherlands.

[53] Under the provisions of Regulation 1408/71, Terhoeve remained covered by the social security legislation of the Netherlands while posted in the United Kingdom.

[54] Para 44 of the judgment.

apply such a ceiling where the income arose in the Netherlands, and one or more other Member States.

The *Volker Graf* case[55] concerned what is at first sight an odd set of facts. German law contained a provision that, on termination of employment after a specified period of service, a compensation payment was payable. Such payments were not made where employees leave by their own choice or where employees bear responsibility for any premature dismissal. Graf, relying on the *Bosman* case, argued that this provision was an obstacle to free movement of workers. It acted as an inhibition to accepting a job[56] elsewhere in the Community. The Court escaped the conclusion which might have flowed from the application of the principles set out in the *Bosman* case by (a) confirming that provisions which are applied equally to all in a Member State which preclude or deter nationals from leaving their country of origin in order to exercise rights of free movement for persons constitute an obstacle to that freedom, but (b) that, in order to be capable of constituting such an obstacle, the measures must affect the access of workers to the labour market. In this case the provision in issue was 'too uncertain and indirect' a consequence of the German law to be capable of being regarded as intrinsically liable to hinder the free movement of persons.

It is sometimes suggested that the distinction between the prohibition of discriminatory rules which can be justified by the derogations in the EC Treaty and of unjustifiable non-discriminatory rules should be abolished.[57] This, it is argued, would avoid the need for classification of measures as distinctly or indistinctly applicable or as non-discriminatory; it would also avoid the need to determine whether measures were 'selling arrangements' when dealing with restrictions applicable to goods. However, the Court would appear to regard as significant the distinction between derogations which are permitted by the EC Treaty and measures which might escape the prohibition on restrictions in relation to goods, persons or services.[58]

Preventing or substantially hindering access to the market

Barnard[59] has suggested that a single question might apply to the areas of the free movement of goods, persons and services in order to determine whether a measure breaches the requirements of the Treaty: does the national measure prevent or

[55] Case C-190/98 *Graf v Filmoser Maschinenbau GmbH* [2000] ECR I-493.

[56] As Graf had done.

[57] Barnard, C, 'Fitting the remaining pieces into the goods and persons jigsaw?' (2001) 26 ELRev 35, at 53.

[58] See Joined Cases C-1/90 and C-176/90 *Aragonesa* [1991] ECR I-4151, paras 12-13 of the judgment.

[59] Barnard, C, 'Fitting the remaining pieces into the goods and persons jigsaw?' (2001) 26 ELRev 35.

impose a direct and substantial[60] impediment of access to the market in another Member State? If it does, then it can only escape the prohibition of restrictions in the Treaty if justified by public interest requirements or one of the derogations contained in the Treaty. Barnard puts forward five arguments in favour of recasting the prohibition in these terms. First, it applies a single rule to all these areas of free movement. Secondly, it avoids the need to classify the measure as (a) direct discrimination, (b) indirect discrimination, or (c) a non-discriminatory obstacle; this is something which has proved controversial. Thirdly, it would bring closer together the basis upon which a measure might escape the prohibition in the Treaty, and would view 'mandatory requirements' as an extension of the derogations in the Treaty. Fourthly, it is more consistent with the objective of integrating the markets of the Member States. Fifthly, a general test based on access to the market 'creates a clearer space in which regulatory competition can operate'.[61]

Barnard also recognizes that there are arguments against such a test, and offers five potential objections. First, it shifts the emphasis from the classification of the restrictive measure to a more economic test which is more difficult for courts to apply. Secondly, it might increase uncertainty since it replaces rules developed by the Court of Justice with standards. Thirdly, the technological, social and economic situations of persons and commodities (goods and services) are sufficiently different that an approach which treats them alike may not be appropriate. Fourthly, it merges an exhaustive list of Treaty derogations with an open list of 'mandatory requirements'. Fifthly, the emphasis on access to the market diverts attention from measures which prevent access to a particular occupation and interfere with its exercise. This might be resolved by regarding the phrase 'access to the market' as reading in the context of the free movement of persons as 'access to the employment market or occupational activity'.

It is the argument of this book that two distinctions should be maintained: that between people and commodities, and that between discrimination and non-discriminatory obstacles. Though issues of classification will remain, the retention of these distinctions is better likely to serve the development of those rights which belong to citizens of the European Union by virtue of that citizenship. Already the case law on citizenship of the Union is indicating quite how powerful a rule prohibiting discrimination can be. The prohibition of discrimination is powerful in all areas, while the law on non-discriminatory obstacles serves to limit the regulatory power of the Member States not by requiring equal treatment, but by requiring special justification for the application of host State regulation in the field of goods, persons and services from other Member States.

[60] This would avoid selling arrangements relating to goods being caught as well as measures which, as in the *Graf* case, are too uncertain and indirect to have a substantial effect on free movement.

[61] Barnard, C, 'Fitting the remaining pieces into the goods and persons jigsaw?' (2001) 26 ELRev 35, at 55.

Twin rules

There is a considerable attraction in the suggestion made by Barnard, but to replace the prohibition of discrimination on grounds of nationality with a rule which is primarily related to the integration of the market would be to deny the fundamental value of equality which is contained in Article 12 EC and reflected in specific articles of the EC Treaty relating to the free movement of persons. That prohibition is having a profound impact upon the development of the rights which flow from citizenship of the European Union. The argument of this book is that it is possible and preferable to draw a distinction between the prohibition of discrimination in all its forms and the prohibition of obstacles to the free movement of goods, persons and services. The argument is that the latter are concerned with the limits of Member State regulatory competence, whereas the former are concerned with fundamental rights for individuals.[62] Their goal is a social rather than an economic one. Respect for the prohibition of discrimination does, of course, restrain certain State conduct but for rather different reasons than the prohibition of unjustified obstacles to free movement which serve a primarily economic end.

It may not always be easy, however, to classify a measure as falling within the scope of the prohibition of discrimination or the prohibition of obstacles to free movement. This is illustrated in the *D'Hoop* case.[63] Marie-Nathalie D'Hoop was a Belgian national. Her parents were Belgian nationals who resided and worked in Belgium. They sent their daughter to France for her secondary education; that secondary education was recognized in Belgium as equivalent to secondary education in a French-speaking school in Belgium. D'Hoop then went to university in Belgium. She subsequently applied for a tideover allowance, which is a special form of unemployment benefit for those who have not found their first job. Her claim for this allowance was rejected on the sole ground that she had not undertaken her secondary education in Belgium. Questions were referred to the Court of Justice concerning her entitlement to the allowance. The Advocate General and the Court took differing views of the questions referred, though the outcome in both instances was that the refusal to grant D'Hoop the allowance was in breach of Community law.

Both the Advocate General and the Court concluded that the provisions of the Treaty on the free movement of workers did not assist D'Hoop since she had never worked. Nor did it appear to the Advocate General, on the information available to him, that the Treaty provisions on services would assist her. He then moved on to the Treaty provisions on citizenship. He concluded that D'Hoop was being denied access to the tideover allowance purely on the grounds of having exercised rights attaching to citizenship of the European Union, namely the opportunity to

[62] And in some cases enterprises.

[63] Case C-224/98 *D'Hoop v Office national de l'emploi* [2002] ECR I-6191, noted at (2003) 28 ELRev 389.

undertake part of her education in another Member State. She was, therefore, the victim of discrimination on grounds of nationality and could invoke the right to equal treatment to secure entitlement to the allowance. The Court's judgment turned on its characterization of the requirements of Belgian law as an obstacle to free movement:

By linking the grant of tideover allowances to the condition of having obtained the required diploma in Belgium, the national legislation thus places at a disadvantage certain of its nationals simply because they have exercised their freedom to move in order to pursue education in another Member State.[64]

The Court then looked at possible justifications for the requirement that eligibility for the tideover allowance be limited to those who have undertaken their secondary education in Belgium. The Court recognized the legitimacy of a Member State wishing to satisfy itself that there is a real link between the applicant for the allowance and the geographic market concerned, but speedily concluded that the requirement 'goes beyond what is necessary to attain the objective pursued'.

The Advocate General's Opinion extended the notion of the prohibition of discrimination on grounds of nationality to one which includes grounds of migration. The distinction was not drawn on the basis of nationality, but on the basis of where secondary education had been undertaken. For this reason, the Court's judgment is to be preferred. It recognizes the growing rights which attach to citizenship, but approaches the issue from the limits of a Member State's discretion to regulate its own social security benefits in relation to citizens of the European Union.

The *Carpenter* case[65] can also be analysed in support of these twin rules as an example of a restriction on free movement which cannot be justified because of its conflict with fundamental values. The facts are simple. Mary Carpenter was the Philippine wife of a United Kingdom national who operated a business under which he provided services in other Member States. He had children from a previous marriage. The United Kingdom immigration authorities wished to deport Mary Carpenter.[66] The reasoning of the Court was as follows. All restrictions on the right of establishment and the freedom to provide services are to be abolished. Community legislation has recognized the importance of ensuring family unity 'in order to eliminate obstacles to the exercise of the fundamental freedoms guaranteed in the Treaty'. The separation of Mr and Mrs Carpenter would be detrimental to the conditions under which Mr Carpenter exercised a fundamental freedom. The Court continued:

[64] Para 34 of the judgment.

[65] C60/00 *Carpenter v Secretary of State for the Home Department* [2002] ECR I-6729, noted at (2003) 28 ELRev 398. See Reich, R and Harbacevica, S, 'Citizenship and Family on Trial: A Fairly Optimistic Overview of Recent Court Practice with regard to Free Movement of Persons' (2003) 40 CMLRev 615.

[66] Prior to marrying, she had overstayed a visitor visa.

That freedom could not be fully effective if Mr Carpenter were to be deterred from exercising it by obstacles raised in his country of origin to the entry and residence of his spouse.[67]

The interference with these rights must strike a fair balance between the competing interests of Mr Carpenter and those of the maintenance of public order and safety in the host State. The Court's advice to the referring Court clearly indicates that it doubted whether the obstacle which would arise consequent upon the removal of Mrs Carpenter could meet the tests of necessity and proportionality applied in testing the national rule which was sought to be applied.

Concluding remarks

This chapter has sought to show that the case law on the prohibition of non-discriminatory obstacles to the free movement of persons and services is distinct from the case law on the prohibition of discrimination. It is, like much of the case law in relation to the free movement of goods, about placing limits on the extent of host State regulation of an activity. To this extent it can be argued that Barnard's new test of whether a measure prevents or substantially hinders access to the market has a considerable attraction. But this test should not also encompass the line of case law on the prohibition of discrimination.

The distinction between these two areas of Community law will, on occasion, be a fine one. However, viewed in this way, the convergence of the case law governing goods, persons and services seems logical in that the focus in on the limits of Member State discretion. The prohibition of discrimination is more rigorous; hence the need to justify discriminatory measures solely by reference to the derogations set out in the Treaty itself. Where indirect discrimination is in issue, the possibility of objective justification comes into play, but the effect of objectively justifying a measure is to take it outside the prohibition of discrimination altogether. The effect of justifying a non-discriminatory obstacles is not to take the measure outside the prohibition of discrimination but to take it outside the scope of the substantive provision of the EC Treaty in relation to the area of free movement in issue.

It could also be said that the objective of the prohibition of non-discriminatory obstacles is primarily economic, whereas the objective of the prohibition of discrimination on grounds of nationality is more social. That is open to the response that it is odd to use the term 'social' in relation to the prohibition of discrimination in the field of goods, and that the prohibition of non-discriminatory obstacles is increasingly having regard to social values in determining whether a measure can be justified. A good example is the *Carpenter* case discussed above. Ultimately, the distinction is one which better enables us to understand, classify and synthesize the case law of the Court of Justice.

[67] C60/00 *Carpenter v Secretary of State for the Home Department* [2002] ECR I-6729, para 39 of the judgment.

11

Services and goods

The context

Much has been written in the literature of Community law about the convergence of the law on the four freedoms.[1] Recurring issues have been whether convergence is appropriate across the areas of goods and persons, and where the similarities and distinctions lie. This chapter looks at the comparison and contrast between the law on goods and services, and posits the argument that convergence here in relation to the regulation of the product is generally to be welcomed.

In his Opinion in the *Säger* case,[2] Advocate General Jacobs raised the pertinent question of treating services by analogy with goods,[3] and went on to note that the provision of services 'covers a vast spectrum of different types of activity'. There are three distinct situations contemplated by the Treaty rules on the provision of services as interpreted by the Court. First, the service provider moves to another Member State in order to provide the service. Secondly, the service recipient moves to another Member State in order to receive a service. Finally, no person moves, but the service moves across national frontiers in a number of forms; it could simply be, for example, a fax or letter containing advice; it might be a set of distance learning training materials, or a language course delivered through audio or video tapes. Equally it could be a service provided by a small trader such as a specialist independent bookshop, or it could be a service provided by a corporate giant, such as an insurance company providing insurance cover for a particular risk, or an airline supplying an airline ticket. In the latter case, the whole transaction may be concluded over the internet.

The two dimensions to services which are not always readily distinguished relate to the marketing of the product on the one hand, and movement of persons for the purposes of providing or receiving a service on the other hand. This is not surprising since the location of the Treaty articles on services forms part of Title III on the free movement of persons, services and capital.[4] Just as there may be

[1] See, in particular, Snell, J, *Goods and Services in EC Law. A Study of the Relationship between the Freedoms* (Oxford, 2002); Barnard, C, 'Fitting the remaining pieces into the goods and persons jigsaw?' (2001) 26 ELRev 35; and Andenas, M and Roth, W-H (eds), *Services and Free Movement in EU Law* (Oxford, 2002), particularly Jarass, H, 'A Unified Approach to the Fundamental Freedoms' at 141.

[2] Case C-76/90 *Säger* [1991] ECR I-4221.

[3] At para 24 of his Opinion, [1991] ECR I-4221, at 4234.

[4] Though the terms of Arts 49 and 50 are not couched in terms of freedom of movement but in terms of the abolition of restrictions.

legitimate regulatory concerns about goods entering a Member State's territory, so too there may be legitimate regulatory concerns about services entering a Member State's territory. So in addition to issues relating to the movement of persons, there may be issues relating to the regulation of the service. This often takes the form of regulation of the service provider, since marketing services fairly more often depends upon both the skill and integrity of the provider than in the case of goods. It is also easier in many ways to regulate the provider because of the intangible nature of much service provision; it is probably impossible to operate border controls to prevent the entry of services whereas goods need to move physically across national borders and border controls are an effective means of controlling the entry of goods.

The development of the law on the free movement of goods

What is now Article 28 EC prohibits quantitative restrictions on imports and all measures having equivalent effect, while Article 29 EC prohibits quantitative restrictions on exports and all measures having equivalent effect. There are exceptions permitted under Article 30 EC which are justified on grounds of:

- public morality, public policy or public health;
- the protection of health and life of humans, animals and plants;
- the protection of national treasures possessing artistic, historic or archaeological value; and
- the protection of industrial and commercial property.

The *Geddo* case[5] defined quantitative restrictions as 'measures which amount to a total or partial restraint of . . . imports, exports or goods in transit,'[6] and the *Henn and Derby* case[7] confirmed that this included a total ban on the importation of a product. Directive 70/50[8] gave the Commission's view on those measures which would constitute measures equivalent to a quantitative restriction. The lists in this directive include both discriminatory measures[9] and non-discriminatory measures which may have the effect of protecting the domestic product.[10]

The early case law concerned, in particular, what constituted a measure equivalent to a quantitative restriction. The *Dassonville* case set out the classic definition of such measures which has come to be known as the *Dassonville* formula:

[5] Case 2/73 *Geddo* [1973] ECR 865. [6] ibid, at para 7 of the judgment.

[7] Case 34/79 *R v Henn and Derby* [1979] ECR 3795, at para 12 of the judgment.

[8] Directive 70/50/EEC of 22 December 1969, [1970] OJ L13/29. This directive applied during the transitional period, though it has had an effect beyond that time frame.

[9] Listed in art 2.

[10] Listed in art 3.

All trading rules enacted by Member States which are capable of hindering, directly or indirectly, actually or potentially, intra-Community trade are to be considered as measures having an effect equivalent to quantitative restrictions.[11]

This definition is very broad indeed. There is no requirement of any intention to protect the domestic product; it is the effect of the measure which determines its characterization. Nor is there any requirement for the measure to hinder trade between the Member States; it is enough if the measure has the capacity to do so either directly or indirectly. The subsequent case law is replete with examples of measures which are capable of favouring the domestic product and so fall foul of the prohibition in what is now Articles 28 and 29 EC. The following gives just a flavour of the range of prohibited measures:

- requirements to obtain import and export licences;[12]
- government-sponsored campaigns promoting national products;[13]
- price-fixing measures;[14] and
- inspections of various kinds.[15]

These examples relate to the removal of discriminatory barriers to markets other than those of the Member State in which the goods are produced. Clearly the creation of an internal market requires the removal of such barriers. But without further development, it would be possible to operate conditions which appear to apply equally to all, but which are framed in such a way that they favour the domestic market. It was the famous *Cassis de Dijon* case[16] which took the law firmly into the arena of non-discriminatory obstacles to the free movement of goods. The brilliance of the judgment lies in its promotion of the free movement of goods, its recognition that differences of national approach producing a variety of products with distinctive national characteristics are to be encouraged, and its balancing of the entitlement of Member States to apply regulatory measures with the obligation to open their markets to goods from other Member States. The case concerned the blackcurrant liqueur produced in France. French producers wished to market their product in Germany, but the product did not satisfy the requirements applicable in Germany on the marketing of alcoholic drinks. To constitute a liqueur in Germany, the product had to have an alcoholic content of 25 per cent, whereas cassis typically has an alcoholic content of only between 15 to 20 per cent. The judgment contains two rules. The first is a powerful rule of mutual acceptance of products:

There is therefore no valid reason why, provided they have been lawfully produced and marketed in one of the Member States, alcoholic beverages should not be introduced into any other Member State; the sale of such products may not be subject to a legal prohibition on the marketing of beverages with an alcohol content lower than the limits set by the national rules.[17]

[11] Case 8/74 *Dassonville* [1974] ECR 837, para 5 of the judgment.
[12] Case 68/76 *Commission v France* [1977] ECR 515.
[13] Case 249/81 *Commission v Ireland* [1982] ECR 4005.
[14] Case 82/77 *Van Tiggele* [1978] ECR 25.
[15] Case 50/85 *Schloh* [1986] ECR 1855.
[16] Case 120/78 *Rewe-Zentrale AG v Bundesmonopolverwaltung für Branntwein* [1979] ECR 649.
[17] Para 14 of the judgment.

This paragraph, taken in the overall context of the case, is sufficiently wide to apply not just to alcoholic drinks but to all products. The starting point is a presumption that goods lawfully produced and marketed in one Member State may be marketed in any Member State.

The second limb of the *Cassis de Dijon* judgment sets out the circumstances in which the Member State may nevertheless regulate the goods in its national market:

In the absence of common rules relating to the production and marketing of alcohol . . . it is for the Member States to regulate all matters relating to the production and marketing of alcohol and alcoholic beverages on their own territory.

Obstacles to movement within the Community resulting from disparities between the national laws relating to the marketing of the products in question must be accepted in so far as those provisions may be recognized as being necessary in order to satisfy mandatory requirements relating in particular to the effectiveness of fiscal supervision, the protection of public health, the fairness of commercial transactions and the defence of the consumer.[18]

The term 'mandatory requirements' is too direct a translation of the French '*exigences impératifs*' to be helpful in English. Later case law use the more helpful phrase 'over-riding requirements of general public importance'. Many commentators have chosen to describe the approach as the 'rule of reason'. The effect of the judgment is that national regulatory measures which serve a legitimate public interest and do not go beyond what is necessary and proportionate to meet that aim will not fall foul of the prohibition of measures equivalent to quantitative restrictions in Articles 28 and 29 EC. But those that do not serve such an interest or go beyond what is strictly necessary to protect that interest will breach Articles 28 and 29 EC. The genius of the *Cassis de Dijon* ruling is to expose national regulatory measures to a test which promotes market integration. Rather than simply being able to rely upon national measures which apply equally to domestic and imported products, Member States would be called upon to show whether those national measures have a legitimate aim, and whether they are strictly necessary and proportionate to the attainment of that aim. In the *Cassis de Dijon* case, the German authorities argued that the rules on minimum alcohol content operated for the protection of public health since the possible proliferation on the market of drinks with a low alcohol content may 'more easily induce a tolerance towards alcohol than more highly alcoholic beverages'.[19] It was also argued that the German rules protected the consumer against unfair commercial practices, since drinks with a lower alcoholic content tend to be cheaper. Neither argument, when subjected to objective scrutiny, convinced the Court that there was a need to give priority to the national regulations over the free movement of goods. The Court noted that there were means that were less restrictive of the free movement of goods which would serve to alert the consumer to the nature of the product and its alcoholic content.

[18] ibid, para 8 of the judgment.

[19] ibid, para 10 of the judgment.

The judgment in *Cassis de Dijon* did not signal any departure from the wide definition of measures equivalent to quantitative restrictions which had been set out in the *Dassonville* formula. The *Cassis de Dijon* decision did, however, make it clear that measures which applied equally to domestic and imported products could breach the prohibition in Article 28 EC. The seminal nature of this case is widely acknowledged. Advocate General Jacobs has stated:

> The importance of the 'Cassis de Dijon' principle cannot be overstated: if a Member State were allowed to prevent the importation and sale of products lawfully manufactured in another Member State, simply because they were not made in the manner prescribed by the law of the importing State, there would be no such thing as a common market, at least until all legislation governing such things as the composition, packaging and labelling of goods had been harmonized.[20]

The case law is, of course, replete with examples of the application of the *Dassonville* formula and of the application of the ruling in the *Cassis de Dijon* case.[21] One trend which emerged from the case law was that of traders seeking to use the prohibitions in Article 28 EC as a right to trade by arguing that any national regulation they found irksome was capable of hindering intra-Community trade. Commentators began to examine the nature of the regulatory regime. So, for example, Weatherill and Beaumont question whether Article 28 EC catches any rule that can be linked, however remotely, to an effect on trade, and note that national regulatory rules can be categorized as potentially dual burden or as equal burden rules.[22] The former require a product to comply with a second set of regulations relating to its access to the market. The latter, however, apply equally to all products and do not impose an additional burden. Weatherill and Beaumont comment:

> A common market requires free trade, but it does not require regulatory uniformity. National rules that do not partition the market should remain unaffected. This regulatory autonomy is an aspect of the principle of subsidiarity, which serves to confine Community intervention to instances where it is efficient.[23]

The dilemma posed by the use of Article 28 EC as a right to trade can be illustrated by the confused saga of the *Sunday Trading* cases.[24] In a series of cases mounted by the do-it-yourself superstore B & Q[25] the legality of the United Kingdom restrictions on Sunday trading were challenged as being in breach of the prohibition on measures equivalent to quantitative restrictions. In one case,[26]

[20] Case C-412/93 *Leclerc-Siplec* [1995] ECR I-179, at 188.

[21] See generally Oliver, P, *Free Movement of Goods in the European Community: under Articles 28 to 30 of the EC Treaty*, 4th edn (London, 2003).

[22] Weatherill, S and Beaumont, P, *EU Law* (London, 1999), at 608.

[23] ibid.

[24] Matters were not helped by the incoherent nature of the United Kingdom legislation on Sunday tradition. See generally Arnull, A, 'What Shall We Do on Sunday?' (1991) 16 ELRev 112.

[25] Among others.

[26] Case 145/88 *Torfaen BC v B & Q plc* [1989] ECR 3851.

B & Q was prosecuted for trading on a Sunday in defiance of the United Kingdom's Sunday trading laws. Questions were referred by the Cwmbran Magistrates' Court to the Court of Justice. The Advocate General proposed that the Court should respond in the following terms:

> A national rule which prohibits retail premises from being open on a Sunday for the sale of goods to customers, save in respect of certain specified items, is not covered by the prohibition laid down in Article 30 [now 28] if the rule does not cause imported good to be discriminated against or placed at an actual disadvantage compared with domestic goods and if it does not screen off the domestic market of the Member State in question or make access to that market substantially more difficult or unattractive for imported goods to which the rule applies.[27]

In the alternative, the Advocate General proposed that the Court should rule that the measures may be justified in the general interest if they did not go beyond what was strictly required to encourage 'non-working activities and social contacts on a specified day which is already devoted to those purposes by a large part of the population'.

The Court did not follow the Advocate General's preferred solution, but rather approached the case through the traditional route of the prohibition on measures equivalent to quantitative restrictions. The national provisions applied equally to domestic and imported products. National rules governing the opening hours of retail premises 'reflect certain political and economic choices in so far as their purpose is to ensure that working and non-working hours are so arranged as to accord with national and regional socio-cultural characteristics.'[28] As such these laws serve a legitimate purpose but must be subject to the necessity and proportionality tests in order to determine whether 'the restrictive effects on Community trade which may result therefrom do not exceed the effects intrinsic to rules of that kind.'[29] This consideration was a matter for national courts.[30]

The problem was that national courts found this test a difficult one to apply. In the United Kingdom some courts found that the Sunday trading laws were compatible with the prohibition on measures equivalent to quantitative restrictions, whereas others concluded that they were not. Following a number of references to the Court of Justice,[31] it was established that Sunday trading rules did not go beyond what was necessary to achieve their objective. However, the approach remained rooted in the *Dassonville* formula and the *Cassis de Dijon* line of authority. Once a trader raised the issue of the application to domestic and imported products alike of a national regulation capable of having an effect on trade between the Member States, the Member State whose law was called into question would be required to show whether the national laws served a legitimate

[27] ibid, para 34 of the Advocate General's Opinion. [28] ibid, para 14 of the judgment.
[29] ibid, para 17 of the judgment. [30] ibid, para 16 of the judgment.
[31] See, for example, Case C-306/88 *Rochdale Borough Council v Anders* [1992] ECR I-6457; Case C-304/90 *Reading Borough Council v Payless DIY and others* [1992] ECR I-6493; and Case C-169/91 *Stoke on Trent City Council v B & Q plc* [1992] ECR I-6635.

aim and whether the way it sought to achieve that aim was both necessary and proportionate. What the later Sunday trading cases did was to indicate that, in applying the test of proportionality, if the effect of a national measure on trade between the Member States was purely uncertain and speculative, the national measure would not thereby be incompatible with the prohibition in what is now Article 28 EC.

The opportunity to re-consider this line of authority in so-called 'equal burden' cases arose in the *Keck and Mithouard* case.[32] The case concerned the prohibition on reselling at a loss under French law, which applied equally to domestic and imported products. The Court was explicit about the need to reconsider its case law:

In view of the increasing tendency of traders to involve Article 30 [now 28] of the Treaty as a means of challenging any rules whose effect is to limit their commercial freedom even where such rules are not aimed at products from other Member States, the Court considers it necessary to re-examine and clarify its case-law on this matter.[33]

The Court's ruling in *Cassis de Dijon* was confirmed, but the range of measures which fall within the *Dassonville* formula was limited:

. . . contrary to what has previously been decided, the application to products from other Member States of national provisions restricting or prohibiting certain selling arrangements is not such as to hinder directly or indirectly, actually or potentially, trade between Member States within the meaning of the *Dassonville* judgment . . . , so long as those provisions apply to all relevant traders operating within the national territory and so long as they affect in the same manner, in law and in fact, the marketing of domestic products and those from other Member States.[34]

Consequently measures which met this test would fall outside the scope of the prohibition in what is now Article 28 EC of measures equivalent to quantitative restrictions. Academic response to the decision in *Keck* has been largely critical,[35] and although there has been a line of cases seeking to clarify the concept of a selling arrangement, the decision did stop in their tracks those claims by traders that Article 28 EC effectively granted a right to trade freely.

In the *Leclerc-Siplec* case,[36] Advocate General Jacobs submitted the state of the case law to scrutiny, and proposed an alternative solution to the need to distinguish between selling arrangements and product requirements. The case arose in the context of the prohibition in France on the distribution sector advertising on television. Leclerc-Siplec distributed motor fuels from garages attached to supermarkets forming part of the same group of companies. Noting that the full effect of

[32] Joined Cases C-267/91 and 268/91 *Keck and Mithouard* [1993] ECR I-6097. This was a case in which the Second Chamber of the Court elected to refer to the Full Court.

[33] ibid, para 14 of the judgment.

[34] ibid, para 16 of the judgment.

[35] Peter Oliver comments that 'the opprobrium which has been heaped on that ruling by a host of authors must be almost without precedent': Oliver, P, 'Some Further Reflections on the Scope of Articles 28-30 [ex 30-36] EC' (1999) 36 CMLRev 783, at 793.

[36] Case C-412/93 *Leclerc-Siplec* [1995] ECR I-179.

the judgment in *Keck and Mithouard* remained uncertain, the Advocate General noted:

> The effect of the *Keck* judgment is still uncertain: perhaps it is best understood as excluding from the scope of Article 30 [now 28] only measures of an entirely general character which do not preclude imports, which operate at the point of sale and which have no effect on trade other than to reduce the overall quantity of goods sold and which in doing so affect imports and domestic products alike.[37]

The Advocate General went on to note that, in the *Hünermund* case,[38] the Court had applied the *Keck* ruling to a restriction on advertising by pharmacists in cinemas, on radio, or television. The Advocate General was clearly concerned that restrictions on advertising have the capacity to pose a serious threat to the integration of the markets.[39] However, he concluded that if the test laid down in the *Keck* ruling is applied to the prohibition arising in the case before him, the prohibition on advertising falls outside the prohibition in what is now Article 28 EC. But he went on to suggest an alternative analysis.[40] His reasoning was as follows.

It is inappropriate to make rigid distinctions between different categories of rules and to apply different tests depending upon the classification of the rules. What is at issue is not so much a distinction based upon classification as a distinction based upon the effect of the application of the rules. Product requirements present a serious obstacle to the integration of the market, while selling arrangements may present little or no obstacle. The *Keck* test introduces a test of discrimination, which seems inappropriate. Simply because a set of national rules is restrictive does not alleviate the adverse effect on the importer:

> Restrictions on trade should not be tested against local conditions which happen to prevail in each Member State, but against the aim of access to the entire Community market. A discrimination test is therefore inconsistent as a matter of principle with the aims of the Treaty.[41]

The Advocate General then posited a new test based on the principle that all undertakings engaged in legitimate economic activity should have unfettered access to the whole of the Community market unless there is a valid reason for denying them full access to a part of that market. The new test would be whether the national measure creates a substantial restriction on access to the Community market. The Advocate General went on:

> Once it is recognized that there is a need to limit the scope of Article 30 [now 28] in order to prevent excessive interference in the regulatory powers of the Member States, a test based on the extent to which a measure hinders trade between Member States by restricting market access seems the most obvious solution.[42]

[37] Opinion of the Advocate General, at para 34.
[38] Case C-292/92 *Hünermund* [1993] ECR I-6787.
[39] See paras 19–21 of the Advocate General's Opinion in Case C-412/93 *Leclerc-Siplec* [1995] ECR I-179.
[40] ibid, paras 38–55 of the Opinion.
[41] ibid, para 40 of the Opinion.
[42] ibid, para 42 of the judgment.

Such a test would not apply to measures which discriminate against imported products, and so the new test would only apply to those measures which apply equally to imported and domestic products. The Advocate General noted that most of the earlier cases in which the effect on trade had been dismissed as the basis for determining whether there was a breach of Article 30 (now 28) EC concerned measures which were discriminatory and so would not, under the proposed test, be excused as not having a substantial effect on access to the market.

The Advocate General's views were not followed by the Court, which decided the case by applying its ruling in *Keck* and concluding that the prohibition on advertising was a selling arrangement and so was outside the prohibition in what is now Article 28 EC. That would appear to have settled matters for some time, although there have been subsequent cases and subsequent developments in the field of advertising restrictions.[43]

Goods and services: similarities and differences

If the perspective from which the free movement of goods and services is viewed is the dismantling of protectionist barriers, or the prohibition of discrimination in all its forms, or securing the completion of an internal market, then the logic of convergence is compelling. Jukka Snell has commented, 'The building of a coherent and transparent European legal system demands a common approach that is based on generally accepted principles, not on dubious distinctions.'[44]

However, there are practical and legal distinctions between the Treaty rules on the four freedoms which demand more than a monochrome view of the landscape.

The rules in the EC Treaty on goods prohibit State measures which favour the domestic market. As Wouter Wills has noted, Article 28 (ex 30) EC is about 'policing the borderline between legitimate and illegitimate national regulation'.[45] The emphasis is on State measures. By contrast, the benefits granted by Article 39 EC are given to individuals and may be asserted against both State actors and private parties. So the prohibition on discrimination based on nationality applies to a private sector employer as well as to State entities; by contrast a private seller of goods may urge consumers to buy national by singing the praises of British cheese or fruit, but the State may not do so.[46]

The Treaty provisions on the right of establishment and on services use the language of prohibiting restrictions, before moving on the specify certain individual

[43] See below, this chapter.

[44] Snell, J, *Goods and Services in EC Law. A Study of the Relationship between the Freedoms* (Oxford, 2002), at 15.

[45] Wils, W, 'The search for the rule in Article 30 EEC: much ado about nothing?' (1993) 18 ELRev 475, at 477.

[46] See Case 249/81 *Commission v Ireland* [1982] ECR 4005, and Case 222/82 *Apple and Pear Development Council v K J Lewis Ltd* [1983] ECR 4083.

or business rights. The Treaty provisions are silent on the source of those restrictions, but we now know from the case law that these Treaty articles are not just about State measures but are about professional and business regulation more generally.[47]

A further difference between the rules on goods and workers is that once goods are lawfully introduced into one Member State from outside the territory of the Member States, they are in free circulation in all Member States. There is as yet no corresponding rule in relation to workers or self-employed persons. Admission of a national of a non-Member State as a worker or self-employed person in one Member State does not grant any rights to enter and work in any other Member State.

There are practical differences too. The tendency in regulating the market in goods is to regulate the product; examples are requirements that the goods meet certain standards if they are to be sold on a particular market. By contrast, the tendency in regulating services is to regulate the provider of the service rather than the service itself. The consumer is protected by the integrity and standing of the service provider.[48] Yet in many respects services share a key characteristic with goods; they are a commodity to be sold in the market place.[49] Such an analysis might take an undergraduate by surprise since services are seen—and are so located in the EC Treaty—as the residual category of the free movement of persons once workers and establishment have been considered. There is justification for that since there is a closer link between service provision and the need for the service provider (or service recipient) to move across Member State borders than in the case of the supply of goods. There are also practical links between goods and services exemplified by the advertising industry. Advertising is a service, but much advertising is carried out through the medium of goods. In some cases, a magazine is wholly advertising material; in other cases, advertising is a feature of a magazine with a broader function. Among the most powerful arguments in favour of a unity of approach to the regulation of goods and services is that Article 94 EC grants a single competence to issue Community secondary legislation for the approximation of laws which directly affect the establishment or functioning of the common market, and Article 95 EC grants a similar competence using qualified

[47] See, for example, Case 107/83 *Ordre des Avocats v Klopp* [1984] ECR 2971; Case C-415/93, *Union Royale Belge des Sociétés de Football Association, ASBL and others v Jean-Marc Bosman and others* [1995] ECR I-4921; and Case C-309/99 *Wouters and others v Algemene Raad van de Nederlandse Orde van Advocaten* [2002] ECR I-1577. See also Snell, J, 'Private Parties and the Free Movement of Goods and Services' in Andenas, M and Roth, W-H (eds), *Services and Free Movement in EU Law* (Oxford, 2002), at 211.

[48] This has given rise to arguments as to which State should regulate the service provider: the State from which the service provider comes (the home State), the State in which the service is provided (the host State), or both.

[49] See, for a compelling argument that the economics of trade in goods and services are the same, Snell, J, *Goods and Services in EC Law. A Study of the Relationship between the Freedoms* (Oxford, 2002), at 15–26.

majority voting in relation to the establishment or functioning of the internal market.

Advertising: goods and services

In his Opinion in *Leclerc-Siplec*,[50] Advocate General Jacobs noted the important role advertising has to play in opening markets:

In a developed market economy, based on free competition the role of advertising is fundamental. Advertising is the means by which manufacturers and distributors of goods, and providers of services, seek to persuade consumers that their goods or services are worth buying.[51]

The Advocate General noted the view taken by the United States Supreme Court that 'the free flow of commercial information is indispensable' to a free enterprise economy.[52] The role of advertising is crucial to the successful introduction of new products onto the market place, or of existing products to a new market:

In short, advertising injects greater fluidity and mobility into the economy and enhances competitiveness. A ban on advertising tends to crystallize existing patterns of consumption, to ossify markets and to preserve the *status quo*.[53]

This would suggest that freedom to advertise is an essential corollary to the fundamental freedoms laid down in the EC Treaty, subject only to prohibitions which meet the tests for derogations from the Treaty freedoms laid down either in the Treaty or recognized in the case law of the Court of Justice. In considering the advertising ban arising in the *Leclerc-Siplec* case, the Advocate General noted that he is concerned with a partial ban on advertising, whose effects must be considered. In relation to the sale of petrol through outlets attached to supermarkets, the impact on access to the market is not regarded as substantial. The Court did not follow the Advocate General's alternative analysis, and decided that the partial advertising ban was not caught by Article 30; it was a legitimate selling arrangement which escaped the prohibition.

The question of advertising bans came before the Court in the *De Agostini* cases.[54] This involved, in one of the cases, the television advertising of a children's magazine about dinosaurs which fell foul of the Swedish law banning television advertising directed at children under the age of 12, and, in the other cases, television advertising of skin-care products and detergents which fell foul of the

[50] Case C-412/93 *Leclerc-Siplec* [1995] ECR I-179.

[51] ibid, para 19 of the Opinion.

[52] *Virginia State Board of Pharmacy v Virginia Citizens Consumer Council*, (1976) 425 US 748.

[53] Case C-412/93 *Leclerc-Siplec* [1995] ECR I-179, para 20 of the Opinion.

[54] Joined Cases C-34–36/95 *De Agostini* [1997] ECR I-3843. See also Greaves, R, 'Advertising Restrictions and the Free Movement of Goods and Services' (1998) 23 ELRev 305. See also Pending Joined Cases C-262/02 *Commission v France* and C-429/02 *Bacardi France*, the Opinion of the Advocate General was issued on 11 March 2004.

Swedish law banning advertising which prohibits misleading statements. The cases were argued both in relation to the free movement of goods and freedom to provide services. In relation to the compatibility of the ban on advertising targeted at children with the EC Treaty rules on free movement of goods and services, the Advocate General referred to the views he had expressed in the *Leclerc-Siplec* case, but nevertheless considered that under the *Keck* ruling it was arguable that the prohibition on television advertising might in fact have a greater impact on imported products than domestic products. So the ban was in principle contrary to Article 30 (now 28) EC. The unlawfulness of the ban could, however, be rescued under the application of the *Cassis de Dijon* authority; in this case, the Advocate General concluded that the advertising ban was not contrary to Article 30 EC. The Advocate General went on to conclude that the rules on services in the EC Treaty did not apply in this case since the relevant elements of the activity are confined within a single Member State.[55]

The Court's response on the relevant question was rooted firmly in Articles 30 (now 28) and 59 (now 49) EC, and uses very similar language. A Member State is not precluded from taking, on the basis of provisions of its domestic law, measures against an advertiser in relation to television advertising, but it is for the national court to determine whether the national measures are necessary for meeting 'overriding requirements of general public importance' or one of the specified derogations in the relevant Treaty article, whether they are proportionate for that purpose and whether the aims or over-riding requirements could be met by measures less restrictive of intra-Community trade.[56]

The ruling is helpful in relation to advertising controls. There is also an important difference on the burden of proof, and there will be shifting burdens in some cases. First,[57] courts will need to determine whether the challenged regulatory measures are selling arrangements or not. Here the burden of proof would appear to be neutral. It will be for each party to adduce such evidence as it considers relevant to resolve this issue. Once a measure has been categorized as a selling arrangement, then it is prima facie permissible under the EC Treaty, unless it can be shown that it discriminates in law or fact. However, if the challenged regulatory measure is a product requirement, then there would appear to be a presumption that it constitutes a restriction to free trade, and so can only be justified by the application of one of the Treaty derogations or as legitimately serving an overriding national interest which cannot be met by less-restrictive measures.

Similar issues were raised in the *Gourmet International* case.[58] The case concerned the Swedish ban on the advertising of alcoholic drinks. The case arose in the

[55] The Advocate General acknowledges that it is for the national court to determine whether this is in fact the case.

[56] Joined Cases C-34/36/95 *De Agostini* [1997] ECR I-3843, paras 47 and 54 of the judgment.

[57] At least in relation to challenges based on the free movement of goods.

[58] Case C-405/98 *Gourmet International* [2001] ECR I-1795. The Advocate General was again Advocate General Jacobs.

context of litigation by the Consumer Ombudsman seeking to restrain the publication of advertisements for drinks in a magazine supplement made available only to subscribers. The Advocate General considered that the advertising ban was not a selling arrangement since 'it seems to me inherent in any rule which prevents producers from advertising directly to the public that it will disproportionately affect imported products.'[59] However, the measure could be justified as being for the protection of the health and life of humans, although the Advocate General questioned whether that aim could not be achieved by less restrictive means.

The Advocate General had no difficulty in concluding that the ban is caught by Article 59 (now 49) EC. Following the decision in *Alpine Investments*,[60] freedom to provide services would be defeated if national measures were permitted which restricted the ability to offer services. In the field of services, there is no analogue to the ruling in the *Keck* case. The wording of the derogations applicable to Article 59 is rather different than those which relate to the field of the free movement of goods,[61] but the Advocate General concluded that the advertising ban is capable of justification for the protection of the health and life of humans subject to the requirement that it must be shown that the same result cannot be achieved by less restrictive means. The Court's judgment and reasoning were to the same effect.

One interesting feature of this case is to treat the grounds of derogation in relation to the provision of services, where the Treaty wording refers to exceptions 'providing for special treatment of foreign nationals on grounds of public policy, public security or public health' as having read into them the wording of the derogations in relation to free movement of goods which refer to measures 'for the protection of the health and life of humans'. Technically, the exceptions to Article 59 (now 49) EC to be found in Article 56 (now 46) EC in relation to public health are heavily circumscribed by reference to the Annex to Directive 64/221.[62] However, the Court uses the term 'the protection of public health against the harmful effects of alcohol' and the Advocate General refers to 'the protection of the health and life of humans', using language more redolent of that used in the Treaty provisions on goods rather than services.

People and products are different

In the context of the free movement of goods, there may, of course, be movement of people. Goods need to be delivered, and people make the deliveries. The EC

[59] Para 34 of the Opinion.

[60] Case C-384/93 *Alpine Investments* [1995] ECR I-1141, para 19 of the judgment. See ch 10 above.

[61] Article 30 contains a reference to grounds of (a) public morality, public policy or public security, and (b) the protection of health and life of humans, whereas Article 46 refers to 'special treatment for foreign nationals on grounds of public policy, public security or public health'. There is no express reference to the protection of health and life of humans, and the public health ground is heavily circumscribed by the provisions of Directive 64/221.

[62] See ch 5 above.

Treaty provisions on goods do not explicitly recognize this because they do not need to do so. The person moving will either be an employee of a larger concern working in a different Member State, or an employee who is providing a service by making the delivery, or a self-employed person. By contrast the provisions on services are located after the provisions on workers and establishment, and so tend to follow the language of people moving rather than products moving. However, as this chapter and chapter 13 on insurance services will show, the nature of services requires careful analysis.

On the one hand the choice of means of delivery of a service will often be in the hands of the service provider, who can choose whether the service provider or the service recipient moves across a national boundary within the Union, or whether no one moves. The classic example would be the delivery of legal advice by a large law firm in London. Either the lawyer can go to the client, or the client can go to the lawyer, or neither moves and the advice is sent by mail, fax or the internet. The freedom to provide and receive services would be restricted if this freedom was not available.

Equally, the provision of services across national boundaries may be a one-off or infrequent transaction, or it may be the essence of the business. The internet seller of airline tickets may be a good example here. Indeed, here the consumer may not know where the ticket seller has set up the internet operation, and may be unaware of where the email confirmation of the necessary travel code validating the ticketless authority to travel has originated. All this indicates that it will be vital to determine in any issue involving services what is being regulated. Is it movement *in connection with* the service, or is it the service itself? If it is the service itself, then there is a strong argument for the regulation of services to parallel, so far as appropriate, the permissible regulation of goods and vice versa. If it is the movement of people, then the cognate rules are those relating to the free movement of employed and self-employed individuals. Where it is a corporation whose movement is in issue, then that artificial legal person may expect more regulatory provisions to surround its movement than the movement of people.

So convergence in relation to the rules concerning the regulation of the service is to be welcomed, whereas there is no need for convergence of the rules relating to the regulation of the product with those relating to the rights of people to move.

12

Case study: lawyers

Introduction

Legal practice is traditionally carried out in the Member States[1] by sole practitioners or partnerships. It is perhaps therefore not surprising that cases involving legal practice have made a significant contribution to the law on the free movement of persons. Lawyers also provide the subject matter for a case study on the free movement provisions because of the significant differences in the structure and organization of national law and national legal orders.[2] This is unlike the practice of medicine, architecture or civil engineering where the underlying knowledge and skills have much more in common. Finally, lawyers make a good case study since the practice of law is heavily regulated; this means that the controlling and constraining influence of Community law might be more clearly seen than in some other areas of professional activity.[3]

Despite the differences in national legal systems, there is one body of Community law which applies in all the Member States. This has provided opportunities for transnational legal practice which has been seized with enthusiasm by some legal practitioners. Legal practice has also in recent years become much less territorial and more transnational.[4]

One of the early cases in which the Court of Justice was required to consider legal practice was the *Reyners* case.[5] This arose in the context of a requirement in Belgium that those admitted to the profession of *avocat* are Belgian nationals.[6] Reyners was a Dutch national who lived in Belgium where he was made *docteur en droit*. He was, however, denied admission to the profession of *avocat* because he was not a Belgian national. He challenged that refusal as being in breach of Article 52 (now 43) EC. At the start of his Opinion, Advocate General Mayras noted:

[1] Indeed perhaps globally.

[2] Of course, there are significant similarities between the legal systems of some of the Member States; good examples are France and Belgium, and the United Kingdom and Ireland.

[3] See in relation to the United Kingdom and Germany, Foster, N, 'European Community Law and the Freedom of Lawyers in the United Kingdom and Germany' (1991) 40 ICLQ 607.

[4] See generally Tyrrell, A and Yaqub, Z (eds), *The Legal Professions in the New Europe. A Handbook for Practitioners*, 2nd edn, (London, 1996).

[5] Case 2/74 *Reyners v Belgium* [1974] ECR 631.

[6] As late as the 1970s, it was not uncommon for admission to legal practice in a country to be conditional on the holding of the nationality of that country. Nationality requirements as a condition of admission to practise law still exist in some countries, but are generally on the wane.

How is it possible not to register some surprise that freedom of establishment for *avocats* has not yet been attained and that it can even be denied them?

In truth, this problem, which brings into question the interpretation of Articles 52 and 55 of the Treaty of Rome, is one of those which have, since the coming into force of the Treaty, given rise to the most lively controversies and the most marked divergencies between the Bars and between the national Governments to the point where action by the Community organs has been paralysed and no positive measures have been able to be taken to free the activities of the *avocat* at the Community level.[7]

The Court first had to decide whether Article 52 had direct effect. The Court concluded that it did, at least in relation to the prohibition of discrimination on grounds of nationality since this is 'one of the fundamental provisions of the Community'[8] and despite the absence of harmonizing measures in the particular sphere contemplated by Articles 54 and 57. The Court then went on to consider whether the activities of *avocats* involved the exercise of official authority such that the activity could be restricted to nationals of the Member State.[9] The Court concluded:

54. It is therefore right to reply to the question raised that the exception to freedom of establishment provided for by the first paragraph of Article 55 must be restricted to those of the activities referred to in Article 52 which in themselves involve a direct and specific connexion with the exercise of official authority.

55. In any case it is not possible to give this description, in the context of a profession such as that of *avocat,* to activities such as consultation and legal assistance or the representation and defence of parties in court, even if the performance of those activities is compulsory or there is a legal monopoly in respect of it.

At a stroke, the Court laid the conditions for the liberalization of legal practice within the Community, and side-stepped the political disagreements which had precluded developments through legislative measures. The continuing use of nationality requirements is evidenced in infringement proceedings taken against Italy.[10] The Commission argued that Italian law retained an ambiguity when it repealed its nationality requirement.[11] The Court rejected the complaint taking a different view of the requirements of legal certainty than that put forward by the Commission.

In December 1974, the Court handed down it decision in the *Van Binsbergen* case.[12] This case, which laid the foundations for the development of the prohibition of non-discriminatory obstacles which restrict the exercise of the freedom to provide services, arose in the context of the provision of legal advice in social

[7] Case 2/74 *Reyners v Belgium* [1974] ECR 631, at 658.

[8] Para 24 of the judgment.

[9] For a broader discussion of the exception, see ch 5 above.

[10] Case C-145/99 *Commission v Italy* [2002] ECR I-2235. Other failures to allow access to the practice of law were also raised in the case.

[11] Paras 32–40 of the judgment.

[12] Case 33/74 *Van Binsbergen v Bestuur van de Bedrijfsvereniging voor de Metaalnijverheid* [1974] ECR 1299, discussed in ch 10 above.

security matters. This is much less regulated than the practice of law under more formally recognized professional titles. This judgment trod the delicate balance between liberalization and appropriate Member State regulation. It affirmed the ability of the host Member State to lay down professional rules (even in the area of the provision of services), but also imposed conditions. The requirements of the professional rules must serve a legitimate purpose and be proportional to that need.

The *Klopp* case[13] concerned a requirement imposed by the Paris Bar on legal practice which had the effect of segmenting the market in legal services. The Paris Bar would only admit those who establish chambers in one place only, which must be within the territorial jurisdiction of the *tribunal de grande instance* with which the *avocat* is registered. Klopp was a German national who held a dual qualification. He was a member of the Düsseldorf Bar, but also qualified to be admitted to the French Bar by virtue of his studies in Paris. He had an office in Düsseldorf and wished to open an office in Paris while retaining his office in Germany. The effect of the French rule was that he could only practise in France if he closed his office in Germany. The issue before the Court was whether the French requirements were compatible with Article 52 of the Treaty. The Court noted that the right of establishment of nationals of other Member States was, in Article 52, expressed as being 'under the conditions laid down for its own nationals by the law of the country where such establishment is effected'. However, that did not give the host Member State *carte blanche* to lay down any rule it wished; the French provisions effectively permitted establishment in only one place and that constituted a denial of the right of establishment. Any rules applicable in the Member State of secondary establishment must respect the Treaty freedom, but it is legitimate to impose special requirements in order to ensure that such lawyers 'maintain sufficient contact with their clients and the judicial authorities and abide by the rules of the profession'[14] having due regard to modern methods of transport and communication.[15] It does not follow from this case that registration with the local Bar may not be a condition of establishment; the problem concerned the requirement that a person have only one establishment. It was established in the *Gullung* case that a person seeking to establish themselves as a lawyer in another Member State where registration is required cannot avoid that requirement on the grounds that they are already registered as a lawyer in the Member State from which they come.[16]

In infringement proceedings brought by the Commission,[17] the Italian Government sought to justify a requirement that members of the Bar reside in the judicial district of the court to which the Bar at which they are enrolled is attached as meeting essential requirements of judicial organization. This could not, in the

[13] Case 107/83 *Ordre des Avocats au Barreau de Paris v Klopp* [1984] ECR 2971.
[14] Para 20 of the judgment. [15] Para 21 of the judgment.
[16] Case 292/86 *Gullung v Conseil de l'ordre des avocats du barreau de Colmar et de Saverne* [1988] ECR 111, paras 24–31 of the judgment.
[17] Case C-145/99 *Commission v Italy* [2002] ECR I-2235.

opinion of the Court, be justified since it prevents members of the Bar established in Member States other than Italy from maintaining an establishment in Italy.

To what extent can national regulation take account of disciplinary action taken against a legal practitioner in another Member State? This issue arose in the *Gullung* case[18] in the context of the application of the Lawyers' Services Directive.[19] It is, however, clear from the Court's judgment in this case that Community law does not permit a person to sidestep requirements that they are of good character and standing with relevant professional bodies through reliance on Community law.

Recognition of qualifications

An alternative means of segmenting the legal profession along national lines is to require anyone wishing to be admitted to a country's professional title to undertake all their legal training in that country.[20] This brings into play Community law on the mutual recognition of qualifications. These rules[21] will only apply where there is a Community element to the claim. Therefore, they are of no assistance where the objective of the litigation is to take issue with provisions of national law by nationals of the Member State concerned in relation to the exercise of the activity in that State.[22]

The *Thieffry* case[23] shows how severely such attempts have in the past adversely affected individuals seeking admission to practise law. Thieffry held Belgian nationality and had obtained a *docteur en droit* in Belgium. He practised as an *avocat* at the Brussels Bar. He sought and was granted recognition of his Belgian doctorate from the Université de Paris I as the equivalent of *license en droit* in French law. This qualified him to take the *Certificat d'Aptitude à la Profession d'Avocat (CAPA)* which he duly took and passed at the Université de Paris II. He then sought admission to the Paris Bar. His application was rejected on the grounds that he did not provide evidence that he held a French *license* or *docteur en droit*. Thieffry challenged the refusal to admit him to the Paris Bar. The Court emphasized the fundamental nature of freedom of establishment in the scheme of the Treaty. This meant that national practices must have regard to the objective of freedom of establishment. The guidance to the referring court had to tread a fine line. There was, at the time,

[18] Case 292/86 *Gullung v Conseil de l'ordre des avocats du barreau de Colmar et de Saverne* [1988] ECR 111.

[19] See below in this chapter where the case is discussed in more detail.

[20] See, for example, the unsuccessful complaint by the Commission in relation to the repeal of the Italian requirement that access to the Italian Bar required the possession of an Italian diploma in law and the completion of two years as a trainee working within the jurisdiction of the Italian courts: Case C-145/99 *Commission v Italy* [2002] ECR I-2235.

[21] Whether flowing from the Court's decisions, or from the Community secondary legislation on the mutual recognition of qualifications.

[22] Joined Cases C-225–7/95 *Kapasakalis and others v Greece* [1998] ECR I-4239.

[23] Case 71/76 *Thieffry v Conseil de l'ordre des avocats à la Court de Paris* [1977] ECR 765.

no directive on the mutual recognition of qualifications, but the facts of the case indicated that universities in France had recognized the equivalence of the Belgian qualification as a prerequisite to the professional stage of training (CAPA) to which Thieffry had been admitted. There was some evidence before the Luxembourg Court that the academic effect and the civil effect of recognition was different; accordingly it was for the national authorities to determine the effect of that distinction 'taking account . . . of the objectives of Community law'.[24] The clear implication of the Court's reasoning is that there would need to be the most compelling reasons for refusing to accept the consequences of the recognition of Thieffry's Belgian qualification in the context of his meeting the requirements for admission to the Paris Bar.[25]

The issue of recognition of qualifications also arose in the *Vlassopoulou* case.[26] Vlassopoulou, a Greek national registered as a lawyer with the Athens Bar, held a German doctorate in law. She had worked for German lawyers for four years, having received permission from the German authorities to deal with foreign legal affairs and Community law; she was, in this regard, subject to the supervision of a German lawyer in the firm in which she worked. She applied for admission as a *Rechtsanwalt*, but her application was rejected because she had not studied law at a German university, passed the First State Examination, completed a preparatory training period, and subsequently passed the Second State Examination. In other words, she had not followed the traditional route to admission to the German legal profession. Vlassopoulou contested the decision, and the case found its way to the Bundesgerichthof, which referred questions to the Luxembourg Court on the interpretation of what was then Article 52 of the Treaty.

In a decision handed down a few months after the deadline for implementation of the first general system directive[27] on mutual recognition of qualifications, and which is clearly influenced by the provisions of that directive, the Court interpreted Article 52[28] to include a duty to consider the equivalence of qualifications in good faith even where the directive did not apply.[29] The Court said:

> . . . a Member State which receives a request to admit a person to a profession to which access, under national law, depends upon the possession of a diploma or a professional qualification must take into consideration the diplomas, certificates and other evidence of qualifications which the person concerned has acquired in order to exercise the same profession in another Member State by making a comparison between the specialized knowledge and abilities certified by those diplomas and the knowledge and qualifications required by the national rules.[30]

[24] Para 22 of the judgment.

[25] See, in particular, paras 25–26 of the judgment. The Advocate General is much more explicit: see [1977] ECR 765, at 794.

[26] Case C-340/89 *Vlassopoulou v Ministerium für Justiz* [1991] ECR I-2357.

[27] Considered in detail in ch 4 above.

[28] Read together with Article 5 (now 10) EC

[29] In this case, the factual situation arose prior to the date for implementation of the directive.

[30] Case C-340/89 *Vlassopoulou v Ministerium für Justiz* [1991] ECR I-2357, para 16 of the judgment.

A number of obligations flowed from this bona fide assessment of equivalence. If the comparison reveals a correspondence of skills and knowledge, the qualifications must be accepted as equivalent to the national requirements. If the comparison shows that the national requirements are only partially met, the applicant can be required to undertake national training to meet the shortfall in the qualifications, but may not be required to begin the process of qualifications all over again. In making the assessment, periods of practical experience are to be taken into account. In the event of any adverse decision as to the equivalence of the qualifications, reasons must be given.

The date for the implementation of the first general system directive[31] was 4 January 1991. This required the mutual recognition of diplomas leading to professional qualification where the activity constituted a regulated profession in the Member States in question. As was explained in chapter 4, the directive deals with situations where there is a shortfall in the training evidenced by the diploma presented for recognition. Here, the general rule is that the applicant must, at their own choice, either complete a period of further training (called an adaptation period in the directive), or undertake assessment in the material which has not been covered in the home State (called an aptitude test in the directive). However, for those 'professions whose practice requires a precise knowledge of national law and in respect of which the provision of advice and/or assistance concerning national law is an essential and constant aspect of the professional activity',[32] it is the regulator who has the choice as to whether an adaptation period is served or an aptitude test is taken. All national bars have chosen to require an aptitude test.[33]

The Commission found it necessary to take infringement proceedings against Italy for incomplete transposition of the requirements of the first general system directive in that Italy (a) had not drawn up any detailed rules for the conduct of the aptitude test in relation to cross-qualification of lawyers with the result that the requirements imposed were unpredictable, and (b) in practice, set a discriminatory aptitude test which was excessively difficult by comparison with the qualifying examination which Italian lawyers are required to sit.[34] The Court upheld these complaints indicating that there was an obligation to set out and publish details of the knowledge and skills which are seen as indispensable for legal practice in Italy, and some indication as to how the aptitude test met those requirements. The Court also found that the practical implementation of the aptitude test lacked coherence and transparency. Italy had failed to fulfil its obligations under the Treaty.

[31] Directive 89/48/EEC of 21 December 1988 on a general system for the recognition of higher-education diplomas awarded on completion of professional education and training of at least three years' duration ('the first general system directive'), [1989] OJ L 19/16, as amended by Directive 2001/19/EC, [2001] OJ L206/1. See also Directive 92/51/EEC of 18 June 1992 on a second general system for the recognition of professional education and training to supplement Directive 89/48/EEC ('the second general system directive'), [1992] OJ L209/25, as amended by Directive 2001/19/EC, [2001] OJ L206/1.

[32] Article 4 of the directive.

[33] In England and Wales for admission as a solicitor, it is the Qualified Lawyers Transfer Test.

[34] Case C-145/99 *Commission v Italy* [2002] ECR I-2235.

An important distinction was made in the *Morgenbesser* case.[35] Christine Morgenbesser held a *maîtrise en droit* which she had obtained in France. She then worked in a law firm in Paris for eight months before joining a firm of *avvocati* in Italy. She sought enrolment in Italy as a *praticanti-patrocinanti*; the Advocate General described this status as that of trainee lawyer. Her application was refused because she did not have a legal diploma issued or confirmed by an Italian university. She also applied to the *Universitá degli Studi* of Genoa for recognition of her *maîtrise en droit*; this was granted subject to her completing two years of study, passing 13 examinations and writing a thesis. This decision is the subject of separate proceedings in Italy. The Court of Justice, in responding to questions raised in the course of national proceedings challenging the refusal to enrol her as a trainee lawyer, ruled that the first general system directive did not apply to her because she had not completed the training required for admission to the legal profession of any Member State, or indeed to trainee status.[36]

That, however, was not an end of the matter. As the Court had ruled in the cases of *Vlassopoulou*[37] and *Fernández de Bobadilla*[38] there must be a good faith assessment of the equivalence of the extent to which the qualifications offered represented evidence of skills and knowledge equal to that required for the purposes for which the applicant sought their recognition. The requirements which can then be applied are those reasonably required to meet any shortfall in skills and knowledge required for the purpose for which recognition is sought.

The Services Directive

The content of the directive

Following the early cases on the free movement of lawyers outlined above, there was increased impetus to conclude a directive on the effective exercise by lawyers of freedom to provide services. In March 1977 a directive was adopted.[39] The directive states that it does not concern freedom of establishment, nor the mutual recognition of qualifications. Its concern is to facilitate the provision of services by those designated as a lawyer under the terms of the directive.[40] Indeed, the directive opens with a derogation:

[35] Case C-313/01 *Morgenbesser*, judgment of 13 November 2003, [2003] ECR nyr.

[36] In addition to her *maîtrise en droit*, the applicant would need to have completed the *certifcat d'aptitude à la profession d'avocat* (*CAPA*) in France to be eligible for access to the status of *stagiaire*.

[37] See above, this chapter.

[38] Case C-234/97 *Fernández de Bobadilla* [1999] ECR I-4773. See ch 4 above.

[39] Council Directive 77/249/EEC of 22 March 1977 to facilitate the effective exercise by lawyers of freedom to provide services, [1977] OJ L78/17.

[40] For the list, see art 1(2). Art 2 requires Member States to recognize persons holding these titles as lawyers for the purposes of the Directive.

Notwithstanding anything contained in this Directive, Member States may reserve to prescribed categories of lawyers the preparation of formal documents for obtaining title to administer estates of deceased persons, and the drafting of formal documents creating or transferring interests in land.[41]

The lawyer providing the service must use the title applicable in his or her home State, and may not use the corresponding title in the host State. The lawyer delivering services is required to comply with the rules of professional conduct of the host State, other than those relating to residence or registration in the host State, as well as those applicable in the home State.[42] Article 5 requires that a Member State may require a visiting lawyer 'to be introduced' to the presiding judge or the President of the relevant Bar in the host State, and to work 'in conjunction with a lawyer who practises before the judicial authorities' in the host State. This poorly drafted provision has given rise to differing interpretations. Article 6 enables the host State to exclude visiting lawyers who are in the salaried employment of a public or private undertaking from activities to which similarly employed lawyers in the host State are excluded. Article 7 sets out the procedure by which a person's status as a lawyer within the directive is established, and for reporting back to the home State any disciplinary matters arising while services are being provided.

Case law on the directive

The infringement proceedings against France[43] concerned provisions of French law implementing the directive which did not include French nationals within its terms. This would mean that a French lawyer practising as a solicitor in England would have been unable to provide legal services in France. The French Government did not contest the Commission's complaint that, in this respect, France had failed to fulfil its obligations under the Treaty.[44]

The interpretation in Germany of the requirements of Article 5 of the directive was considered by the Court of Justice in infringement proceedings brought by the Commission against Germany.[45] German law implementing the directive provided the following:

(a) A lawyer from another Member State providing services[46] must act in conjunction with a German lawyer even in those cases where, under German law, there is no requirement to be represented by a lawyer.
(b) The German lawyer with whom the visiting lawyer is acting in conjunction must be the authorized representative on the record.
(c) The visiting lawyer may not appear in oral proceedings or at criminal trials unless accompanied by the German lawyer.

[41] Article 1, second sentence. [42] Article 4.
[43] Case C-249/89 *Commission v France* [1991] ECR I-3591.
[44] See below for other aspects of this case.
[45] Case 427/85 *Commission v Germany* [1988] ECR 1123.
[46] For convenience described in this chapter as a 'visiting lawyer'.

(d) The visiting lawyer may not visit as defence counsel a person held in custody unless accompanied by the German lawyer.
(e) The necessary co-involvement of the German lawyer must be proved whenever some step in the proceedings is taken. If this is not done, the step in the proceedings is of no effect. But where the proceedings are oral, such co-involvement is presumed unless the German lawyer immediately countermands or amends the step in the proceedings.
(f) In cases in which German law requires a client to be represented by a lawyer admitted to practise before the judicial authority in question, the visiting lawyer is merely entitled to submit observations during the oral phase by delegation from the German lawyer on the record.[47]

It will be observed that the German rules affect the scope of the work which can be done by the visiting lawyer, the manner in which that work is done, and the restriction to a specific geographic area of the right to plead. In relation to the first question concerning the scope of the work done by the visiting lawyer, the Court said:

> . . . Article 5 of the Directive may not have the effect of imposing upon a lawyer providing services requirements for which there is no equivalent in the professional rules which would apply in the absence of any provision of services within the meaning of the Treaty. It is undisputed that, in proceedings for which German law does not make representation by a lawyer mandatory, the parties may conduct the cases themselves; in such proceedings, German law also allows representation to be entrusted to a person who is neither a lawyer nor a specialist, provided that that person does not act in a professional capacity.[48]

It followed that, by imposing these extra requirements in respect of a visiting lawyer, Germany had failed to fulfil its obligations under the Treaty. The Commission also considered that the requirements for much of the work to be done by a German lawyer reflected a misunderstanding as to the concept of working 'in conjunction with' a German lawyer. The Court said:

> . . . the lawyer providing services and the local lawyer, both being subject to the ethical rules applicable in the host Member State, must be regarded as being capable, in compliance with those ethical rules and in the exercise of their professional independence, of agreeing upon a form of cooperation appropriate to their client's instructions.[49]

Any national regulation in this area must be proportionate to the objectives of the freedom to provide services and appropriate national regulation of the activity.

[47] Described in the case as the rule of territorial exclusivity.
[48] Case 427/85 *Commission v Germany* [1988] ECR 1123, para 13 of the judgment. See also Case C-249/89 *Commission v France* [1991] ECR I-3591.
[49] Para 24 of the judgment.

The final issue concerned the territorial exclusivity of audience before certain courts. The position in Germany is that lawyers are admitted with rights of audience before courts in particular localities. Rights of audience before other courts are limited to the submission of observations during the oral phase of the proceedings. This rule was applied by analogy to lawyers from other Member States providing services. The limitation is clearly more restrictive than a requirement to work in conjunction with a local lawyer. The German Government also drew attention to the limitation of rights of audience before the Bundesgerichthof to those with established experience in dealing with appeals involving a point of law. The Court appeared to conclude that this type of limitation is justified.

The Commission considered that the directive entitled the visiting lawyer to the same rights as those enjoyed by local lawyers with rights of audience before the courts in question. The Court of Justice considered that this issue fell outside the scope of the services directive. In somewhat complex reasoning which is not always easy to follow, the Court concluded:

> The rule of territorial exclusivity . . . is precisely part of national legislation normally relating to a permanent activity of lawyers established in the territory of the Member State concerned, all such lawyers having the right to gain admission to practise before one, and sometimes two, German judicial authorities, and to pursue before them all the activities necessary for representation of clients or their defence of their interests. On the other hand, a lawyer providing services who is established in another Member State is not in a position to be admitted to practise before a German court.
>
> In those circumstances, it must be stated that the rule of territorial exclusivity cannot be applied to activities of a temporary nature pursued by lawyers established in other Member States, since the conditions of law and fact which apply to those lawyers are not in that respect comparable to those applicable to lawyers established on German territory.[50]

The effect of this decision would appear to be that visiting lawyers do enjoy rights of audience before the courts where they are delivering services subject only to the requirement to work in conjunction with a local lawyer in accordance with the principles laid down by the Court earlier in this judgment.[51]

The issue in the *Gullung* case[52] concerned the potential use of the services directive to evade requirements that lawyers be of good character. Gullung, the holder of French and German nationality, found himself the subject of disciplinary proceedings in France in relation to his practice as a *notaire*. He resigned. Subsequent applications in France to be admitted as a *conseil juridique* and as an *avocat* failed on the grounds that he was not of good character. Gullung was admitted in Germany as a *Rechtsanwalt*. He then set up an office in Mulhouse in France offering legal advice. The Mulhouse Bar responded by prohibiting any member of the Mulhouse Bar from 'lending assistance' to Gullung. Gullung's action against this decision was dismissed as being without foundation. Gullung subsequently found

[50] Paras 41–2 of the judgment.
[51] See also Case C-249/89 *Commission v France* [1991] ECR I-3591.
[52] Case 292/86 *Gullung v Conseil de l'ordre des avocats du barreau de Colmar et de Saverne* [1988] ECR 111.

himself in trouble with the Colmar Bar Council and the Saverne Bar Council which issued similar prohibitory orders. It was his challenge to these orders which resulted in questions being referred to the Court of Justice.

The Court first had to deal with the implications of Gullung's dual nationality. Unsurprisingly, the Court ruled that this did not preclude his ability to rely on the provisions of the directive. The Court's ruling on the effect of the prior finding in France that Gullung was not of good character is equally unsurprising:

> By requiring compliance with the rules relating to professional ethics of the host Member State the directive assumes that the person providing the service has the capacity to comply with the requirements of those rules. If the competent authority of the host Member State has already found in the course of proceedings concerning access to the legal profession that the person lacks such capacity so that he is barred from access to the profession on that ground, he must be considered not to satisfy the very conditions laid down by the directive with regard to freedom to provide services.[53]

The distinction between service provision and establishment

The *Gebhard* case[54] concerned the attempts of a German lawyer to practise in Italy. He lived in Italy with his Italian wife and their family. He had worked in collaboration with an Italian law firm for a number of years. He then opened his own chambers in Milan in which Italian *avvocati* and *procuratori* worked in collaboration with him. Gebhard indicated that almost all his work was non-contentious; two-thirds of his business was for German speakers and about one-third for Italian speakers in Germany or Austria. About five per cent of his business was accounted for by assistance to Italian practitioners whose clients faced problems relating to German law. Complaints were made that his practice was called 'Studio Legale Gebhard' and that he described himself as an *avvocato*.[55] Disciplinary action was begun against him on these grounds by the Milan Bar Council. The outcome was to prohibit him from using the Italian titles. He appealed against these rulings arguing that the services directive permitted him to pursue his professional activities from his own chambers in Milan.

As has already been made clear, the services directive does not address any issues relating to freedom of establishment for lawyers, so the directive would only be of assistance to Gebhard if he could show that he was doing no more than providing services in Italy. This was patently not the case here; he was established in Italy. Accordingly, he would be subject to the national rules on the practice of law, and could draw no support from the provisions of the directive. However, the Court

[53] Para 21 of the judgment.

[54] Case C-55/94 *Gebhard v Consiglio dell'Ordine degli Avvocati e Procuratori di Milano* [1995] ECR I-4165, discussed in some detail in ch 10 above.

[55] Both professional titles used by Italian lawyers.

did make some important observations on the distinction between services and establishment. In particular, the Court indicated that it was not incompatible with the provision of services to have some infrastructure in the Member State in which services are provided. The Court said:

> . . . the temporary nature of the activities in question [which constitute the provision of services] has to be determined in the light, not only of the duration of the provision of services, but also of its regularity, periodicity or continuity. The fact that the provision of services is temporary does not mean that the provider of services within the meaning of the Treaty may not equip himself with some form of infrastructure in the host Member State (including an office, chambers or consulting rooms) in so far as such infrastructure is necessary for the purposes of performing the services in question.[56]

It followed from this case that legislation in Italy which precluded a lawyer from another Member State who provides services in Italy from having any form of infrastructure in Italy was incompatible with Article 59 (now 49) EC.[57]

The *AMOK* case[58] concerned the costs rules applicable in Germany in cases where rights were exercised under the services directive. A party to proceedings in Germany was represented by a lawyer who was established in Austria, and who acted in conjunction with a lawyer established in Germany. That party was successful in the litigation and sought reimbursement of their lawyers' costs. AMOK Verlags raised objections on two grounds; either that it was unnecessary to use a lawyer established in Austria in the proceedings, or, in the alternative, that the cost of the second lawyer with whom the lawyer in Austria worked in conjunction should be discounted. The Court ruled that it was not incompatible with Community law or the services directive for the host Member State to have a judicial rule limiting the recoverable fees to those which would have resulted from representation by a lawyer established in that State. But this response was coupled with the answer to a second question which specifically asked about the permissibility of a restriction on recovery of the costs of the local lawyer with whom the foreign lawyer acted in conjunction. The Court noted that such a restriction was likely to make trans-frontier legal services less attractive. The question accordingly was whether such a restriction could be justified; that was not the case in Germany where the costs were clearly stated in national legal provisions. The Court ruled that Article 49 EC and the services directive are to be interpreted as precluding a rule which prevents recovery of the costs of the local lawyer required by national rules in addition to the costs of the lawyer from another Member State who is representing a party to litigation.[59]

[56] Case C-55/94 *Gebhard v Consiglio dell'Ordine degli Avvocati e Procuratori di Milano* [1995] ECR I-4165, para 27 of the judgment.

[57] Case C-145/99 *Commission v Italy* [2002] ECR I-2235, paras 20–24 of the judgment.

[58] Case C-292/02 *AMOK Verlags GmbH*, Judgment of 11 December 2003, [2003] ECR nyr.

[59] Presumably in those legal systems which permit recovery of costs from the losing party.

The Establishment Directive

After many years of gestation, a directive on lawyers' establishment was finally concluded.[60] This directive does not attempt to harmonize qualification to practice, but does, if the requirements of the directive are met, permit the permanent practice of law in another Member State under home title,[61] and integration into the host Member State community of practising lawyers on the basis of a qualification acquired in another Member State. The directive only applies to those who are fully qualified for legal practice in one of the Member States; it is of no assistance to trainee lawyers.

Under Article 3 of the directive, a lawyer[62] from one Member State wishing to establish a practice in another Member State must register with the professional body in the host Member State, and the professional body in the host Member State is obliged to register the migrant lawyer on presentation of proof of qualification from the home Member State. The host Member State must then notify the professional body in the home Member State of the registration. This provides authority to practise on a permanent basis in any form permitted under local rules,[63] but only using the home Member State title; there must be no translation to the local equivalent. The obvious purpose of this provision is to ensure that consumers in the host Member State are aware that they are dealing with a lawyer from another Member State.[64]

As is usual for those exercising freedom of establishment, migrant lawyers are subject to the professional rules in the host Member State while practising there.[65] Furthermore, if representation is reserved to a nominated profession, then representation in court is only permitted where the migrant lawyer works in conjunction with a local lawyer. If professional indemnity insurance is required in the host Member State, the migrant lawyer must purchase such cover, although, on proof of adequate cover through cover in the home Member State, the migrant lawyer is exempted from obtaining additional insurance in the host Member State. Under Article 7 the disciplinary rules of the host Member State apply and any disciplinary matters are to be reported to the professional body in the home Member State, which has a right to intervene in any proceedings under the rules of the host Member State.

[60] European Parliament and Council Directive 98/5/EC of 16 February 1998 to facilitate practice of the profession of lawyer on a permanent basis in a Member State other than that in which the qualification was obtained, [1998] OJ L77/36. The Directive entered into force on 14 March 2000. See also Lonbay, J, 'Lawyers bounding over the borders: the Draft Directive on lawyer's establishment' (1996) 21 ELRev 50.

[61] Without restriction on the areas of legal practice: art 5 of the Directive.

[62] As defined in art 1(2) of the directive.

[63] Even if not permitted under home Member State rules: art 8.

[64] Except perhaps in the case of Belgium, France and Luxembourg where the title of *avocat* is used.

[65] Conflicts between the host Member State and home Member State rules of professional conduct are determined in favour of the rules of the host Member State.

As the discussion in chapter 4 above indicated, qualifying as a local lawyer is probably the least harmonized area under the system established by the general system directives. The establishment directive makes it clear that its rules must not preclude anyone from seeking admission on the basis of qualifying as such under the general system directives. However, the establishment directive offers a much easier route[66] for full integration into the local legal profession after he or she has been exercising rights under the directive in relation to the practice of the law of the host Member State on an 'effective and regular'[67] basis for three years.[68] It is for migrant lawyers to establish that they meet the requirements of the directive. Upon such proof being presented, the applicant is to be admitted to the local profession without further examination or assessment.

If they have practised for three years but cannot show effective and regular practice of host Member State law, but only sporadic practice of such law, migrant lawyers may nevertheless apply for admission to the local legal profession. In such cases, the host Member State must make a good faith assessment of the skills and experience of national law acquired by applicants on the basis of training they have undertaken as well as professional business conducted. No examinations may be required.

The establishment directive remained controversial to the end. Luxembourg sought its annulment in proceedings before the Court of Justice[69] essentially on the grounds that the directive favoured home Member State regulation to the detriment of the interest of the consumer and the proper administration of justice. Underlying the challenge was a deep concern that there would be no requirement for any knowledge of national law before lawyers qualified in another Member State could set up offices in Luxembourg and practise the law of Luxembourg. The plea was not successful. The legislature had not gone beyond what was permitted by the EC Treaty in setting up the scheme in the directive.

France and Ireland have been brought before the Court for failure to implement the directive.[70]

The work of the CCBE

The CCBE[71] is the officially recognized representative organization for the legal profession in the European Union and the European Economic Area. It liaises

[66] This may be more apparent than real save where the legal systems are very similar, since the ability to practise national law on an effective and regular basis will require a significant command of local law which may not be acquired without undertaking training in the relevant national law.

[67] Defined in art 10(1) as 'actual exercise of the activity without any interruption other than that resulting from the events of everyday life'.

[68] Article 10 of the Directive.

[69] Case C-168/98 *Luxembourg v European Parliament and Council* [2000] ECR I-9131.

[70] Case C-351/01 *Commission v France* [2002] ECR I-8101; Case C-362/01 *Commission v Ireland* [2002] ECR I-1433.

[71] Council of the Bars and Law Societies of the European Union. See www.ccbe.org. Oddly none of the language versions produce the acronym CCBE. There are eighteen Member States representing the Member States of the European Union plus Iceland, Liechtenstein and Norway.

between the Bars and Law Societies from the Members States of the European Union and the European Economic Area. It represents all these professional bodies and so represents the interests of around half a million European lawyers.

On 16 September 1977 the CCBE passed the Declaration of Perugia on the principles of professional conduct of the Bars and Law Societies of the European Community. This was a first attempt to distil the essence of the ethical requirements of legal practice. It is now of merely historical interest, though many of the headings will remain familiar as hallmarks of rules of professional conduct.[72]

The CCBE now produces a much more substantial *Code of Conduct for Lawyers in the European Union*.[73] It is divided into five sections: preamble; general principles; relations with clients; relations with the courts; and relations between lawyers. The Preamble indicates that the purpose of the code is to state 'common rules which apply to all lawyers from the European Economic Area . . . in relation to their cross-border practice'.[74]

Conclusion

The size of the legal services sector in the Member States does not appear to be well known, but it is substantial. Trends in recent years have been for cross-border legal services including mergers of law firms across national boundaries, so that law firms have the resources to meet the needs of their large corporate clients. The focus of both legislation and case law at Community level has focused on access to the profession in terms of the mutual recognition of qualifications, coupled with measures designed to facilitate both the delivery of services and establishment as a legal practitioner in another Member State. The principle of home Member State regulation has triumphed in the field of establishment in relation to access to qualification to practise, but only under the home title, in another Member State coupled with subjection to the professional rules of the host Member State. These developments have necessitated some significant changes to the practices of Member State professional bodies in the regulation of legal practice.

[72] Such as personal integrity, independence and confidentiality. By contrast the provisions on advertising seem positively antiquarian with their recognition of a prohibition on personal advertising of lawyers' services.

[73] The latest edition can be found at http://www.ccbe.org/doc/En/code2002_en.pdf. See also Tyrrell, A, 'Professional Duties and Privileges' in Tyrrell, A and Jacub, Z, *The Legal Professions in the New Europe*, 2nd edn, (London, 1996), at 23.

[74] CCBE Code, para 1.3.1.

13

Case study: insurance services

Background

Financial services are generally considered to include banking, insurance, and transactions in securities. Such activities are generally carried out by large corporations. Individuals, in so far as they are concerned with such activities, are usually involved as consumers. The primary actors in exercising the freedom of establishment and freedom to provide services in these areas are business entities. This chapter looks at the way in which Community law has regulated insurance services. These have a particular significance for the United Kingdom since the British insurance market is the largest in Europe, and the third largest in the world. The industry employs 354,000 people: 806 insurance companies are authorized to carry on insurance business in the United Kingdom.

The British insurance market accounts for 28 per cent of total premium income across Europe, and accounts for nearly one-third of the life insurance market. The insurance industry's investments constitute just over one-third of all the investment in Europe and equal that of France and Germany combined.[1] Total premium income for both general insurance business[2] and long-term insurance business[3] was £125.5 billion in 2002. The largest 10 motor insurers handle 87 per cent of motor insurance business, and the largest 10 property insurers account for 85 per cent of that market. The largest 10 companies in the long-term insurance market account for just over two-thirds of the market. This is business on a very large scale indeed.

Developing a single market for insurance

The right of establishment and the right to provide services in other Member States includes rights for business organizations. Insurance companies wished to set up branches or agencies in other Member States in order to develop their businesses, and also wished to sell insurance to those wishing to buy cover in another Member

[1] Source: Association of British Insurers. See www.abi.org.uk.
[2] Excluding Lloyd's.
[3] Life insurance, individual and group pensions, life annuities, and income and critical illness protection.

State as a provision of services. The process of achieving something which might be described as a single market in insurance services took over 30 years to achieve and required a significant amount of Community legislation. The process was largely achieved by 1 July 1994. As Merkin and Rodger point out,[4] the complexity of achieving a single market is explicable by the significance of insurance for both businesses and individuals:

> Insurance, which has as its objective the spreading of risk and loss, is one of the most important forms of economic activity. Businesses rely upon insurance to protect their assets and to enable them to undertake new ventures which are too speculative for them to risk unprotected exposure. Consumers rely upon insurance to safeguard their possessions and to plan their future income levels. . . . However, insurance is also a difficult activity to conduct successfully, as the process of underwriting should involve a deep knowledge of markets, probabilities and statistics: indeed, the history of insurance throughout the world is characterised by regular, and on occasion spectacular, failures of insurance companies.[5]

National regulation of insurance services has generally involved the application of rules relating to four areas. First, businesses wishing to carry on insurance activities require prior authorization to do so. The purpose is to ensure that the insurance provider has both the skill and knowledge to provide the service, as well as the means to meet the liabilities that will arise. Secondly, businesses are required to demonstrate their solvency. Thirdly, there is ongoing regulation to ensure that the guarantees which led to the grant of the initial authorization to engage in the business remain. Fourthly, regulation can take the form of requiring prior approval of the terms of insurance policies, and in some instances this will include a requirement for certain provisions to be included in the cover. This is known as 'material control' of the activity. While prior authorization is an almost universal form of regulation, material control is much more frequently met in Continental legal systems than in common law systems. The challenge therefore in establishing a single market in insurance services was to provide a common regulatory framework which would avoid the need for multiple regulatory frameworks to be satisfied when an insurance provider in one Member State wished to expand the activities into another Member State either by way of establishment or the provision of services. As we have seen in other areas, there is a tension between home State and host State control. The home State will believe that its regulatory system is sufficient to provide all the protections needed, but the host State will be concerned at both the effectiveness and content of the home State supervision. Sometimes this concern will be a genuine concern to protect consumers, but sometimes it can be a device to protect the domestic market in insurance services. A substantial programme of directives has sought to level the playing field so that the internal market can operate in the field of insurance services.[6]

[4] Merkin, R and Rodger, A, *EC Insurance Law* (Harlow, 1997), ch 1. [5] ibid, at 2.
[6] The printed list of legislation in force on the europa website runs to some eight pages of text.

As in other areas, the approach has been sectoral. The market has been divided into life and non-life insurance. Non-life insurance which tends to be less heavily regulated than the life insurance market was the subject of the first round of directives. The literature sub-divides the directives into three generations of directives:

> The Single Insurance Market was achieved by means of three 'generations' of insurance Directives: the first generation was concerned with the right of establishment; the second generation dealt with freedom to provide insurance by way of services; and the third generation converted these two basic principles into the single market.[7]

The route to the introduction of a single market in insurance services can only be understood by examining the three generations of directives. The later generations have not always replaced the earlier directives, but have tended to amend them and add supplemental provisions. The result does not aid clarity, since what is left is a mass of amended and re-amended legislation, though parts have now been drawn together in a single instrument.

The life insurance sector is now principally governed by Directive 2002/83/EC.[8] Non-life insurance remains regulated by a series of directives, and there are directives in specific areas, such as motor vehicle insurance, legal expenses insurance, and credit and suretyship insurance. The Community has set up an Insurance Committee[9] made up of representatives of the Member States and chaired by the Commission's representative to assist the Commission in its work in the insurance field with a view to establishing closer co-operation between the national supervisory authorities and the Commission.

The first generation directives

The first generation directives were concerned with freedom of establishment, and the very first of these concerned non-life insurance other than motor vehicle insurance.[10] The directive sought to establish a common regulatory structure so that national restrictions on establishment could be abolished, and freedom of establishment for such insurers assured. The approach was essentially one of harmonization so that the system of regulation would be very similar in every Member State. Prior authorization for engaging any of the 17 classes of non-life insurance covered by the directives was required, and this would only be granted

[7] Merkin, R and Rodger, A, *EC Insurance Law* (Harlow, 1997), at 3. The material in this chapter draws significantly on this work.

[8] Directive 2002/83/EC of the European Parliament and the Council of 5 November 2002 concerning life assurance, [2002] OJ L345/1.

[9] Council Directive 91/675/EEC of 19 December 1991 setting up an Insurance Committee, [1991] OJ L374/32.

[10] Council Directive 73/239/EEC of 24 July 1973, [1973] OJ L228/3, known as the 'first non-life directive' and Council Directive 73/240/EEC of 24 July 1973, [1973] OJ L228/20.

where the insurer submitted a 'scheme of operations' setting out a business plan and the financial resources available to support it, and where the insurer had a minimum guarantee fund. A solvency margin was required. Authorization in one Member State entitled the insurer to establish in any Member State subject to its maintaining sufficient technical reserves realizable in the host Member State to enable it to meet claims there. The directives did not address the issue of material control.

It was some years before a similar directive was adopted in the field of life insurance, but when it did arrive, its provisions closely paralleled those of the non-life directives.[11]

The second generation directives

The second generation directives sought to open up the single market for insurance services rather than establishment of the insurance businesses in more than one Member State. The intention was to permit any authorized insurer established in one Member State to provide insurance services in any other Member State without the need for further authorization and without the need to be established in that other Member State. The first of the second generation directives was the directive[12] on co-insurance.[13] This measure was designed to open the borders to co-insurance arrangements by enterprises from more than one Member State. Several Member States failed to implement the directive in full, and the Commission took infringement proceedings against them for this failure to fulfil their obligations. So began the famous insurance cases.[14] The national legislation at issue had the effect of excluding insurers from other Member States from being the lead insurer in respect of risks located in that State unless they were established in, or authorized by, that State. Intermediaries[15] could arrange cover for risks located in the host State only with insurers established in, or authorized by, that State. Thresholds had been introduced which had the effect of excluding insurers from other Member States from participating in the insurance of risks below a specified level.

The case had the potential to throw the programme of directives into disarray. On the one hand the Commission was arguing that any requirement for

[11] See Council Directive 79/267/EEC of 5 March 1979, [1979] OJ L63/1, known as the 'first life directive'.

[12] Council Directive 78/473/EEC of 30 May 1978, [1978] OJ L151/25.

[13] A common arrangement under which risk is shared by insurers, one of whom will then have delegated authority to administer the co-insurance contract and deal with any claims arising under the insurance.

[14] Case 252/83 *Commission v Denmark* [1986] ECR 3713; Case 205/84 *Commission v Germany* [1986] ECR 3755; Case 206/84 *Commission v Ireland* [1986] ECR 3817; and Case 220/83 *Commission v France* [1986] ECR 3663. See generally Edward, D, 'Establishment and Services: An Analysis of the Insurance Cases' (1987) 12 ELRev 231.

[15] For example, insurer brokers.

authorization by, or establishment in, the Member State where the services were to be delivered constituted an infringement of the Treaty.[16] On the other hand, the Member States argued that the maintenance of some national regulation of service provision in the insurance sector was justified in the general interest having regard to the multifarious nature of insurance contracts. In particular, there were genuine concerns to protect insured persons and third parties who might be affected by the materialization of the risk for which the insurance cover had been obtained. Since the German legislation was the most restrictive, the Court took the proceedings against Germany as the lead case. However, the Court also made it clear that it was only concerned with situations in which the risk against which the insurance cover was taken arose in the Member State of the insured person.

The Court's judgment took a very broad view indeed of establishment. Arrangements short of the establishment of a branch or agency could be enough to bring the activity within the scope of establishment rather than service provision. An office managed by the insurance company's own staff, or the presence of a broker authorized to act on a permanent basis for the insurer would be sufficient to constitute establishment.[17] This would, of course, open the door to much more intrusive host State control than in the case of service provision. Equally, if it could be shown that the business arrangement was designed to avoid the national regulatory regime and that the activity was entirely or principally directed towards the territory, the situation could be treated as falling within the Treaty provisions on establishment rather than services.[18]

The Court went on to stress that the provisions of what were then Articles 59 and 60 on the free movement of services are not conditional on the harmonization or co-ordination of the laws of the Member States, and require the removal in respect of a service provider established in another Member State of 'all restrictions on his freedom to provide services imposed by reason of the fact that he is established in a Member State other than that in which the service is to be provided'.[19] Nevertheless, some national regulation may be permissible:

> . . . the freedom to provide services, as one of the fundamental principles of the Treaty, may be restricted only by provisions which are justified by the general good and which are applied to all persons or undertakings operating within the territory of the State in which the service is provided in so far as that interest is not safeguarded by the provisions to which the provider of a service is subject in the Member State of his establishment. In addition such requirements must be objectively justified by the need to ensure that professional rules of conduct are complied with and that the interests which such rules are designed to safeguard are protected.[20]

[16] And the cases had implications far beyond co-insurance transactions.

[17] Case 205/84 *Commission v Germany* [1986] ECR 3755, para 21 of the judgment. The law on the distinction between establishment and services has probably been changed as a result of the decision in Case C-55/94 *Gebhard* [1995] ECR I-4165; see ch 2 above.

[18] ibid, para 22 of the judgment.

[19] ibid, para 25 of the judgment.

[20] ibid, para 27 of the judgment.

The Court identified a number of aspects of insurance arrangements which justify special measures: the need to be certain that an insurance provider will be able to meet the indemnity provided for if the risk materializes at some time in the future; the nature of insurance as a mass phenomenon; and the inability of a policy holder to judge the future financial viability of the insurer. The Court considered that the directives which then existed did not provide full guarantees in respect of all the matters covered by national schemes of regulation, and conceded that in some circumstances a requirement for prior authorization in relation to service provision in the insurance market may be justifiable. However, the necessity for establishment in the host State was not considered to be met, particularly as a requirement for establishment actually operates to deny the possibility of providing services in that Member State.

The Court's view of the permissibility, at least for certain categories of insurance, of requiring service providers to be authorized by the host State meant that the legislators could not continue with a system in which establishment and authorization in one Member State opened up the possibility of providing services in another Member State without meeting regulatory requirements in that State. The legislators adopted a different approach for non-life and life insurance.

The second non-life directive[21] dealt with issues flowing from the insurance cases by adapting the regime set up by the first generation directive in this area. It initially excluded compulsory insurance,[22] though this was brought within the regime by a 1990 amendment to the directive. A crucial distinction made by the directive is between the insurance of 'large risks'[23] and the insurance of 'mass risks'.

Under Article 5 of Directive 88/357/EEC, large risks are those relating to the insurance of railway rolling stock, aircraft and liability arising out of use of an aircraft, ships and liability arising out of use of ships, goods in transit, credit and suretyship where the policy-holder is engaged professionally in an industrial or commercial activity or in one of the liberal professions, and certain classes of insurance where the policy-holder's assets exceed stated criteria. The classes of insurance concerned are fire and natural forces, other damage to property, general liability and miscellaneous financial loss. From 1 January 1993 the asset-based criteria are that the policy-holder exceeds the limits of at least two of three criteria: (1) a balance sheet total of 6.2 million ecu, (2) a net turnover of 12.8 million ecu, and (3) an average number of employees of 250 during the financial year. The notion is that the policy-holder is not in these circumstances a consumer who is the weaker party in the transaction, and is therefore less in need of protection than the individual consumer. The insurance here is essentially commercially based, rather

[21] Council Directive 88/357/EEC of 22 June 1988, [1988] OJ L330/44. A consolidated version of this directive is available on the europa website. This directive did not replace Directive 73/239/EEC but amended it. It remains in force, and again a consolidated version is available on the europa website.

[22] Common examples of compulsory insurance are motor vehicle insurance and employers' liability insurance.

[23] Article 5 of Directive 88/357/EEC.

than consumer-based. In these cases an insurance provided established in one Member State is permitted to provide services in another Member State subject only to a requirement to notify the regulatory authorities of that other Member State of its intentions and of the classes of insurance business in which it proposes to engage.

The remaining classes of insurance business are regarded as consumer insurance and the second non-life directive left Member States free to require authorization by their regulatory authorities before insurance services could be provided. There are also additional protections which operate for the consumer in these cases. Article 7 of the directive provides that the law governing the contract should be the law of the consumer's home State subject to the possibility of the parties contracting for different arrangements if the law of the consumer's home State permitted this. Article 19 allowed Member States to impose material control over the terms of the policy and over premium levels. Article 21 required notification to be given to a consumer that the insurer is established in another Member State. Finally, Article 24 permitted host State regulations to require the service provider from another Member State to make financial contributions in the host State to policy-holder protection schemes designed to provide a guarantee fund to meet liabilities under the policy in the event of the insolvency of the insurance provider.

The so-called second life directive[24] followed the scheme in the second non-life directive in liberalizing the market in insurance services, but the distinction between large risks and mass risks could not be applied so easily to this sector of the insurance market. However, there remained a need to distinguish between those policy-holders who needed special protection and those for whom this was less important. The basis of the distinction adopted was whether a policy-holder had taken the initiative in seeking the commitment. To constitute such a policy-holder, one of two conditions had to be satisfied. Either policy-holders had to have approached a provider or intermediary with a view to taking out life insurance provided by an insurer in another Member State and had signed a standard form statement to that effect, or the policy-holder had taken out the insurance other than in response to advertising or any form of direct approach by the insurance provider and the contract was made in the insurer's home State or by each of the parties in their own home States. These policy-holders were regarded as not needing any special protection, whereas other policy-holders were deemed to need such protection. In the latter cases, authorization could be required by the host State. Additional protection was also provided for in the following terms: (1) there was a rebuttable presumption under Article 4 that the applicable law was that of the consumer's country; (2) the consumer had to sign a statement in standard terms acknowledging that the insurer was established in another Member State; (3) under

[24] Council Directive 90/619/EEC of 8 November 1990, [1990] OJ L330/5. This directive has been repealed and replaced by Directive 2002/83/EC.

Article 15 there was a mandatory cooling-off period during which the consumer could withdraw from the insurance; and (4) Member States could elect to retain material control over the terms of the policy and over premium rates.

In short, the effect of the second generation directives was to make home State regulation dominant in relation to the provision of insurance services for those types of insurance where special protection of the consumer was not considered necessary, but to permit limited host State regulation of service providers established in other Member States for those classes of non-life and life insurance where the general good justified a degree of host State regulation in the interests of protection the consumer.

The third generation directives

The objective of the third generation of insurance directives was to complete the internal market in insurance services through the introduction of the single insurance licence. The single insurance licence[25] would enable companies to establish themselves in other Member States and to provide insurance services in Member States in which they were not established on the basis of a single authorization and supervision in the Member State in which their head office or centre of operations is located. This required the abolition of the distinction between commercial and consumer insurance transactions, though this did not mean that the interests of the consumer were sacrificed in favour of the single insurance market. The interests of the consumer are adequately protected through the system of home State control which lies at the heart of the single market in insurance. The Commission's view is that it is not open to the host Member State to seek to monitor whether the home Member State is checking that an insurance company is meeting all the requirements of its authorization to engage in insurance business. Any doubts about compliance should be referred to the Commission, which can, if necessary, use its infringement powers to secure compliance.[26]

The two central directives were the third non-life directive[27] and the third life directive.[28] Article 4 of the third non-life directive amends Article 6 of Directive 73/239/EEC to read as follows:

The taking up of the business of direct insurance shall be subject to prior official authorization. Such authorization shall be sought from the competent authorities of the home Member State by:

[25] Sometimes called the 'Insurance Single Passport', see Donohue, J, *The Insurance Single Passport. A Guide to the Implementing Regulations* (London, 1995).

[26] Commission Interpretative Communication, Freedom to provide services and the general good in the insurance sector, [2000] OJ C43/5, at 12–13.

[27] Council Directive 92/49/EEC of 18 June 1992, [1992] OJ L228/1. This directive, as amended, is still in force. A consolidated version can be found on the europa website.

[28] Council Directive 92/92/EEC of 10 November 1992, [1992] OJ L360/1. This directive has been repealed and replaced by Directive 2002/83/EC.

(a) any undertaking which establishes its head office within the territory of that State;
(b) any undertaking which, having received the authorization referred to in the first subparagraph extends its business to an entire class or to other classes.

Article 7 of Directive 73/239/EEC is amended to read as follows:

1. Authorization shall be valid for the entire Community. It shall permit an undertaking to carry on business there, under either the right of establishment or the freedom to provide services.

2. Authorization shall be granted for a particular class of insurance. It shall cover the entire class, unless the applicant wishes to cover only some of the risks pertaining to that class, as listed in point A of the Annex.

However:

(a) Member States may grant authorization for the groups of classes listed in point B of the Annex, attaching to them the appropriate denominations specified therein;
(b) authorization granted for one class or a group of classes shall also be valid for the purpose of covering ancillary risks included in another class if the conditions imposed in point C of the Annex are fulfilled.

Articles 4 and 5 of Directive 2002/83/EC concerning life insurance closely parallel these provisions. Both directives specify the basis upon which authorization is to be granted. There are specified forms for each Member State which the insurance company must take.[29] Before authorization can be granted the insurance company must provide a scheme of operations which must include evidence of:

(a) the nature of the commitments which the insurance company proposes to cover;
(b) the guiding principles as to reassurance;
(c) the items constituting the minimum guarantee fund;
(d) estimates relating to the costs of setting up the administrative services and the organization for securing business and the financial resources intended to meet those costs.[30]

Authorization is not to be granted until the identity of the shareholders or members[31] has been disclosed, and authorization is to be refused if 'taking into account the need to ensure the sound and prudent management of an assurance undertaking', the competent authorities in a Member State are not satisfied as to the qualifications of the shareholders or members.

The provisions of Title IV of Directive 2002/83/EC typify the approach adopted under the single insurance licence for establishing a branch in another

[29] So, for example, in the United Kingdom the insurance providers must be one of the following: a company incorporated by shares or by guarantee or unlimited; a society registered under the Industrial and Provident Societies Acts; a society registered or incorporated under the Friendly Society Acts; or a member of the association of underwriters known as Lloyd's.
[30] There are additional requirements for the first three financial years.
[31] With qualifying holdings, which are defined as 10 per cent of the capital or voting rights: Art 1(g) of Directive 92/49/EEC and art 1(j) of Directive 2002/83/EC.

Member State or for providing insurance services in a Member State other than that where authorization to undertake insurance provision has been granted.

An insurance company intending to open a branch in another Member State must notify the competent authorities in its home Member State of its intention to do so. Specified details must be supplied to the competent authorities. Unless those authorities have any doubts about the adequacy of the proposed arrangements, they must communicate the information to the competent authorities in the Member State where the branch is to be opened and attest to the solvency margins of the insurance company. If the competent authorities refuse to communicate this information to the other Member State, they must give reasons for their refusal to the insurance company within three months of receiving all the information in question. There is a two-month period following receipt in the host Member State of the information from the competent authorities in the Member State of authorization during which the host State may 'inform the competent authority of the home Member State . . . of the conditions under which, in the interest of the general good, that business must be carried on in the Member State of the branch'.[32]

An insurance company intending to provide services for the first time in another Member State must notify the competent authorities in the Member State of authorization of its plans. Within one month, the competent authorities must communicate to the Member States in which the insurance company proposes to provide services a certificate attesting that the insurance company has the minimum solvency margin calculated in accordance with the directive; of the class of insurance the insurance company is authorized to offer; and of the nature of the insurance services the insurance company proposes to offer in the other Member State or Member States. In the case of the provision of services, the host Member State may apply conditions in the general good, although there is no obligation (as is the case with the provisions concerning establishment) for notification of these requirements. Regulation by the home Member State is deemed sufficient. The ability of Member States to impose material control over policy terms and premium rates disappears.

Under the third generation directives, an insurance company can simultaneously carry on business in the same Member State under the freedom of establishment provisions and under the freedom to provide services provisions of the secondary legislation even if it is the same activity. The Commission has indicated that in such cases, it will be for the insurance company to be able to relate any given activity to one or other of the methods of carrying on its business.[33]

Not unsurprisingly, the directives contain a wealth of technical detail about the operation of insurance business in the European Union, but those provisions are not central to the issues addressed in this book.[34]

[32] Article 40(4) of Directive 2002/83/EC.

[33] Commission Interpretative Communication, Freedom to provide services and the general good in the insurance sector, [2000] OJ C43/5.

[34] Such as, for example, the information to be supplied to consumers; see Case C-386/00 *Axa Royale Belge* [2002] ECR I-2209.

The Commission found it necessary to take action against three Member States for failure to fulfil their obligations in relation to Directive 92/49/EEC.[35] In all three cases, the Member States in question were found to have failed to fulfil their obligations under Community law. The proceedings against France concerned a requirement for the systematic notification of the general conditions of contracts which insurance companies propose to market for the first time in France. The French Government sought to justify the requirement as a sampling mechanism, but conceded that there was ambiguity in the wording of the French legislation. The Court concluded that the French requirement was for the systematic notification to the authorities in the host Member State of the general and special conditions of insurance policies. This is expressly prohibited by the directive and so France had failed to fulfil its obligations.

The proceedings against Belgium concerned the exclusion from the scope of the Belgian implementing legislation of any insurance fund or company covering accidents at work. The defence of the Belgian Government was that such insurance is regarded in Belgium as covered by the statutory scheme of social security. The Court did not agree with the arguments of the Belgian Government about the scope of the directive and found Belgium to have failed to fulfil its obligations.

The infringement proceedings against Italy concerned the maintenance of rate-freezing rules in relation to third party liability claims in motor vehicle insurance, and the introduction of a mandatory excess system. The Italian Government sought to defend its actions as part of a general programme of anti-inflationary measures. This view was not accepted by the Court and a failure to fulfil obligations under Community law was found. A separate head of complaint related to the requirement of Italian law that insurance companies supply information to the competent authorities in Italy. This was sought to be justified on the grounds that it aided the prevention of fraud and that requesting the information from the competent authorities in the home Member State might not forestall fraud because of the inherent delays in such a system. The Court rejected this part of the complaint, not on the broad merits, but because the Commission's reasoned opinion had challenged it only under Article 44 of Directive 92/49/EEC which pursued a different aim from that of anti-fraud measures.

Taxation and equal treatment

Two cases decided in 2002 and 2003 showed that the general requirements of equality of treatment still retained force in the field of insurance. The *Danner* case[36] concerned the tax treatment of pension insurance contributions paid by a doctor who held both German and Finnish nationality who had established himself in

[35] Case C-296/98 *Commission v France* [2000] ECR I-3025; Case C-206/98 *Commission v Belgium* [2000] ECR I-3509; and Case C-59/01 *Commission v Italy* [2003] ECR I-1759.

[36] Case C-136/00 *Danner* [2002] ECR I-8147.

Finland, but continued to pay pension insurance contributions to a German insurance company. The Finnish tax authorities permitted him only to deduct his contributions to the extent of 10 per cent of his taxable income. He would have enjoyed a higher deduction if he had made similar contributions to a Finnish insurance company. The Court noted that, although direct taxation falls within the competence of the Member States, the Member States must exercise their tax competence consistently with Community law. The effect of the differential tax treatment of contributions to a pension fund depending upon the nationality of the insurance company to whom the contributions were paid clearly constituted a restriction on the freedom to provide services. It put non-Finnish enterprises at a disadvantage. The Finnish Government sought to argue that the coherence of the national tax system and the effectiveness of fiscal control justified the legislation in issue. The argument was not accepted. There was differential treatment in breach of Community law.

The *Skandia* case[37] raised similar issues. Ramstedt was an employee of Skandia. He was a Swedish national and worked in Sweden for Skandia. Skandia made provision for Ramstedt's pension partly through its Danish, German and English insurance companies, which were all part of the Skandia group. The Swedish tax authorities determined that there would be no immediate tax deductions for the pensions contributions made to these companies. The deductions would arise at the later date when the pension was paid. Contributions paid to a Swedish company would be treated differently and, it was argued on behalf of Ramstedt, more favourably. The Court ruled that Article 49 EC precludes a Member State from treating in a potentially different way for tax purposes a policy issued by an insurance company established in another Member State as compared with an insurance policy issued by an insurance company established in that Member State.

Some lingering issues

In February 2000, the Commission issued an interpretative communication relating to a number of issues arising in the insurance sector.[38]

Distinguishing establishment and services

The development of the case law on the dividing line between establishment and services through the *Gebhard* case[39] has made it more difficult to draw that dividing line, and certainly calls into question the continuing validity of certain

[37] Case C-422/01 *Försäkringsaktiebolaget Skandia* [2003] ECRI-6817.

[38] Commission Interpretative Communication, Freedom to provide services and the general good in the insurance sector, [2000] OJ C43/5.

[39] Case C-55/94 *Gebhard* [1995] ECR I-4165.

statements made in the *Insurance* cases.[40] The starting point is, of course, that establishment 'involves the actual pursuit of an economic activity through a fixed establishment in another Member State for an indefinite period'.[41] By contrast, the provision of services (where the service provider moves to another Member State) involves presence of a temporary character and the *Gebhard* case tells us that we must measure this having regard 'not only to the duration of the provision of the service, but also of its regularity, periodicity or continuity'.[42] Furthermore:

> The fact that the provision of services is temporary does not mean that the provider of services within the meaning of the Treaty may not equip himself with some form of infrastructure in the host Member State (including an office, chambers or consulting rooms) in so far as such infrastructure is necessary for the purposes of performing the services in question.[43]

Where the service provider does not move but provides the services on a continuing basis from the home Member State, the rules on services apply rather than those on establishment.[44] However, if it can be established that the provision of services is being used to circumvent national law in the target Member State, then the activity might fall within the scope of the Treaty provisions on establishment rather than services. But the case law on abuse of Community law means that it will be difficult to prove the intention to avoid national law and so this possibility will only be met very rarely. The Commission's interpretative note expresses its view on when the use of intermediaries, such as insurance brokers, will bring the activity within the rules on establishment rather than services. In the view of the Commission, an enterprise which uses intermediaries will bring itself within the scope of the Treaty rules on establishment where all three of the following conditions are met:

(a) the intermediary is subject to the direction and control of the insurance company;
(b) the intermediary is able to commit the insurance company; and
(c) the intermediary has a permanent brief.

An intermediary who meets these three requirements is, in effect, an extension of the insurance company.[45] The interpretative note goes on to suggest the sort of checks which should be carried out in order to come to a conclusion on the applicability of each of the three conditions. However, the following examples of the use of local services[46] are some of those given by the Commission which will not, in its view, bring the activity within the scope of the rules on establishment:

40 See above, this chapter.
41 Case C-221/89 *Factortame* [1991] ECR I-3905, para 20 of the judgment.
42 Case C-55/94 *Gebhard* [1995] ECR I-4165, para 27 of the judgment.
43 ibid.
44 See Case C-56/96 *VT4 Ltd* [1997] ECR I-3143, a case concerning broadcasting.
45 But will not in the Commission's view thereby constitute a 'branch' of the insurance company.
46 Described as being upstream or downstream of the main transaction.

- the use of a local expert to assess the risk to be covered under the provision of services;
- the use of local legal, medical or actuarial services established in the Member State where the services are provided; and
- a permanent structure for managing files relating to claims.

The Commission's view is that it would be contrary to Community law for a host Member State to oblige an insurance company which has been providing insurance services in its territory for a given length of time to become established there as a precondition of its continued pursuit of economic activity there.

e-Commerce

In recent years, there has been a significant increase of the direct selling of insurance products, particularly over the internet. The Commission is alert to these developments and says:

> The existing legal framework governing the single insurance market rests on mechanisms which did not envisage the use of information technology for carrying on insurance business in the single market. For this reason, the Commission already stated in its communication to the Council on the Financial Services Action Plan that it intended to bring out a Green paper to examine whether the existing provisions of the directives in the field of financial services provided a regulatory framework that is propitious to the development of electronic commerce in financial services while ensuring that the interests of consumers are fully protected.[47]

Applicability of rules promoting the general good

Most of the remainder of the interpretative note concerns issues arising in relation to the requirement that an insurance company meets in the host Member State conditions applied for the general good. The concept of requirements for the general good is not a closed one, and the Court has not defined the concept though it is clear that it cannot replicate a matter which has already been harmonized by Community law.[48] The interpretative note lists the following matters as having been acknowledged by the Court as having as their objective the pursuit of the general good:

- professional rules designed to protect the recipient of services;[49]
- protection of workers,[50] including social protection;[51]

[47] Commission Interpretative Communication, Freedom to provide services and the general good in the insurance sector, [2000] OJ C43/5, at 13.

[48] Although it would seem that a Member State could in certain circumstances require a higher level of protection than the minimum harmonized level of Community law, provided always that the requirement met all the other conditions for constituting a legitimate measure for the general good.

[49] Joined Cases C-110–111/78 *Van Wesemael* [1979] ECR 35.

[50] Case 279/80 *Webb* [1981] ECR 3305.

[51] Case C-272/94 *Guiot* [1996] ECR I-1905.

- consumer protection;[52]
- preservation of the good reputation of the national financial sector;[53]
- prevention of fraud;[54]
- the preservation of social order;[55]
- the protection of intellectual property;[56]
- the preservation of national historical and artistic heritage;[57]
- cultural policy and protection of cultural diversity in the audiovisual sector;[58]
- the cohesion of the tax system;[59]
- road safety;[60]
- the protection of creditors;[61]
- the fairness of commercial transactions;[62] and
- the protection of the proper administration of justice.[63]

Any such requirement must apply equally to insurance companies established in the Member States as to those established elsewhere. Any requirements which did not apply equally would need to be justified on the grounds of public policy, public security or public health. Even here, the Court will look at the extent to which there are national measures which seek to meet the risk against which the requirements are aimed. The Commission's view is that it is difficult to see what measure in the field of insurance could constitute a serious threat to the interests of society, and so 'it is reasonable to believe . . . that discriminatory measures are unlikely to be justified in the insurance sector.'[64]

Any measure for the general good must be objectively necessary and proportionate to the objective pursued, and must not be the subject of protection under the system of regulation operated by the home Member State.

A number of examples of the application of the general good principles in the insurance sector are given. It seems that, despite their prohibition except where expressly permitted, some Member States are continuing to require prior notification of the particulars of policy conditions on the grounds that they are needed to

[52] Case 252/83 *Commission v Denmark* [1986] ECR 3713; Case 205/84 *Commission v Germany* [1986] ECR 3755; Case 206/84 *Commission v Ireland* [1986] ECR 3817; and Case 220/83 *Commission v France* [1986] ECR 3663.

[53] Case C-384/93 *Alpine Investments* [1995] ECR I-1141.

[54] Case C-275/92 *Schindler* [1994] ECR I-1039

[55] ibid.

[56] Case 62/79 *Coditel* [1980] ECR 881.

[57] Case C-180/89 *Commission v Italy* [1991] ECR I-709.

[58] Case C-148/91 *Veronica Omroep Organisatie* [1993] ECR I-487.

[59] Case C-204/90 *Bachmann* [1992] ECR I-249.

[60] Case C-55/93 *van Schaik* [1994] ECR I-4837.

[61] Case C-3/95 *Reisebüro Broede* [1996] ECR I-6511.

[62] Case C-384/93 *Alpine Investments* [1995] ECR I-1141.

[63] ibid.

[64] Commission Interpretative Communication, Freedom to provide services and the general good in the insurance sector, [2000] OJ C43/5, at 18.

protect their consumers, to guarantee transparency of the products available and to facilitate substantive control of insurance products by the supervisory authorities. The Commission's view is that such requirements constitute a breach of Community law, since this is an area which has been fully harmonized by the Community in the insurance directives.

A number of Member States have detailed legislation in the motor vehicle insurance sector on the scale of no-claims bonuses which are gained and lost according to a driver's accident record. These are sought to be justified on the grounds that they contribute to preventing road accidents, since drivers facing increased premiums will drive more carefully. These systems are also said to aid transparency by permitting a more ready comparison between different policies. The Commission notes that freedom as regards scales of premiums is a feature of the insurance directives, and the maintenance of mandatory tariffs is contrary to the letter and spirit of the third generation directives. The Commission therefore queries whether other less restrictive measures might meet the benefits claimed for such schemes.

Though there are other examples in the interpretative note, the final example which will be mentioned here is the imposition of standard claims or minimum insurance conditions. These tend to be justified on the basis that they protect the consumer as the weaker party in the transaction, and protect third party victims who are intended beneficiaries of the insurance of the particular risk. The Commission notes, first, that requirements flowing from a desire to protect the consumer as the weaker party should be carefully examined to check that they are applied only in those circumstances where they are objectively necessary. They are likely to have the effect of making access to the market of a Member State with such requirements more difficult because the insurance product needs to be tailored to the specific needs of that market.

Concluding comment

This creation of a single insurance licence has largely been achieved by requiring sufficient harmonization of national systems of regulation to permit mutual recognition of systems of supervision to be accepted among the Member States. The result has been to open the market for both suppliers and consumers of insurance products. However, it took 30 years to achieve sufficient trust among the Member States to enable the single insurance licence to operate. It has also required more Community-level regulation of the product than in the case of goods. The reasons are clear. In the case of goods, it is usually possible to examine them. A person buying a car has ready access to a wealth of information about which is the best car for the price. Though there are parallel sources of information in relation to services, the comparisons are generally much harder for the consumer to make.

The risks of getting it wrong may be much more catastrophic than simply buying a car you do not like or which lacks some feature you might have considered if you were better informed. The controls are essentially exercised through control on the supplier of the services rather than on the services themselves. Indeed, one feature of the Community provisions on insurance products has been some liberalization of the terms of the insurance. The controls consist of authorization to enter the market and ongoing supervision of the actor in the market. The material in this chapter is some distance away from the consideration of individuals moving, or supplying services, across national boundaries. It is all about big business being able to operate in the European market represented by the territories of the Member States under a uniform regime. We are in the realm of commercial law rather than social law, and in the realm of regulation.

14

Distinguishing personal rights from business regulation

Introduction

This book has divided the exposition of the law relating to workers, establishment, and services into three parts: a general part in which issues of definition, entitlement and remedies were discussed; a synthesis of the personal rights which citizens now carry around with them when moving; and a discussion of the regulation of market access. It is argued that this synthesis of Community law in the area offers a means through which divergences and convergences across the free movement of persons and services, particularly when viewed alongside some developments in the field of the free movement of goods, are recognized but which offers a more coherent legal framework than may be apparent from other analyses.

It is also inherent in this synthesis of Community law that there is an alternative to an analysis which concentrates on whether the underlying basis of the prohibition on restrictions to the four freedoms is on the one hand discrimination or on the other on prevention or hindrance to market access. Clearly both equality of treatment and market integration are central to the system of control the EC Treaty puts in place. The prohibition of discrimination on grounds of nationality has always been at the heart of the Community legal order, but there are also economic, and increasingly, social objectives in the Community legal order.

A constitutional right to freedom of movement

One part of the argument in this book is that the Court has fashioned a constitutional right to freedom of movement out of the provisions of the EC Treaty on the free movement of persons when read in conjunction with the provisions of the Treaty of citizenship of the Union.

In the early years of Community law, the rights in the Treaty were principally for those exercising economic activity. Hence there was a line of cases determining what sort of activity was sufficient to bring someone within the scope of the Treaty provisions on workers, establishment, and services.[1] A rich case law largely

[1] See generally ch 2 above.

providing guidance for national courts on what constituted being a worker for the purposes of Article 39 (ex 48) EC developed. This was of particular importance since those who were workers obtained the protection set out in particular in Regulation 1612/68,[2] whereas those who were merely work seekers enjoyed lesser protection.[3] The case law has not yet reached the position that the nature of the activity in which a person engages in moving from one Member State to another is wholly irrelevant, but the significance of the nature of the activity is less. This can be illustrated by comparing the positions of a worker, a work seeker, and a retired person in the context of a number of rights. In terms of entry into another Member State, it matters not whether a person is a worker, work seeker or a retired person; there is in each case a right to enter the Member State of his or her choice, subject only to the ability of the host Member State to apply one of the Treaty derogations to exclude the person. In terms of residence in the Member State the person has entered, there will be differences. For the worker, it will depend on the nature of the work obtained; is the job a permanent one? Is it seasonal work, or short-term work? For the work seeker, it is limited in time, though the Member State of residence cannot remove a person whose job prospects are very good even at the end of the initial period of residence. For the retired person, entry will have been conditional on showing sufficient financial resources and health insurance; it remains unclear what rights of residence a retired person would have if subsequently their income falls unexpectedly or if they can no longer obtain, for financial or other reasons, the required health insurance. In other areas, the watchword is now equal treatment with nationals. Here the case law remains somewhat equivocal. In the *Grzelczyk* case[4] the Court re-affirmed what it had said in the *Martínez Sala* case[5] that 'a citizen of the European Union, lawfully resident in the territory of a host Member State, can rely on Article 6 [now 12] of the Treaty in all situations which fall within the scope *ratione materiae* of Community law.'[6] The caution with which the Court proceeded becomes clear on a careful reading of paragraphs 40 to 46 of the judgment. The Court noted that the Directive 93/96/EEC does not require a student to have a specified level of financial resources. However, a host Member State remains free to conclude that a student who has recourse to social assistance no longer fulfils the conditions of his or her residence and so can take measures 'within the limits imposed by Community law, either to withdraw his residence permit or not to renew it'.[7] But such measures cannot be the automatic consequences of a student having to have recourse to social assistance. The directive

[2] And this was more specific and detailed than, for example, the rights of self-employed persons.
[3] See generally ch 8 above.
[4] Case C-184/99 *Grzelczyk v Centre public d'aide sociale d'Ottignies-Louvain-la-Neuve* [2001] ECR I-6193; see generally ch 7 above.
[5] Case C-85/96 *Martínez Sala v Freistaat Bayern* [1998] ECR I-2691.
[6] Case C-184/99 *Grzelczyk v Centre public d'aide sociale d'Ottignies-Louvain-la-Neuve* [2001] ECR I-6193, para 32 of the judgment.
[7] Para 42 of the judgment.

speaks of a student not becoming an unreasonable burden on the host Member State. The Court said that this:

. . . accepts a certain degree of financial solidarity between nationals of a host Member State and nationals of other Member States, particularly if the difficulties which a beneficiary of the right of residence encounters are temporary.[8]

The Court concluded:

It follows . . . that Article 6 [now 12] and 8 [now 17] of the Treaty preclude entitlement to a non-contributory social benefit . . . from being made conditional, in the case of nationals of Member States other than the host State where they are legally resident, on their falling within the scope of Regulation 1612/68 when no such condition applies to nationals of the host Member State.[9]

That is getting close to a principle of equal treatment in every respect. That it is not quite there is confirmed by the Court decision in the *Collins* case.[10] Brian Collins held dual nationalities: that of Ireland and of the United States. He had worked in the United Kingdom in 1980 and 1981,[11] and returned to the United Kingdom in 1998 in order to look for work.[12] He claimed a means-tested benefit which was refused. As an Irish national, he had a right of entry into the United Kingdom to seek work. The United Kingdom conditions of entitlement to the benefit he claimed required claimants for means-tested benefits to be 'habitually resident' in the United Kingdom unless they were workers for the purposes of Regulation 1612/68 or had a right of residence by virtue of Directive 68/360. The Court noted that the term 'worker' is not used in a single sense in Regulation 1612/68. Under Title II of Part 1, it refers to a person who has entered the employment market, but elsewhere appears to have a broader sense. The Court concluded that there is no right of residence to look for work under Directive 68/360/EEC; such a right flows from Article 39 (ex 48) EC itself, and may be limited in time; the right of residence referred to in Directive 68/360/EEC is for those who have found work. This brought the Court squarely up against the arguments based on citizenship of the Union. The Court acknowledged its rulings in *Grzelczyk* and *Garcia Avello*[13] and signalled a move beyond what had been decided in its earlier case law:

63. In view of the establishment of citizenship of the Union and the interpretation in the case-law of the right to equal treatment enjoyed by citizens of the Union, it is no longer possible to exclude from the scope of Article 48(2) [39(2)] of the Treaty—which expresses the fundamental principle of equal treatment guaranteed by Article 6 [now 12] of the Treaty—a benefit of a financial nature intended to facilitate access to employment in the labour market of a Member State.

[8] Para 44 of the judgment. [9] Para 46 of the judgment.
[10] Case C-138/02 *Collins*, Judgment of 23 March 2004, [2004] ECR nyr.
[11] The Court concluded that this period of work was too remote from the later work to leave any Community rights in place. There was no link between that activity and the current job search: see para 28 of the judgment.
[12] Which it seems he subsequently found: para 50 of the judgment.
[13] Case C-148/02 *Garcia Avello*, Judgment of 2 October 2003, [2003] ECR nyr.

64. The interpretation of the scope of the principle of equal treatment in relation to access to employment must reflect this development, as compared with the interpretation followed in *Lebon* and in Case C-278/94 *Commission v Belgium*.

However, the conditions of entitlement to the benefit claimed in the United Kingdom do not exclude the claimant on grounds of his nationality, but on the basis of a rule which applies equally to United Kingdom nationals, namely that the person must be 'habitually resident' in the United Kingdom. That requirement was challenged on the grounds that it might constitute indirect discrimination in that such a requirement places Member State nationals who have exercised their rights of free movement at a disadvantage. Residence requirements, such as this, will only be lawful if they can be justified on objective grounds not connected to the nationality of claimants and are necessary and proportionate in effect. The Court had recognized in other cases[14] that it is legitimate to demand a link between an applicant for a means-tested benefit and the geographic employment market in question. The residence requirement must, however, meet the test of necessity and proportionality. There must be clear criteria for the application of the test, and the period of residence required must not exceed that which is necessary in order for the national authorities to satisfy themselves of the genuine link with the employment market of that Member State.[15]

The judgment in *Collins* both gives and takes away. It recognizes the competence of the Member States to attach conditions to access to means-tested benefits for work seekers who have not yet attained the status of worker but subjects them not only to a requirement of equal treatment but also to a requirement of objective justification if they appear to have the effect of placing those who have exercised Community rights of free movement at a disadvantage.

Read expansively, the case law on citizenship of the Union grants a constitutional right to movement[16] to a Member State of choice without the need to establish economic activity. On entry to a Member State, there is a guarantee of equality of treatment. That right remains qualitatively different from the right nationals of a State enjoy under international law in relation to the right to leave and enter their State of nationality. This right is absolute. The constitutional right under the EC Treaty is subject to the exceptions both in relation to entry and in relation to the possibility of removal on grounds of public policy, public security or public health included in the EC Treaty. It is also clear that, depending upon the purpose of the entry, there may be some differentiation in the right the migrant enjoys or in the security of the right of residence.

[14] Notably Case C-224/98 *D'Hoop* [2002] ECR I-6191.

[15] So the proposal to require residence for a continuous period of 12 months in the draft Social Security (Habitual Residence) Amendment Regulations 2004 may face some difficulties of justification in the light of the decision in the *Collins* case.

[16] Even in circumstances not formally within the terms of the EC Treaty or the secondary legislation, as in Case C-413/99 *Baumbast and R v Secretary of State for the Home Department* [2002] ECR I-7091.

Another way of putting this is that the Court is increasingly treating the right to free movement as a constitutional right and more favourably, in that it is subject to the satisfaction of fewer conditions. The expansive reading of the rights of individuals to move is justified by reference to the constitutional language used in Part Two of the EC Treaty.

Perhaps the most dramatic example of an expansive reading is the *Carpenter* case.[17] Here even the most liberal commentator would have to accept that the link with the free movement of services was slender indeed. This, however, had the dramatic result that national immigration law was trumped by Community rights to enable Mr Carpenter to avoid the risk of deportation of his Philippine wife. Although only a small proportion of the total population of the Member States take up employment or self-employment in a Member State other than that of their nationality, a much larger proportion take holidays abroad on a regular basis by virtue of which they are receiving services.[18]

It can be argued that the key incident of citizenship is the right to leave and enter the State of your nationality free from immigration control. Citizenship of the Union gets close to such a right. The provisions of Directive 2004/38/EC[19] on the right of permanent residence define with considerable clarity the circumstances in which the right of residence becomes permanent for a range of individuals.

Fundamental rights

The distinction between nationals, citizens of the European Union from other Member States, and third country nationals becomes less marked when the issue of fundamental rights is considered. It has always been the case that nationality of a Contracting Party is not a prerequisite for enjoyment of the rights protected under the European Convention on Human Rights. The rights are guaranteed for all who are within the jurisdiction of the Contracting Parties.[20] The approach adopted within the European Union parallels this, though the parallelism has not often been noted. This is only as it should be. If rights are fundamental, then they are accorded to individuals as such regardless of their nationality. A particular reflection of this approach within the context of Community law is the trend to grant third country

[17] Case C-60/00 *Carpenter* [2002] ECR I-6729.

[18] Since the purpose of using the services provisions of the EC Treaty was to determine whether Mr Carpenter's circumstances fell within the scope of the EC Treaty, there is no logical reason to distinguish between service provision and service receipt: see Case 186/87 *Cowan* [1989] ECR 195.

[19] Directive 2004/38/EC of 29 April 2004 on the right of citizens of the Union and their family members to move and reside freely within the territory of the Member States, [2004] OJ L158/77. See generally ch 8 above.

[20] See generally Ovey, C and White, R, *The European Convention on Human Rights*, 3rd edn, (Oxford, 2002), ch 2.

nationals the same rights that are available to citizens of the Union once they have been admitted to a Member State.[21]

The development of the fundamental rights agenda which itself has the prohibition of discrimination at its heart reinforces the idea that certain rights are inherent rather than linked to the exercise of economic activity. Both the *Carpenter* case[22] and the *Akrich* case[23] show the Court having great concern for fundamental rights in the form of family unity in their reasoning and conclusions. There is beginning to emerge a European right to family life recognized by Community law and inspired by Article 8 of the European Convention on Human Rights.

Taken to their logical destination, current developments in the case law would remove the need for much of the secondary legislation guaranteeing equality of treatment. So, for example, much of Regulation 1612/68 would no longer be needed. But any area where Community law wished to go beyond entitlement available under national law would need to be retained since Community law steadfastly retains its liking for the doctrine of reverse discrimination. This sits uncomfortably with notions of constitutional protection attaching to citizenship of the Union. Specific measures of harmonization and co-ordination would also need to be retained. Examples of current measures that would need to be retained are the directives on mutual recognition of qualifications and on the co-ordination of social security entitlements.

Business entities as nationals of the Member State

The distinction between individuals and business entities is becoming wider. The first sentence of Article 48 EC provides:

> Companies or firms formed in accordance with the law of a Member State and having their registered office, central administration or principal place of business within the Community shall, for the purposes of this Chapter, be treated in the same way as natural persons who are nationals of Member States.

However, the Court has not given business organizations the same generous treatment that it accords to individuals on the basis that business entities are artificial legal persons. The free movement of business organizations remains subject to much greater limitations than the movement of individuals, even when the movement is for the same purpose. So a company moving its centre of administration may be subject to control, for example in relation to treasury consent, in a manner which would be regarded as a prohibited restriction if applied to an individual. This

[21] The case law on the interpretation of Association Agreements and the Europe Agreements demonstrates this tendency.

[22] Case C-60/00 *Carpenter* [2002] ECR I-6729.

[23] Case C-109/01 *Secretary of State for the Home Department v Akrich*, judgment of 23 September 2003, [2003] ECR nyr.

may simply be an inherent feature of the various forms of corporate personality under which businesses operate. However, it is argued that a justification can be found in the distinction the EC Treaty now makes between individuals and business entities as artificial legal persons. Though not wholly free from doubt, the language of Part Two of the EC Treaty on citizenship of the Union would appear to be limited to people and does not extend to business entities with legal personality. Consequently, people have the constitutional right to move whereas businesses have a lesser Community right to move under the free movement provisions of the EC Treaty.

The entitlement of business organizations to protection of their fundamental rights is also different; there are clearly some fundamental rights which cannot be enjoyed by business entities, whereas others are perfectly suited to application to them. Examples would be the right to a fair trial and the right to property.[24]

Discrimination *versus* non-discriminatory obstacles

Much has been written on whether the fundamental freedoms are based on the prohibition of discrimination against products or nationals of other Member States or the abolition of restrictions on the exercise of the fundamental freedoms.[25] Making these sorts of distinctions can be a semantic exercise which is ultimately of limited value. The purpose of the fundamental freedoms is to reduce the barriers which go with nation States and to encourage integration of the market. Excluding goods or people solely on the basis of their country of origin is the crudest form of obstacle to the free movement of goods and persons. A Member State which applies conditions which apply to all but which favour its own nationals or national products as a means of seeking to protect the domestic market in goods or jobs achieves the same end by different means. A Member State which applies conditions which cannot be justified objectively in the context of the aim to have an internal market is simply discriminating in a different way. If a measure is operating to restrict free movement, its effect is to discriminate against the product or person affected by the measure.

The creation of the *Dassonville* formula as the definition of measures having an effect equivalent to a quantitative restriction was appropriate to its time as the case law on the free movement of goods demonstrates. But it was too sweeping. The boundaries were rolled back in the *Keck* case. The reasoning in that case was defective, but the impact was satisfactory. Something akin to the *Dassonville* formula could have been developed in the context of the free movement of persons. It might read as follows: 'All regulatory provisions within a Member

[24] The right to freedom of expression is more controversial. See generally Shiner, R, *Freedom of Commercial Expression* (Oxford, 2003).

[25] Much of the literature is referred to in the footnotes in Barnard, C, 'Fitting the remaining pieces into the goods and persons jigsaw?' (2001) 26 ELRev 35.

State which are capable of hindering, directly or indirectly, actually or potentially, free movement of persons constitute restrictions prohibited by the EC Treaty.'

Such a formula could, in the extreme, be applied to the nationality laws of a Member State, so just as it was necessary to narrow the definition of trading rules under the *Dassonville* formula, so too it would be necessary to narrow the definition of regulatory provisions under such a formula. It is no accident that the provisions of the EC Treaty concerning free movement of workers speak largely in terms of rights for workers, whereas the provisions on establishment and services speak essentially to the abolition of restrictions. Perhaps too little has been made over the years on the effect of these provisions on a distinction between measures affecting individuals moving for the purpose of the envisaged economic activity and the regulation of the activity itself.

The EC Treaty provisions on the free movement of goods apply to State measures, whereas many of the provisions on the free movement of persons apply to private actors. This calls for some comment. In some areas, the application to private actors arises as a result of a requirement for the Member State to put in place provisions prohibiting discrimination on grounds of nationality. In other areas, the private actor is a body with significant regulatory authority over a particular area of activity, such as a professional body. Indeed in some Member States the regulatory authority may enjoy some statutory authority to regulate the activity. At the very least, they are organizations with considerable power to regulate the activities of individuals.[26] So the distinction may be more apparent than real when real-world situations are carefully analysed.

Controlling the regulators

Wouter Wils noted that Article 30 (now 28) EC is about 'policing the borderline between legitimate and illegitimate national regulation'.[27] The same may be true of aspects of Article 39 EC, and of Articles 43 and 49 EC. Here there is convergence between the approach adopted in relation to measures affecting the free movement of goods and the free movement of persons. First, discrimination, whether direct or indirect, in favour of nationals or national products is prohibited. Secondly, the so-called 'obstacles' approach will apply where there is a requirement which applies equally, in the case of goods, to domestic products and to imported products, and, in the case of the free movement of persons and services, to nationals of the host Member State and nationals of the other Member States.

[26] For example, football associations. See also Snell, J, 'Private Parties and the Free Movement of Goods and Services' in Andenas, M and Roth, W-H (eds), *Services and Free Movement in EU Law* (Oxford, 2002), at 211.

[27] Wils, W, 'The search for the rule in Article 30 EEC: much ado about nothing' (1993) 18 ELRev 475, at 477.

The first question will be to establish whether there is a restriction on the rights of free movement. Since the term restriction contains the assumption that the measure is prohibited, it might be better to frame the first question in terms of whether there is an interference with one of the fundamental freedoms. Here a definition like that propounded in the *Dassonville* case may be helpful in relation to goods, persons and services, but it needs to be modified by adding a requirement that the interference operates as an interference with the freedom to an appreciable extent. This would accommodate the 'selling arrangements' case law in the field of the free movement of goods,[28] and minimum impact cases in the field of the free movement of persons.[29] The nature of the enquiry here will vary considerably. In some cases, the issue will be whether the interference hinders access to the market,[30] while in others it will be whether the person who has exercised Community rights is placed at a disadvantage.[31]

The next question would be to ask whether the interference can be justified under the derogations permitted in the EC Treaty. It is logical to address this issue before considering the application of the case law on non-discriminatory obstacles.[32]

Finally, the enquiry turns to the possible justification for the interference in the general good. In order to avoid the prohibition on restrictions on the freedoms contained in the EC Treaty, the following conditions must be met:

- the contested measure must apply equally to domestic and imported products, or equally to nationals of the host Member State and of other Member States;
- the contested measure must have a legitimate aim which is compatible with the EC Treaty;[33]
- the requirements in the contested measure must be necessary to attain that aim;
- the requirements must be proportionate in that no measure which is less restrictive of the freedom will suffice to meet the legitimate aim; and
- the legitimate aim is not already addressed under an effective system of regulation applicable in the home Member State.

This methodology is redolent of the approach taken in the field of the protection of human rights when considering the rights contained in the European Convention which are subject to limitations.[34] Just as the Court in Strasbourg frequently finds itself having to determine whether an interference with one of the rights protected by the European Convention is 'necessary in a democratic society',

[28] Joined Cases C-267/91 and 268/91 *Keck and Mithouard* [1993] ECR I-6097.
[29] For example, Case C-190/98 *Graf* [2000] ECR I-493.
[30] As in Case C-190/98 *Graf* [2000] ECR I-493.
[31] As in Case C-224/98 *D'Hoop* [2002] ECR I-6191.
[32] Joined Cases C-1/90 and C-176/90 *Aragonesa* [1991] ECR I-4151, paras 12–13 of the judgment.
[33] Case C-250/95 *Futura Participations SA* [1997] ECR I-2471, para 26 of the judgment.
[34] Notably Arts 8–11 ECHR.

so the Luxembourg Court is frequently called upon to determine whether an interference with one of the fundamental freedoms is necessary in an internal market.

As we have seen from the case law, the sorts of requirements that are applied in the context of the free movement of persons and services principally concern the exercise of the activity, though this may include concerns about the suitability of the person to engage in that activity. This is because the regulation of services tends to involve the regulation of the provider of those services rather than the services themselves. In some areas, notably the mutual recognition of qualifications, Community harmonization measures have been necessary. In others comprehensive regulatory schemes have had to be put in place at Community level; examples here are the services directive and establishment directive for lawyers,[35] and the three generations of directives in the field of insurance.[36]

It might be objected that the introduction of a threshold of requiring any interference to operate to an appreciable extent is to introduce a vague and unpredictable threshold which will lead to uncertainty and which would be difficult for courts to apply.[37] The response is to argue that it is not that difficult to apply such a test; in considering any measure found potentially to be an interference with the fundamental freedoms, it would be appropriate to question the extent to which the contested measure hindered access to a market but that would not be the sole test. It would be for the parties contesting and defending the measure to argue the point in their pleadings. Threshold questions are commonly put before courts. One example from the case law of the Court of Justice in setting out a test for national courts will make the point. In determining whether someone is a worker for the purposes of Article 39 EC, national courts have to consider whether the work being undertaken is genuine and effective to the exclusion of work that is purely marginal or ancillary.

Home State *versus* host State regulation

The principle of subsidiarity may help us to understand the relationship between home State and host State regulation of an activity. Subsidiarity would tend to favour host State regulation; the place where the activity takes place is best able to regulate that activity. It will have familiarity with the economic and social culture of the place, and will know what needs to be done both to promote business and to

[35] See generally ch 12 above.
[36] See generally ch 13 above.
[37] See arguments posited by Catherine Barnard in relation to her proposed test of 'direct and substantial hindrance of access to the market' in Barnard, C, 'Fitting the remaining pieces into the goods and persons jigsaw?' (2001) 26 ELRev 35. See also Barnard, C and Deakin, S, 'Market Access and Regulatory Competition' in Barnard, C and Scott, J, *The Law of the Single European Market. Unpacking the Premises* (Oxford, 2002), at 197.

protect the consumer. However, the principle of subsidiarity also indicates that in certain circumstances, the local level is not the best place to locate regulation, since the objective of creating an internal market may require regulation at a different level. The difficulty is that the creation of an internal market requires multi-level regulation. There will also be regulatory competition. An economic actor wishing to operate in more than one Member State will face competing systems of regulation with conflicting demands which will operate as an interference with the exercise of one or more of the four freedoms. The only solution to the multiple burdens is either a system which gives priority to one of the competitors for being regulator or which harmonizes the system of regulation so that the regulatory competition is removed.

The tendency in Community law in the field of goods and services has been to favour home State regulation. The producer will naturally comply with the regulations operative in the place of production, and the supplier of services will comply with the system of regulation in the business's home State. A further complication arises in the field of services. The supplier's expertise is much more likely to be ongoing in the field of services than in the field of goods. The distinction should not be exaggerated since after-sales service is an important feature of the purchase of expensive goods, such as cars, and many electrical goods. As a result, the compromise solution has been to give home State regulation priority where the supplier is 'merely' engaging in delivering services, while giving priority to host State regulation where a business becomes established in that State. However, the State which is the later in time in seeking to regulate an activity is obliged to take account of the system of regulation to which the business has already been subject and may not require additional safeguards where the system of home State regulation already offers safeguards in respect of the risks that concern the host Member State. Respect for the regulators in another Member State is now deeply rooted in the Community system, since mutual recognition will avoid the requirement for multiple regulatory burdens which constitute an interference with the fundamental freedoms.

Final remarks

The thesis of this book is that a modern exposition of the law relating to workers, establishment, and services is best served by recognizing convergences and divergences. The introduction of citizenship of the Union has given citizens a constitutional right to move, which is having a profound effect on the bundle of personal Community rights citizens carry with them as they move between the Member States whether as employees, self-employed persons, students or tourists. The language of rights is helpful in analysing the current state of the law,[38] but also

[38] See de Búrca, G, 'The Language of Rights and European Integration' in Shaw, J and More, G, *New Legal Dynamics of European Union* (Oxford, 1995), at 29.

highlights tensions between economic rationality and social concerns. The constitutional right to free movement which flows from citizenship of the Union also explains the expansive approach being taken by the Court when it is called upon to deal with issues of personal movement and of the rights which citizens enjoy in every Member State. Separation of this line of case law from that which is essentially concerned with the regulation of interferences with the exercise of the four freedoms through State measures and cognate measures of regulation reveals greater coherence in the case law than some of the literature might suggest. It is certainly possible to posit an argument that the case law taken as a whole, when dealing with interferences with the four freedoms, is broadly consistent and does not make distinctions which are unsustainable. It is in the nature of case law that anomalies will arise which do not fit the model which academic commentators synthesize from the raw material of the Court's judgments. That reflects both the nature of courts and the serendipity which brings particular disputes to courts in the first place.

Select Bibliography

Books

Ackers, L, *Shifting Spaces. Women citizenship and migration within the European Union* (Bristol, 1998).

Alston, P, *The EU and Human Rights* (Oxford, 1999).

Andenas, M and Roth, W-H (eds), *Services and Free Movement in EU Law* (Oxford, 2002).

Apap, J, *The Rights of Immigrant Workers in the European Union* (The Hague, 2002).

Apap, J, *Freedom of Movement of Persons. A Practitioner's Handbook* (The Hague, 2002).

Arnull, A, *The General Principles of EEC Law and the Individual* (Leicester, 1990).

Arnull, A, *The European Union and its Court of Justice* (Oxford, 1999).

Arnull, A, Dashwood, A, Ross, M and Wyatt, D, *Wyatt & Dashwood's European Community Law*, 4th edn (London, 2000).

Audretsch, H, *Supervision in European Community Law*, 2nd edn (Amsterdam, 1986).

Baquero Cruz, J, *Between Competition and Free Movement. The Economic Constitutional Law of the European Community* (Oxford, 2002).

Barnard, C, *EC Employment Law*, 2nd edn (Oxford, 2000),

Barnard, C, *The Substantive Law of the EU. The Four Freedoms* (Oxford, 2004).

Barnard, C and Scott, J, *The Law of the Single European Market. Unpacking the Premises* (Oxford, 2002).

Beenen, N, *Citizenship, Nationality and Access to Public Service Employment. The Impact of European Community Law* (Groningen, 2001).

Bell, M, *Anti-Discrimination Law and the European Union* (Oxford, 2002).

Blainpain, R, *European Labour Law*, 8th edn (The Hague, 2002).

Böcker, A and Guild, E, *Implementation of the Europe Agreements in France, Germany, the Netherlands and the UK: Movement of Persons* (London, 2002).

Craig, P and de Búrca, G, *The Evolution of EU Law* (Oxford, 1999).

Craig, P and de Búrca, G, *EU Law. Text, Cases, and Materials*, 3rd edn (Oxford, 2003).

Curtin, D and O'Keeffe, D (eds), *Constitutional Adjudication in European Community and National Law* (Dublin, 1992).

Dashwood, A and O'Leary, S (eds), *The Principle of Equal Treatment in EC Law* (London, 1997).

Donohue, J, *The Insurance Single Passport. A Guide to the Implementing Regulations* (London, 1995).

Douglas-Scott, S, *Constitutional Law of the European Union* (Harlow, 2002).

European Commission, *Social Protection in Europe 2001* (Brussels, 2002).

European Commission, *Your social security rights when moving within the European Union. A practical guide* (Luxembourg: Office for Official Publications of the European Communities, 2002 update).

Everling, U, *The Right of Establishment in the Common Market* (Chicago, 1964).

Gil Ibáñez, A, *The Administrative Supervision and Enforcement of EC Law* (Oxford, 1999).

Green, N, Hartley, T, and Usher, J, *The Legal Foundations of the Single European Market* (Oxford, 1991).

Guild, E, *The Developing Immigration and Asylum Policies of the European Union* (The Hague, 1996).

Guild, E, *European Community Law from a Migrant's Perspective* (The Hague, 1999).

Handoll, J, *Free Movement of Persons in the EU* (Chichester, 1995).

Hartley, T, *The Foundations of European Community Law*, 5th edn (Oxford, 2003).

Hervey, T, *European Social Law and Policy* (Harlow, 1998).

Jørgensen, E, *Union Citizens. Free movement and non-discrimination* (Copenhagen, 1996).

Kostakopoulou, D, *Citizenship, Identity and Immigration in the European Union. Between Past and Future* (Manchester, 2001).

Majone, G, *Deregulation or Re-regulation? Regulatory Reform in Europe and the United States* (London, 1990).

Mancini, G, *Democracy and Constitutionalism in the European Union* (Oxford, 2000).

Martin, D and Guild, E, *Free Movement of Persons in the European Union* (London, 1996).

Mei, A P van der, *Free Movement within the European Community. Cross-Border Access to Public Benefits* (Oxford, 2003).

Merkin, R and Rodger, A, *EC Insurance Law* (Harlow, 1997).

Nielsen, R and Szyszczak, E, *The Social Dimension of the European Union*, 3rd edn (Copenhagen, 1997).

O'Leary, S, *The Evolving Concept of Community Citizenship. From the Free Movement of Persons to Union Citizenship* (The Hague, 1996).

Oliver, P, *Free Movement of Goods in the European Community: under Articles 28 to 30 of the EC Treaty*, 4th edn (London, 2003).

Ovey, C and White, R, *The European Convention on Human Rights*, 3rd edn (Oxford, 2002).

Pennings, F, *Introduction to European Social Security*, 4th edn (Antwerp, 2003).

Pertek, J (ed), *General Recognition of Diplomas and Free Movement of Professionals* (Maastricht, 1992).

Poiares Maduro, M, *We The Court: The European Court of Justice and the European Economic Constitution* (Oxford, 1998).

Rogers, N, *A Practitioner's Guide to the EC–Turkey Association Agreement* (The Hague, 1999).

Schermers, H *et al*, *Free Movement of Persons in Europe* (Dordrecht, 1993).

Shaw, J and More, G (eds), *New Legal Dynamics of the European Union* (Oxford, 1995).

Shiner, R, *Freedom of Commercial Expression* (Oxford, 2003).

Snell, J, *Goods and Services in EC Law. A Study of the Relationship between the Freedoms* (Oxford, 2002).

Szyszczak, E, *EC Labour Law* (Harlow, 2000).

Tyrrell, A and Yaqub, Z (eds), *The Legal Professions in the New Europe. A Handbook for Practitioners*, 2nd edn (London, 1996).

Walker, N (ed), *Europe's Area of Freedom, Security and Justice* (Oxford, 2004).

Watson, P, *Social Security Law of the European Communities* (London, 1980).

Weatherill, S, *Law and Integration in the European Union* (Oxford, 1995).

Weatherill, S and Beaumont, P, *EU Law*, 3rd edn (London, 1999).

Weiler, J *The Constitution of Europe* (Cambridge, 1999).

Weiss, F and Wooldridge, F, *Free Movement of Persons within the European Community* (The Hague, 2002).

White, R, *EC Social Security Law* (Harlow, 1999).

Williams, D, *EC Tax Law* (London, 1998).

Winter, J *et al* (eds), *Reforming the Treaty on European Union. The Legal Debate* (The Hague, 1996).

Wyatt, D and Dashwood, A, *Wyatt & Dashwood's European Community Law*, 3rd edn (London, 1993).

Chapters and essays in books, and working papers

Arnull, A and Jacobs, F, 'Applying the Common Rules on Free Movement of Persons' in Schermers, H *et al*, *Free Movement of Persons in Europe* (Dordrecht, 1993), at 272.

Armstrong, K, 'Mutual Recognition' in Barnard, C and Scott, J, *The Law of the Single European Market. Unpacking the Premises* (Oxford, 2002), at 225.

Barnard, C and Deakin, S, 'Market Access and Regulatory Competition' in Barnard, C and Scott, J, *The Law of the Single European Market. Unpacking the Premises* (Oxford, 2002), 197.

Búrca, G de, 'The Language of Rights and European Integration' in Shaw, J and More, G, *New Legal Dynamics of European Union* (Oxford, 1995), 29.

Búrca, G de, 'The Role of Equality in European Community Law' in Dashwood, A and O'Leary, S, *The Principle of Equal Treatment in European Community Law* (London, 1997), 13.

Cath, I, 'Free Movement of Legal Persons' in Schermers, H *et al* (eds), *Free Movement of Persons in Europe. Legal Problems and Experiences* (Dordrecht, 1993), 450.

Curtin, D, 'Integrating the "Schengen Acquis" into the Legal Order of the European Union; Opaque Legal Practice and Unidentified Objects' in Vandamme, T, and Reestman, J-H, *Ambiguity in the Rule of Law. The Interface between National and International Legal Systems* (Groningen, 2001).

Everson, M, 'The Legacy of the Market Citizen' in Shaw, J and More, G (eds), *New Legal Dynamics of the European Union* (Oxford, 1995), 73.

Jacobs, F, 'An Introduction to the General Principles of Equality in EC Law' in Dashwood, A and O'Leary, S, *The Principle of Equal Treatment in European Community Law* (London, 1997), 1.

Jarass, H, 'A Unified Approach to the Fundamental Freedoms' in Andenas, M and Roth, W-H (eds), *Services and Free Movement in EU Law* (Oxford, 2002), 141.

Kupiszewski, M, *Consequences of EU Enlargement for Freedom of Movement between Council of Europe Member States*, Central European Forum for Migration Research Working Paper 1/2003 (Warsaw, 2003).

O'Keeffe, D, 'Judicial Interpretation of the Public Services Exception to the Free Movement of Workers' in Curtin, D and O'Keeffe, D (eds), *Constitutional Adjudication in European Community and National Law* (Dublin, 1992).

O'Leary, S, 'The Free Movement of Persons and Services' in Craig, P and de Búrca, G, *The Evolution of EU Law* (Oxford, 1999), at 377.

Snell, J, 'Private Parties and the Free Movement of Goods and Services' in Andenas, M and Roth, W-H (eds), *Services and Free Movement in EU Law* (Oxford, 2002), 211.

Tyrrell, A, 'Professional Duties and Privileges' in Tyrrell, A and Jacub, Z, *The Legal Professions in the New Europe*, 2nd edn (London, 1996), 23.

Weiler, J, 'European Citizenship and Human Rights' in Winter, J *et al* (eds), *Reforming the Treaty on European Union. The Legal Debate* (The Hague, 1996), at 57.

Weiler, J, 'To be a European Citizen: Eros and Civilization' in Weiler, J *The Constitution of Europe* (Cambridge, 1999).

Articles

Anagnostaras, G, 'Not as unproblematic as you might think: the establishment of causation in governmental liability actions' (2002) 27 ELRev 663.

Arnull, A, 'References to the European Court' (1990) 15 ELRev 375.

Arnull, A, 'What Shall We Do on Sunday?' (1991) 16 ELRev 112.

Arts, K, 'ACP-EU relations in a new era: The Cotonou Agreement' (2003) 40 CMLRev 95.

Barber, N, 'Citizenship, nationalism and the European Union' (2002) 28 ELRev 241.

Barnard, C, 'Fitting the remaining pieces into the goods and persons jigsaw?' (2001) 26 ELRev 35.

Barrett, G, 'Family Matters: European Community Law and Third-Country Family Members' (2003) 40 CMLRev 369.

Berghman, J and Okma, K, 'The Method of Open Co-ordination: Open Procedures or closed circuit? Social policy making between science and politics' (2002) 4 EJSS 331.

Bernard, N, 'Discrimination and free movement in EC Law' (1996) 45 ICLQ 82

Bleckmann, A, 'German Nationality within the Meaning of the EEC Treaty' (1978) 15 CMLRev 435.

Bleckmann, A, 'The Personal Jurisdiction of the European Community' (1980) 17 CMLRev 467.

Búrca, G de, 'The Drafting of the European Union Charter of Fundamental Rights' (2001) 26 ELRev 126.

Colvin, M, 'The Schengen Information System: a Human Rights Audit' [2001] EHRLR 271.

Craig, P, '*Francovich*, Remedies and the Scope of Damages Liability' (1993) 109 LQR 595.

Daniele, L, 'Non-Discriminatory Restrictions to the Free Movement of Persons' (1997) 22 ELRev 191.

Dashwood, A and White, R, 'Enforcement Actions under Articles 169 and 170 EC' (1989) 14 ELRev 388.

Davies, P, 'Posted Workers: Single Market or Protection of National Labour Law Systems?' (1997) 34 CMLRev 571.

Davis, R, 'Citizenship of the European Union . . . rights for all?' (2002) 28 ELRev 121.

Docksey, C, 'The Principle of Equality between Women and Men as a Fundamental Right under Community Law' (1991) 20 ILJ 33.

Dougan, M and Spaventa, E, 'Educating Rudy and the non-English patient: A double-bill on residency rights under Article 18 EC' (2003) 28 ELRev 699.

Drury, R, 'Migrating Companies' (1999) 24 ELRev 354.

Dyrberg, P, 'Full free movement of companies in the European Community at last?' (2003) 28 ELRev 528.

Editorial, 'The Tampere summit: The ties that bind *or* The Policeman's Ball' (1999) 36 CMLRev 1119.

Edward, D, 'Establishment and Services: an Analysis of the Insurance Cases' (1987) 12 ELRev 231.

Ellis, E, 'Social advantages: A new lease of life?' (2003) 40 CMLRev 639.

Foster, N, 'European Community Law and the Freedom of Lawyers in the United Kingdom and Germany' (1991) 40 ICLQ 607.

Friedl, A, 'Fixed Term Contracts for Foreign language Lecturers—A Proportionate Restriction on Free Movement of Workers' (1996) 25 ILJ 66.

Giesen, R, 'Posting: Social Protection of Workers vs. Fundamental Freedoms?' (2003) 40 CMLRev 143.

Greaves, R, 'Advertising Restrictions and the Free Movement of Goods and Services' (1998) 23 ELRev 305.

Guild, E, 'How can social protection survive EMU? A United Kingdom perspective' (1999) 24 ELRev 22.

Hall, S, 'Loss of Union Citizenship in Breach of Fundamental Rights', (1996) 21 ELRev 129.

Hall, S, 'The European Convention on Nationality and the Right to have Rights' (1999) 24 ELRev 586.

Handoll, J, 'Article 48(4) EEC and Non-National Access to Public Employment' (1988) 13 ELRev 223.

Hanlon, J, 'Pensions integration in the European Union' (2004) 29 ELRev 74.

Jacqueson, C, 'Union citizenship and the Court of Justice: something new under the sun? Towards social citizenship' (2002) 27 ELRev 260.

Johnson, E and O'Keeffe, D, 'From Discrimination to Obstacles to Free Movement: Recent Developments concerning the Free Movement of Workers 1989–1994' (1994) 31 CMLRev 1313.

Lonbay, J, 'Lawyers bounding over the borders: the Draft Directive on lawyers' establishment' (1996) 21 ELRev 50.

Marenco, G, 'The notion of restrictions on the freedom of establishment and provision of services in the case law of the court' (1991) 11 YEL 111.

O'Keeffe, D, 'Equal Rights for Migrants: The Concept of Social Advantage in Article 7(2), Regulation 1612/68' (1985) 5 YEL 93.

O'Keeffe, D, 'Is the Spirit of Article 177 under Attack? Preliminary References and Admissibility' (1998) 23 ELRev 509.

O'Leary, S, 'Putting Flesh on the Bones of European Union Citizenship' (1999) 24 ELRev 68.

Oliver, P, 'Some Further Reflections on the Scope of Articles 28-30 [ex 30-36] EC' (1999) 36 CMLRev 783.

Peers, S, 'Indirect Rights for Third Country Service Providers Confirmed' (1995) 20 ELRev 303.

Peers, S, ' "Social Advantages" and Discrimination in Employment: Case Law Confirmed and Clarified' (1997) 22 ELRev 157.

Pertek, J, 'Free movement of professionals and recognition of higher education diplomas' (1992) 12 YEL 293.

Rawlings, R, 'Engaged Elites, Citizen Action and Institutional Attitudes in Commission Enforcement' (2000) 6 ELJ 4.

Reich, R and Harbacevica, S, 'Citizenship and Family on Trial: A Fairly Optimistic Overview of Recent Court Practice with regard to Free Movement of Persons' (2003) 40 CMLRev 615.

Ross, M, 'Mutual recognition of professional qualifications' (1989) 14 ELRev 162.

Shaw, J, 'The Many Pasts and Futures of Citizenship in the European Union' (1997) 22 ELRev 554.

Simmonds, K, 'The British Nationality Act 1981 and the Definition of the Term 'National' for Community Purposes' (1984) 21 CMLRev 675.

Stanley, P, 'Note on *Asscher*' (1997) 34 CMLRev 713.

Steiner, J, 'From Direct Effect to *Francovich*' (1993) 18 ELRev 3.

Temple Lang, J, 'The Duties of National Courts under Community Constitutional Law' (1997) 22 ELRev 3.

Temple Lang, J, 'The Duties of National Authorities under Community Constitutional Law' (1998) 23 ELRev 109.

Theodossiou, M, 'An analysis of the recent response of the Community to non-compliance with Court of Justice judgments' (2002) 27 ELRev 25.

Tridimas, T, 'Liability for breach of Community law: growing up and mellowing down' (2001) 38 CMLRev 301.

Vanistendael, F, 'The Consequences of *Schumacker* and *Wielockx:* Two Steps forward in the Tax Procession of Echternach' (1996) 33 CMLRev 255.

Van Overbeek, P, 'AIDS/HIV infection and the free movement of persons in the European Economic Community' (1990) 27 CMLRev 791.

Watson, P, 'Minimum income benefits: social security and social assistance' (1985) 10 ELRev 335.

Watson, P, 'Equal treatment in the award of family allowances' (1989) 14 ELRev 346.

Watson, P, 'Free movement of workers: recent cases' (1989) 14 ELRev 415.

Wattel, P, 'The EC Court's Attempts to Reconcile the Treaty Freedoms with International Tax Law' (1996) 33 CMLRev 223.

Weatherill, S, 'After *Keck:* Some Thoughts on How to Clarify the Clarification' (1996) 33 CMLRev 885.

Wils, W, 'The search for the rule in Article 30 EEC: much ado about nothing?' (1993) 18 ELRev 475.

Wyatt, D, 'Social security benefits and discrimination by a Member State against its own nationals' (1978) 3 ELRev 488.

Useful Websites

europa.eu.int	The European Union
citizens.eu.int	The European Union's dialogue with citizens. Provides detailed practical information on rights and opportunities in the European Union and its internal market plus advice on how to exercise these rights in practice.
curia.eu.int	The Court of Justice of the European Communities and the Court of First Instance.
www.eurovisa.info	Covers the Schengen arrangements.
www.ccbe.org	CCBE is the officially recognized representative organization for the legal professions in the European Union and the European Economic Area.
www.ilo.org	International Labour Organization.
www.coe.int	The Council of Europe.
www.echr.coe.int	The European Court of Human Rights.
www.abi.org.uk	Association of British Insurers, which is the trade association for the United Kingdom's insurance industry.

Index